"Jack Balswick, Judith Balswick, and Thomas Frederick present a Christian perspective on the significance and purpose of the contemporary family. Through a unique blend of biblical theology, systems theory, and the social sciences, they address the many facets of the modern-day family relative to marriage, parenting, sexuality, communication, and the social dynamics of family life. As a teaching professor in the Christian academic setting, I have used the earlier editions of this extraordinary text for both graduate and undergraduate classes in marriage and family studies. In addition, as a licensed marriage and family therapist, I have found the biblical and theoretical concepts helpful and applicable. I greatly recommend this book to instructors, students, counselors, or pastors who are seeking to develop an overarching theological and sociological framework for the family."

—**Brad Overholser**, chair of human development, Hope International University

"This updated edition of *The Family* presents recent research to continue the important contribution of this book to our thinking about families from a distinctly Christian viewpoint. It's based on a systemic developmental perspective that captures the reality of our relationships in our families across the life span, with a special focus on the attributes of grace, empowerment, and intimacy within Christian covenantal love that can permeate those relationships and impact the larger social environment."

—**Mark Stanton**, professor of psychology, Azusa Pacific University

"The reason for the longevity and influence of Balswick and Balswick's *The Family* is based in two things: the clarity of their writing on topics of interest to the Christian community and their engagement with recent scholarship. This fifth edition of what is now a standard text on family life continues this pattern of thoughtful Christian scholarship. The result is a stimulating text whose relevance extends beyond the classroom to the front lines of Christian engagement with families, whether it be in a clinical, parachurch, or congregational setting."

—**Kelvin Mutter**, associate professor of counselling and spiritual care,
McMaster Divinity College

"*The Family* is a unique resource in the study of marriage and family: it adeptly integrates theology with sociological perspectives and proven family therapy models. I highly recommend this text for marriage and family studies in Christian colleges and universities and can personally attest to how helpful it's been to both educators and students alike."

—**Yvonne Thai**, ch   Sciences and professor
of sociology, C   d Professional Studies

T0339020

The Family

The Family

A Christian Perspective
on the Contemporary Home

FIFTH EDITION

JACK O. BALSWICK,
JUDITH K. BALSWICK,
AND
THOMAS V. FREDERICK

Baker Academic

a division of Baker Publishing Group
Grand Rapids, Michigan

Published by Baker Academic
a division of Baker Publishing Group
PO Box 6287, Grand Rapids, MI 49516-6287
www.bakeracademic.com

Printed in the United States of America

Library of Congress Cataloging-in-Publication Data
Names: Balswick, Jack O., author. | Balswick, Judith K., author. | Frederick, Thomas V., author.
Title: The family : a Christian perspective on the contemporary home / Jack O. Balswick, Judith K. Balswick, Thomas V. Frederick.
Description: Fifth edition. | Grand Rapids, Michigan : Baker Academic, a division of Baker Publishing Group, 2021. | Includes bibliographical references and index.
Identifiers: LCCN 2021009288 | ISBN 9781540963000 (paperback) | ISBN 9781540964489 (casebound) | ISBN 9781493432035 (ebook)
Subjects: LCSH: Families—Religious life. | Marriage—Religious aspects—Christianity. | Parenting—Religious aspects—Christianity.
Classification: LCC BV4526.2 .B357 2021 | DDC 261.8/3585—dc23
LC record available at https://lccn.loc.gov/2021009288

Baker Publishing Group publications use paper produced from sustainable forestry practices and post-consumer waste whenever possible.

24   25   26   27   7   6   5   4   3   2

Contents

Contents

Detailed Contents

Illustrations

Preface

We (Jack and Judy) initially wrote *The Family: A Christian Perspective on the Contemporary Home* to present an integrated view of contemporary family life based on current social-science research, clinical insights, and biblical truth. The biblical integration reflects broad theological truths woven throughout the Scriptures rather than specific proof texts. We chose to present the social-scientific knowledge in an easy-to-read style rather than one that was academic but more cumbersome. The positive response to the previous four editions of our book has warranted this updated fifth edition. And we brought on a coauthor, Tom, to partner with us in the task. Building on the previous material, this new edition incorporates the most current research to date—with over one hundred additional references incorporated into the fifth edition—and our response to the continued changes that are taking place in modern society and family life, the increasing role of grandparents in parenting their grandchildren, and work and family life. And in recognition of the importance of biosocial influence, we highlight the interactive effect of bio-psycho-socio-cultural factors that help us understand family dynamics.

Our book is divided into seven parts. In part 1, "Theological and Social Perspectives on Family Life," we put forward a basic theology of relationships and theoretical perspectives on the family as a developing biosocial system. Part 2, "Marriage: The Foundation of Family Life," is devoted to the topics of mate selection, cohabitation, and the establishment of a strong Christian marriage. In part 3, "The Expansion of Family Life: Parenting and Beyond," we focus on the development and rearing of young children, the particular challenges of midlife parents and their adolescent children, and the joys and challenges of the later-life family. In part 4, "Gender and Sexuality: Identity in Family Life," we consider the changing definitions of masculinity and femininity and the implications they have for family relationships, and we discuss the complex dimensions of becoming an authentic sexual self as part of God's design and intention. Part 5, "Communication: The Heart of Family Life," describes the expression of love and intimacy as well as the expression of anger and normal conflicts that inevitably occur between family members. In part 6, "The Social Dynamics of Family Life," we attend to the critical aspects of family life such as work-family dynamics, life stressors, divorce, single parenthood, remarriage, and building new family forms. Part 7, "Family Life in Postmodern Society," deals with the effects that modern industrialized society and postmodern thinking have had on family life. Suggestions are made for changing social structures to create a more family-friendly environment.

Rather than taking a piecemeal approach, devoting each chapter to a specific topic, we have attempted to make every chapter an integral part of the overarching theme of the book. The foundation for this theme is the theology of family relationships expounded in parts 1 and 2. Therefore, we have aspired to weave into the content of each chapter our theological basis for family relationships from the perspective of the family as a developing system.

Coauthorship and teamwork make this book a collaborative project. A marriage and family therapist for over forty years, Judy is senior professor at Fuller Theological Seminary in the Marriage and Family Therapy Department. Jack, a professional sociologist with forty-five years of teaching, research, and writing experience at the university and seminary level, is also a senior professor at Fuller. They have each had postdoctoral seminary training in theology and biblical studies and they speak throughout the United States and abroad on marriage and family life. Tom Frederick has known Jack and Judy since 1997, when he came to Fuller Theological Seminary as a marriage and family therapy student. It was there that he was introduced to the Balswick's theology of family relationships and witnessed their authentic Christian commitment to personal and spiritual growth as mentors and scholars. Tom is currently a professor of psychology and the program director for the online Master of Science in Counseling Psychology program at California Baptist University.

Although we have attempted to blend academic, clinical, and theological understandings of the family, our interest in family life is not merely as scholars. The core of our lives has been experienced in the context of family, and our joint calling is to minister to families. We feel most fortunate to have been reared and nurtured in loving Christian homes. Our parents modeled unconditional love and grace that provided secure foundations and brought profound spiritual meaning to our lives.

Being married for sixty years has taught us (Jack and Judy) much about what it takes to live out the principles we propose in this book. Our adult children, Jacque and Joel, have challenged and continue to challenge us to grow throughout every life stage. We have tried to maintain balance through the joys and pains, ups and downs, ebb and flow, stress and elation of family living. Forty years ago our beloved ten-year-old son, Jeff, died of bone cancer. Working through that loss as well as remembering the delight of his life has changed us all. We spent three years living in an extended-family arrangement with our daughter Jacque, her first husband, and our two- and three-year-old grandsons, Curtis and Jacob, who have now graduated from college and are working full time. We have two additional grandsons, Taylor and Liam, from our daughter's marriage to Dana Kirk. Our adopted Korean son Joel is married to Uyen Mai, a Chinese Vietnamese woman, who has enriched our multicultural perspective. In addition they have gifted us with our first granddaughter, Elizabeth, and their adopted Korean son, Benjamin. We've been through the agonizing illnesses and deaths of all four parents and had the privilege and challenge of living with Judy's aging mother for nine months prior to her death at age ninety-two.

I (Tom) have been married to Gail Frederick for twenty-three years, which has taught me much about the transformative nature of marriage. Gail's Taiwanese background has added a crucial multicultural dimension to family life. We have had to practice careful listening and other communication strategies. Further, it has been enriching to see both sets of in-laws accept us as part of the family. We have enjoyed the hospitality of our Taiwanese family while making our lives in California. Raising two children, Nathaniel and Zoe, has provided many opportunities to practice empowerment, grace, and intimacy. Being a teenager is challenging under normal circumstances; however, there are no manuals for parenting or being a teen during a global pandemic.

All in all, the three of us have learned a lot and continue to learn as we encounter the blessings and struggles of each unique stage of family life. Having preached on the fragility of the isolated nuclear family, we are constantly reminded of our need for God as our strength as well as for those who have walked alongside us on the journey. Our friends, family, and communities of faith add a wealth of wisdom and perspective. We want to offer a warm and heartfelt thanks to Nathaniel Frederick, who assisted in compiling and updating the bibliography. Robert Hosack at Baker Academic provided needed encouragement for us tackling this revision. We would be remiss without thanking editor James Korsmo and copyeditor Stephanie Juliot. Their thorough review, attention to detail, and helpful suggestions have greatly improved this fifth edition. Finally, we would like to thank Paula Gibson from the visual communication department whose work on the front cover captured beautifully the content of the book. We trust that what we have learned will benefit our readers.

Visit www.bakeracademic.com/professors
to access study aids
and instructor materials for this textbook.

PART 1

Theological and Social Perspectives on Family Life

Some observe a crisis in the Christian family in the United States today. There are challenges to how Christians define the nature and function of the family, and many are confused with how to incorporate the best sociology research into understanding this bedrock of society. Our approach is to consider the biblical, theological, cultural, and sociological perspectives on family life in an attempt to integrate secular knowledge with the truth of Scripture. In chapter 1 we present a theology of family relationships based on what the Bible says about relationality through the Holy Trinity: God as parent in relationship to the children of Israel, Christ as groom in relationship to the church as bride, and the Holy Spirit in relationship to all believers who are empowered to live in rightful relationships as brothers and sisters in Christ. The emergent theology of family relationships highlights the elements of covenant, grace, empowerment, and intimacy as family members strive to maintain their unique individuality within family unity.

In chapter 2 we introduce two sociological perspectives. The systemic perspective, which views the family as a unit of interrelated parts, concentrates on the relationships between family members. The developmental perspective focuses on the bio-psycho-socio-cultural impact and various stages of individual and family life. By integrating these sociological perspectives, we will discover some of the basic marks of a resilient family.

1

A Theological Foundation
for Family Relationships

Developing a Theology of the Family

How can we best use Scripture to learn God's intention for family life during the new millennium? A common approach is to pick out the key verses from the various scriptural passages dealing with the family. These verses are then arranged as one would arrange a variety of flowers to form a pleasing bouquet. However, such use of Scripture presents problems when Christians come up with different bouquets of verses and then disagree as to what the Bible says about family life. This method of selecting certain verses about the family can be compared to strip mining. Ignoring the historical and cultural context, the strip miner tears into the veins of Scripture, throws the unwanted elements aside, and emerges with selected golden nuggets of truth. Too often, this type of search for God's truth about the family produces a truth that conforms to the preconceived ideas of the miner doing the stripping.

Prominent among the golden nuggets that are typically mined are New Testament regulations regarding family and household relationships (e.g., Eph. 5:22–6:9; Col. 3:18–4:1; 1 Tim. 2:8–15; 6:1–2; Titus 2:1–10; and 1 Pet. 2:18–3:7). These passages indicate early Christianity's concern for order in three basic household relationships: between husband and wife, between parent and child, and between master and slave. New Testament scholar James Dunn (1996), however, emphasizes the importance of considering the total context of scriptural passages about family life. Dunn notes the problem when scriptural texts are read without considering the social, historical, and cultural context of the time of writing. Although the motive of discovering hard-and-fast rules for household life is understandable, a "problem arises here when we try to make the household codes into timeless rules which can be simply transposed across time to the present day without addition or subtraction" (62). Doing so would mean that we accept slaves as part of God's intention for family households. Dunn concludes that such an approach is an abuse of Scripture.

In contrast to a strip-mining mentality, we take a broad view by considering relevant biblical references as well as a theology that offers deeper meaning and concrete principles of living in our complex, postmodern world. By way of analogy, we base our theology of family relationships on *relationality within the Holy Trinity* and throughout the Old and New Testament descriptions of *God in relationship*. The use of analogy is crucial to understanding the correspondence between God and humanity. Relying on analogy to build our theological model is based on a more theological interpretation of Scripture (TIP). One of the main ways to engage in TIP is using typological approaches that identify types or prototypes in one passage of Scripture that are developed in later passages. Further, these typological approaches allow us to develop a *biblical theology* associated with the type or prototype by connecting passages across the Scriptures. This is very different from citing one or two passages as proof texts for one's position. There are two main dimensions of typology in interpreting Scripture (Parker 2018). The primary type in this kind of reading is horizontal typology, which occurs when an Old Testament figure or institution corresponds to or is an adumbration for a New Testament figure or institution. The initial analogy is between God and Adam. That is, God makes Adam as an image bearer and covenant partner, which foreshadows Christ as the Covenant Keeper on humanity's behalf.

Trinitarian Relationality

The first humans were created to be covenant partners with God, entailing stewardship of God's creation. What we read in Genesis 1 and 2 reflects the formation of covenants between lords and vassals (Horton 2006). God as the Lord declares his works; he speaks, and his empowering Word accomplishes his will. Then, God creates and appoints humans—Adam and Eve—to represent him in his covenant relationship to the creation. "With God's act of creation, the relations between the persons of the Trinity finds its analogy between God's relations with his people and the relations between the people themselves and the covenant community" (Horton 2012, 124).

As with all covenants, there are blessings, responsibilities, and consequences for violation.

We believe humans are created by a relational, triune God to be in meaningful and edifying relationships. The good news is that Scripture presents a model of relational life in the Trinity—God is one yet composed of three distinct persons. Stanley Grenz puts it this way: "The same principle of mutuality that forms the genius for the human social dynamic is present in a prior way in the divine being" (2001, 48). Building on this truth, our starting point in developing a theology of family relationships is to recognize that, by way of analogy, relationships between family members reflect the relationality within the Holy Trinity.

Relationality is the primary vehicle for humans to carry out their covenant responsibilities. Image bearing does not connote ontology; in other words, the *imago Dei* describes our status in covenant relationship with God (Grenz 2001; Horton 2012; Strachan 2019), not necessarily humanity's psychological makeup. Genesis 1:26–27 states, "Then God said, 'Let *us* make humankind in our image, according to our likeness. . . . So God created humankind in his image, in the image of God he created them; male and female he created them." The *us* connotes the triune Godhead (Father, Son, and Holy Spirit), who in unity created humankind in the image of God (*imago Dei*). Throughout the Bible, *unity* and *uniqueness* are simultaneously described as the relational aspects of the Godhead.

The task of image bearing entails a threefold commission from the Creator (Fowler 1987). First, Adam and Eve—and then all people—are to govern or be responsible stewards of the creation. Second, image bearers engage in developing or liberating creation. In other words, humans function as image bearers in developing the potential of the created order. Finally, image bearing entails redemption of the aspects of creation that have been marred due to human fallenness and sin (Gen. 3). Humans do this redemptive work when they remove or ameliorate the effects of sin (e.g., when teachers support at-risk students to achieve academically). Middleton summarizes the threefold commission this way: "The imago Dei designates the royal office or calling of human beings as God's representatives and agents in the world, granting authorized power to share God's rule or administration of earth's resources and creatures" (2005, 27). Unity with God as image bearers means exercising one's unique ability to govern, liberate, and redeem creation.

Applying image bearing to family relationships, Gary Deddo (1999) draws on Karl Barth, when he states that "the nature of the covenantal relationship between God and humanity revealed and actualized in Jesus Christ . . . [is] grounded in the Trinitarian relations of Father, Son, and Spirit" (2). As distinction and unity coexist in the Godhead, so are they to exist among family members. Deddo states, "In the revelation by the Son of the Father through the Spirit we come to recognize the activity of the one God apportioned to each person of the Trinity. The Father is the Creator, the Lord of life; the Son is the Reconciler, the re-newer of life; the Spirit is the Redeemer, the giver, the conveyor of this life which is given, sustained and renewed" (36). Family relationships are analogous in human form to this divine model. As the three distinct persons—Father, Son, and Holy Spirit—mutually indwell a trinitarian fellowship, so are family members to mutually indwell a family fellowship in similar ways.

Miroslav Volf expands on this concept by examining the Greek word *peri-choresis*, which "connotes mutual interpenetration without any coalescence or commixture" (1998, 208–13, 19). *Perichoresis* (from *peri*, meaning "around," and *chorea*, meaning "dance") pictures the "divine dance" or union of Father, Son, and Holy Spirit, which has gone on from the beginning and continues forever. This fellowship of three coequal persons perfectly embraced in love and harmony is the ultimate intimate union. This is affirmed in passages such as John 10:38, "so that you may know and understand that the Father is in me and I am in the Father," along with John 16:13–15, when Jesus refers to God's glory as the Spirit reveals the truth that the Son is of the Father. Divine unity is expressed as the distinct persons mutually indwell the Godhead.

The trinitarian model reflects the nature of covenantal relationality (distinction and unity) and becomes a core ideal and a central theme of understanding family relationships. However, we acknowledge that, unlike God, we are not perfect, and therefore in applying these principles, we will have to struggle with our human imperfections. We must look to God for grace and strength to attain personal distinction in relationships. The relational process—be it the initial forming of the marital relationship, nurturing and guiding in the child-rearing years, building new family structures, or dealing with the end of life—involves the fundamental issues of forming unity while embracing each person's distinctiveness. We use the biblical analogy in terms of how the members of the Godhead act in unity through distinctiveness with the themes of covenant, grace, empowerment, and intimacy.

God in Relationship

The Old and New Testaments use familial language by way of analogy to describe the relationship between the creator God and the created ones, including God as parent relating to the children of Israel, Christ as groom in relation to the church as bride, and the Holy Spirit indwelling and empowering

6

believers to be brothers and sisters in the Lord. God's actions toward Israel are characterized by compassionate love, discipline, guidance, pursuit, generosity, nurture, respect, knowledge, and forgiveness. Jesus welcomes little children, women, the disenfranchised, and his disciples into close, intimate connection. The Spirit prays in and through us when we cannot find the words to speak. In other words, familial relationships are analogies for describing the covenant relationship between God and his people.

A covenant is a type of relationship, usually between a king or queen and vassals. The covenant intends to bind the lord to a particular group of people, where protection would be offered for loyalty. Covenants entail stipulations and consequences for violation of the terms by either side. Michael Horton (2006) describes covenants as containing six components: (1) a preamble describing the one great king making the treaty; (2) a historical prologue describing the events and reasons (and justification) for the covenant; (3) stipulations between the king and the vassal; (4) sanctions or consequences for failing to uphold the treaty; and the final two aspects of covenant making, are (5) depositing the covenant on tablets and (6) periodically celebrating or reviewing them publicly. Genesis 1 and 2 should be read with this formulation in mind. God announces his covenant with Adam and Eve. This covenant is based on the Creator's word of power in establishing the universe, and it culminates with a blessing. In this way, Genesis 1:26–28, partially quoted above, describes the covenant representative being a differentiated humanity with covenant expectations—stewardship, fruitfulness, and multiplication (Gen. 1:28).

Ray Anderson (1982) uses the concept of cohumanity to build a theological anthropology. Beginning with the theological truth that "humanity is determined as existence in covenant relation with God" (37), Anderson applies the concept of covenant to all human relationships. He considers covenantal relationships in the family as a "secondary order, made possible by the primary order of differentiation as male or female" (52). Differentiation achieves the godly purpose of interdependence and cooperative interaction between people. In other words, unity and uniqueness become the primary vehicles for embodying the image of God.

In applying covenant as a paradigm for the family, Anderson and Guernsey (1985) highlight the unconditional quality of covenant: "It is covenant love that provides the basis for family. For this reason, family means much more than consanguinity, where blood ties provide the only basis for belonging. Family is where you are loved unconditionally, and where you can count on that love even when you least deserve it" (40).

Similarly, Stuart McLean (1984, 4–32) suggests the following ways that covenant can be used as a metaphor for marriage and family relationships: (1) people are social and live in community; (2) the basic unit of family and of covenant is the dyad; (3) people living in community experience struggle and conflict as well as harmony; (4) people living in covenant must be willing to forgive and be forgiven by one another; (5) people living in covenant must accept their strong bond to one another; (6) people living in covenant accept law in the form of patterns and order in relationships; and (7) people living in covenant have a temporal awareness as they carry a memory of the past, live in the present, and anticipate the future.

Covenant forms the foundation of our theology of family relationships. Covenant results in image bearing, and image bearing entails fulfilling the covenant stipulations of dominion or stewardship—that is, ruling over the birds of the air and fish of the sea—and fecundity regarding offspring and culture development (Wolters 2005). Finally, image bearing results in blessings for fulfilling the covenant—provision and blessing from God.

Elements in a Theology of Family Relationships

We propose a theology of family relationships that involves four dimensions or characteristics of Christian relating: covenant, grace, empowerment, and intimacy. Covenant is the core or meta-virtue of relating which grounds and supports the others. We further suggest that family relationships will be either dynamic and maturing or stagnant and dying. Family relationships, and all relationships for that matter, are oriented toward God's intended *telos* (or goal) or away from that goal, and any trajectory away from God's intended ideal is an outcome of sin (Wolters 2005). A model of this process of family relationships is presented in figure 1.

FIGURE 1 **Theological Characteristics of Family Relationships**

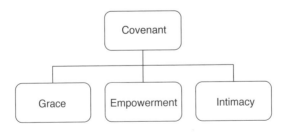

The logical beginning point of any family relationship is a covenant commitment, which has unconditional love at its core. Unconditional love as the bedrock love of one's relationship to the other creates responsiveness and accessibility to the other. Grace emerges from this covenantal foundation. Mercy and forgiveness, aspects of grace, are extended in relating with others—a result of the loving forgiveness received from God. In this atmosphere of grace, family members have the freedom to empower one another. Empowerment leads to the possibility of intimacy among family members. Grace, empowerment, and intimacy deepen as the foundation of covenant is solidified.

Covenants form the basis for grace, empowerment, and intimacy. As the three secondary relationship virtues are experienced, the covenant is increasingly solidified. For example, the relationship between a parent and an infant child begins as a unilateral (one-way) love commitment, but as the parent lives out that commitment, the relationship grows into a bilateral (mutual) love commitment. Grace, empowerment, and intimacy are expressed in this relationship. The covenant motivates the parents to offer grace to their offspring (food, housing, daily needs, interaction). Empowerment is expressed in the covenant as children learn the stipulations (household rules) that are embedded in the family. Finally, intimacy develops as partners learn more and more about one another. These three virtues feed back into the covenant, making it grow and bear fruit.

For such growth to take place in any relationship, there must be mutual involvement. Growth in family relationships can be blocked or hampered when one person in the relationship is unable or unwilling to reciprocate covenant love, grace, empowerment, or intimacy. Thus, growth in a relationship can come to a standstill at any point in this cycle. Because relationships are dynamic and ever changing, if a relationship does not move to deeper levels of commitment, grace, empowerment, and intimacy, it will stagnate and fixate on contract rather than covenant, law rather than grace, possessive power rather than empowerment, and distance rather than intimacy.

These theological relationship characteristics are derived from an examination of biblical writings that show how God enters into and sustains relationships (covenants) with humanity. The Bible teaches that God desires to be in relationship with humankind and also longs for humans to engage in a reciprocal relationship. We recognize, however, that although we are created in the image of God, we are fallen creatures who will fail in all aspects of relationship with God and others. In a sense, no person can ever make a covenant commitment in the way that God covenants with us, nor can anyone foster an atmosphere of grace in the same way God gives grace. Our empowerment attempts often resemble possessive power, and our attempts at intimacy pale in comparison to God's knowing and caring. Yet we are hopeful because God has been revealed perfectly in Jesus Christ. He is our model and enabler as we live out our lives and relationships according to God's purpose.

Covenant: To Love and Be Loved

Covenant—God's steadfast commitment to creation—forms the basis for the other relationship virtues. As the trunk of the proverbial tree, covenant is the core feature of relationship virtues from which grace, empowerment, and intimacy branch out. The central point of covenant is that it is an unconditional commitment, demonstrated supremely by God to the creation.

Although the concept of covenant has a rich heritage in Christian theology, the biblical meaning has been eroded by the modern notion that commitment is no more than a contract. Covenant is basic to the structure of the first two chapters of Genesis (Horton 2006), even though the first biblical mention of a covenant is found in Genesis 6:18, where God says to Noah, "But I will establish my covenant with you; and you shall come into the ark." God tells Noah to take his wife and sons and daughters-in-law, along with all living creatures, and Noah does everything that God commands. In Genesis 9:9–10, God repeats this promise of covenant: "As for me, I am establishing my covenant with you and your descendants after you, and with every living creature that is with you." The covenant is even extended to nonhuman creatures. Next, God makes a covenant with Abram: "I am God Almighty; walk before me, and be blameless. And I will make my covenant between me and you, and will make you exceedingly numerous" (Gen. 17:1–2). Upon hearing this, Abram falls down on his face. God continues in verse 7, "I will establish my covenant between me and you, and your offspring after you throughout their generations, for an everlasting covenant, to be God to you and to your offspring after you." Then in verse 9, the role of Abram (whose name is now changed to "Abraham") in the covenant is specified: "God said to Abraham, 'As for you, you shall keep my covenant, you and your offspring after you throughout their generations.'"

What can we learn from these two accounts of God's establishing a covenant with Noah and with Abraham? First, we see that God is not offering either of them any choice in the matter. That is, God is by no means saying, "Now I am going to commit myself to you if this is your desire." Instead, the establishment of the covenant is based entirely on God's action. Second, God's offer is in no way contractual; that is, it is not based on Noah or Abraham keeping their end of the bargain. God's commitment stands firm and solid (immutable would be the theological descriptor) no matter what their response. However, God desires and even commands a response—covenants come with expectations. Does this make God's covenantal offer conditional? Is God free to retract the offer if it is not reciprocated? The answer is a resounding no! The covenant God offers is steadfast and true, "an everlasting covenant," regardless of the response to it. Third, although the covenant itself is not conditional, the benefits or blessings are determined by the response. Both Noah and Abraham are given a choice to respond. If they are to benefit from the covenant, they need to make a freely determined response of obedience. Although the continuation of God's love is not conditioned on their response, the blessings of the covenant are conditional. Now that they receive and respond to God's covenant, they also receive the fulfillment of the promise. Fourth, we notice that God extends the covenant to their families from generation to generation. Neither Noah nor Abraham can anticipate obedience on the part of their descendants, further evidence of the unconditional nature of the covenant. In the same way, the blessings of the covenant are conditional, depending on whether the descendants decide to respond to and follow God.

Indeed, the Old Testament account in the book of Hosea conveys the central theme of the covenant relationship between God and the children of Israel. The cycle is as follows: The children of Israel turn away from God and get into all kinds of difficulty. God pursues them with a love that will not let them go, offering reconciliation and restitution when they respond. And then comes the incredible blessing of being in relationship with the Almighty God, who mothers like a hen and leads with cords of human kindness. The children of Israel reap the satisfaction of basking in the intimate presence and profound connection with their loving God.

The life of Jesus is the supreme expression of unconditional love. It is noteworthy that Jesus tells the story of the prodigal son (Luke 15) in response to the Pharisees' and the scribes' criticism of his sitting with sinners. Just as the father in the story welcomes his wayward son home with open arms, Jesus demonstrates unconditional love to a people who have rejected his Father. The unconditional nature of God's love is perhaps most clearly expressed in 1 John 4:19, "We love because he first loved us," and 1 John 4:10–13, "In this is love, not that we loved God but that he loved us and sent his Son to be the atoning sacrifice for our sins. Beloved, since God loved us so much, we also ought to love one another. No one has ever seen God; if we love one another, God lives in us, and his love is perfected in us. By this we know that we abide in him and he in us, because he has given us of his Spirit." Here is the promise of the mutual indwelling of God's unconditional love in us as we dwell in God's love through the sacrifice of Christ and the presence of the Spirit. And as we have received that unconditional love represented in the unity of the Godhead, we offer that unconditional love to others as God's image bearers.

Having discussed the unconditional quality of God's covenant commitments, we now turn to a related consideration—the issue of reciprocity. Whereas the unconditional nature of covenant love is unquestionable, in a familial context the concept of covenant can be used to refer to both unilateral and bilateral relationships. Figure 2 depicts the different types of commitment found in family relationships.

FIGURE 2 **Types of Commitment in Family Relationships**

	Conditional	Unconditional
Unilateral	Modern Open Arrangement	Initial Covenant
Bilateral	Contract	Mature Covenant

Any covenantal relationship is based on an unconditional commitment. However, covenantal relationships can be either unilateral (one-way) or bilateral (two-way). We have labeled a unilateral unconditional relationship an initial covenant and a bilateral unconditional relationship a mature covenant. All biblical references to the covenant God initiates are examples of initial covenants. It would be erroneous to think of an unconditional unilateral relationship as partial, dependent, or even immature because, from the individual's perspective, a personal covenant without restrictions is given. From a relational perspective, unilateral unconditional commitment entails the attractive possibility of someday becoming a two-way street. The desire of God in each initiated covenant is that the unconditional commitment will eventually be reciprocal and mutual—that one day, humanity will be able to ultimately consummate and fulfill the covenant stipulations.

When a child is born, the parents make an unconditional commitment of love to that child. The infant or young child is unable to make such a commitment in return. However, as the child matures, the relationship that began as an initial (unilateral) covenant can develop into a mature (bilateral) relationship. True reciprocity occurs as parents themselves age and become socially, emotionally, and physically more dependent on their adult child. Here, in a mature bilateral commitment, reciprocal and unconditional love is especially rewarding.

Our ideal for marital and mature parent-child relationships is an unconditional bilateral commitment. As shown in figure 2, there are two types of conditional family relationships. One type we call the *modern open arrangement*, which is symptomatic of a society in which people are hesitant to make commitments that do not inherently offer benefits. A typical example is a person who begins a marriage with the unspoken understanding that as long as his or her needs are being met, all is well, but as soon as those needs are no longer met, the relationship will end. When both spouses adopt this conditional stance, the marriage amounts to a contract, a quid pro quo arrangement. In modern open arrangements, the couple believes they have fulfilled the marital contract when they get from the relationship a little more than they give to the relationship. That is, modern open arrangements are viewed as successful if one gives slightly less than one receives.

In reality, much of the daily routine in family life is carried out according to informal contractual agreements. When we advocate relationships based on covenant, we must recognize the importance of mutuality, fairness, and reciprocal processes that lead to interdependence. Yet there are extraordinary dimensions of loving unconditionally, such as sacrificing oneself for the other and going the second mile even when things aren't equal. It is a matter of being willing to be *unselfish* rather than thinking only of self (*selfish*) or only of others (*selfless*), as Stephen Post (1994) defines the terms. Any mature relationship based on contract alone will forgo the incredible acts of love that far exceed any contract made by two individuals and ultimately reflect the fulfillment of God's covenant in the saving work of Christ on the cross.

Grace: To Forgive and Be Forgiven

By its very nature, covenant is grace—unmerited favor. From a human perspective, the unconditional love of God makes no sense except as it is offered in grace. *Grace* is truly a relational word. One is called to share in a gracious relationship with God. Due to God's unshakable covenant, grace is extended. God condescends to the creature and the creature is elevated (see Ps. 8).

John Rogerson (1996) takes the understanding of grace as a natural extension of covenant love and applies it to family life. He cites Old Testament texts suggesting that God desires the establishment of structures of grace to strengthen family life. These structures of grace are defined as "social arrangement[s] designed to mitigate hardship and misfortune, and grounded in God's mercy." The following example is from Exodus 22:25–27: "If you lend money to my people, to the poor among you, you shall not deal with them as a creditor; you shall not exact interest from them. If you take your neighbor's cloak in pawn, you shall restore it before the sun goes down; for it may be your neighbor's only clothing to use as cover; in what else shall that person sleep? And if your neighbor cries out to me, I will listen, for I am compassionate." From his analysis of Old Testament teachings about the family, Rogerson concludes, "What is really important is that theologically-driven efforts were made to counteract the forces that undermined the family" (41).

Family relationships, as designed by God, are meant to be lived out in an atmosphere of grace, not law. Family life based on contract leads to an atmosphere of law and is a discredit to Christianity. Law keeps a tally of credits and debits. Family members take an account of how much they give and how much they receive from the family. Fairness in this sense is based on balancing this ledger (Boszormenyi-Nagy and Krasner 1986; Boszormenyi-Nagy and Spark 1984). On the contrary, family life based on covenant leads to an atmosphere of grace and forgiveness. There must be a willingness to forgive if right relationships are going to develop in family life (Borrowdale 1996). Just as the meaning and joy of being a Christian would be deadened if we conceived of our relationship with God in terms of law and not grace, so would meaning and joy be constrained in family relationships. On both the individual and the family level, law leads to legalism, whereas grace offers freedom. In an atmosphere of grace, family members learn to act responsibly out of love and consideration for one another.

The incarnation is the supreme act of God's grace to humankind. Christ came in human form to reconcile the world to God. This act of divine love and forgiveness is the basis for human love and forgiveness. Forgiveness bridges grace offered horizontally and vertically (Shults and Sandage 2003), meaning that Christians are able to extend grace, mercy, and forgiveness as they have received them. We can forgive others as we have been forgiven, and the love of God within makes it possible for us to love others in the same unconditional way.

One may ask if there is any place for law in family relationships. Are we to believe that when grace is present in the family there is no need for law at all? Our answer must be the same as that given by the apostle Paul: "For Christ is the end of the law so that there may be righteousness for everyone who believes" (Rom. 10:4). It is not that the law itself is bad, for it points the way to God. But because humans are limited and fallen, we can never fulfill the law. Christ is the end of the law because he is the perfect fulfillment of the law. We are righteous by faith alone! No one can keep the law perfectly.

We are free from the law because of Christ's perfection and righteousness, which leads to our salvation.

The same can be said concerning family relationships. Through Scripture we can know something of God's ideal for family relationships, but none of us can expect to measure up perfectly to that ideal. In a family based on law, the members demand perfection of one another. Rules and regulations are rigidly set to govern relationships. This kind of pressure for flawlessness adds guilt to the failure that is inevitable in such a situation.

The application of the concept of grace in family relationships is a challenge when we are working out family structures, roles, and rules. Although the covenant of grace rules out law as a basis for family relationships, family members living in grace accept structure, forms, patterns, order, and responsibility in relationships. In reality, much of the daily routine of family life must be performed according to agreed-upon rules, regularity, and order. Grace means having consistently applied, developmentally appropriate rules and expectations for each family member. Grace is also the ability to be reflective about those rules and make changes as necessary. Grace does not repress needs or limit lives, but offers order and regularity so that family members' needs are met and their lives enhanced.

Empowerment: To Serve and Be Served

The most common and conventional definition of *power* is the ability to influence another person. In such a definition, the emphasis is placed on one's ability to influence and not the actual exercise of the authority. Most research on the use of power in the family has focused on a person's attempt to influence or control the behavior of another. An underlying assumption in such analyses is that people using power try to decrease rather than increase the power of those they are trying to influence. They tend to use power in a way that assures the maintenance of their own more powerful position. In this sense of power, a suitable synonym may be *control*.

Empowerment, however, is a biblical model for the use of power that is completely contrary to its common use in the family or in society at large. Empowerment can be defined as the attempt to establish power in another person. Empowerment does not necessarily involve yielding to the wishes of another person or ceding one's own power to someone else. Rather, empowerment is the active, intentional process of helping another person to become empowered. The person who is empowered has been equipped, strengthened, built up, matured, and has gained skill because of the encouraging support of the other. Empowerment flows out of the covenant between partners because covenant relationships seek the best of the other. Empowerment as an offshoot of the covenant encourages the other to develop into the person God intends. Empowerment facilitates the development of authentic, Christlike individuals.

In a nutshell, empowerment is the process of helping another person recognize his or her potential and then reach that potential through one's encouragement and guidance. It involves coming alongside a person to affirm their gifts and build their confidence to become all that they can be. Sometimes the empowerer must be willing to step back and allow the one being empowered to learn through experience and not through overdependence. An empowerer respects the uniqueness of each person and equips that person according to his or her individual ways of learning. Empowerment never involves control, coercion, or force. Rather, it is a respectful, reciprocal process that takes place between people in mutually enhancing ways.

A great example of this in the Scriptures is the story of the prodigal son in Luke 15. In this familiar story, a wealthy father has two sons. The younger son asks for his share of the family estate before the father passes away. The father assents to this request, and the younger son takes his money and moves to a faraway country. In the meantime, the older son remains steadfast at his father's side, engaged in the family business. After his inheritance runs out and he is forced to perform tasks unthinkable for an Israelite, the younger son returns home. The father welcomes him with open arms, throwing a lavish party. The older son, who was working out in the fields, did not know his younger brother had returned. The older son confronts his father when he finds out the party was for the younger son—the one that wished his father was dead! Empowerment, as the lens for this story, indicates that the father empowers the younger son by giving him the inheritance. He allows him to make a decision as an adult and experience the consequences of that decision. Luke even records the younger son's development while feeding the pigs: "He came to his senses" (Luke 15:17 NIV).

If covenant is the basis of grace, and grace is the underlying atmosphere of acceptance and forgiveness, then empowerment is the action of God in people's lives. We see it supremely in the work of Jesus Christ. The celebrated message of Jesus is that he has come to empower: "I came that they may have life, and have it abundantly" (John 10:10). The apostle John puts it this way: "But to all who received him, who believed in his name, he gave power to become children of God, who were born, not of blood or of the will of the flesh or of the will of man, but of God" (John 1:12–13). Ray Anderson (1985) insightfully exegetes this text by noting that power "of blood" is power in the natural order, and "the will of the flesh" refers to tradition, duty, honor, obedience, and everything that is part of conventional power. In this passage, then, it is clear that the power is given by God and not by either physical or conventional means.

The power given by Jesus is of a personal order—power that is mediated to the powerless. To us in our sinful and powerless condition, God gives the ability to become children of God. This is the supreme example of human empowerment. Jesus redefined power by his teaching and by relating to others as a servant. Jesus rejected the use of power to control others and instead affirmed the use of power to serve others, to lift up the fallen, to forgive the guilty, to encourage responsibility and maturity in the weak, and to enable the unable. His empowerment was directed to those who occupied the margins.

In a very real sense, empowerment is love in action. It is the mark of Jesus Christ that family members need to emulate most. The practice of empowerment in families will revolutionize the view of authority in Christian homes. Sadly, authority in marriage continues to be a controversial issue today because of a widely accepted secular view that power is a commodity in limited supply; therefore, a person must grab as much power as possible in relationships. Whether through coercion or manipulation, striving for power leads to antagonizing competition rather than to the cooperative building up of people. Power becomes a distortion that distances, in contrast to mutual empowerment, which leads to unity.

But the good news for Christians is that the power of God is available to all persons in *unlimited supply*! Ephesians 4 reminds us that unique spiritual gifts are given to everyone for the building up of the body of Christ, "until all of us come to the unity of the faith and of the knowledge of the Son of God, to maturity, to the measure of the full stature of Christ" (v. 13). In a similar vein, Galatians 5:22–23 contrasts the works of the flesh against the fruit of the Spirit, which is freely given and defined as love, joy, peace, patience, kindness, generosity, faithfulness, gentleness, and self-control. In verses 25 and 26, we are encouraged and admonished: "If we live by the Spirit, let us also be guided by the Spirit. Let us not become conceited, competing against one another, envying one another." This is the character of God, and it is available to all family members who draw on the inexhaustible resources in Christ Jesus!

Empowerment is born out of God's covenant love, and it thrives in the gracious relational context experienced in Christ Jesus. The Spirit of God empowers us to empower others. And when mutual empowerment occurs among family members, each will be stretched in the extraordinary ways of servant love and humility. Family members will grow in the stature of Christ as they mature into the character of Christ in their daily interactions. When they use their areas of strength to build up one another, they are placing unity and interdependency at the heart of their relationships. It has nothing to do with having power over others but rather involves taking great delight in building up one another to become all God wants us to be. This is the essence of what we read in 1 Corinthians 8:1: "Knowledge puffs up, but loves builds up."

Traditional thinking about parent-child relationships is also based on the false assumption that power is in limited supply. Thus, parents often fear that as children grow older and gain more power, their parental power will automatically be reduced. In contrast, a relationship-empowering approach to parenting begins by reconsidering the nature of power and authority. In the biblical sense, parental authority is an ascribed power. The Greek word for authority, *exousia*, literally means "out of being." It refers to a type of influence that is not dependent on any personal strength, achievement, or skill but that comes forth "out of the being" of a person. The Greek word for power, *dynamis*, is the word from which *dynamo* is derived. The authority of Jesus flowed from his personhood. It was dynamic.

Dynamic parents have authority that flows from their personhood as they earnestly and responsibly care for their children's physical, social, psychological, and spiritual development. The process of empowering children certainly does not mean giving up a position of authority, nor does it mean that parents will be depleted or drained of power as they parent. Rather, parents and children will both achieve a sense of personal power, self-esteem, and wholeness. Successful parenting involves building a relationship in which children gain personal power and parents retain personal power throughout the process.

Once again, human fears and personal or cultural needs may stand in the way of parental empowerment of children and adolescents. In the frailty of human insecurity, parents may be tempted to keep their offspring dependent on them. In the attempt to use their power over their children, they may inadvertently have a false sense of security in their parental position. When children obey out of fear and under coercion, it is likely to backfire. An emotional barrier develops when children are loyal out of obligation rather than by choice. The parental demand for unreasonable obedience and loyalty may be culturally motivated, but it is often related to selfish needs as well. In contrast, covenant love and empowerment lead to a mature interdependency in which there is both freedom and a continued sense of belonging for adult children. This kind of love remains faithful, honorable, and predictable even when differences threaten to endanger the relationship.

All parents have experienced the temptation to keep a child dependent, which is often rationalized as something we do for the child's own good. Many times, however, the child is kept in a dependent position for the parents' own convenience. Empowerment is the ultimate goal, where parents release the child to self-control. Of course, mistakes will be made, and failure will be the occasional consequence of trying out new wings. Parents have a hard time letting their children make mistakes (especially the same mistakes they themselves made when young), so this transition to self-reliance is difficult for parents and children alike. It is important for parents to remember that the key to their authority lies not in external control but in internal control that their children can integrate into their own personhood. When this integration occurs, it is a rewarding and mutually satisfying achievement.

On the community level as well, Christians are called to live according to extraordinary social patterns. Even though we are sinners, God provides us with the ability to follow the empowerment principle in our relationships. God empowers us, by the Holy Spirit, to empower others. The biblical ideal for all our relationships, then, is that we be Christian realists in regard to our own sinfulness and tendency to fail, but Christian optimists in light of the grace and power available to live according to God's intended purposes.

Intimacy: To Know and Be Known

Humans are unique among living creatures in our ability to communicate through language, a capacity that makes it possible for us to know one another intimately. Our Christian faith is distinct from Eastern religions in its teaching that God has broken into human history to be personally related to us. A major theme that runs through the Bible is that God wants to know us and to be known by us. We are encouraged to share our deepest thoughts and feelings through prayer. We are told that the Holy Spirit dwells within us and that God understands the very groaning within that cannot be uttered (Rom. 8:26–27).

Adam and Eve stood completely open and transparent before God, "naked, and . . . not ashamed" (Gen. 2:25). The intimacy that Adam and Eve felt enabled them to be themselves without any pretense. They had no need to play deceptive games. Only after their disobedience did they try to hide from God out of a feeling of nakedness and shame—to which God responded with care and gracious provision of animal skins. Shame is often born out of a fear of unworthiness or rejection. Shame entails the experience of personal wrongness—I am wrong or broken. When shame is present, family members put on masks and begin to play deceptive roles before one another. By contrast, as we examine the nature of the pre-fall human family (which is the only social institution that belongs to the order of creation), we find an emphasis on intimacy—on knowing and being known. This is what it means to be a servant, to empty oneself as Jesus did when he took the form of a servant. This is how one is to be submissive and loving in relationships. It is also true that to have any union or partnership or interdependence with another person, one must always be willing to give up some of one's own needs and desires. When family members come to one another with this kind of attitude and perspective, they will find a common ground of joy, satisfaction, and mutual benefit.

When family members experience grace and empowerment flowing out of covenant love, they will be able to communicate confidently and express themselves freely without fear. Family members will want what is best for one another. They will make a concerted effort to listen, understand, accept differences, and value and confirm uniqueness. Family members will develop and express themselves (uniqueness) in their family relationships without the pressure to change or modify themselves (unity).

The capacity for family members to communicate feelings freely and openly with one another is contingent on trust and commitment. They are not afraid to share and be intimate with one another. John gives us insight into this: "God is love" (1 John 4:16); "There is no fear in love, but perfect love casts out fear" (v. 18). God expresses perfect love, and we can respond in love because God loved us first (v. 19).

This brings us back to the unconditional covenant love that is the cornerstone for family communication and honest sharing without the threat of rejection. As family members offer their love unconditionally to one another, the security that is established will lead to deeper levels of intimacy.

The unconditional love modeled by Jesus gives a picture of the type of communicative intimacy desirable in family relationships. Recall how Jesus, at the end of his earthly ministry, asked Peter not once but three times, "Do you love me?" (John 21). Peter had earlier denied Jesus three times; Jesus was giving Peter the opportunity to assert what he had previously denied and to reaffirm his love three times. Perhaps the relationship between Jesus and Peter had not been the same since Peter's triple denial. Likewise, family relationships become strained as we disappoint, fail, and even betray those whom we love the most.

Forgiving and being forgiven are important aspects of renewal. There is a need to confess as well as to receive confession. This is a two-way street that can resolve the unfinished business between family members. Being willing to admit failures and to acknowledge being offended by another person opens intimacy between two people as they seek reconciliation. Intimacy will bring relationships to full maturity.

Applying the Theological Model: From Hurting to Healing Behaviors

In examining biblical themes that have a bearing on the nature of family relationships, we have suggested that (1) commitment should be based on a mature (i.e., unconditional and bilateral) covenant love; (2) family life should be established and maintained within an atmosphere of grace, which embraces acceptance and forgiveness; (3) the resources of family members should be used to empower rather than to control one another; and (4) intimacy is based on a knowing that leads to caring, understanding, communication, and communion with others. These four elements of Christian family relationships are part of a continual process: intimacy can lead to deeper covenant love, commitment fortifies the atmosphere of freely offered grace, the climate of acceptance and forgiveness encourages serving and empowering others, and the resultant sense of self-esteem leads to the ability to be intimate without fear.

Table 1, which represents a summary of our theological model, illustrates how a family that places its allegiance in Jesus Christ can move toward God's paradigm for relationships. Although believers experience different levels of maturity in Christ, each of them has a capacity to follow God's way because of the spiritual power within. Inasmuch as all family members are imperfect, with their own individual temperaments and experiences, they progress at different rates in the process of realizing God's ideals of unconditional love, grace, empowerment, and intimacy. That is to say, all family members fall on a continuum between hurting and healing behaviors. As long as they move in the direction of healing, they will grow and the family will benefit. When they choose hurting behaviors and move away from God's way, however, the entire family will be negatively affected.

Among the hurting behaviors in a family environment are conditional love, self-centeredness, perfectionism, faultfinding, efforts to control others, unreliability, denial of feelings, and lack of communication. With such behaviors, the focus is on self rather than on the best interests of the other family members. In hurting families, each individual is affected on the personal level. For example, one may not feel loved or worthy of being loved by the other family members. Such individuals are limited in their ability to love others unconditionally. A vicious circular pattern emerges. Such problems at the personal level cause the individual to view interpersonal relationships as potential threats. The result is behavior that perpetuates the root problem. For example, an individual who does not know what it is to be loved unconditionally is prone to approach others defensively.

Hurting families tend to withhold grace, often demanding unreasonable perfection and blaming those members who don't measure up. Individuals in these families fear they will make a mistake and be rejected because of their failure to meet the standards. So they try harder to be perfect. What they need is acceptance for who they are and forgiveness when they fail.

TABLE 1 **From Hurting to Healing Behavior**

Hurting Behavior	Problem at the Personal Level	Obstacle to Interpersonal Relationships	Behavior Perpetuating the Problem	Healing Behavior: The Cure
From Conditional Love to Unconditional Love				
Conditional love	Feeling unloved	Fear of not being loved	Loving others in order to be loved in return	Unconditional love
Self-centeredness	Feeling unworthy of love	Fear of being thought worthless	Focus on self	Christ-centeredness
From Shame to Grace				
Perfectionism	Fear of making a mistake	Fear of not being accepted	Trying harder	Acceptance
Faultfinding	Expectation of perfection in self and others	Fear of being criticized	Blaming others	Forgiveness
From Control to Empowerment				
Efforts to control others	Lack of confidence in one's ability to influence	Fear of losing others	Overcontrol	Building others up
Unreliability	Lack of control of oneself	Fear of disappointing others	Being out of control	Reliability
From Lack of Feeling to Intimacy				
Denial of feelings	Fear of feelings	Fear of rejection	Avoidance of feelings	Experience of feelings
Lack of communication	Distrust of others	Fear of being hurt by others	Superficial conversation	Open and honest communication

Hurting families also tend to control rather than empower their members. Individuals in these families lack the confidence that they can influence others; they fear they will be discredited because of their inadequacies. The result is a desperate attempt to get power by coercing and controlling less powerful family members. What is needed instead is affirmation and validation by the family. Empowerment will build confidence so that all family members can reach their greatest potential.

Hurting families are characterized at the individual level by their members not being in touch with their feelings. Their fear of rejection keeps them in denial of their emotions. What they need most is a safe atmosphere in which they can express their feelings, thoughts, wants, and desires and be heard and understood by the other family members. Open communication helps each person share more honestly rather than hide feelings and thoughts from others. In turn, this experience increases one's capacity to be known by others and to know oneself at deeper levels.

A cure is needed to break the perpetual cycle found in hurting families. An individual who has been loved only conditionally needs to experience unconditional love in order to feel lovable enough to give love and to support others. The breakthrough comes when one receives God's unconditional love. Being cherished by God gives a sense of self-worth and a new self-perception ("I am lovable"). Drawing on the Holy Spirit and maturing in the faith, the individual now has reason to follow God's paradigm and to adopt healing behaviors.

We have seen that living in covenant love is a dynamic process. God has designed family relationships to grow from hurting to healing behavior—that is, to a maturity analogous to that of individual believers who attain the full measure of perfection found in Christ (Eph. 4:13). This maturing of relationships eventually enables family members to reach out to people beyond the boundaries of the family.

2

The Family as a Developing Biosocial System

Experience shows that it is possible to observe family life, or even be actively involved in family life, and yet be limited in our understanding of it. In fact, active involvement in family life may be the very reason we fail to understand it from a wider perspective.

In this chapter, we introduce two theoretical perspectives that family clinicians and sociologists have found helpful in gaining a wide-angle view of family life. The first one is called family-systems theory because it views family life not merely as the sum total of the actions of all the individual members but rather as the interactions of all family members operating as a unit of interrelated parts. Individuals are considered in the context of their relationships. We describe this theory at length. Parenthetically, it should be noted that by including biological factors relevant to family life, our focus is on the family as a *bio*social system. The other theoretical perspective is family-development theory, which views the family as developing over time through natural life-cycle stages. Both family-systems theory and family-development theory emphasize the interrelationships between the individual's bio-psycho-social development and the relationship context in which he or she is embedded. We explain these two perspectives, which will serve as a basis for focusing attention on family life as a whole.

Family-Systems Theory

A major cultural theme in modern society is individualism. Individualism has caused us to focus on the individual's needs and perspective rather than on relationships and groups. Current psychological approaches largely focus on individual differences or individual psychology as opposed to groups or networks of individuals (which more correctly belongs in social psychology and sociology). The clinical profession is shifting the focus from the individual to the broader family system and beyond to include multileveled systems. This relational or systemic perspective allows clinicians to understand the embedded social dimension of human nature and flourishing. Both family therapists and sociologists now view family life from a broader systems perspective.

What is a family-systems perspective? Basically, it is a holistic approach that understands every component of family life in terms of the family as a whole. A *system* is by definition any identifiable whole composed of interrelated individual parts. To understand any system, one must begin by identifying the various levels within that system. Think of a series of concentric circles. At the core is the individual (bio-psycho-social dimensions); the next level includes the nuclear family (the family one lives within); then comes the extended family (grandparents, relatives, significant others); the next level includes school, work, friends, neighbors, and faith communities; and the final multicultural level includes socioeconomic, cultural, ethnic, racial, geographical, religious, and historical context. All these systems are interrelated. They influence and are influenced by one another simultaneously. The boundary around each of these multileveled systems involves belonging and membership. Western societies usually define the boundary of the family system as a husband, a wife, and their children. In many other societies, the extended family is considered the basic family system.

Resilience and constraints are embedded within the relationships among these levels. For example, a toddler is developing competencies related to walking, talking, and increasing personal autonomy (bio-psycho-social dimensions). This competence is supported and encouraged by parents (nuclear family). The nuclear family is also embedded in a context that supports their care and nurture (resilience factor) or constrains it (due to limited economic opportunities, high levels of crime, and/or high levels of divorce or out-of-wedlock childbearing). Finally, all the previous subsystems are embedded in a macrosystem that provides meaning-making, values, and spiritual perspectives either supporting the previous subsystems or constraining them. The impetus for change in order to accommodate various competencies can derive from any of the subsystems.

The fundamental concepts of systems theory are illustrated in figure 3. Notice that there are several semipermeable boundaries: (1) around the entire family, (2) between subsystems like the parents and children, and (3) around each individual. Anything within the boundary is considered part of the system, and anything that falls outside the boundary is identified as part of the environment. These boundaries indicate that inputs may come from outside the family as well as within each subsystem in the family. Input includes any message or stimulus that enters the system from the environment. Output includes any message or response from the system to the environment. Boundaries around a system can be relatively open or closed. In an open family system, boundaries are said to be permeable, allowing for significant input from and output to the environment. In a closed family system, boundaries serve as barriers to limit such interaction.

Parents form the leadership system that determines how open or closed the boundaries with the environment are. Once a boundary has been established, objects within the system are identified as units of the system. In the newly established family, there are two units (individuals), the husband and the wife, each with identifiable positions and roles within the family. As children enter the family, the system becomes more complex, since each new member (whether biological, adopted, or fostered) occupies a given position in the system and is assigned a role to play within it, and now subsystems are created.

A family that includes children has at least two subsystems: the parental subsystem, composed of the spouses or adult relationship partners, and the

FIGURE 3 **Family-Systems Theory**

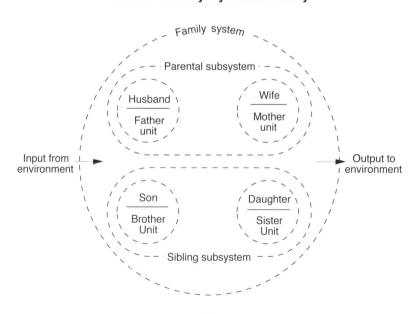

sibling subsystem, composed of the children (or, in the case of an only child, the child subsystem). Each sibling is also identified as an individual unit with unique traits, qualities, and biological makeup. An extended-family system includes grandparents, relatives, and nonrelatives who are considered part of that system. For example, when a divorced father of two children unites with a widowed mother of three, a broad definition of this family system includes relatives and friends from all sides of that family.

In most systems, rules of hierarchy exist between the subsystems. The major rule is that the adult subsystem (parents/adult members or nonfamily members) is considered to have authority and responsibility over the children in the home. It can be problematic when a child takes on a parental position in the home rather than remaining part of the sibling subsystem. In fact, the pattern of children becoming parents, or what we call parentified children or parentification indicates a serious concern with the family. When a child emerges as an authority and becomes the boss, an incongruent hierarchy emerges. According to Nuttall, Valentino, and Borkowski (2012), a *parentified child* can experience problems after marriage when parenting their own children. This negative effect of parentification may depend upon the nature of the sibling relationships (Borchet et al. 2020). Older siblings can periodically take responsibility when parents aren't present, but they relinquish that position after the parents return.

Multilevel systems theory developed in large part because of the inadequacies of a simplistic cause-and-effect model for complex social behavior, such as that of a family. The difference between a more complex system and a simplistic system can best be seen in the various ways in which behavior can be controlled, balanced, or changed through a feedback process. The many levels of feedback in a complex system, such as a family, are embedded within one another and build on one another. There are four major levels of feedback: simple feedback, cybernetic control, morphogenesis, and reorientation.

Simple Feedback

Simple feedback is identical with a cause-and-effect model. For example, to assist parents in toilet training a child, a behavior-modification therapist focuses on the behavior itself. Giving the child candy intermittently when the task is accomplished reinforces the desired behavior. By contrast, withholding the reward (candy) conditions the child to relinquish undesired behavior. Family members frequently use simple feedback as a stimulus for change. It is a simple exchange between the system and the environment.

Cybernetic Control

Cybernetic control is somewhat more complex. Here an output from the system feeds back to a monitoring unit within the system, which sets in motion a systemic adjustment to the original output. Perhaps the best example of cybernetic control is the self-monitoring action of a thermostat. On a cold winter day, we may set the thermostat at 70 degrees. When the room temperature gets below a certain point (say 68 degrees), then the needle in the thermostat makes electrical contact and the heater turns on. The heater will stay on until the needle rises to the point (say 72 degrees) where it loses electrical contact; then the heater turns off. This is cybernetic control because the heating system has a built-in mechanism to control itself. Cybernetic control functions around a *homeostatic balance*—optimal functioning occurs within a range. For example, the thermostat may have a five-degree range in which it will not start the furnace or shut it off.

Family life can be understood in much the same way. Families have rules or norms that define expected behavior for each family member. Each of these rules has a tolerance limit beyond which one cannot go without the family as a system taking some counteraction. In our thermostat analogy, the tolerance limits were 68 and 72 degrees. The family will need some flexibility in setting its tolerance limits, for if they are set too rigidly, there will be a constant need to correct, and normal family living will be impossible. For example, imagine what would happen to the heater if the tolerance limits were set at 69.999 and 70.001 degrees. The heater would be turning on and shutting off constantly, and all the energy would be exerted in that endeavor.

Consider a family that has a rigid rule that everyone must be home and be seated at the table at exactly 6:00 p.m. for the evening meal. The family may be willing to wait for about thirty seconds for Maria to get off the phone so they can begin, but they most certainly will not tolerate a five-minute delay. The system will draw on its storehouse of memories and choose an action to correct the undesirable behavior. It may be that Maria's siblings will pressure her to hang up or that her parents will warn her that she won't get anything to eat unless she hangs up immediately. In either case, the system works as a whole to shape her behavior.

All families have rules that each member obeys for the good of the whole. The system monitors deviance from these rules. Cybernetic control is the action the system takes to maintain the rules or status quo (referred to as *homeostasis* in systems-theory language). In other words, families exert a certain amount of social pressure (called *homeostasis* in systems-theory language) to maintain the current levels of family functioning. For the most part, individuals in the family are able to develop competencies as long as these competencies do not require the family's nature or structure to change. Adding a child, for example, means that the structure of the family needs to change. New rules and communication patterns are needed as the new family member is cared for. As the child develops, more and more competencies are acquired. These new competencies will eventually require a change in the nature of the family's relationships—parenting strategies of teens should be very different than for younger children; the parents' relationship needs to change to accommodate a teen; the family's relationship with the social world needs to change as well. The ways in which families respond to these changes vary dramatically. Sometimes problematic responses to these changes become homeostatic, meaning that the family becomes resistant to trying a different coping mechanism to deal with the changes. This is known as *reification* in family therapy. These reified functional patterns, sometimes called *overfunctioning/underfunctioning reciprocity*, limit the effectiveness of the individual and family development (Bowen 2004).

On the one hand, cybernetics is ultimately functional—concerned with the accomplishment of tasks in the family. Function allows family members to be responsive to one another while addressing inputs from the outside environment. Sometimes, these functional changes incorporate more acute challenges from outside the family, allowing children and more vulnerable members to cope with the challenges. On the other hand, function may become a more persistent pattern. In family therapy language, these functional responses are reified and become the homeostatic balance in the family. The issue here is that these challenges prevent others from developing needed competencies themselves.

Morphogenesis

Families often go beyond cybernetic control, however, for they are continually redefining and changing their rules, regulations, and procedures. The system's rule changes often result in a change of form or function (*morphogenesis*) in the family. Expanding our illustration, let's suppose that the family is determined not to begin eating without Maria and that none of their tried and proven techniques succeed in getting her off the phone. A system that functions only at a cybernetic level can do absolutely nothing. It must either resort to a past response or not respond at all. However, a system that operates on a morphogenetic level is capable of generating or creating new ways of responding to the situation. New responses are created whenever tested methods no longer work or the system is facing a situation for the first time.

One advantage that effective family systems have over ineffective family systems is the ability to operate at this higher level. The overly rigid family is usually incapable of morphogenetic responses because the family lacks flexibility. However, chaotically structured families with few rules or boundaries have similar difficulty because they do not possess the cohesiveness to act in a united way.

The family is usually required to generate new response patterns whenever unpredictable or unexpected changes occur. For example, when a member of the family loses a job, gets sick, or dies, new response patterns are demanded. This is also true for positive life-cycle changes, such as the birth or adoption of a child into the family, a wedding or anniversary celebration, or an unexpected inheritance of money. The family will be challenged to form new response patterns to these events as well. For instance, when we (the Balswicks) adopted our nine-year-old Korean son, each family member (sister, father, and mother) needed to make space for and welcome him into our family of three. Joel, in turn, needed to make space for us as he came to know us through interactions as a brother and son and the newest family member. We each were challenged in different ways as individual family members through the process of becoming a newly formed family. In the Frederick family, we also had to make changes with the adoption of a new pet. The process is the same in this more lighthearted example. Each member of our family provided input into the decision to adopt a kitten, we discussed the impact this would have on our daily schedules, and we devised a chore list with everyone contributing.

Another important aspect of a more complex model is that people bring meaning to their behavior. We must do more than understand a person's actions; we must pay attention to the beliefs (perspectives) of that person in relation to his or her behavior. So Maria may have a very good reason to ask the family to make an exception for her lateness; for example, she is working hard on an important project for school and needs the family to be flexible. If family togetherness is the mother's priority, however, she and Maria will have to negotiate change according to the meaning each one brings to the issue. In general, there is no right or wrong way for a family to be organized, but the family must determine how its system will function by considering the best interest of each family member in addition to what is in the best interest of the family system itself. This is how the many levels of a system are embedded within and build on one another.

The tendency in most families is to respond in old, familiar ways to new situations (homeostasis). These old ways will likely be inadequate, and the family will become stuck in them rather than be motivated to operate on the morphogenetic level. It is also true that most families do not stagnate—

because changes are always occurring in the family, whether at an individual, a relational, or a family level. In other words, family members constantly need to be in tune with the complex changes happening at all levels as they make adjustments in their daily living. The effective family understands that flexibility in structure, as well as relational connection between family members, is needed to operate on the morphogenetic level. Members of these families are alert and responsive to one another in the realm of individual differentiation and in keeping family togetherness a priority.

A unique perspective on morphogenesis developed from family-systems theory is known as differentiation of self (DoS). DoS focuses on how families function over time in response to one another. As described above, families sometimes develop a cybernetic pattern of under- and overfunctioning. Challenges to this pattern that disrupt the homeostatic balance often require internal resources to change the rules of the system or engage in morphogenesis. DoS is an internal resource, as well as a relational strength, developed in families. DoS may be conceptualized as the balance between individuality and togetherness (Bowen 2004; Kerr and Bowen 1988). DoS provides the resources to live out one's core values and beliefs (individuality) while maintaining relationships with others (togetherness). Challenges to homeostasis create intense anxiety, which exerts pressure to maintain the status quo in the family. DoS helps individuals to remain authentic to their values and beliefs while engaging in the change process, thus preventing rigid relational patterns like overfunctioning/underfunctioning reciprocity to develop while encouraging open and authentic intimacy to characterize the family's relationships.

The following is a brief illustration of differentiation of self and work based in Tom's clinical practice. Carlos was a typical teen, and he regularly questioned his parents' desire and expectation that he would attend college in preparation for a career. Education was immensely important to his parents, Letty and Mario—they both graduated from college, Letty was a middle-school teacher, and Mario was an administrator for the local school district. To a large extent being in the Mendoza family meant that education was important. Carlos was questioning the family's very identity by stating his desire to not pursue college. This questioning created a significant amount of stress and tension that challenged the family's homeostasis. Both parents began to exert pressure on Carlos to be faithful to his Mendoza identity and attend college. Our clinical work focused on supporting the family while making space for Carlos to explore the potential of not going to college. Differentiation helps each family member to maintain their relationships with each other while allowing each to solidify their core values and beliefs. For Carlos, this means that it is important for him to have space to ask the questions and clarify and choose his core values while remaining part of the family.

Reorientation

The fourth and highest level of feedback is reorientation; here the family changes its entire goal. In morphogenesis, new ways of responding are generated, but in reorientation, the goals themselves are changed. Reorientation involves a dramatic change in family life in which the entire system converts to new ways of thinking and behaving. For example, reorientation may occur when the family of an alcoholic comes to grips with an understanding of how every member contributes to the problem. Treatment affects not only the alcoholic but also each and every family member, so change occurs at all levels. Another example is a radical change in an entire family's belief system, such as when an individual religious conversion spreads to all members, resulting in an entirely new pattern of family living.

Major systemic change is fairly rare, and most families operate out of morphogenesis (generating new response patterns) or homeostasis (maintaining the status quo). Reorientation is most needed when a family's existing patterns of behavior prove to be totally unworkable and damaging to its members.

Biological Influences on the Family

In their article "Biosocial Influences on the Family," D'Onofrio and Lahey (2010, 762) state, "There has been a growing acceptance of the importance of biological factors in the study of family and social influences, as many researchers are now studying how biological and social factors act and interact." Before the emergence of the social sciences, it was assumed that nature rather than nurture was primarily responsible for human behavior. Evidence for the importance of nurture ushered in a social determinism in the form of behaviorism—recall John B. Watson's (1930, 82) famous boast, "Give me a dozen healthy infants, well formed, and my own specific world to bring them up in and I'll guarantee to take any one at random and train him to become any type of specialist I might select—doctor, lawyer, artist, merchant-chief and, yes, even beggar-man and thief, regardless of his talents, penchants, tendencies, abilities, vocations and race of his ancestors." While few behavioral scientists accepted such a strong social deterministic position, they do include the influence of social and relational factors, along with biological and neurological factors, in order to understand the embodied nature of human existence.

A newer understanding of the biological and genetic influences on individual and family life concerns interpersonal neurobiology. Based on Dan Siegel's (2020) work on it, aspects of interpersonal neurobiology include (1) the brain and neuron functioning and (2) neuroplasticity. The focus here is how both genetics and environments, especially parent-child relationships, collaborate to enhance individual functioning. This perspective also emphasizes how the brain and relationships are fluid or malleable (neuroplasticity), allowing individuals to adapt to trauma and negative experiences.

Considering biological influences on the family is important for at least two reasons. First, and most obvious, is to give a more complete and true understanding of the family. Second, on a more practical level, is to recognize that behavior by family members must be understood in terms of biological as well as social factors. This helps members of the family to be less self-blaming when certain difficulties arise. Parents of a child struggling with mental illness, addiction, or any one of a number of other developmental difficulties are empowered by knowing about the biological factors that contribute to any particular behavioral problem. This liberates parents from feeling overly responsible for their child's difficulties. An *oversocialized* view of child development leads to an undue burden of guilt and shame for many parents or caregivers.

Because of the complex ways in which biological factors operate, assessing the relative importance of biological versus sociocultural factors is challenging. To begin with, it is necessary to move beyond a mere additive model in which one simply assesses the amount of separate influences of nature and nurture. Instead, what is needed is an *interactive* model that takes into account how biological and social factors impact and are being impacted by each other, and how the interactions impact family life. Although the role of biological factors will be included throughout the book, a few examples of genetic or neurological factors may be helpful at this point.

Genetic Factors

A simplistic view of the role of heredity in human behavior can be heard in such comments as, "He's just like his grandfather," or "She's just like her aunt Betty." In reality, the role of genes in human behavior is very complex. We now know that genes influence behavior by controlling very complex biological and developmental functions. D'Onofrio and Lahey (2010, 768) conclude, "It has become clear that genes and environments influence our behavior in a complex interplay that often involves the genetic moderation of environmental influence." Further, it is not simply that genes and the environment interact, for as Adele (2009, 2) points out, "Experience affects which genes are turned on (or off) and when," and "the environment participates in sculpting expression of" genes. Genetic disposition, therefore, might be thought of as necessary but not sufficient for the display of complex behaviors.

An example relevant to family life is the finding that the same gene has been linked with alcohol dependence, decreased probability of marrying, and an increased risk of divorce (Dick et al. 2006). Rendering these associations much more complex, however, are follow-up analyses that revealed that "personality characteristics, such as reward dependence, may partially explain how the gene is associated with both alcohol dependence and marital status" (D'Onofrio and Lahey 2010, 765). It should be noted, however, that the associations between these behaviors were small. That is, neither genetic nor personality factors *completely* explain the causes of alcohol dependence and marital status. Behavioral scientists emphasize the multidimensional nature of human problems like divorce and alcoholism, and addressing these human concerns requires incorporating both the medical and psychological aspects of human existence.

Another aspect in understanding the role of genetics is the idea that genes may also influence behavior differently according to the social context of behavior. For example, "Youth who are genetically predisposed to be aggressive who live in sparse rural environments may be less likely to engage in violence than youth living in urban environments because of the greater density of gangs in densely populated environments" (D'Onofrio and Lahey 2010, 768–69). Again, we must recognize the complexity of these matters as well as acknowledge that with more study there will be more clarity.

Neurological Factors

Largely due to technological advances, including the use of brain imaging, immunology, and endocrinology, much research has been done on how the neurological system influences human behavior. The areas in which research has shown neurological factors to be important in family life include the role of human stress (D'Onofrio and Lahey 2010).

An understanding of the role of stress has been found to be important in the following family processes: (1) during times of rapid change in the family, such as pregnancy, early childhood, and puberty; (2) during parent-child relationships, where stressful relationships can shape a child's stress neurobiology; (3) during conflict encounters where stress reactivity or the lack of it can either escalate or dampen conflict and correspondingly the stress levels of family members; and (4) in documenting how stress impacts each individual family member in different ways (D'Onofrio and Lahey 2010).

34

Accumulated research shows that hormone levels influence and are influenced by social environments. The implications for family life are many, beginning with a better understanding of adolescent behavior when hormones are raging, to showing how hormonal changes affect women during menopause, to explaining changes in sexual relationships among elderly couples as hormone levels diminish.

The use of MRI and other brain-imaging techniques has brought forth new information on how the brain and neurological system impact human behavior. For instance, we now know that the brain "is still undergoing normative developmental changes during late adolescence and early adulthood" (Casey et al. 2005, 45). The brain simply is not engaging in higher-order brain processing until the mid-twenties. This knowledge may not stop the parent-teen battles about teen behaviors, but it does give reason to have dialogue about the concern.

Interpersonal neurobiology focuses on how the brain and relationships mutually influence one another. For example, early positive interactions fostering secure attachment between a caregiver and child support neurological development. Further, this neurological development—increasing neurons and connections in various parts of the brain—feeds back into the parent-child relationship, enhancing the attachment bond (Cozolino 2014).

So, taking into account recent advances in knowledge about the influence of biology on family life, we offer several guarded conclusions. First, the influence of biological factors is very complex and interactive with sociocultural factors. Second, the relative importance or amount of biological influence is difficult to detect. Third, the amount of influence, although important, is often quite small. For all of these reasons, the number of citations given in this book for biological factors will be limited in comparison to the evidence cited regarding the impact of sociocultural factors on family life. We encourage readers to maintain an awareness of the possible implications of biological factors for a more balanced and comprehensive understanding of family life in the twenty-first century.

Family-Development Theory

Imagine that we had access to a time machine and could view the Lee family at different points in its development. Let us suppose that we could view Mr. and Mrs. Lee during their first month of marriage, the year their first child was born, the year their youngest child was born, the year their youngest child became a teenager, the last year that child lived at home, and the year their youngest grandchild was born. Altogether, we would have six slices from the life of this family. They would look quite different at each of those points, but there would also be certain elements of continuity: the basic organization of the family, the siblings' birth order (family constellation), the family's history and traditions, the presence of extended family, and so on. It should be noted that each stage of family life has predictable times of tension, and certain stages require more family structure than do others.

The developmental perspective allows us to view the typical family's progression through various stages of life. The family is not only responding to its current environment and trying to adapt to inputs (family-systems theory), but the family is also embedded in time (sequences) producing inputs and responding to global challenges throughout history. Within each stage, the family must accomplish certain key developmental tasks (notice that changes in family development primarily focus on membership changes like engagement or birth). Likewise, each individual family member must master developmental tasks at a particular stage. A degree of variation and oscillation is normal in this process, since both the family as a unit and individual family members must accomplish their respective tasks before the family can move on to the next stage of development. To the extent that the developmental tasks are not accomplished, the family will be less prepared to move on. It is helpful to think about developmental tasks in terms of age appropriateness for each unique family member and determine when an individual is over- or underdeveloped in a particular area. While one is working toward a balance in many areas of development, it is always important to recognize the natural ebb and flow that occurs as an individual family member proceeds through the life stages.

Some developmental tasks are stage specific, while other tasks are accomplished throughout the phases of family life. For example, in the first year of marriage it is important for a couple to make joint decisions about finances and household chores, but this becomes less important once a pattern is established. However, interpersonal communication is a skill that will be important throughout married life.

Table 2 lists the basic developmental stages of a family, the major task associated with each stage, and the event that initiates it. It should be noted that all families are unique and that these stages do not happen as precisely as the chart indicates.

In general, a family can be said to have moved from one stage to the next when a major transition takes place. We begin our list with the premarital stage because of the importance of differentiation from one's family of origin (the family into which a person was born). The goal of differentiation is to develop a clear sense of self that enables one to relate to and interact with

TABLE 2 Family Development

Stage	Major Task	Initiating Event
Premarital	Differentiating from family of origin	Engagement
Marital dyad	Adjusting to marital roles (establishing a household)	Marriage
Triad	Adjusting to new child	Birth/adoption of first child
Completed family	Adjusting to new family members	Birth/adoption of youngest child
Family with adolescents	Increasing flexibility in family system	Children's differentiation from the family
Launching	Accepting departure of family members	Children initiating a move for college, career, or marriage
Postlaunching	Establishing new patterns and embracing new members	Departure of last child from home
Retirement	Accepting aging process and regenerating meaning	End of employment

others in interdependent ways. This sense of self is based on one's identity. That is, one's true self is based on values and beliefs that ground human action. DoS entails authentically living out one's core beliefs while engaging in meaningful relationships. Such a capacity for self-sufficiency leads to deeper levels of connection. Note that differentiation does not negate intimacy in favor of autonomy. It allows for intimacy and autonomy, for both are intriguingly dependent on each other. The process of differentiation begins in childhood, intensifies during late adolescence, and continues throughout the life stages. Success in differentiation gives one the best chances for achieving mature marital intimacy and forming an interdependent union.

The most obvious and important transition in the family life cycle is marriage. When two people marry, a new family begins in the form of a dyad. The major developmental task involves the husband's and the wife's adjustment to each other in their new roles as married rather than single people. This interaction brings a differentiated marital unity. That is, each spouse forms a meaningful, values-driven family based on their shared beliefs. Each partner maintains this relationship while living authentically according to their values. This unity forms the basis for engaging in other social contexts, especially with in-laws.

There is an incredible agenda to be accomplished during this stage: setting up a new household, dividing up household chores, creating a budget, establishing work and career roles, meshing together sexually, developing friendships and planning social events, making decisions about church involvement and spiritual growth, and so on. On top of this, values and meaning-making are also crucial. Partners need to identify the core beliefs that will inform how the family engages with the social world. This is an important time of establishing a sound foundation for future stages. The couple will face questions about whether or when to have children, and some will face infertility questions and decisions.

In view of the amount of energy and cooperation needed to accomplish the items on this agenda, it is vital that the newly formed couple follow the biblical mandate to "leave and cleave." If they are to make these many decisions, the couple must clearly define their united relationship. They need encouragement and support from their respective families in this process, but if the families interfere, the foundation will be weakened.

The third family stage, the triad, begins with the birth, adoption, or fostering of the first child. Many couples benefit from having at least a few years together to form the spousal union and accomplish the tasks required of newlyweds before having children. The early arrival of a child can prematurely shift the focus of attention from the tasks of the marriage relationship to those of the parent-child relationship. When a child is born, adopted, or fostered into a family, the existing system must make necessary changes to welcome the new member. New boundaries will need to be defined and established between members and subsystems; physical space must be made to accommodate the new member.

When children reach adolescence, increased pressure is placed on the family system to accommodate itself to greater demands for flexibility. At this time, differentiation is especially pronounced because of the emotional and physical separation taking place. The drive toward adulthood for the adolescent generates internal pressure for the family to incorporate another adult into the family. This pressure toward differentiation on behalf of the adolescent encourages the family to expand its membership to include the values and beliefs of the developing adolescent. It is also the time when parents approach midlife, which often involves stress. Many challenges arise when the stressful stages of adolescence and midlife occur simultaneously. This may also be the time when a person builds a new family, made up of a new spouse with the spouse's children and/or one's own.

The launching stage begins when children are hankering to make it on their own. The parents must allow their children to leave the family of origin while supporting this rather shaky interim period. It is crucial for parents to be open to their adult child's decisions, such as finding a place to live, entering the military, choosing a college or training for a career, entering the workforce, choosing a mate, taking a trip, and so on. In some cases, the adult children are not ready to launch, and new rules for household living must be instituted.

The postlaunch stage brings new challenges, depending on one's life circumstances. Due to the expanded life expectancy in our society, the postlaunch stage accounts for nearly half the lifespan of the typical family system. This can be a period of renewed closeness and/or struggle between husband and wife as they refocus their spousal relationship and develop meaning without children in the home. It may be an exciting time of searching for a job or pursuing a new career. Perhaps one is grappling with life after a divorce, the death of a spouse, or life as a single parent. If children were previously the major focus, it can be a period of disillusionment and loneliness (the empty-nest syndrome). Another complication involves caring for elderly parents and working through their deaths. Often there is time for sibling relationship connection or reconciliation. Then, just when it looks as if there is plenty of freedom to progress, spousal illness or financial responsibilities pose a problem. Dealing with boomerang kids who return home for one reason or another can become an unexpected focus. It is also a time to plan retirement, make decisions about where to live and travel, and prepare for a fixed-income lifestyle. A delightful aspect of this stage might involve developing relationships with grandchildren.

An Integration of Systems and Development Theories

In this book, we use both the systems and the developmental perspective in discussing family life. The family is a developing system that embraces the arrival of new members and then releases them when they depart. It must be able to tolerate and respond to the changing needs of its individual members while providing a sense of belonging. At the same time, the family must be responsive to the environment. It must maintain a stability that can provide a firm foundation while remaining flexible enough to adapt to changing circumstances. This is not an easy feat, especially with the enormous demands made on the family in our postmodern urban society. A multitude of extra-familial systems (the work world, the educational system, the church, clubs, and organizations) all contend with the family for the time and devotion of family members. Only effective families can survive the intrusiveness of our contemporary society.

To understand how to build effective families, we must begin with a definition of what it takes to be an effective family. Table 3, which is based on clinical and sociological literature, presents a summary of various characteristics of strong and weak families. There are four major areas of analysis:

TABLE 3 **Characteristics of Effective and Ineffective Families**

	Effective Families	Ineffective Families
Cohesion	Individuation Mutuality	Fusion Disengagement
Adaptability	Flexibility Stability	Rigidity Chaos
Communication	Clear perception Clear expression	Unclear perception Unclear expression
Role Structure	Agreement on roles Clear generational boundaries	Conflict over roles Diffused boundaries

cohesion, adaptability, communication, and role structure. In each area, two characteristics mark the resilient family.

Cohesion

Cohesion refers to the degree of emotional closeness existing in a family. In fact, family cohesion has been found to be related to a number of positive family outcomes, including child social competence (Leidy, Guerra, and Toro 2010). Additionally, young adult children transitioning to college tend to have less depressive symptoms provided they have adequate cohesion with their parents (Moreira and Telzer 2015). In effective families, the members are differentiated (have a healthy degree of separateness) and have a strong sense of belonging (a healthy degree of connection and interdependence). There is mutual respect for the unique qualities and personalities of the other family members. At the same time, there is family togetherness; members belong to one another and realize they are interdependent in their family unity. When family members are overly cohesive (fusion), family members lack a sense of separate identity or individuality; each member is overly dependent on the family or other members for identity, and individuals are discouraged from developing values and beliefs in disagreement with the family's values. An example of fusion is when one member's problem devastates an entire family. The family members are so overly involved and concerned that they lose perspective. In the process, the problem worsens, and the chance of finding a solution lessens as they are pulled down together as a group.

The opposite extreme is a very low level of cohesion, which can be described as disengagement or emotional cutoff. In the disengaged family, the life of each member rarely touches the other members in a meaningful way. The members lack involvement, and they do not contribute to or cooperate with one another. In times of personal crisis, the members of a disengaged family are likely to be indifferent and uninvolved. In fact, they may not even be aware of the problem because it hasn't been shared. Here the system cannot provide help or support for the hurting member. Each individual is too busy or is uninterested in what is happening with the others, sometimes refusing to acknowledge or even relate to one another.

Effective families, by contrast, have a degree of mutuality and involvement that is supportive but not intrusive. This cohesion is based on the identity of the family—its core meaning and values. Cohesion around this identity

FIGURE 4 **Disengagement, Differentiation, and Fusion**

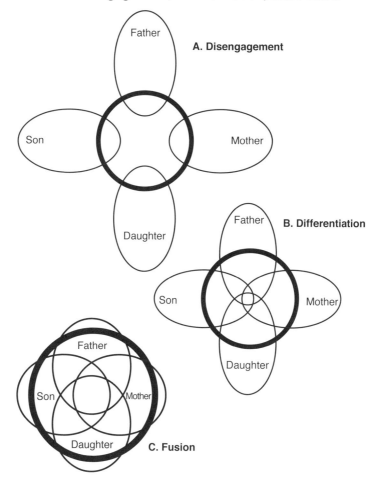

Adapted from David Olson, *Prepare/Enrich Counselor's Manual, Version 2000* (Minneapolis: Life Innovations, 1998), 81.

allows each member to incorporate and expand the family identity while maintaining membership in the family. This quality is lacking in both fused and disengaged families, which are at the opposite ends of a continuum: fused families do not allow individuals to expand or even question the family's identity, and disengaged families have no center around which members orbit. In the middle of this continuum are resilient families, which display an appropriate degree of cohesion and engagement.

For analytical purposes, individuation and mutuality can be discussed separately, but in actuality they overlap in what we refer to as differentiation. Figure 4 illustrates disengagement, differentiation, and fusion. The bold lines in the figure represent the boundaries around the family, and the light lines indicate the boundaries around each individual family member. In the disengaged family (A), the lives of the individual members very rarely touch one another. Cohesion is so low that each person lives in psychological isolation from the others.

In the differentiated family (B), daily lives overlap, but each individual is also involved in activities outside the family. Each member has a separate life and identity and, therefore, is actively and meaningfully engaged with others. Although a vital part of each member's identity and support is found within the family, much is also found beyond the family boundary.

In the fused family (C), the lives of all members are hopelessly entwined. Each family member has little identity beyond the boundary of the family. Even within the family, there is little space for a given member to be independent of the others. A member of an enmeshed family who tries to separate is likely to be labeled disloyal and to experience pressure from the others to remain enmeshed.

Needless to say, the amount of cohesion varies from family to family and from one life stage to another. For example, the degree of cohesion is higher with young children when the emotional bonding between parent and child is a primary focus. When children become teenagers and are working toward self-identity, it is fitting that they separate emotionally in preparation for the independence necessary to eventually leave home. But even when they achieve suitable autonomy, they view themselves as part of—and keep close ties with—the family throughout life.

Adaptability

A second important criterion for judging family life is adaptability. Families that have too high a level of adaptability tend to be chaotic. They lack the needed structure and predictability that provide stability and security. At the opposite extreme, inflexible families have a very low degree of adaptability and can be equally unbalanced. These families have created such a tight, unbending system that they neither have nor give grace, a strength especially needed during periods of change and transition in the family life cycle.

A balanced level of adaptability characterizes strong family life. The two dimensions of flexibility and stability mark the orderly family. In resilient families, there is a sense of orderliness that entails both flexibility and structure. The difference between families in this particular area can be observed in

FIGURE 5 **Adaptability and Cohesion within Families**

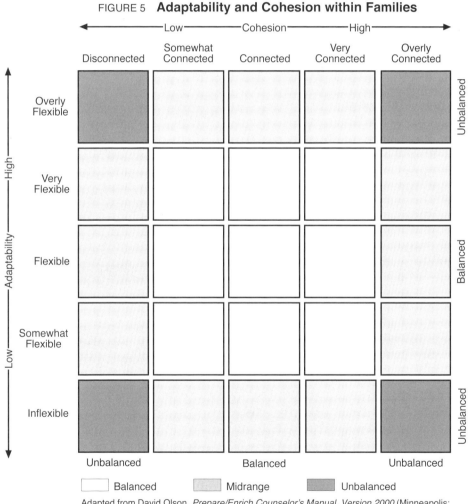

Adapted from David Olson, *Prepare/Enrich Counselor's Manual, Version 2000* (Minneapolis: Life Innovations, 1998), 81.

the dinner patterns. In the chaotic family, dinner is at no set time, and family members come and go from the dining table whenever it is convenient. In the inflexible family, it is understood that dinner is at 6:00 p.m. sharp and that time will never be altered. In the stable yet flexible family, dinner is scheduled for a certain time because the members value family togetherness, but exceptions are made when needed and determined by the family as a whole.

David Olson (1988, 1998, 2011) has combined cohesion and adaptability in the Circumplex Model, in which he describes balanced and unbalanced family systems. The families at the center of figure 5 are balanced. They experience satisfying degrees of cohesion and adaptability. The four corners represent four types of unbalanced or extreme family systems, combinations of disconnectedness or inordinate connectedness with either inflexibility or excessive flexibility. Families that experience life in these extremes need better balance and more appropriate levels of cohesion and adaptability in their relationships. It is important to note that the balanced category includes a broad range of family styles. There is room for a variety of styles. The family needs to determine what is good for itself according to cultural values, input from all family members, age appropriateness, and what is best for the unique family members as well as the unique family system. Families at the extremes have the most difficulty satisfying both individual and family needs. Validation and suggested usefulness of the Circumplex Model can be found in an article by Olson (2011). When couples and family members are made aware of the disadvantages of the extreme categories of relating, they can make necessary changes that bring a more satisfying balance to their home.

Communication

There are probably more self-help books on family communication than on any other topic. Because communication contributes in such an important way to effective family life, this is probably as it should be. The dynamics of good communication boil down to clarity of perception and clarity of expression. Clarity of perception pertains especially to the receiver of communication. It involves good listening skills, the ability to pick up on the sender's intonations and body language, and the willingness to ask for clarification when needed. In effective families, members have empathic skills, which include the ability to put oneself in the other's shoes and to understand what it feels like to be in that person's situation. This enables the communication to be on target so the receiver can make a response that helps the communicator feel understood and keeps him or her connected.

The more obvious dimension of good communication—clarity of expression—pertains to the sender. In resilient families, members are able to communicate feelings, opinions, wishes, and desires in a forthright and unambiguous manner. Clarity in sending messages is often a result of congruency between the person's words and body language. Care in this area goes far to ensure effective communication.

Role Structure

Each family member has a role to play in the family. The family as a whole usually defines this role. In a family with two parents and two children, every member has at least two roles: the adults take the roles of spouse and parent, while the children take the roles of child and sibling. And, of course, each person has roles outside the family (student, employee, etc.). One challenge is that roles sometimes become one's identity: who the person is in the family consists only of what they do in the family. That is why cybernetics is important but is not the most important aspect of family life.

Higher levels of role conflict are a common characteristic in less effective families. Contention arises when the role expectations of one member conflict with the role expectations of another member. For example, conflict is evident if both spouses want to work outside the home and have the other be totally responsible for the housekeeping and childcare. The expectations cause great distress and provide little room for compromise or negotiation. Highly effective families, in contrast, are characterized by expressing and negotiating role expectations. In the case cited above, for example, spouses strive toward a decision that works for both of them. They decide to share responsibility in the home in a way that allows both to be fulfilled by work outside the home. Note that the issue is not who plays a particular role but whether there is mutual agreement about the roles.

A second dimension in regard to role structure concerns the generational boundaries in the family. Strong families are characterized by clear boundaries around the parental subsystem and clear boundaries around the sibling subsystem. However, these boundaries are too diffuse when one sibling begins to play the role of parent to a brother or sister. Of course, in the single-parent home or when Mom and Dad are away, the oldest child may be put in charge. However, this role is relinquished readily when a parent returns home. When the oldest child is saddled with this role and continues to parent the younger siblings when the adults are present, it becomes a problem. This is a blurring of generational boundaries.

Boundaries in effective families are clear but permeable. This means that family members have the freedom to take on different roles. For example, a parent can become playful and childish at times, while children may sometimes act as nurturers to their parents. For a parent or a child to occasionally break out of a fixed role is a sign of flexibility. A mother may playfully stand on the coffee table and perform for her children, or a child may comfort the parent who comes home discouraged and needs consideration and support. Though these are not their dominant roles, family members have the freedom to take them on occasionally.

Flexibility in roles and permeable boundaries are important, but a problem arises when generational boundaries are crossed. For example, it is confusing when one of the marriage partners assumes the role of parent to the other or when a child becomes a parent to the parent. In a single-parent home, it is quite natural for the oldest child to take on extra responsibility to provide the support needed. However, the single parent must be careful not to overburden the child with adult responsibilities, because taking on inappropriate responsibility infringes on the child's sibling relationships. Another example is siblings who jump out of their age-appropriate roles and either regress to a younger role or assume an unsuitably older role in their sibling relationships. In another scenario, grandparents may attempt to parent grandchildren, thereby taking over the role that rightfully belongs to the parents. This may occur because the grandparents desire control or because their own adult child has abdicated responsibility. But whatever the case, it can disrupt the relationships among family members.

The biblical basis for family relationships presented in chapter 1 combined with the social-scientific developmental systems approach laid out in this chapter provide the overarching framework for an integrated view of marriage and family relationships. The initial task of integration is delicate. Our Christian presuppositions include values and biases that influence our response to the social-science literature. Likewise, our social-science presuppositions will be present as we attempt to understand how Scripture applies to the contemporary family. We encourage the reader to join with us in the demanding task of integrating biblical and social-science knowledge about the family.

PART 2

Marriage

The Foundation of Family Life

Marriage continues to be the foundation on which the family is established. Family therapist Virginia Satir (1983) refers to the marital partners as the *architects* of the family. There is certainly deep concern about the state of marriage today and what needs to be done to ensure permanency. The negative impact of marital fragility on our children and our society is increasingly evident. In addition, research indicates that individuals who marry benefit from this relationship in terms of physical and mental health when compared to persons who remain single (Carr and Springer 2010). The crucial question is what must be done to strengthen marriage across the life cycle.

Chapter 3 focuses on the coming together of two individuals and their respective families. The couple who forms a family has already experienced family life prior to their relationship. Each person brings with him or her recollections and experiences from their family of origin that have greatly impacted him or her. The saying that there are "six in the marriage bed" is a way of alerting spouses that each brings a set of parents into their union.

The marriage ceremony proclaims to family, friends, and members of the community that a new union has been formed. The reception provides an opportunity for these groups of people to be introduced to one another in anticipation of their support for the couple. Undoubtedly, the wedding day can be a stressful time for families. Disparate emotions related to separation, endings, and beginnings acknowledge a change in family dynamics. When both families approve and support the union, the "leaving and cleaving" aspects give the couple the best chance to flourish and establish a firm foundation. Unfortunately, lacking family support means the couple is more likely to start out on shaky ground as they try to achieve a stable marriage.

Chapter 4 is devoted to the process of establishing a firm marriage. The essential supports in a solid foundation include the strengths of the two families of origin, the character strengths that each spouse brings into the marriage, the strength of the relationship itself, and the strength that comes from friends and community. These sources of support are all crucial in establishing a solid foundation. And in Christian homes, of course, the cornerstone is Christ.

Although the foundation is established early in marriage, it is important to recognize that the marital dyad is a dynamic and growing relationship. There is no such thing as a static marriage, because, like any living organism, marriage is in either a state of growth or a state of decline. Chapter 5 presents the constituent elements of a marriage relationship that is based on and grows in accordance with biblical principles.

3

Mate Selection and Cohabitation

Romance and Reality

Western society has been based on the nuclear family, and the foundation of that family is marriage. This means that the beginning of the family life cycle occurs when a new family is formed, especially by marriage. All societies have a process whereby unmarried people come to be married. This process is called mate selection. While the beginning phase of marriage is technically the first stage of family life, mate selection is a necessary preliminary. Understanding mate selection is an important starting point for understanding all other stages in the life cycle of the family. The traditional understanding of mate selection as a transition to marriage has become much more complex as a result of premarital practices like "'hooking up,' internet dating, visiting relationships, cohabitation, marriage following childbirth, and serial partnering" (Sassler 2010, 557). Given the changes and prevalence of cohabitation, some scholars are choosing to eliminate "mate selection" in favor of descriptions such as "relationship formation and development" (see Hadden, Agnew, and Tan 2018).

Few developments related to family life have been as dramatic and controversial as the rise in premarital cohabitation. The majority of marriages in North America and European countries today are preceded by the couples living together as sexual partners sharing a household. Unfortunately, cohabitation as a precursor of marriage is a significant predictor of divorce. Some evidence suggests that for the first year of marriage, cohabitation is associated with increased satisfaction. However, over the long term, cohabitation is associated with increased likelihood of divorce (Rosenfeld and Roesler 2019). Our presentation of the mate-selection process will include the consideration of whether cohabitation is a *step toward* marriage or an *alternative to* marriage.

Mate Selection in Traditional Cultures

In the United States, selecting a mate is usually an individual matter. Unmarried people date and then choose the person they will marry. Contrary to popular opinion, this approach is actually a fairly recent development. In most societies throughout history, selecting a mate was a decision made solely by the parents, whose age, experience, and cultural heritage brought the wisdom to make this important decision. Often, these arranged marriages included neighbors and communities in the mate-selection process as well.

In societies that practice parental arrangement, mate selection is more a link between two extended families than a uniting of two individuals. There is great variability across cultures in the mate-selection process, extending along a continuum from parent-arranged marriage at one end to total individual free choice at the other. In societies where marriages are arranged by parents, the two dominant approaches are the bride-price system and the dowry system. The bride-price system is the norm in subsistence economies where the labor performed by women is greatly valued and the daughter is seen as the property of her father. In exchange for the bride, the groom's family gives her family various material goods. The dowry system is the norm in agricultural societies, where organized family units live and work on their own property. A dowry consists of goods that parents give to their unmarried daughter to make her an attractive commodity on the marriage market. In such a system, the wife brings the dowry with her into the marriage.

These approaches to mate selection are associated with important *economic* aspects of the family. We will discuss some of these trends later in this book. For now, we note that the family in traditional societies played an important economic role (Frederick and Dunbar 2019; Sweet 2014). The family in these societies was an economic producer, and children would be taught the family's business, making them productive members of the community. Additionally, arranged marriages would benefit both families as they would be joined via the new marriage. In the maintenance of the family and community, arranged marriages played an economic, not emotional, role.

In this postmodern world, the modernization process has challenged the tradition of parent-arranged marriages. Rapid advancements in technology have driven profound changes in the workplace, which resulted in a transformation in the family (Frederick and Dunbar 2019; Lee 1998). This transformation of economics and the family is referred to as industrialization. As a result of industrialization, families have been transformed from centers of economic production to centers of consumption. More time away from the family and going to work has allowed for individuals to maximize personal choice and benefit. As societies increasingly value individual freedom, mate selection becomes a personal choice instead of a parental one. A by-product of accepting these modern trends has been the gradual erosion of parent-arranged marriages and the emergence of romantic love as the basis for marriage.

Young people in traditional societies are increasingly exposed to a Western view of romantic love through the mass media. Many of these youth are quite familiar with American and Western European movies, popular music, and magazines that glorify romantic love. When youth in traditional societies begin to embrace the concept of romantic love, they do not immediately challenge the time-honored mate-selection procedure, but on an unconscious level these new ideas begin to undermine the old ways. Acceptance of these new ideas occurs in a sequential order: (1) two people should be romantically in love before they marry; (2) only the two people directly involved can determine if romantic love is present in their relationship; and (3) romantic love is most effectively cultivated within a social environment where unmarried youth can become acquainted with members of the opposite sex through dating.

In response to these modern notions of mate selection, parents may be willing to consider the opinion of their children and even seek their approval of a selected mate. They may even allow a courtship time for the young people to become acquainted and fall in love. However, most often these young people gradually assert themselves regarding their future mate and demand a say in the matter. This changes the entire process. The Western value that compatibility of personality should be a factor in mate selection is adopted. Thus, unmarried youth want the freedom to become acquainted with potential partners for the purpose of determining whether they are in love and compatible. It is at this stage that dating enters the picture. Dating is often a major point of contention between parents and children because it signals that control of the mate-selection process is passing from the hands of the parents to the hands of the unmarried youth. When two unmarried young people believe that they are in love and want to marry, the parental arrangement will be only a formality. In time, perhaps over several generations in traditional cultures, the formality of parent-arranged marriages will most likely cease to exist.

Mate Selection and the Role of Romantic Love

As we transition to discussing mate selection in postmodern cultures, we will focus on mate selection as a prerogative of the two people directly involved. In our postmodern era, many people believe finding a mate is primarily about personal attraction and romantic love. The popular internet matchmaking business also emphasizes personality compatibility as a major factor, so taking personality tests, indicating preferences, writing autobiographies, and viewing photographs are all part of the mate-finding process.

Although some would argue that romantic love is not unique to Western cultures, the concept of romantic love is generally thought to have had its beginnings in European societies during the eleventh century, when "courtly love" became fashionable among the privileged class. Courtly love usually involved a romantic relationship between a married aristocratic lady and an unmarried knight or troubadour. The concept of courtly love introduced the element of affection into male/female relationships. Affection was uncommon in most marriages of the day because they were primarily economic arrangements. By the sixteenth century, courtly love had changed to include sexual involvement between the lady of nobility and her paramour. The emerging middle class of European society during the sixteenth and seventeenth centuries came to value romantic love yet held to faithfulness as a value in marriage. This dilemma was solved when the love object changed from a married person to a single person. Thus, during the seventeenth and eighteenth centuries, parent-arranged marriage and romantic love existed side by side. By the twentieth century, it became proper and somewhat of a formality for a man to ask for parental permission to marry the daughter.

Romantic love and erotic love are very similar. We can understand their relationship in three ways. First are feelings of longing for the other person and the desire to be sexually and psychologically intimate; second, the beloved is idealized and regarded as necessary for one's happiness; and finally, preoccupation with the relationship results in an overestimation of the other person.

In fact, romantic love leads to rather dramatic changes in one's character. Studies suggest that an area of the brain known as the caudate is associated with romantic passion. Neuroscientists have produced brain images of this fevered activity prior to long-term commitment. Brain imaging reveals that pictures or thoughts of the object of one's desire are the only things that can "light up" certain areas of the brain. Based on these findings, Helen Fisher and her colleagues (2002) suggest that what we call romantic love develops over three sequential stages, beginning with *lust* (sexual drive), then *attraction*, and finally *emotional attachment*. Such "falling in love" is a romantic attachment that differs from one's relationship with family or friends and changes one physiologically as the body increases the production of hormones and chemical substances known as peptides, vasopressin, and oxytocin (Fisher et al. 2002). Romantic love is similar to drives such as hunger, thirst, or drug craving rather than to emotional states such as excitement or affection. During this intense time, emotions may shift from euphoria to anger to anxiety and become even more intense when love is withdrawn or one is rejected. As a relationship deepens, the neural activity associated with romantic love alters to long-term attachment.

Some have argued that romantic—or what is better considered erotic or lustful—love should not be the sole basis for mate selection. Rational decision-making and identification of other loving behaviors is important to this process. Aaron Beck (1989), the father of cognitive therapy, wrote a book called *Love Is Never Enough*, emphasizing the cognitive aspects of being in love and how these cognitions either increase or decrease marital satisfaction. Christians have traditionally understood three dimensions of love from ancient Greek culture: *agape*, *philia*, and *eros*. C. S. Lewis has written eloquently about these dimensions in *The Four Loves* (1960a). The self-giving *agape* corresponds to commitment; *philia*, brotherly friendship, corresponds to soul-mate connection; and *eros*, deep desire to know and be known by a specific person, corresponds to passion and desire for that person.

Using these three dimensions, four types of love relationships can be conceptualized. The first, *complete love*, embraces an equal portion of all three loves: commitment/*agape*, intimacy/*philia*, and passion/*eros*. In most cases, passion is likely to dominate at the beginning of a relationship, followed by a surge in emotional and friendship intimacy, and finally, commitment. While all three dimensions of love are important for a Christian marriage, it is a commitment to the other person that provides an environment in which intimacy and passion can grow to full maturity. The ideal relationship exhibits equal amounts of commitment, intimacy, and passion prior to marriage.

In *self-giving love*—a second type of love relationship—commitment/*agape* is dominant. In many societies (including those with parent-arranged marriages), the resolution of a couple to be faithful and self-giving in their love is the most desired prerequisite for marriage. It is noteworthy that marriages based on faithful commitment end in divorce far less frequently than those based solely on romantic love. However, this fact should not imply that parent-arranged marriages are more likely to achieve the Christian ideal than love-based marriages. For while intimacy and passion may develop in arranged marriages, the familial structure and cultural values promoted in traditional societies may also hinder such development. The commitment that keeps these marriages together may be less a self-giving commitment to one's spouse than a commitment to the extended family and community. When marriages lack a personal covenant, it is unlikely that the spouses will achieve true intimacy.

A third type of love relationship, *friendship love*, is when emotional intimacy/*philia* is dominant. Although few relationships move into marriage on the basis of friendship alone, it is an essential factor in a good marital relationship. Many people describe their spouse as their best friend, an indication of being an emotional companion to one's mate. Others complain that the friendship is so strong they find it difficult to feel passionate with their partner, and it compromises the sexual passion.

In *infatuation love*, a fourth and final type of love relationship, passion/*eros* is dominant. Some relationships get off to a passionate start: two people connect on the basis of immediate attraction and sexual response, which may lead to an impulsive marriage. Such relationships do not ordinarily have the emotional core and stability of commitment to sustain the marriage. But since passion by itself cannot carry a relationship over time, infatuation often burns itself out before a couple decides to marry.

Theories of Mate Selection

In view of the flexibility and complexity of the modern courtship system, family researchers have been challenged to explain the mate-selection process. One of the most studied aspects of present-day mate selection is the degree to which people choose mates who are similar or different from them. If we believe both clichés, "like marries like" and "opposites attract," there will be similarities *and* differences in the couple. In this section, we will describe several theories of mate selection.

"Like Marries Like" Theory

Studies have shown that endogamous factors, or similar social backgrounds, are key components in mate selection. These factors include race, ethnicity, religion, education, occupation, and geographical proximity. It should be noted that some of these factors directly relate to the opportunity to get to know another person. Close contact in the workplace, for example, affords the opportunity to view someone as a potential marriage partner. For this reason, it is fairly common for people in the same occupation to marry. It has also been shown that homogamous factors, or similar personal characteristics and interests, are of importance. Included here are religious and political beliefs, moral values, hobbies, intelligence, height, weight, and physical appearance.

Another important finding is that most people seem to marry partners with a similar amount of ego strength; that is, a person with low self-esteem tends to marry a person with low self-esteem, and a person with high self-esteem will marry another person with high self-esteem. Internet matchmaking sites that take these important factors into account are more likely to yield good matches than those that rely on more superficial indicators, such as photographs or autobiographies.

Bowen Family Systems Theory

In chapter 1 and 2, we introduced the concept of differentiation of self (DoS), which is part of Bowen Family Systems Theory (BFST). Bowen (2004) developed a clear understanding of the role of DoS in mate selection. For mate-selection purposes, Bowen theorized that individuals would marry those who have similar levels of DoS. This is based in part on the idea that individuals would have similar propensities to manage anxiety and maintain certain relationship roles. As marital relationships have a high survival level, meaning that marriages perform important psychological functions, DoS allows individuals to cope with anxiety while maintaining these crucial relationships. The research on this aspect of Bowen's theory is mixed at best (Rodríguez-González et al. 2016). There have been four studies that have demonstrated a connection between levels of DoS and mate selection (Bartle 1993; Kear 1978; Rovers et al. 2007; Tuason and Friedlander 2000) and four studies that do not support this connection (Day, St. Clair, and Marshall 1997; Lal and Bartle-Haring 2011; Peleg and Yitzhak 2011; Skowron 2000).

Theoretically, BFST understands that as individuals develop in their families of origin, DoS mediates the relationship between maintaining one's relationships to others, especially one's parents, and anxiety. One's level of differentiation is highly influential on one's ability to manage anxiety while engaging in relationships with others. In families with higher levels of DoS, individuals are able to maintain developmentally appropriate responsibility—that is, children learn to feed themselves while parents provide the meal and maintain their relationships with their families. When anxiety arises, rigid relational patterns emerge in an attempt to manage anxiety. These rigid relational patterns demand that individuals maintain relationships with parents at the expense of personal autonomy and development. As an example, a child may develop and maintain more chronic behavioral issues that function to distract family members from developing peer relationships based on mutuality and interdependence. That is, chronic behavioral issues function in relationships so that parents and children maintain rigid relationship patterns characterized by over- and underfunctioning. These rigid patterns prevent both the parents and children from developing relationships based on mutuality and interdependence. When disagreements arise between parents, anxiety increases, which is disseminated throughout the family. The child responds symptomatically, creating a distraction from the differentiation work the parental partners need to engage in. When this child leaves his or her family of origin, BFST posits that a spouse with similar relational patterns and lower levels of DoS will be sought.

Personality Theory

Personality characteristics have been an increasing focus for understanding mate-selection preferences. This research has highlighted three sets of characteristics (Fletcher et al. 2004): (1) warmth/trustworthiness, (2) attractiveness/vitality, and (3) status/resources. Research suggests that trustworthiness is an important factor in mate selection for both males and females (Fletcher et al. 2004; Valentine et al. 2020). Women tend to emphasize warmth/trustworthiness and resources as compared to men. Attractiveness/vitality are important characteristics for short-term relationships (hook-ups) more for men than women. For long-term relationships, attractiveness/vitality are not important characteristics.

Filter Theory

In their classic work, Alan Kerckhoff and Keith Davis (1962) have suggested that endogamy, homogamy, and complementary needs are three different filters through which a potential mate must pass (see fig. 7). The first and broadest filter in the mate-selection process is endogamy, as most people date and establish relationships with individuals from similar backgrounds. The second filter is homogamy, which is narrower and more selective. Only those people who have similar interests and characteristics pass through this filter. Casual dating allows individuals to discover which potential partners have compatible interests and characteristics. The last filter, complementary needs, is the narrowest. Whereas a number of potential mates may pass through the endogamous and homogamous filters, only a few will have the exact personality traits to meet one's most pressing needs.

Marriage Markets Theory

Marriage markets refers to the idea that there is a discrete number of potential partners in a given population. This population has traditionally been defined in terms of neighborhoods or communities. In other words, marriage markets are geographically and demographically homogeneous places where individuals find mates. Before the advent of the internet, individuals would generally seek mates that were geographically close (Rosenfeld and Thomas 2012). The thinness or thickness of these markets would be determined by the numbers of potential partners and the selectivity of mate preferences. The advent of the internet has moved these markets from local to international in focus, making one's internet search skills an important variable in identifying potential mates. Of course, geographical proximity is still important. After all, individuals will need to physically meet potential mates at some point in the process.

Other Theories

Furnham (2009) noted a gender difference in what is valued in the mate-selection process. In a study based on 250 adults in their early twenties, he reported that "females rated intelligence, stability, conscientiousness, height, education, social skills, and political/religious compatibility significantly higher than males, whereas males rated good looks higher than females" (262).

Wenzel and Emerson (2009, 341) report that socially anxious individuals believe others are less likely to select them when compared to socially non-anxious individuals. McGee and Shevin (2009, 67) found that persons with a good sense of humor are perceived as more attractive as potential mates. Montoya (2008, 1315) indicates that "attractive perceivers expected to date more attractive targets while unattractive perceivers expected to date less attractive targets."

A Christian Perspective on Mate Selection

Taken together, the various sociological theories of mate selection comport well with the theological model of family relationships that we presented in chapter 1. This will become clear as we describe what mate selection would be like if it developed according to the principles suggested in our theological model: commitment, grace, empowerment, and intimacy.

At the beginning of a dating relationship, there is a minimal degree of commitment between the partners. With an increased degree of commitment comes an increased sense of trust and security. Commitment being the foundation for the relationship, it is important to consider what is being committed *to*. In other words, mate selection should focus on the end result of marriage as opposed to a more culturally consonant understanding of dating and relationship formation as a way of meeting personal needs and avoiding loneliness.

This means that human initiative and decision-making are foundational for mate selection. Marriage requires something more than human love and desire. Bonhoeffer (1997b, 41) describes weddings as a place where people can be "celebrating their triumph [in getting married]" because "the course [they] have taken at the outset is one that [they] have chosen for [themselves]." The wedding is a place where God blesses the marriage so that it can persevere throughout all of life's challenges. God blesses a marriage so that "it is not [their] love that sustains the marriage, but from now on, the marriage that sustains [their] love" (Bonhoeffer 1997b, 43). With the goal of marriage in mind, individuals should assess their ability to commit to a specific partner in covenantal terms. The point here is that the marriage becomes the covenantal context for living out one's identity with another. Making the covenant of marriage entails embarking on a lifelong relationship that sustains and transforms each partner into a one-flesh reality (see Gen. 2:22–25).

As each partner increasingly commits toward establishing a covenantal relationship, grace can be expected to grow proportionately. Grace is experienced through acceptance and appreciation by the partner. The presence of grace promotes a feeling of security because differences are respected and because there is an atmosphere of forgiveness whenever failure occurs. Partners share more of their characteristics, desires, and dreams as they enter deeper into commitment with one another. The partners are increasingly valued and accepted for who they are and not for what they might be or do for the other.

Out of grace emerges a mutual empowerment process. In the early stages of dating, the couple may operate on a quid pro quo basis (something for something), with each attempting to have personal needs met through the relationship. Where there is a minimal degree of commitment and acceptance, partners are likely to think more in terms of what they can get from a relationship rather than what they can contribute to it. The empowerment model is hopeful in that it shows that love can be elevated above self-centered exchange. A depth of commitment and grace can imbue each partner with a genuine desire to empower by both giving to and receiving from the other. This involves being interested in the growth of the other person and finding ways to encourage the partner to reach his or her greatest potential and thus to be all that God created him or her to be.

Some relationships are not empowering but rather are based on mutual dependency. When couples are overly dependent on each other, they tend to demand that the partner meet their every need. Codependency is the exact opposite of differentiation as noted in trinitarian theology, where distinctiveness and unity are intermingled. Differentiated partners are responsible to God for their lives and therefore bring unique gifts to the couple relationship. In other words, each partner has based his or her identity on Christ, who accepts and values them. Christian identity facilitates a marriage covenant between partners and God, and grace, empowerment, and intimacy deepen. Partners act in their relationship out of strength rather than deficit. They are able to ask for what they would like without demanding the partner provide it. Being centered in Christ gives them confidence that God is the best resource to guide, empower, nurture, inspire, and soothe. They look to God for personal growth but also openly share and offer themselves to each other in that process. When spouses cling to each other for dear life in a raging river, they perpetuate an enabling system in which they both are likely to drown together. But when sufficiently differentiated, they are a strong resource for each other so that when one is struggling, the partner is standing on solid ground to extend a helping hand.

Ecclesiastes 4:9–12 refers to this idea that two sufficient persons are better than one alone. Because they bring their unique strengths to the union, they can be there for each other rather than be dragged down in an overly dependent relationship. "Two are better than one, because they have a good reward for their toil. For if they fall, one will lift up the other; but woe to one who is alone and falls and does not have another to help. Again, if two lie together, they keep warm; but how can one keep warm alone? And though one might prevail against another, two will withstand one. A threefold cord is not quickly broken." Being united in unique strengths and making God the center of their relationship (a threefold cord) presents a wonderful image of marital partnership and union.

We live in a society that encourages people to think that they can have instant gratification. This mentality carries over into the dating relationship, where people look for instant sexual intimacy. The prevalence of an instant sexual gratification ethic has resulted in the emergence of the concept of "hooking up," defined as intimate physical behavior outside of a committed relationship. Hooking up seems to be less about dating in order to get to know the other and more about sexual fulfillment. Research on hooking up among college students reports that it can result in both positive and negative experiences, "with women being more likely to report it as a negative experience than men" (Owen and Fincham 2011). Negative emotional reactions were related to "reports of depressive symptoms and feelings of loneliness," while positive emotional relations had to do with hope for the possibility of a committed relationship (321). This finding seems to point out the importance of the biblical wisdom that sexual involvement is best when part of a committed relationship.

In our theological model, intimacy entails a deep level of knowing and being known through understanding, listening, caring, and sharing. It is not only a physical or sexual encounter but a deeply felt process of becoming known. Sexual intimacy is one of many facets of intimacy, and it is certainly not the most important one. Accordingly, intimacy builds on commitment, grace, and empowerment. Using these foundational biblical concepts, people who trust the commitment, who experience acceptance and forgiveness throughout dating, and who find their partner interested in and actively affirming empowerment during the dating process will feel safe enough to be more honest and revealing. They are willing to take off their masks and resist the temptation to put on pretenses. They share a desire truly to know each other. The couple is more interested in a relationship with the other person than in the mere pleasure that person can give in a superficial sexual encounter. Intimacy of this nature leads to deeper levels of commitment, grace, and empowerment.

Certain beliefs about mate selection, such as "love is enough" or "there is a one and only for me," are a serious hindrance in discerning God's will. A research study has identified seven such *constraining beliefs* that limit, inhibit, hinder, or perpetuate exaggerated or false expectations about mate selection (Cobb, Larson, and Watson 2003). The beliefs that "there is a one and only, that love is enough, that cohabiting before marriage will improve chances of being happily married, that I will have complete assurance, that the match will make a perfect relationship, that choosing should be easy and effortless, and that one should choose someone to marry whose personal characteristics are the opposite of their own" seem to adversely affect mate selection. These myths blur the clarity of vision needed when choosing a mate. The study discovered that "men and women were found to be equally susceptible to constraining beliefs about mate selection, with the exception of the One and Only belief, the Idealization belief, and the Complete Assurance belief, all of which women appear to endorse to a slightly greater degree" (229).

Cohabitation: A Path toward or Alternative to Marriage?

Virtually all industrialized societies in the last fifty years have experienced a dramatic increase in cohabitation. This increase is true for premarital cohabitation and cohabitation following divorce or the death of a spouse. In the United States, cohabitation has increased seventeenfold between 1960 and 2010—from about 450,000 people in 1960 to more than 7.5 million today

(Wilcox 2011, 75). Most marriages and remarriages taking place today will be preceded by a cohabiting arrangement.

Our goal in this section is to develop a Christian perspective on the topic. We draw on existing research—mainly self-reported responses to survey research questionnaires or interviews—to understand this phenomenon more fully. We consider the reasons people choose to cohabit and examine the impact of this trend. We offer a response to cohabitation that is informed by both biblical and social-scientific literature. We begin by addressing the question of whether premarital cohabitation is an *alternative to* marriage or a *step toward* marriage.

Is Cohabitation a Step toward Marriage?

Actually, premarital cohabitation is not a new idea, for as early as 1966 anthropologist Margaret Mead proposed a two-step plan for single adults. The first step, *trial marriage*, would be a time for the couple to determine whether they were compatible; and the second step would be to *legalize the union* when the couple decided to have children. A few years later, Scriven (1968) proposed a three-stage plan whereby a relationship progressed from *sexual satisfaction*, to *social security*, to *sensible spawning*. The idea was for couples to establish contracts for stated periods of time and periodically renew them as they saw fit. In 1997, McRae surmised that cohabitation would serve as a type of marriage preparation, a stage that occurs between courtship and marriage. He reasoned that cohabiting would give the couple a chance to test the degree of compatibility, and if their personalities "fit" they would move to marriage. This idea of cohabitation as being a trial for marriage persists in the literature today (Rosenfeld and Roesler 2019).

What Does Culture Have to Do with It?

In terms of acceptability of cohabitation in various cultures, Heuveline and Timberlake (2004) found that cohabitation had different meanings with respect to family formation, values, and cultural sanctions. They describe a continuum of attitudes, based on their study of cohabitation in sixteen industrial societies. At one end of the spectrum, cohabitation is *marginal* because it is culturally rejected or even penalized in these societies. Societies with a more moderate view may accept cohabitation as a prelude to marriage but expect the legalization of marriage prior to bringing children into the home. More open cultures distinguish cohabitation as an *alternative to marriage* or a *stage in the marital process*; and at the other end of the spectrum are cultures that give total acceptance (northern European countries), where cohabitation is actually *indistinguishable from marriage* with certain legal rights.

North America is moving toward the more open aspects of this continuum, where cohabitation is considered an alternative lifestyle or even alternative to marriage. In the United States, age seems to make a difference in that "older cohabiters are more likely to view their relationship as an alternative to marriage, whereas younger cohabiters view their relationship as a prelude to it" (King and Scott 2005, 271). Since 1970, we have seen an increase in cohabitation and a decrease in the social stigma associated with it (Rosenfeld and Roesler 2019). In general, the more accepting a society's attitude toward cohabitation, the more cohabitation will be defined as an alternative to marriage (Perelli-Harris and Gassen 2012).

Making the Decision to Cohabit

In an effort to answer the question about why couples choose to cohabit, Huang et al. (2011, 876) report that the primary motives for cohabiting include "spending time together, sharing expenses, and evaluating compatibility." Many couples admittedly decide to cohabit for the convenience, companionship, and exclusive sexual relationship with a chosen partner, regardless of whether there is an intention to marry or not.

WHAT DOES LOVE HAVE TO DO WITH IT?

Since the role of romantic love was addressed previously, we note only that what distinguishes modern forms of relationship coupling from the past is the greater freedom young adults have to pursue sexual/romantic relationships without parental involvement. Marriage is no longer an economic arrangement, controlled and arranged by parents, but a participant-run system in which the concept of love drives the relationship. A decoupling of economics, sex, and commitment from marriage has led to a growing number who choose to cohabit and delay marriage (the median age for first marriage now stands at 28.1 for women and 30.5 for men, according to the US Census Bureau). Copen et al. (2012) note, "If entry into any type of union, marriage or cohabitation, is taken into account, then the timing of a first union occurs at roughly the same point in the life course as marriage did in the past." In other words, relationship unions occur when individuals complete education and or job-training expectations and are ready to join the workforce, while individuals have greater freedom to engage in less-committed sexual and emotional relationships allowing them to fulfill their emotional needs while completing education and job training.

What Does Commitment Have to Do with It?

By its very nature, a cohabiting relationship is one in which commitment is ambiguous. Popenoe and Whitehead (2002) believe a high commitment ethic is necessary for marital stability, so they warn against cohabitation for that very reason. Marriage researcher and Christian therapist Scott Stanley and colleagues (2006) describe cohabiting as "relationship inertia" in which cohabiters are "sliding" rather than "deciding" on a marital partner. He concludes that men who live with women they eventually marry are not as committed to the union as those who did not live with their mates before marriage.

Smock (2000) discovered that cohabiting men and women differ in the way they conceptualize commitment. She found that women tend to perceive cohabitation as a step prior to marriage, whereas men are inclined to view cohabitation as a step prior to making a commitment. When it comes to drawbacks of cohabiting, Huang et al. (2011) found that "men [are] more concerned about loss of freedom, while women are more concerned with delays in marriage," pointing out that gender norms about relationship intimacy govern cohabiting unions (876).

Rhoades, Stanley, and Markman (2006, 553) report that "men who cohabited with their spouse before engagement were less dedicated than men who cohabited only after engagement or not at all before marriage," and after marriage, these husbands were "less dedicated to their wives than their wives were to them." These researchers wonder if some couples who otherwise would not have married end up married due to what they refer to as "the inertia of cohabitation." In other words, the couple simply remains in a relationship regardless of quality or fit. The obvious implication is that persons do not make their expectations about marriage explicit prior to cohabiting, and that becomes a problem after they marry.

In a representative sample of 1,294 unmarried individuals comparing cohabiting with noncohabiting (dating) relationships, Rhoades, Stanley, and Markman (2012, 348) found that initially "cohabiting relationships were characterized by more commitment, lower satisfaction, more negative communication, and more physical aggression than dating [noncohabiting] relationships." These authors summarize that the transition from dating to cohabitation is declining "in most indices of relationship quality as well as in interpersonal commitment after cohabitation began, though the frequency of sex increased temporarily."

Eventual Outcomes

While these studies are quite bleak when it comes to marital outcomes, a couple's or partner's view and understanding of a unique cohabitation agreement is certainly an important factor in whether they will end up in a stable marriage. It is probably wise to recognize that for some couples, cohabitation is an *alternative* to marriage and for others it is considered a *stage* in the relationship that leads to marriage. Johnson and colleagues (2011) describe the role that dedication and constraints play in choosing to marry after cohabiting. On the more positive side, partners may have higher levels of commitment to the relationship. On the other hand, there may be constraints that deter the dissolution of the relationship (children or a joint-owned business). Both factors influence the decision to marry after cohabiting as well as the decision to dissolve the relationship.

Does Premarital Cohabitation Lead to Marital Adjustment?

Social scientists have been interested in the effects of cohabitation on the institution of marriage since the early 1970s, when they began tracking the increasing rates of cohabitation and out-of-wedlock births. As a result of cohabitation redefining the nature of marriage and the family, the social-scientific study of cohabitation became an important aspect of family sociology.

The initial prediction by social scientists on premarital cohabitation was that it would lead to better marriages (Trost 1975). This stemmed from the idea that cohabiting would serve as a screening device that would later ensure the compatibility of prospective spouses (Danzinger 1976). It was further reasoned that cohabiters would gain experience in intimacy and therefore develop a greater degree of relational competence necessary for an enduring and fulfilling marriage (Peterman 1975). An accumulation of research on the outcome of marriage satisfaction preceded by cohabitation has failed to support those optimistic predictions in the long term (Rosenfeld and Roesler 2019; van Houdt and Poortman 2018).

However, cohabitation may be more closely related to marital satisfaction and adjustment in the first year of marriage. In the first year of marriage after cohabitation, the evidence suggests that cohabitation affords some relationship skills associated with conflict resolution. These benefits disappear around the fifth year of the marriage (Rosenfeld and Roesler 2019).

When compared to married persons, cohabiters had poorer relationships with parents and expressed lower levels of commitment and happiness with comparable married individuals. These factors also influence the dedication and decision to marry after cohabiting (Johnson, Anderson, and Aducci 2011). Kulu and Boyle (2010, 881) indicated that cohabitation prior to marriage was related to lower commitment to the partner, increased incidence of divorce, lower marital satisfaction, and higher rates of wife infidelity. Treas (2000) reported that cohabiting couples are more likely to experience infidelity, while Binstock and Arland (2003) found that cohabiting couples were more likely to separate and less likely to reconcile after a separation when compared to married couples. Aarskaug, Keizer, and Lappegard (2012) gathered a large sample of 41,760 marital and cohabiting unions across Europe and have confirmed that cohabitation is related to relationship instability in European societies. They report that "in all countries cohabiters more often had breakup plans and were less satisfied with their relationships than individuals who married" (389). These researchers further report that the differences in relationship satisfaction were greatest in those countries where cohabitation was least prevalent.

Thomson and Colella (1992) conducted some early research into the effects of cohabitation on relationship and marital satisfaction. Among the couples in their study, greater dissatisfaction in previously cohabiting marriages had more to do with the unconventional attitudes and lifestyles of these couples than the fact that they had cohabited. Individuals with more liberal social values toward premarital sex and commitment have a greater freedom to express dissatisfaction and to separate or divorce when things do not go well. However, DeMaris and MacDonald (1993) disagreed with this conclusion, stating that "controlling for unconventionality had only a minimal impact on the cohabitation effect" (406), and they pointed out that "although family attitudes and beliefs tend to predict the attractiveness of a cohabiting lifestyle, they do not account for differences between cohabiters and non-cohabiters in instability" (399). The role of more liberal social attitudes has been included in much of the more recent research as well. Early research demonstrates that cohabitation was more constraining on those couples that married after cohabiting.

As pastors and Christians wanting to help, understanding the effects of cohabiting—both positive and negative—on later marriages may identify certain qualities that contribute to eventual marital success. It is important to understand the relationship dynamics and the challenges associated with cohabiting before marriage. However, it is also important to understand the dynamics that occur for those cohabiters who eventually marry to build a successful marriage and remain married. At this point, it may be helpful to attempt to decipher some of the more complex factors linking premarital cohabitation and eventual marital stability or instability.

In the article "Reassessing the Link between Premarital Cohabitation and Marital Instability," Steffen Reinhold (2010) gives "some support to the thesis that the once-strong association between premarital cohabitation and marital instability has weakened over time." Copen et al. (2012, 2) likewise surmise that although "it has been well documented that women and men who cohabit with their future spouse before first marriage are more likely to divorce than those who do not . . . recent research suggests that the association between premarital cohabitation and marital instability for first marriages has weakened over time."

Is There a Selective Factor?

Certainly there are cohabiting couples who have been successful in forming quality marriages, so we ask the question about selective factors that might be at work. Brown et al. (2006, 454) conclude that "selection factors largely account for the deleterious effects of premarital cohabitation on marital success." For example, certain individual characteristics (less traditional, more independent, less culturally constrained, etc.) may put some cohabiters at higher risk for marital instability. Kulik (2011, 120) found that "the noncohabiting women reported better levels of adjustment of spousal cohesion and display of affection, and they used strategies of concession to resolve marital conflicts to a greater extent than did women who cohabited."

Pootman and Mills (2012, 357) found that "joint investments increased as interpersonal commitment increased." Cohabiters who have no marriage plans invest the least while couples who directly married without prior cohabitation invested the most. This research would raise the question about joint commitment in the relationship and degree of investment a couple makes in their future relationship and eventual marital success after cohabitation. Kulu and Boyle (2010, 881) agree that it is important to consider the prior commitment factor while reporting general increased incidence of divorce, lower marital satisfaction, lower commitment to the partner, and higher rates of wife infidelity.

Other researchers make the point that a single-factor explanation between premarital cohabitation and marital instability is faulty. Gender, age, and ethnicity have also played a role in the effects of cohabiting on later marriages. Phillips and Sweeney (2005) found that premarital cohabitation was positively associated with subsequent marital disruption among non-Hispanic White populations but not among non-Hispanic Black or Mexican Americans. King and Scott (2005, 271) discovered that "older cohabiters report significantly higher levels of relationship quality and stability than younger cohabiters, although they are less likely to have plans to marry their partners."

Based on a sample of 2,737 respondents, Musick and Bumpass (2012, 1) found that the change in "a range of measures tapping psychological well-being, health, and social ties" is similar in cohabiting and marriage relationships. They conclude, "Overall, differences tend to be small and appear to dissipate over time, when the greater instability of cohabitation is taken into account."

The National Center for Health Statistics reported evidence from the National Survey of Family Growth (from a sampling of nearly 13,000 people) that the differences in marital adjustment and outcome between married persons who had and who had not cohabited is small (Jayson 2010).

Rosenfeld and Roesler (2019) conducted one of the largest studies on cohabitation before marriage. This study is based on six waves of data from the National Surveys of Family Growth. The data from this study are representative of individuals throughout the United States from 1970 until 2015. For women in this study, the rate of cohabiting with the man they eventually married was 11 percent in 1970. By 2015, the rate was 70 percent, indicating the growing popularity of cohabiting. In more positive terms, this study indicates that couples who cohabited before marriage have higher satisfaction scales compared with couples that do not cohabit. However, these gains are also maintained among couples who cohabit and do not marry. This suggests that premarital cohabiting allows couples to learn how to negotiate conflict and adjust to living together compared with noncohabiting couples who do not have that opportunity. The long-term effects of cohabitation prior to marriage are more negative (i.e., associated with marital dissolution).

As the above discussion demonstrates, some of the research is mixed on the overall negative effects of cohabiting on marriages. There are important factors to keep in mind as a couple transitions from cohabitation to marriage. Care must be taken to resist the assumption of a strong *causal relationship* between cohabitation and marital failure. Viewing the connection between cohabitation and relationship dissolution as the death knell of a relationship may be a self-fulfilling prophecy. Factors to take into account include the following: the degree of commitment; valuing and making marriage and family life a priority; communication and conflict-resolution life skills, recognizing marital expectations, and developing a differentiated unity; making joint decisions about children, roles, and careers; and being involved in an extended family and/or faith community that supports and encourages covenant vows.

How Does Cohabitation Impact Children?

Thinking beyond the pros and cons of premarital cohabitation for a couple, we now consider how children are impacted. Heuveline and Timberlake (2004) cite studies estimating that between 25 and 40 percent of all children spend some time in a cohabiting arrangement. Brown et al. (2006) report that when compared to children growing up with married couples, children growing up with cohabiting couples tend to have worse life outcomes. Since cohabiting parents break up at a much higher rate than married parents, the impact of cohabiting on children can be devastating.

Aronson (2004) finds that among mothers with infants, those in cohabiting relationships tend to fare far worse economically than married mothers. Popenoe and Whitehead (2005) point to evidence of higher risk of sexual abuse and physical violence among children in cohabiting unions. DeLeire and Kalil (2005, 286) report the rather sobering finding that "cohabiting-parent families, compared to married-parent families, spend a greater amount on two adult goods (alcohol and tobacco) and a smaller amount on education." The implications are that cohabiting parents invest less in the welfare of their children than married parents do.

In a study of 2,160 families, Schmeer (2011, 181) reports "worse health for children born to cohabiting parents . . . than for children with stable married parents." In addition, it seems that stable cohabitation is no better for child health than cohabitation dissolution, and a child's health is better among the cohabiting parents who marry than for those who do not marry.

Sociologists David Popenoe and Barbara Whitehead (2003, 2004, 2005) at Rutgers University have completed a comprehensive review of research on cohabitation before marriage in their yearly report on the state of marriage in the United States. They caution young adults to think twice about cohabiting prior to marriage, offering the following four principles. First, *consider not living together at all before marriage, since there is no evidence to support the view that cohabiting will result in a stronger marriage.* The evidence, they suggest, shows that living together before marriage increases the chance of divorcing after marriage. The exception may be for those couples who are committed to marriage, have formally announced their engagement, and have chosen a wedding date.

The second principle is *don't make a habit of cohabiting.* They see the evidence as refuting the popular myth that persons learn to develop better relationships from a number of failed cohabiting relationships. Rather, multiple cohabitation is repeatedly found to be a strong predictor of the failure of future relationships.

The third principle is *limit cohabitation to the shortest possible period of time.* The intent and spirit of this advice is based on their conclusion that the longer one lives together with a partner, the more likely it is that the low-commitment ethic of cohabitation will take hold. Participation in a cohabiting relationship can have an eroding effect not only on the participants' view of the importance of commitment but also on societal ethics, which value unconditional commitment as a basis for marriage and family life.

The fourth principle is *don't cohabit when children are involved*. The spirit of this principle is based on the value that children need and should have parents who are committed to staying together for them.

While Popenoe and Whitehead write as social scientists, not as advocates for a Christian view of marriage, their advice certainly comports well with the biblical wisdom that marriage is to be based on lifelong covenant commitments. Those who make a marital covenant with their partner will have a better chance for stability and happiness than those who merely slide into marriage through default.

A Christian Perspective on Cohabitation

A Christian response to cohabitation needs to be *pastoral* in intent, understanding three important things: sin or violation of God's ordinances is serious; there is a difference between understanding sin and its effects and living with sinners; and we are all sinners. Our discussion thus far has been on the theoretical and empirical evidence related to cohabitation. But Christians must go further, acknowledging that cohabitation is not God's sexual standard for relationships. Committed to this standard, we seek to exude grace when dealing with others. Given that many congregants may be living in cohabiting relationships, how can pastors come alongside and support congregants and families in this family arrangement? In this pastoral posture, we organize our response around four questions: (1) What is the nature of commitment in cohabiting relationships? (2) When are two people married in the sight of God? (3) Is cohabitation a threat to the institution of marriage? (4) How should the church respond to cohabiting couples?

What Is the Nature of Commitment in Cohabiting Relationships?

The prominent reasons people enter cohabiting relationships include love, companionship, sexual exclusivity, economics, ambivalence toward marriage, loneliness, and peer pressure. Whereas many of these are understandable reasons for living with a companion, the critical missing piece is commitment. Knowing that there is a conditional, reciprocal relationship adds a level of instability to cohabiting relationships. A conditional relationship is inherently less stable than a covenant relationship because the commitment is on a trial basis. Cohabiting partners are ambivalent toward vowing before God to commit themselves to each other for a lifetime. This impermanence brings more anxiety to the relationship, making daily life more uncertain and adding a level of worry to conflict negotiation.

The biblical concept of a "one-flesh union" blessed by God is the essential missing piece in a cohabiting arrangement. Whereas an exclusive sexual union is an important aspect of cohabitation, just as it is in marriage, covenant provides an enduring, ongoing, faithful commitment through all aspects of married life. It is *hesed* ("steadfast love" or "loyalty," a Hebrew word often used to describe covenant commitment) that promises faithful giving of oneself to the other and keeping the best interest of the other in mind "for better or worse, richer or poorer, in sickness and health, and till death do us part." The model of unconditional covenant commitment is a scriptural ideal for marriage.

The cohabiting couple may have a difficult time grasping the value of covenant love. Independence instead of mutual interdependence limits the deepest possibilities of acceptance, empowerment, and intimacy. When partners are uncertain about permanent commitment, they are prone to keep some distance and protect themselves rather than open up in vulnerable ways to one another. A relationship of reluctance, a fear of becoming too attached, puts emotional barriers up rather than breaking them down. Thus, one of the biggest problems with cohabitation is that it can inhibit deeper levels of personal sharing and knowing. Holding oneself back limits growth through mutual empowerment in the relationship and keeps partners from developing the deepest capacity for intimacy and loving.

It takes courage to know oneself and then reveal that self to a partner. A clarified sense of self allows a partner to surrender in self-giving ways. The "forever" covenant commitment provides a capacity to share without fear. Differentiation gives partners freedom to express personal longings and fears as well as respond to the partner's thoughts, feelings, needs, and desires. Communicating covenant love through thought and action, regardless of obvious flaws and failures, means partners are able to be "naked and not ashamed." There is no longer a need to protect oneself from a deeper attachment. Grace-filled love gives partners the courage to risk letting themselves be known. Covenant, grace, empowerment, and intimacy are the essential ingredients of a committed relationship.

When Are Two People Married in the Sight of God?

The covenantal basis for Christian marriage is modeled after the covenant God made with Israel. God is pictured as trustworthy and forever faithful in expressing unconditional love to the people of God. This translates to the importance of permanence or covenantal love for human relationships as the basis upon which sexual and emotional intimacy are developed. This Christian view of marriage must be differentiated from the legal, civil definitions. In the United States, there has been a conflation of these two meanings so that pastors are able to perform *legally recognized* marriages. To help cement the Christian understanding of marriage in the sight of God, there are several important considerations.

First, does the couple need consent from parents or family before they can be considered married before God? While parental consent was part of Jewish marriage during biblical times, this was a cultural practice based on the mate-selection process. Whereas parental consent is certainly desirable, it would be difficult to find scriptural evidence that it is a requirement for marriage.

Second, does a couple need to make their commitment before a community of believers before they are married in God's sight? The covenant of marriage is entered by relational partners, officiated by a minister or pastor, and sealed by God. One could argue that while it is wise to have support from a faith community, it is not a scriptural directive. There is not a mandate or decree regarding the presence of the church for the wedding ceremony.

Third, is the consent of civil authorities needed? Those who believe that persons should have the consent of the civil authorities point to health concerns—for example, blood tests for negative Rh factor or sexually transmitted diseases—that have ramifications for each partner and their future children. Also, it gives spouses certain legal, financial, and property rights. While there are excellent reasons to seek the consent of civil authorities, it would be difficult to support this as a scriptural mandate.

Following a "letter of the law" interpretation of Scripture, one could argue that none of the above conditions are required to be married in God's sight. At the same time, we think it is important to understand the spirit of the law, which recognizes family, community, and civil authorities as structures that support marriage. Cohabiting couples who say they are married "before God" but fail to make it public miss out on a vital source of collective encouragement. The strength of a commitment multiplies when it is made before Christian witnesses who offer resources as well as a place of accountability. The wisdom of making commitments within a believing community is especially noticeable during times of trouble. A couple depends on others to keep them resilient when life stresses come their way.

Partners who fail to legalize their "marriage" lose out on the government's obligation to look out for the welfare of each partner, the couple, and their children. This especially has ramifications for spouses and their children in regard to financial and property rights, benefits that occur when a relationship has the legal support of society. There is a sense in which a personal commitment is maintained through a supportive community and society.

Some endorse a mutual covenant commitment made between an unmarried man and woman before God and sealed through sexual intercourse as the minimal biblical standard; others believe there is a need for the commitment to be made in the presence of the Christian community and/or within the accepted formal structure of civil society. The ceremony and the license are aspects that serve to integrate a couple into society. Evidence points to the fact that the individualistic ethic in our society keeps people from fully realizing the importance of personal commitments that are embedded in a community context.

Is Cohabitation a Threat to the Institution of Marriage?

At the societal level, we do believe that cohabitation poses a threat to marriage and family stability. In response, the church can offer an informed voice to support societal practices that undergird marriage and family life. At present, marriage in the United States is the accepted way of recognizing a social and legally binding relationship between two consenting adults, and cohabiters do not have that protection.

The negative impact of cohabitation on children continues to be a grave concern to the church. Children born to cohabiting couples are less likely to spend their childhood in a two-parent home than are children born to married couples. There is ample evidence that the economic and emotional impact of divorce on children has deleterious effects on them.

How Should the Church Respond to Cohabiting Couples?

The church must make a distinction between how it responds to individuals who are in cohabiting relationships and how it responds to cohabitation as a *practice* or *lifestyle*. We advocate that Christians should offer grace to cohabiting couples over law. Churches may want to encourage congregants that are cohabiting to live into God's covenant with the church and make a covenant commitment to one another.

A detailed discussion of how the Christian community can wisely respond to each of these cohabiting situations is beyond the limits of this chapter. We do offer some general guidelines, however, about how the Christian community can best respond to these different scenarios.

1. The Christian community promotes and encourages the biblical standard of a permanent covenant commitment between two people before

God, presenting this through the compelling influence of modeling. The church as a faithful community demonstrates living into commitment, grace, empowerment, and intimacy. This community encourages each congregant to live out these experiences in daily life.

2. The Christian community offers hospitality, lovingly reaching out to all who enter their doors, offering covenant, grace, empowerment, and connection, which provides a place of belonging and security.

3. The Christian community openly receives children and family members into the church family, giving them a glimpse of the faithful, trustworthy presence of love and support among God's people.

4. The Christian community offers a public ceremony within the community of faith to celebrate the covenant union when couples decide to marry, with no stigma or shame placed on them or their children.

5. The Christian community continues to show love and grace, accepting people as they are in the love of Christ without coercion.

6. The Christian community becomes a trustworthy place and loving community and never turns away anyone who seeks God.

We believe that the church often deprives cohabiting couples of a genuine place of caring and belonging and that we have so much to offer them in our communities of faith. If there is a decision to make covenant vows, it behooves the church to support them through a meaningful public ceremony. Elaborate and expensive wedding ceremonies may keep some from moving toward this. Helping with a simple, culturally appropriate ceremony that includes congregation and family members as a witness to the covenant vows is really the important thing.

Here are just a couple personal examples of the faith community providing support in small but significant ways. Judy's mother wore a simple gold dress for her wedding ceremony after the Sunday night church service. Her aunt and uncle stood with them, and the church provided cake and coffee for a small reception afterward. Jack's parents had a similar ceremony after the Sunday morning church service. They invited the family and a few special friends over to the house for a light Sunday brunch reception. A wedding was an occasion to support the couple's covenant commitment without all the fuss and flair of an expensive, elaborate wedding. Both sets of parents were married more than sixty years, a covenant commitment that lasted over their long lives. Tom and Gail also had a very simple ceremony. They were blessed to have Tom's father, an ordained minister in the Church of the Nazarene, officiate the ceremony. The wedding was followed by a small celebration with close friends and family.

Perhaps the greatest challenge to the Christian community is to offer grace in the midst of the tension felt when those who enter the church to learn of God and God's ways have a different set of value systems. The discouraging truth is that living outside of biblically based norms can negatively affect one's attitudes toward those norms. Individuals grow accustomed to lifestyles outside of God's intention for humanity, yet they experience glimpses of the blessings God intends for relationships even while living outside the standard. For example, cohabiting couples meet intimacy and relationship needs for one another. Joy and love are present. But ambivalence toward God's intended design leads to devaluing marriage and covenant commitment. Discipling individuals and couples in situations like this means we need to extend the hand of hospitality and friendship first. As the church exposes individuals and families in this situation to more and more biblical truth, the relationship of grace and fellowship aids in the discipleship process. Rather than reacting with judgment or fear, the church is the place that opens wide its doors, welcoming all to come and learn of the ways of Jesus.

In its stance toward the practice of cohabitation, we believe that the church can err in two ways: either by failing to uphold the sacred purpose of marriage or by condemning and shutting out those who cohabit. In upholding marriage as God's way with one hand, we should extend God's grace with the other. Our gospel must be full of truth and grace. The church needs to be the very place that reaches out to seekers, both those living outside biblical norms and those for whom biblical behavior has not yet become part of their lives. The church will have a minimal impact on the lives of those who are cohabiting until it clearly offers the hands of both truth *and* grace.

A couple may be on a path to Christ without even knowing it. When a cohabiting couple establishes a covenant commitment, they have understood something essential about God's way. The Christian community can nurture a couple's natural inclination to continue to move in God's way through patience, respect, and love that points them in that direction. Being compassionate rather than judgmental comes out of the assurance that God, who is the final judge, is the one who loves most fully. "Christ's love sees us with terrible clarity and sees us whole. Christ's love so wishes our joy that it is ruthless against everything in us that diminishes our joy" (Buechner 1992, 58). Striving to help cohabiting couples find the joy of covenant love is a great privilege. The Christian community needs to show forth God's love in faithful, engaging ways that will draw those who cohabit closer to the way, the truth, and the more abundant life.

Discerning God's Will

Marriage is an important, sacred event in most societies. Marriage is pivotal because it is necessary to the psychological well-being of the individuals involved, the social well-being of the married couple and family, the economic well-being of communities, and the survival of society itself. One advantage of parent-arranged marriage is that it protects young people from the pressure, confusion, and agony of having to make such a major decision on their own. The obvious disadvantage is the impact of excluding the couple from this critical process, which has enormous implications for the rest of their lives. This leads us to the question of how Christians are to approach the mate-selection process.

To answer this question, we must begin by considering how one comes to discern God's will in the matter of choosing a mate. First, a couple contemplating marriage will want to view their relationship through the theological and biblical relationship lenses we have presented in this chapter. As they look at their relationship history in light of these values, they will begin to answer the mate-selection question through their experiences with each other. Many couples already recognize trouble in their relationship as they are dating but deny the seriousness of the problems. For this reason, long engagements are predictive of successful marriage. When the couple gets beyond the romantic stage during the months and years prior to marriage in a long engagement, they gain a more realistic idea about managing their relationship. They will have experienced conflicts and struggles during this time and have a good understanding of how they deal with each other in the process. They will have had time to see each other in all sorts of situations and been willing to discuss their expectations about roles and future plans.

Premarital counseling with a licensed therapist or pastor is a great way to discern how marriage with a particular individual could grow. We strongly suggest that a couple intentionally learn all they can about their relationship through a premarital inventory, identifying strengths and weaknesses in their relationship. David Olson's *Prepare/Enrich* (1998) is a 125-item questionnaire used by clergy and counselors to assess a couple's chances for a successful marriage. The inventory matches each person's responses to questions in major areas such as personality, friendships, conflict, communication, finance, sex, views on children, and family of origin. It has proven to be quite accurate in predicting whether a couple will be successful or eventually divorce (Fowers, Montel, and Olson 1996). Another helpful inventory is the "Preparation for Marriage Questionnaire" (Holman, Larson, and Harmer 1994). It consists of 178 items that evaluate the following five areas that are predictive of marital satisfaction and stability: (1) degree of unity in values, attitudes, and beliefs; (2) personal readiness for marriage (the indicators include emotional health and maturity, self-esteem, and independence from one's family of origin); (3) partner readiness (communicating ability and skills, self-disclosure, and empathic behavior); (4) couple readiness (agreement on basic issues, stability of the relationship, approval of each other's friends and relatives, and realistic expectations); and (5) background and home environment (satisfaction with the home environment, the quality of the home environment, the quality of the parent-child relationship, and absence of physical and sexual abuse). Sue Johnson's helpful resource (2008) outlines important conversations relational partners need to have to benefit their relationship. Another important tool for premarital counseling is "Saving Your Marriage before It Starts" (SYMBIS), developed by Les and Leslie Parrott (2015). (More information is available on the Parrotts' website, https://www.symbis.com/couples/.)

These assessments and discussion tools can provide concrete information that will help a couple determine the potential success of their future together. Couples should spend time discussing these relationship dynamics; process the results of the inventories with a trusted counselor or minister; grapple honestly with family of origin and multicultural challenges; take time to work out a financial budget; attend workshops on relationship skill development; be aware of personality differences and consider how they might affect the relationship; deal openly with sexual relationship issues with a counselor and read and discuss an informative book on the subject.

No one particular way of finding God's will is best for everyone, but in most cases a combination of activities is advisable. Here are four specific guidelines for couples to consider when seeking God's direction about marriage. First, look to God directly through prayer, Bible study, and meditation. Second, seek wisdom and input from parents, significant family members, and good friends. Trusted people who know and are willing to be honest about each partner's individual strengths and weaknesses will prove invaluable. Third, as mentioned earlier, go through a premarital counseling process in which all aspects of the relationship are examined honestly, and spend time clarifying expectations with an objective professional or pastor. Fourth, seek wisdom from trustworthy Christians in their community of faith. Those in the body of Christ provide a communal perspective that will help affirm or disaffirm the couple's decision-making process.

Based on these suggestions, we advise that a couple can best discern God's will through a biblically balanced approach that is open to input from three sources—the individuals directly concerned, family and close friends, and the Christian community, which together can serve as a check against an incorrect decision. When decisions are made without input from all three sources, there is a greater probability of error. Given the power of passion and the contemporary emphasis on intimacy in romantic relationships, the individualistic bias is the most likely to have fatal consequences. Family bias is typical of parental arrangements. When parents are discerning Christians, they can be an invaluable source of wisdom, though they may have a limited perspective because of personal or cultural biases. Christian-community bias is probably the most difficult to detect since it is generally felt that a corporate body is less prone to bias. However, an obvious danger is the power a particular leader (or leaders) may wield. Leaders also have human limitations and are therefore capable of using their influence in misguided ways. Particularly troubling are communities in which congregants are required to submit to an authoritarian leader out of loyalty.

Even if one concedes the wisdom of this model, there is always the possibility of disagreement. Consequently, the individuals, family, and Christian community should work together to bring about a congruous decision that will enhance the probability of a lasting covenant.

4

Establishing Marriage

Moving toward Differentiated Unity

Each spouse's experiences growing up in his or her particular family of origin are major preparations for marriage, for good and for ill. Accordingly, marriage involves more than a uniting of two individuals; it is also a uniting of two extended families. Bringing aspects of two culturally diverse families into a new unit is a process of affirming the best of both cultures (sense of belonging) and discovering the spouses' own sense of identity as a couple. In the process, they may choose to discard some of their heritage, expand aspects of it, and create a unique union that exceeds what either of them would be on their own. Forming a new relationship as a couple distinguishes each of them from their family of origin (the family each grew up in) and at the same time keeps each of them connected with it. We begin this chapter by recognizing the impact of family of origin as well as other important factors that contribute to marital quality.

Factors That Predict Marital Quality

Researchers have identified several factors from the family of origin (FOO) that affect marital satisfaction and quality. These factors include conflict-resolution style, relationship self-regulation based on family-of-origin climate (Hardy et al. 2015), and background and contextual factors (Larson and Hickman 2004).

First, FOO experiences highly influence a marital partner's conflict-resolution style, which partially affects marital satisfaction (Dennison et al. 2014). This indicates that individuals learn relationship strategies from their family of origin, such as how to resolve conflict, and these habits are incorporated into conflict resolution in one's family of choice. These resolution strategies influence the overall satisfaction and quality of marriage.

Second, FOO climate can be thought of as one's perceptions of the safety, warmth, and fairness in the family of origin. This climate entails one's emotional experience of the support, empathy, and availability of parents. One important aspect of this climate relates to how individuals learn to self-regulate in their relationships. That is, more positive experiences in one's FOO lead to greater capacities to self-regulate in one's marital relationship. This relational self-regulation (RSR) provides important strategies for engaging in relationships that facilitate marital satisfaction. Individuals learn how to manage emotional experiences while maintaining their relationships with their FOO. These are important skills needed for each spouse to learn as they adjust to one another while creating a new sense of family identity. One important RSR is the ability to manage one's anxiety or anger in responding to one's spouse. Additionally, RSR allows individuals to interpret their spouse's behavior more positively, enabling conflict to be avoided or resolved without relying on more negative conflict-resolution strategies.

Finally, sociocultural and contextual factors that affect the quality of marriage include age at time of marriage, level of education and income, and occupational stability. Being similar (homogamy) in race, socioeconomic status, religion, intelligence, and age are factors that affect a new marriage in a positive way. Individual characteristics such as physical and emotional health, lack of neurotic traits, conventionality, and level of self-esteem contribute to the quality a couple can achieve in their new union. Also, having similar values, attitudes, and beliefs seems to bring out the best in both spouses.

When it comes to interpersonal dynamics, good communication and conflict-resolution skills bring strength and quality to the marriage (Gottman 2011). Not having cohabited and low participation in premarital sexual intercourse also contribute to a couple's quality of marriage and sexual satisfaction (Larson and Hickman 2004; Strait et al. 2015).

Research regarding the effects of the family of origin demonstrate that one's family of choice is significantly influenced by one's family of origin. When parents have had a high-quality marital relationship, the couple has a better chance of developing quality in their own marriage. When both sets of parents have achieved a long-lasting marriage (no divorce), are relatively free of mental illness, demonstrate positive conflict-resolution strategies, and provide a warm, caring, and nurturing home environment, chances for high quality in the newly formed marriage increase. Also, when families are supportive and refrain from pressuring the couple, marital quality is more likely. The new couple needs time and space to develop their relationship. In the next section, we will consider in more detail the family-of-origin dynamics.

Resolving Issues Related to the Family of Origin

The influence of families of origin on the family of choice is generally referred to as intergenerational transmission (Bowen 2004; Kerr and Bowen 1988). This is one of the most important contributions from Bowen Family Systems Theory (BFST). Intergenerational transmission refers to the communication patterns and strategies children learn from their parents as well as the emotional tone of the family. The main ways that communication and relationships merge with emotional experience occurs via differentiation of self (DoS).

DoS is a key component in the adaptability of families. It allows each individual family member, with the sure identity of belonging to their family, to understand his or her values and beliefs and engage in family relationships based on these beliefs. Further, as stressors arise within the family and children develop increasing competencies, parents need to support these competencies by increasing parental expectations for the children. Stressors outside the family demand the family to adapt to pressures as well. Taken together, DoS provides the psychological and relational strengths needed to respond to these challenges in a values-based manner.

DoS provides the individual with the tools to manage emotional experience while maintaining one's relationships with others. DoS should be conceptualized along two dimensions (Frederick and Dunbar 2019). First, intrapersonal DoS focuses on one's ability to be attentive and responsive to one's emotional experience while not being overwhelmed by that experience. Individuals with high levels of DoS are able to acknowledge their emotions while responding to them in a values-based manner. Second, DoS has an interpersonal dimension focusing on the balance of individuality and togetherness (Bowen, 2004; Kerr and Bowen, 1988). Interpersonal DoS enables individuals to maintain their values commitments while remaining in relationships with others. Both these aspects of DoS are transmitted in one's FOO as described above.

Parents as Role Models

Parents are powerful role models. They teach through verbal communication, but their nonverbal behavior is probably even more influential. Children learn important lessons about marriage by observing how their parents communicate with each other—how they express their feelings of love, affection, and anger. Everything that parents do in their role as marriage partners will profoundly influence their children's behaviors and attitudes as marriage partners. Although true for both husbands and wives, there was a stronger correlation between wives' positive experience in their family of origin and reported marital adjustment. On the other hand, more negative FOO experiences had more negative effects on conflict resolution and marital satisfaction for women as compared to men (Dennison et al. 2014).

Research indicates that regardless of whether or not we agree with the way our parents handled their marriage or parenting responsibilities, when a similar situation arises in our own family, our spontaneous reaction will be to behave as our parents did. The young wife who witnessed her mother's temper whenever her father was running late may be determined to give her husband the benefit of the doubt rather than lash out in anger. However, when a similar situation arises, she finds herself scolding her husband before he has a chance to explain his tardiness. The husband, who remembers that his father was less than considerate in not calling home about being detained, nevertheless forgets to call his wife. In many ways, relationship partners replicate relational patterns from their families of origin.

Spouses must make an effort to recognize and correct faulty attitudes and behaviors they unthinkingly bring into their marriage. It is imperative to avoid the fatalistic attitude that denies responsibility for one's own behavior by saying, "My parents have been such a strong influence on my behavior that there is nothing I can do about it!" To make excuses of this nature is tempting. A husband may say, "My wife wants me to be more open in communicating my feelings to her; she just doesn't realize that we didn't do that in my family." A wife may say, "I can't help worrying about you when you go on a trip; my mother always worried about my father." These defeatist attitudes do not facilitate needed change.

Equally detrimental is the naive belief that one's family of origin does not affect one's marital life. Such thinking leads to a denial of behavioral patterns that have similar negative outcomes in one's marriage. Without personal awareness of these patterns, change is unlikely.

Parental Support

As noted at the beginning of this chapter, research indicates that social, emotional, and financial support from parents and other relatives—what is known as family climate—is very important in helping a newly married couple establish a solid marriage. In fact, more positive experiences in family climate are associated with better self-regulation (Hardy et al. 2015). Children with more supportive and warm family climates internalize the ability to regulate anxiety and anger in these early relationships. RSR is cultivated in supportive families and translates to increased marital satisfaction.

In an ideal situation, children have the freedom to move some distance from home for schooling or employment, and their parents remain available to them for emotional and even financial support. This involves both appropriate differentiation (no strings attached) and support (we want to empower you). Some parents make their support conditional on the new couple reciprocating in some way. For support (financial or emotional) to be empowering, it must be unconditional and freely given. For example, financial arrangements should be clearly negotiated in an attitude of mutual respect and agreement. If there are expectations such as paying back a loan later, these conditions must be specified up front so that responsibility becomes part of empowerment.

Some parents are threatened by their children's independence and want to keep control. The demands they make can undermine the newly established unit, forcing the couple to concentrate on meeting the expectations of the family of origin rather than on building the newly formed marital dyad. The couple that continually needs parental financial or emotional help has failed to accomplish the important task of establishing autonomy, which includes the ability to manage financially and to become functionally independent of parents. The manner in which supportive arrangements are made and the accompanying attitudes and expectations of both parents and married children determine whether such help will have positive or negative effects.

The principle of empowerment can be demonstrated by asking the following question: Does the support lead to responsible action and mutual respect or to indebtedness, dependency, and obligation? If parents use their resources to control, the result is emotional distance and resentment. If parents use their resources to empower, they help the couple establish a strong marital bond along with a desire to maintain solid ties and connection with extended family.

A person's identity is formed in the family of origin. In fact, until puberty it is hard to think of ourselves apart from our family. In our families, we acquire the majority of our attitudes, beliefs, and values. What we believe our parents think of us shapes our self-concept. One's identity is connected with being from a particular family, and this identity forms the main psychological vehicle for living. Identity is so important psychologically that Dan McAdams (1997) describes identity achievement as the crux of human development.

At puberty, however, differentiation begins to intensify. Through this process, teenagers establish an identity separate from the family. Differentiated individuals are both connected to their families and, at the same time, sufficiently separated socially and psychologically. On the one hand, differentiated individuals have a strong sense of belonging or togetherness with their families. On the other hand, differentiated individuals know themselves—their beliefs, values, and desires—and are able to live out those aspects of their self-concept, or what we would call core self (Bowen 2004), while maintaining relationships with others. This core self takes personal responsibility and is able to respond to experiences and relationships in a manner consistent with its values while maintaining those relationships. It takes a great deal of emotional, intellectual, and spiritual energy to accomplish this extremely important task of sorting out and determining one's own values and beliefs rather than indiscriminately taking on the values and beliefs of one's parents. We describe the process of adolescent differentiation in greater detail in chapter 9. At this point, it is sufficient to say that people are not ready for marriage until they have clearly differentiated themselves from their parents.

There are two types of undifferentiated individuals: those who are overly close and dependent on their family of origin and those who are disengaged or emotionally severed from it. In overly close (fused) relationships, people are so tightly involved with their families that there is no healthy separateness. People who are emotionally cut off, however, are so emotionally removed from their families that there is no healthy connectedness. Notice how these two types are utilizing similar relationship strategies: both fused and cutoff people are using their relationships alone to define their identities. The fused individual often modifies or disavows aspects of the core self so that membership with the family is maintained. On the other side, those who are cut off emotionally are trying to define themselves in contrast to the FOO.

Genesis 2:24 describes differentiation for the marital couple: "Therefore a man leaves his father and his mother and clings to his wife, and they become one flesh." A person cannot leave mother and father if he or she clings to or is fused with them. People overly connected with their parents have difficulty creating a new marital dyad. Yet leaving mother and father is equally impossible if there has never been a sufficient connectedness with them. In cutoff families, children lack the skills to make close emotional connections with others, even a new spouse. In both extremes, it is highly difficult to establish a meaningful "one flesh" union.

The concepts of fusion and cutoff are illustrated in the parable of the prodigal son (Luke 15:11–32). The younger son cuts himself off from his family, demanding his full inheritance and severing all connections. In the process, he cuts off all cultural, social, economic, and psychological ties by moving to a far country and working among swine (which are unclean for Jewish people). On the surface, this may appear to be a sign of independence, but it proves to be premature.

One might also wonder if the elder son who stays home is somehow fused with his family. As the story unfolds, he appears to be undifferentiated. We see this fusion when he complains to his father about his obedience not being rewarded. The older brother is not willingly doing his father's will; he is biding his time until he receives the reward of his inheritance and is obedient to his father only on the surface. His reaction to his father's acceptance of his lost brother is indicative of fusion. A differentiated son would have established a solid connection with a clearly defined self and thus would have celebrated his brother's return. Additionally, his service to the father and family would not be intrinsically based in identity and motivated by the expectation of reward. His jealous and angry reaction suggests that he is threatened by his erroneous belief that his father has only so much love to give and that giving love to the younger brother means that the father loves him less. He is not sufficiently separated from his family of origin, and his dependency leads to possessiveness and jealousy.

Empowerment facilitates personal responsibility and empathy for the other. Each brother would take ownership of his choices, both appropriate and inappropriate. They would be able to allow others to experience the consequences of their behavior while maintaining a relationship with them. The father exemplifies this, understanding the sons' choices and avoiding interference when the consequences of those choices affect his sons. This is not a cold, detached, unfeeling attitude on the part of the father. This is a father empowering his adult sons by allowing them to experience the effects of their choices.

The way God parented the children of Israel afforded them the possibility of achieving differentiation. God offered covenantal love, which is the basis of identity, and the building blocks of grace, empowerment, and intimacy. On the one hand, when the children of Israel went their own way (cut off), he held them accountable and responsible for their actions. On the other hand, God continually offered grace in the form of reconciliation and restoration. This balance of both offering emotional support and affirming differentiation leads to interdependence in relationships.

We have seen that a very important factor in establishing a solid foundation in marriage is the differentiation of both spouses from their families of origin. There can be no cleaving without leaving. When two individuals are differentiated and secure in their own identities, they can give themselves to each other and make room in their selves for the distinct other that contributes toward forming a differentiated unity. Their close and stable relationships with their families of origin promote a loyalty to the old while creating a new and distinct system.

Adaptability

In general, people need order in their lives. Scripture teaches that a human community should be an orderly one. One of Paul's qualifications for church leaders is that they should have orderly home relationships (1 Tim. 3:1–7). Effective families function well with a certain amount of routine and structure. Yet the desired degree of order varies greatly among families and cultures. Some families demand an excessive amount of order; others have almost no structure at all. For example, children's bedtimes may be observed so precisely in some families that if the youngsters are not in bed with the lights out at the prescribed minute, punishment is sure to follow. Other families have such little regard for order that bedtimes are not even prescribed, let alone enforced. These two extremes are examples of very low and very high degrees of adaptability. Degree of adaptability is an important dimension that marriage partners bring with them from their family of origin (see chap. 2).

Most often, effective families have a healthy degree of structure and flexibility (i.e., they are neither overly rigid nor chaotic). Marriages with a capacity for adaptability endure well over time because they are more open to and can adapt better to the changes that continually occur in family life. This ability is especially important because change is inevitable, whether it occurs in the development of individual members, in relationship dynamics, throughout the family life stages, or because of an unexpected internal or external stressor.

But what happens when a person from a rigid home marries a person from a chaotic home? Both spouses will naturally attempt to implement their own family style, and this presents interesting clashes, to say the least. Spouses who come from more balanced and similar backgrounds will undoubtedly have an easier time of it. All couples need to develop a system that works best for them. Even such matters as how to celebrate particular holidays or how to implement daily family routines such as eating, sleeping, and playing, or rituals such as manners or prayers at the table or reading stories at bedtime will need to be negotiated. The couple will begin to establish their own routines, household rules, roles, and rituals. Once again, they may take certain things from each of their family traditions to enrich their homes and mutually create new ways of organizing their family life.

The Dilemma of Modern Marriage

The high rate of divorce in most Western cultures supports the notion that it is difficult to establish a strong marriage in a postmodern society. Although a variety of explanations can be proposed, such as urbanization, industrialization, changing gender roles, and high social and geographical mobility, surely a key factor is high expectations that marriage will fulfill personal needs. One expectation that Tim and Kathy Keller (2013) describe is the belief that personal happiness and fulfillment is the most important aspect of one's life. Marriage is unable to guarantee personal happiness because it is inherently a give-and-take between relational partners. Personal happiness takes a back seat to maintaining the marriage. This is an affront to the postmodern belief that individual fulfillment and happiness is the most important aspect of life. Up to one hundred years ago, marriage was primarily a social institution designed to meet economic needs and provide a place for rearing children. This view of marriage as an institution has been replaced by the concept that marriage is a companionship grounded on romantic attraction, self-fulfillment, and ego-need gratification (Coontz 2004; Frederick and Dunbar 2019). As the marriage expectation bar continues to be raised, fewer marriages are capable of delivering what they promise in the way of personal fulfillment and satisfaction.

The tremendous expectations placed on marriage today are further exacerbated by the notion that each spouse must compete for power and a separate identity while in the marriage. In the past, wives simply yielded their individual identity and rights to their husbands. As late as the mid-1800s, ownership of any property contributed by the bride's family transferred to the husband. In the traditional marriage, the goal of two becoming one was met by the bride giving up her own identity and taking on a new identity as the husband's wife. While few would want to return to this kind of arrangement, the "challenge in modern marriage is to build a relationship that is mutual, reciprocal, and balanced by equal regard for each spouse and mutual sacrifice for the good of the relationship" (Balswick and Balswick 2006).

One response to the contemporary marriage crisis is to abandon the ideal that marriage is a lifelong commitment. When marriage is defined as a business contract between two partners, the focus becomes maximizing one's benefits and minimizing expenditures. This implies that marriages are primarily for the individual's benefit and that the marriage should be ended when costs exceed benefits. Family sociologists have documented this response in the literature as the "deinstitutionalization of marriage" (Cherlin 2004), the "retreat from marriage" (Smock 2004), and the view that lifelong marriage is "something of an aberration that existed" in the past (Gillis 2004). Ellen Lewin (2004) challenges the idea that marriage is the only legitimate conjugal arrangement. John Gillis (2004) welcomes the new trend of a wide range of formal and informal marriage arrangements and asserts that "seen in the larger historical and global perspective, there is nothing particularly alarming in the tendency. In fact, there is much to recommend it" (991). A careful observer might note that these comments are based on naturalistic assumptions that society should accept what is happening (such as higher rates of cohabitation and divorce) as normative and not make value judgments about what marriage should be. Contrary to a biblical view, much contemporary writing views marriage as a relationship of convenience, formed according to what the two people decide to make of it.

Differentiated Unity: Becoming One and Retaining Uniqueness

The contemporary crisis in marriage is real. But rather than cave in to postmodern marital ethics, we believe the dilemma of modern marriage can be solved by recapturing a biblical view of marriage. Whereas God intends for marriage to constitute a *unity* as in "two become one," it is not God's intent for either the husband or the wife to lose his or her own identity in the process of forming that union. Tim and Kathy Keller (2013) describe how the beauty of a biblical definition of marriage and Christian sexual ethic is that it challenges premodern notions of marriage (marriage functions economically) and modern (marriage is a contract) and even a postmodern view (marriage is a remnant of a long bygone area that impeded on personal flourishing). God intends marriage to reflect the unique type of relationality found in the Holy Trinity. This truth is a core derivative of Genesis 1:26–27: "Then God said, 'Let *us* make humankind in our image, according to our likeness.' . . . So God created humankind in his image, in the image of God he created them; male and female he created them." The *relationality* between the distinct human beings (male and female) reflects the *imago Dei*—the image of God.

We bring this emphasis on relationality into our model for marriage. The relational nature in marriage is analogous in human form to the divine Trinity. As the Father, the Son, and the Holy Spirit (three distinct persons) mutually indwell the Godhead in a trinitarian fellowship, so do spouses (two distinct selves) mutually indwell the marriage union. Ever mindful of our human limitations, we believe this model offers great promise. It is in their distinctiveness that spouses mutually permeate each other when they form their union. Unity and distinction coexist. Reciprocal and mutual interdependency is what God had in mind for marriage. A *differentiated unity* brings great satisfaction to both spouses and to their relationship. In this context, to be human in marriage is to be a particular spouse in a relationship, distinct and unique and yet inextricably intertwined and interdependent with the other. Mutual indwelling never negates but rather enhances the particularity of each spouse. As Gary Deddo asserts, "The unity and the distinction are each unimpaired by the other" (1999, 23).

DoS, or as we will argue later, differentiation in Christ, is about identity. We are called into relationship with Christ during conversion. We are given a new identity, one based on membership in Christ's family. This new identity in Christ forms the core self and is the basis for relating to others. Thus, our differentiation in Christ is the key factor in determining the effectiveness of spousal differentiation. Both spouses are more than they can ever be by themselves, because they have become something bigger in their union. In marriage, spouses are both distinct (male and female differentiation) and equal (directed to be fruitful and have dominion) in their created purpose. They find ultimate meaning in and through their relationship with God and each other. The supreme meaning of being created in the image of God is that spouses reflect a relationship of *unity* without absorbing one into the other. Marital mutuality is reached through a reciprocating relationship in which spouses encounter their own uniqueness in relation to God and the other.

Assimilation is a process in which two separate entities become one, while accommodation is an agreement by two separate entities to be different. From the lens of BFST, assimilation is fusion. The biblical concept of one flesh might appear to be assimilation. However, the Bible also describes the relationship of the believer with Christ as becoming one with him. Does this mean that we lose our identity and personhood when we become Christians? Of course not! In fact, this is the difference between the various Eastern religions and Christianity. Salvation according to the Eastern religions is to acknowledge the self as an illusion and then to recognize oneness with the eternal force in the universe. The dissolution of the self and the cosmos is described in the psychology of mindfulness (Grabovac, Lau, and Willett 2011). In Christianity, salvation is relational. It comes when the person is rightly related to God, the Creator and provider of eternal life.

Assimilation in marriage, where the personhood of one spouse is given up, is not what God intended. Christian marriage is more like accommodation, where two separate people each maintain a distinct personhood but choose to come together in unity and oneness of commitment, meaning, and service. It is noteworthy that the key verses in Ephesians 5, which speak about the marriage relationship, are introduced by the directive, "Be subject to one another out of reverence for Christ" (v. 21). Ideally, in Christian marriage each spouse is subject to the other; that is, each makes room for the other to love and be loved, to forgive and be forgiven, to serve and be served, and to know and be known. A marriage in which one partner, the husband or the wife, is asked to give up his or her personhood for the sake of the other denies God's expression in and through that unique member of the creation. The relationship is remarkably more fulfilling when both people are equally expressed in their union, providing others an opportunity to know two distinct people as well as to relate to the couple as a unit.

Just because a couple forms a union does not mean there are no differences between the spouses. Quite the contrary! Precisely because they bring unique perspectives to the union, they will need to navigate through their differences. In fact, Genesis 2 emphasizes the complementary nature of the relationship—male and female. At a minimum, biological differences foster opportunities to esteem the uniqueness of each spouse as well as incorporate these differences into the marriage. In navigating these differences, it's important that each spouse be open and responsive in an attitude of humble respect. Conflict is to be expected when two distinct and unique individuals express themselves equally. Marriage without conflict can signify that one spouse has given up personhood. In a vital relationship, conflicts are viewed with an eye to finding a solution that is in the best interest of each spouse and the relationship as a whole. Agreement is never at the expense of one spouse over the other. Being subject to one's spouse does not mean giving in for the sake of avoiding conflict or maintaining harmony. In fact, giving in for the sake of avoiding conflict may be a way of letting a spouse down.

Commitment involves a willingness to express your desires and opinions, to confront a partner in love, to listen with openness to your spouse's desires and opinions, to have compassion, and to affirm the other's ideas. Differentiated unity assures a mutual love that works out differences for the good of the relationship.

Learning New Roles in the Marital Dance

Perichoresis is the Greek word used to describe the relationality among members of the Trinity. Eugene Peterson (2005, 44–45) points out that, in the original language, *perichoresis* literally means "a round dance." Like a round dance, marriage can be described as two people moving rhythmically together as they repeatedly embrace, release, hold on, and then let go of each other. Partners will dance in unity when they share an understanding of their roles in relation to each other as they perform their particular dance. It may be an ever-changing dance with new moves as circumstances alter, but when spouses are in step there is great joy in observing the graceful movements. We find it helpful to think of spouses being in tune with each other as they anticipate, construct, change, and live out their roles throughout their marriage.

Prior to marriage, most spouses have already formulated in their minds a role for themselves and a role for the person they are to marry. How husbands and wives define their respective roles can be important. High expectations often lead to disappointment. It was discovered by DeMaris, Sanchez, and Krivickas (2012, 989) that "couples characterized by more traditional attitudes toward gender roles were significantly less satisfied." Discussing role expectations prior to marriage will hopefully counter the unexpected or unrealistic ideals that hinder rather than help the couple work out their respective roles. This subjective anticipation of new roles before entering marriage is known as *role taking*. A rat running a maze is limited to learning by trial and error. It must randomly follow each corridor in search of food until it either reaches a dead end or finds the reward. Humans use their rich vocabulary and elaborate thinking ability to run a maze in their minds. In fact, before two people decide to marry, they each probably run through an elaborate symbolic maze by imagining what it would be like to be married to the other person for the rest of their lives. We constantly engage in role taking when anticipating the new roles we eventually assume.

An important ingredient in the achievement of marital adjustment is the ability to take on the role of another person. This requires empathy—the ability to view the world from someone else's perspective and to stand in that person's place. Research shows that people with role-taking ability score high on marital-adjustment tests. It is extremely important that partners be able to see things from the viewpoint of their spouses. This is what understanding the other is about.

After marriage, spouses engage in *role playing*. Role playing is the process of actually assuming the role of spouse and dancing out the part that has been only imagined up to this point. The first part of role playing can be thought of as *playing at a role*. Spouses play at a role to the extent that they are self-conscious and unsure of themselves in marriage. We can engage in role playing hundreds of times. However, when we actually assume a role, we find it to be somewhat different from what we imagined. A newly married couple will experience some awkwardness in playing at their new roles as spouses. Even though they are acutely aware that they are newlyweds, they are not yet accustomed to their new roles as married people. It takes time to become comfortable with the role so that it feels natural.

People who begin marriage by playing at a role will eventually become comfortable with it and spontaneously engage in playing the role of marital partner. Meanwhile, because of the expectations formed prior to role taking, the early stages of marriage often bring *role conflict*. Both people enter marriage with their personal and family-of-origin definition of what their role and their spouse's role should be. This can lead to confusion and difficulty.

Much emotion is invested in one's new role as husband or wife, and consequently there is also great potential for conflict. A husband and wife may disagree about the definition of the spouse's role. He may enter marriage thinking that husbands do not do dishes, while the wife may consider this to be his role. Similarly, a wife may view her role as including responsibility for the budget, but the husband may see this as his territory. As the couple begins to clarify these messages, tension is likely to occur. If they resort to pulling or pushing while learning this dance, they will appear uncoordinated and will likely step on each other's toes. Finding the mutual rhythm and coordinating the right steps is worth every effort it takes to create a harmonious pattern of movement.

Role conflict arises naturally and not necessarily because a person is immature or unprepared for role skirmishes. Role conflicts need to be worked out in an atmosphere of grace, acceptance, and dialogue. Spouses who have good skills in problem-solving and conflict resolution will have a head start. Resolving role conflicts throughout marriage gives the couple a solid base of operation. Those who cannot achieve solutions are likely to struggle with these same role conflicts, and the marriage will resemble a wrestling match more than a dance.

The marital-role dance is an ever-changing dynamic that must evolve as new patterns emerge. Role definitions appropriate in the beginning stages of marriage may become outmoded two or three years later; roles will change over time and in response to family life-cycle changes. In the daily acts of being husband and wife, new ways of playing out roles are constantly attempted. Role taking does not stop when a couple marries but continues throughout the life cycle. For example, even among very egalitarian couples, the transition to parenthood is associated with a return to more traditional gender roles in marriage (Frederick and Balswick 2011). A couple may have decided early in the marriage that one spouse would stay home with the children when they are young. But when that spouse begins to imagine what a full-time job outside the home would be like (role taking), a role conflict is evident. When any new course of action is taken, the couple must carefully consider its impact on household chores and responsibilities, cooking, childcare, socializing, and so on. A small step now can make a huge difference down the road.

The most troublesome adjustments in marriages are those not clearly worked out ahead of time. In such situations, each spouse may have unspoken expectations of which the other is unaware. Assuming that spouses can read each other's minds is a recipe for relationship breakdown. A typical example is the wife who assumes that her husband's agreement that she be employed outside the home means that he will take on household responsibilities. When he fails to do so, she finds herself doing double duty, a common complaint in marriage that understandably leads to resentment. Many women who imagine they are entering an egalitarian marriage have been disillusioned to find that they are expected to be the superwoman who does it all.

A spousal role can be defined objectively by spouses, family, culture, church, community, and society at large, but the one who performs the role defines it subjectively. And there is rarely a one-to-one correlation between the general definition of a role and how that spouse actually defines it. Because each individual person is unique, role playing is always *role making*.

Each person plays the role of husband or wife according to one's own distinctive taste and style—a person embellishes the marital dance with his or her unique flair. Marriages in which either partner has a prescribed definition of what the other's role should be will most likely encounter trouble. It's best to recognize individual differences and unique personalities in taking on roles. During the Balswicks' early years, Jack complained that Judy was too much like her mother, a very spontaneous and expressive person. Judy's spontaneous ways would embarrass Jack, who was more reserved, and he would reprimand Judy for her behavior. Talking about this helped him see how his role expectation for Judy dampened her free spirit. In fact, he realized that her outgoing personality was one of the things that attracted him to her in the first place. Judy, in turn, was willing to be more considerate of Jack in these situations. It led to an acceptance and appreciation of each other as unique persons with unique personalities and became a significant stepping-stone of growth in the relationship.

Tom and Gail married in May, moved across the country in July, and started seminary in August. They had to rely on one another for help because Tom's parents were in Pennsylvania and Gail's family of origin was in Taiwan. One early adjustment involved negotiating dealing with others. For example, Gail would interactive with wives and Tom would interact with husbands separately at social events. In the car on the way home, Gail would have a list of details and other information from the wives with whom she interacted. She would then ask Tom about details from the husbands. He would frequently respond, "I don't know," since he did not want to pry into other mens' lives. Initially, it was a little frustrating that Gail would learn things about others that Tom would not. But eventually they learned to appreciate how each of them uniquely interacts with those who would become friends.

Adjustment in the Marital Dance

Throughout the marriage, role adjustments must be made for the sake of the relationship. Whatever the reason, both partners must recognize the continual need for flexibility. On occasion, a marriage is adjusted at the expense of one or the other. Although this may occur from time to time out of particular circumstances and by mutual decision, when one spouse always gives in to the demands and needs of the other, it is a one-sided proposition. This is contrary to *perichoresis*, which involves two people agreeing to make room in themselves for the needs and desires of the other. Each learns to honor and not compromise the unique contribution of the other. Reaching mutual satisfaction through assuming marital roles is the goal. This occurs when both spouses derive fulfillment and pleasure from the marriage union. Their commitment to each other, the relationship, and the marriage permits flexibility and creative openness to change that is in the best interest of both spouses and the relationship.

5

A Model for Biblical Marriage

While the previous chapter dealt with some of the social and psychological issues involved in marriage, this chapter applies our theological basis for family relationships, as presented in chapter 1, to marriage in postmodern society. Both modern and postmodern ideologies have influenced today's marriages. For the sake of simplicity, we use the term *modern marriage* to refer to contemporary marriages that have been affected by both, in contrast to the traditional marriage preceding these influences.

It is a common mistake for Christians to defend a cultural version of marriage as the biblical ideal. They fall into this trap by reading the customs of their own culture into biblical passages or by regarding the biblical accounts of specific historical marriages as normative instead of descriptive. Records of marriages during biblical times do not necessarily reflect God's intention for today.

While one mistake is to assume that what our society regards as traditional marriage is biblical, another mistake is to uncritically endorse secular humanistic ideals and ignore what the Bible and Christian tradition have to say about the nature and purpose of marriage. Somewhere between these extremes is what we believe to be the biblical model. Table 4 summarizes the major characteristics of traditional marriage, biblical marriage, and modern marriage, comparing them in terms of the four aspects of our theological model: covenant (commitment), grace (adaptability), empowerment (authority), and intimacy (communication). We will explore each of these characteristics in depth. Close examination will show that both traditional and modern relationships fall short of the ideal. Parenthetically, we believe

TABLE 4 **Traditional, Biblical, and Modern Views of Marriage**

Traditional	Biblical	Modern
Nature of Relationship		
Commitment (to the institution)	**Covenant** (between partners)	Contract (self-fulfillment)
Coercive	Cohesive	Disengaged
Nature of Sexual Intimacy		
Dutiful	**Affectionate**	Self-centered
Male pleasure	Mutual pleasure	Personal pleasure
Adaptability		
Law	**Grace**	Anarchy
Predetermined (segregated roles)	Creative (interchangeable roles)	Undetermined (undifferentiated roles)
Rigid/Stilted	Adaptable/Flexible	Chaotic
Leadership and Decision-Making		
Ascribed power	**Empowerment**	Possessive power
Authoritarianism (dependence)	Mutual submissiveness (interdependence)	Absence of authority (independence)
Male-centered	Relationship-centered	Self-centered
Communication		
Inexpressiveness	**Intimacy**	Pseudo-intimacy
Pronouncement (legislation)	Discussion (negotiation)	Demand (stalemate)
Nonassertive/Aggressive	Assertive	Aggressive

that social-science research will reveal the practical wisdom contained in a biblical model of marriage. Recently, Day and Acock (2013, 164) noted that "relational spiritual framework theory posits that religiousness is associated with couple well-being through relational virtues (e.g., forgiveness, commitment, and sacrifice)."

Commitment

Because Western laws have come to treat marriage as a contract rather than as a covenant, the common statement "Marriage is a commitment!" is often misunderstood. A traditional view of the nature of the marital relationship focused on the notion that a couple should stay married for life; it viewed marriage as a sacred institution that must be upheld at all costs. Preserving the marriage took priority over each spouse's individual well-being. There was also a collective emphasis on loyalty to the group (family or community) rather than to the individual. The individual sacrificed his or her (usually her) preferences in order to maintain the institution and support the collective. Over the years, this collective emphasis has given way to an individualistic, "me-oriented" emphasis—the hallmark of modern marriage. Tim and Kathy Keller (2013) report the results of a survey that describes how many respondents feel marriages impeded personal freedom. From a modern perspective, the marriage should be dissolved when the relationship's demands outweigh the benefits. The focus has shifted to the individual's right to personal happiness. Thus, commitment to marriage as an institution is rejected when it interferes with the individual's perceived right to self-fulfillment.

Prevalence of divorce is one way to gauge the transition from viewing marriage as an institution to marriage as a contract intended to maximize one's personal happiness. It was rare under the traditional system because of an intrinsic commitment to marriage as an institution. Divorce was unthinkable because it transgressed a strongly held belief that violating the institution was morally wrong. The youth counterculture movement of the 1960s challenged these traditional ideas and asserted that commitment to the institution was an invalid reason to stay married. Sexuality was ideally confined to traditional marriage, but with the advent of birth control and increasingly promiscuous sexual behavior, the individual's happiness and personal satisfaction were becoming more important. These shifting values helped transform the nature of marriage (and divorce) from a traditional institution to a relationship contract between two equal partners. Our postmodern culture continues strongly to emphasize this self-absorption.

Accordingly, in the early 1970s, the divorce rate began to rise dramatically and continued to do so for nearly ten years. We have seen a flattening of the divorce rate beginning around the 2000s to around 50 percent. Social scientists now believe that one of the major reasons for this phenomenon was that people who were unhappy increasingly turned to divorce as a way to remove themselves from their past and to find happiness. This turning to divorce was accelerated by several factors. First, we did not know the negative consequences of divorce until much later, especially with the publication of works like *The Unexpected Legacy of Divorce* (Wallerstein, Lewis, and Blakeslee 2001). Second, social stigma regarding divorce diminished as the definition of marriage changed. That is, marriage is no longer considered an institution, so the dissolution of the marriage is like the ending of other contracts. Divorce was pursued without fear of shame or failure because the partnership simply did not fulfill its contract. Finally, therapists tended to encourage the trend. In some ways, therapy reifies the hyperindividualism of modern and postmodern views. Therapists would subtly and not so subtly encourage people to end marriages that were no longer satisfying so an individual could find his or her personal happiness. Since therapists generally believed individuals had a right to personal happiness, this value took precedence over commitment to the sanctity of marriage as an institution.

In the modern marriage, continued commitment is contingent on self-fulfillment. Indeed, one of the main criteria that sociologists now use to measure marital success is happiness or personal satisfaction. A common phrase describing marriage is that it is a 50/50 agreement where each partner supports exactly half of the entire marriage. Dissatisfaction or unhappiness occurs when an individual perceives their load to be greater than 50 percent. A marriage is considered successful if the partners describe themselves as happy or satisfied. Realizing that something is missing in the concept of commitment to marriage as an institution, many people have discarded the whole concept of commitment in favor of individual happiness. This is a tragedy because commitment is the cornerstone of the marriage relationship. The problem lies with too narrow a definition of marriage: in the past, it was solely a commitment to the institution; in the contemporary secular view, it is solely for self-fulfillment.

One way to frame this issue is to emphasize either the togetherness aspects of the relationship (marriage is an institution) or the individualistic aspects of the relationship (personal happiness is all that matters in the marriage). Neither of these approaches the beauty of the biblical perspective that God created humans in his image in the context of relationship. Genesis 2 recounts that God saw it was not good for the man to be alone, so God created the woman. The man recognized her as equal and complementary, bone of his bones and flesh of his flesh; they became one flesh and were naked and not ashamed (vv. 23–25). This is a beautiful picture of interdependency built on complementarity and sacrifice.

Marriage is not only a commitment to the institution but also a commitment to the relationship and the well-being of the marital partner. The relationship is vital in and of itself and needs to be nourished to grow into all God intended it to be. The commitment of Yahweh to Israel as depicted in the book of Hosea provides a profound example of a commitment that endures, renews, forgives, and restores. Marriages are strong when both partners are committed to the institution, to the relationship, and to each other as persons. Commitment only to the institution results in legalism; commitment only to the other person results in humanism. A commitment to all three (person, institution, and relationship) fosters a transformative, authentic marriage that reflects or images (*eikon* in Greek) the trinitarian God of the Bible. This biblical model takes into account the importance of caring for the needs of the individual, the relationship, and the social system.

In the complex interplay (*perichoresis*) of the life of the Trinity—our model for relationality—identity is not diminished in the relationships among the Father, Son, and Holy Spirit. *Modalism* is a trinitarian heresy (Horton 2012) that views God as a single person in three different forms—Father, Son, and Spirit. This distortion is reflected in traditional approaches to marriage, in which the individual is subsumed in the marriage. *Tritheism*, another heresy, views each person of the Trinity as a distinct, separate divine being (Horton 2013). This distortion is reflected in humanistic or modern approaches of maximizing individuality; the partner and his or her "needs" and desires for self-fulfillment take precedence over the relationship. As the church has rejected both *modalism* and *tritheism*, so should Christians reject their implications for developing a trinitarian view of marriage.

A trinitarian view of God shapes our view of marriage as a covenantal relationship between two complementary relational partners. Because of the mutual interplay of the relational partners, their love expressed in the covenant fosters individual growth and becoming. Each partner desires the best for the other. Further, each partner learns to "take up their cross" (Mark 8:34) in denying one's immediate, self-centered desires in order to benefit the covenant relationship. Over time, individual needs are balanced with togetherness needs as the covenant marriage grows over the course of the partners' lives.

The core passage in Genesis 2:24 reads, "Therefore a man shall leave his father and his mother and hold fast to his wife, and they shall become one flesh" (ESV). This "one flesh" perspective emphasizes both the individual identity aspect of husband and wife while also highlighting their "one flesh" unity. When these passages are used in the New Testament by Paul (in Ephesians 5:22–33, for example), the emphasis is not on either one (husbands or wives) or the one-flesh nature of the relationship. The focus is on both the relationship and the individuals in the relationship.

This biblical model also speaks directly to a Christian view of marital sexuality. In traditional marriage, sex is viewed as a right to pleasure for the man but as a duty to be endured by the woman. In modern marriage, sex tends to be self-centered, with the emphasis placed on each individual's right to personal pleasure. There is much to be said for the idea that married people are to be fulfilled sexually, but when this becomes the dominant emphasis, the relationship suffers and the real meaning of sexuality is lost.

The biblical response emphasizes person-centered, affectionate sex in marriage. Scripture advocates mutual pleasure and mutual benefit. This involves a mutual decision to give and receive in love. First Corinthians 7:3–4 clearly states that our bodies are for each other as the ultimate expression of ourselves to each other.

The security that stems from a commitment to the marriage relationship provides an atmosphere of freedom and willingness to learn together through the sexual expression of love. Spouses learn to mesh their lives as sexual persons in the security of relationship commitment. The biblical ideal, then, is much more than personal sexual pleasure or one spouse submitting to the other out of commitment to the institution of marriage. It is relating to each other on all levels: physical, mental, emotional, and spiritual. The scriptural concept of one flesh entails a mutual commitment to one's mate, the relationship, and the institution of marriage.

Relevant to covenant commitment is the finding by Ellison et al. (2011, 404) that although general religiousness "bears a weak relationship to marital outcome—sanctification strongly predicts desirable marital outcome . . . [and] appears to buffer the deleterious effects of financial and general stress on marital quality." We would propose that couples who define their marriage as a sacred relational union—what we call a covenant relationship or marriage—relate to each other in sanctified and sanctifying ways such as "going the second mile" when it comes to handling various marital stressors. Likewise, in their study of marriages Day and Acock (2013) report a positive association between couple well-being and the relational virtues of commitment and sacrifice.

Adaptability

In traditional marriage, roles are inflexibly segregated. The husband usually assumes the role of working outside the home, and the wife assumes the role of homemaking and caring for the children. Most people who argue for separation in marital roles are not aware of how recent this phenomenon is. Until the Industrial Revolution, 90 percent of all families lived on farms, and even as late as one hundred years ago, two-thirds of all families in the United States did so. That the marital roles were far from segregated will be no surprise to anyone who has lived on a farm. Whereas some kinds of work were designated as the man's or the woman's province, both husbands and wives performed manual labor on the farm, and both shared the responsibility in raising their children.

The Industrial Revolution transformed the nature of the family and economy, which had a profound effect on familial roles (Frederick and Dunbar 2019). Industrialization fostered the view that the family is a separate sphere from work and that men could earn enough money so that the wife would not have to work outside the home. These separate spheres of work and family life directly led to the segregation in marital roles developed in the urban family, where home life and work life are divided. In this type of family, the husband works outside the home, leaving childcare to the wife. One would be hard-pressed to argue, on the basis of either historical or biblical evidence, that woman's place is in the home and that man's place is in the business world outside the home.

The modern view that spouses can take on any role in marriage in many ways is refreshing, yet at the same time, undifferentiated roles may result in chaos or conflict about what will get done and who will assume a given responsibility. In the modern world, who does what is often worked out according to a system of social exchange. This system is based on the simple assumption that all relationships involve costs and rewards. What one gives to a relationship is experienced as a cost, and what one receives is experienced as a reward. Marriages thrive when the rewards outweigh the costs for each partner. As long as one gets more than or as much as one gives, there is reason to stay married. The concept of social exchange can be stated as a formula: *rewards* minus *costs* equals *profit*.

Let's imagine a couple trying to decide who will cook the evening meal. The conversation may begin with the husband suggesting that his wife cook, pointing out that he has had a hard day at the office and that he cooked the previous night. The wife may respond that she has had an equally hard day at work and that she cooked dinner three out of the last four evenings. The husband may then agree that he will cook if she cleans up, washes the dishes, and takes out the garbage. The point here is that this arrangement demands constant bargaining and negotiating skills. Each partner keeps a running tally of rewards and cost and they are constantly calculating the profit margins. Disaster looms around the corner when roles are not agreed on beforehand.

We suggest that roles be clearly defined but interchangeable in terms of gender and subject to change (with the obvious exception of biologically determined roles like childbearing). In the case of segregated roles based on a traditional view of marriage, tasks are predetermined according to gender, with no room for change. In modern marriages, roles are often undetermined. Determining roles through mutual agreement opens up creative possibilities for husbands and wives to serve each other through their roles. They are committed together in cooperative efforts to take on certain tasks of daily living. They agree to periodically review how things are going so that they can make changes when necessary in order to maximize their relationship profit.

Although no Bible verses deal explicitly with marital roles, Scripture does teach that everything ought to be done with a sense of order and harmony.

Assigning tasks on the basis of a person's interests, skills, and availability is a loving way to work out marital roles. It also respects differences and recognizes the unique talents of each spouse and his or her special contribution to the marriage.

Of the various tasks to be performed, parenting is without question one of the most crucial. In the traditional family, the mother automatically does most parenting and caregiving. Unfortunately, this leads to the neglect of fathering, a major problem in our society today. In the traditional family, the distinct division of gender roles and responsibilities leaves the emotional nurture to wives and economic development to husbands. Modern families remove the role of economic training from families and foster the male being removed from the family as he is breadwinning. Both of these approaches to fathering contribute to fatherlessness. In modern marriages, parenting roles and responsibilities may be avoided or excused because of overinvolvement in work and extracurricular roles, to the detriment of parenting. These parents should increasingly prioritize the needs of children over and against their career goals. Single- and dual-earner parents often rely on excellent childcare facilities to fill in for them while they are bringing in the income.

In a biblical marriage, both the mother and the father are actively involved in the parenting process. There is no biblical evidence that would lead one to believe that a mother's involvement with children is more important than a father's involvement. Scripture refers to the responsibility of both parents, as in Ephesians 6:1–4: "Children, obey your parents in the Lord, for this is right. 'Honor your father and mother.' . . . And, fathers, do not provoke your children to anger, but bring them up in the discipline and instruction of the Lord." Coparenting seems especially critical in our day and age, as the lack of effective fathering often relates to breakdown in the family system (Lindsey, Caldera, and Colwell 2005) and many other social ills (Lamb 2017).

In the traditional marriage, roles are stilted and rigidly defined. There is very little flexibility as to how they may be performed. In the modern marriage, expectations are so loose that marital roles can be truly lacking. Without any set procedures to bring stability to these roles, the marriage relationship lacks integrity. The biblical marriage has flexible and interchangeable roles as each occasion calls forth what is needed. These roles are intended to foster authentic Christian character, leading us to resemble Christ and his work in the world.

Since change can be expected throughout the cycles of family life, it is vital that spouses be flexible and adaptable. Married life and family life are at their best when they are neither predetermined nor undetermined but provide structured security. This structured security allows spouses and family members to experience the exciting process of each member working for the good of the whole. Family members are empowered to serve others in collaborative efforts.

Leadership and Decision-Making

Authority in marriage is persistently a controversial issue among Christians. Until very recent times, authority in marriage exclusively meant a strong male headship approach. Christians and non-Christians alike have adhered to the idea that the husband is to be the head of the home, whereas the wife is expected to submit to her husband. Recently in Christian circles, a renewed philosophy of authority has emerged involving mutual submission. The husband is challenged to love, serve, and submit to his wife, just as Christ gave his life for the church. Paul argues that family authority should be based on the model of Christ and the church. Ephesians 5:21 reads, "Submit to one another out of reverence for Christ" (NIV), which prefaces perhaps the most famous passage regarding family authority (5:21–33). Everything that follows—husband-wife dynamics, parent-children relationships, and even master-slave roles—is based in the context of the church's submission to the authority of Christ.

Modern marriages are opposed to the traditional male headship arrangement and emphasize individual spousal power in marriage. While this may present power dilemmas for spouses, it enhances equality, freedom, and personal power. In particular, the postmodern perspective recognizes that there are a variety of authority styles, determined mainly by cultural values, and, therefore, not just "one" way to define authority in marriage. Each couple, considering their generational and culture values, will determine authority issues accordingly.

The system of social exchange plays an integral part in dealing with personal power struggles in modern marriage. The focus is on the quid pro quo notion of getting something for something—"if you scratch my back, I'll scratch yours." Spouses are satisfied as long as everything comes out equal and neither partner perceives things as unfair. However, it is hard to define *equal*, and therefore authority and decision-making power may cause conflict.

Under a system of social exchange, negotiation is the best way to deal with conflict. Each partner tries to maximize the returns on his or her investments in the marriage. Accordingly, research shows that in this system, wives who work outside the home have greater power in the marriage relationship than wives who do not. The money earned can be converted into power, thus elevating the authority of the wife in the marriage.

It should be noted that the system of social exchange is built on an assumption about humans that is consistent with Christian thought—namely, that people are basically self-centered by nature. In reality, social exchange is a fairly good model to describe how many marriages operate. We would, however, question the assumption that fighting for your own rights without regard for a partner is ideal. The Christian worldview, by contrast, values unselfish giving, mutual exchange, and even going beyond what is expected. The goal is not to maintain power over one's partner but to empower and be empowered through the relationship.

Authority in Christian, biblical marriage includes dual submission to the lordship of Jesus Christ and to each other. The chain-of-command view that a wife should submit to her husband, who in turn should submit to God, is popular in some Christian circles. This faulty authoritarian persuasion fails to take into account the great news of the New Testament promotion of mutual love, joyful service, and reciprocal submission.

Ephesians 5:25 reads, "Husbands, love your wives, just as Christ loved the church and gave himself up for her." From this, it is clear that headship is to be understood not in the hierarchical sense of the husband's lording it over his wife but rather as taking the role of a suffering servant who gives himself out of his love. Christ's example as a compassionate servant who gave his life for his bride, the church, is the model of how the husband is to be a *source* for his marriage. Wives too are called to this same self-giving, suffering-servant role. Mutual submissiveness, then, is the overriding message of Ephesians 5.

In place of mutual submissiveness, the biblical marriage is based on the concept of mutual regard. That is to say, the biblical view is for marital love to regard the other as one would want to be regarded. This mutual regard emphasizes empowering the other to submit to Christ in discipleship and sacrifice. One way to conceptualize this is the idea of Christ as mediator. Christ mediates one's relationship to others (Bonhoeffer 1995)—in this case, the spouse. When one is a Christian, he or she experiences a separation from the world and an immediacy with Christ: "Although the direct way to our neighbor is barred, [Christians] now find the new and only real way to him—the way which passes through the Mediator [Christ]" (Bonhoeffer 1995, 100). In a Christian marriage, each interaction, each engagement between the spouses, expresses Christ to the other. This mediation of Christ challenges each partner to become more like Jesus in love and self-sacrifice. Stanley et al. (2006, 289) report that sacrificial attitudes were found to predict the maintenance of relationship adjustment over time.

At times one partner may be required to give much more than an equal share to the marriage. God calls both spouses to give generously for the sake of the other when sickness or some other circumstance makes it difficult for one to give much at that time. Putting the interests of the spouse first out of regard for his or her needs is the extraordinary way of the cross.

Communication

In the traditional marriage, there is little need for verbal communication. What communication exists tends to take the form of pronouncements—talking at, rather than with, one's spouse. The husband as head of the marriage legislates without consulting his wife. When conflicts or delicate matters arise, they are often dealt with by sidestepping the issue. Verbal communication is de-emphasized because meeting socio-emotional and companionship needs is not considered a major part of marriage. Marriage is regarded as an institutional arrangement that provides for economic needs and social status.

Communication in the modern marriage can be characterized as a series of declarations and demands that each spouse makes to the other. When conflicts arise, confrontation is the way to get one's needs and disappointments out on the table. The motto is "Openly express what you need from your mate." While such openness can be refreshing when compared to the traditional pattern, a combative posture and insistence on satisfying personal needs will obviously obstruct a sensitive caring for the other. Making aggressive demands, such as "I want my needs met regardless of how you are affected," results in counterdemands that ultimately lead to a stalemate.

In a biblical marriage, the partners communicate by expressing themselves in an open manner. When one talks, the other listens. They care about what is best for their partner. Differences are dealt with by respecting each other's needs and desires. They make an effort to understand each other's point of view and to respond accordingly. There is an attitude of submission and a willingness to consider giving up one's own needs and desires for the sake of the other and the relationship. Both spouses work together to seek solutions through mutual and reciprocal decision-making.

Dual-Earner Marriage

Dual-earner couples bring a new dimension to marriage and parenting roles in today's world (Bianchi and Milkie 2010). Based on data from 2019, half of all couples are dual career or dual earner. The rate of dual-earner families with children has risen to 63 percent. Balancing career and family obligations creates unique challenges for dual-career couples (Su 2019). Economic necessity leaves many families little choice but for both parents to work outside the home. As they consider what is in the best interest of everyone concerned, they must decide whether both the husband and the wife should work. If a couple decides that they will both work outside the home, then the question is how to accomplish this in the most satisfactory way. In a recent study, husbands with more traditional gender-role ideology had lower marital satisfaction if their wives had higher levels of work and family role conflicts (Minnotte, Minnotte, and Pedersen 2013). Additionally, husbands' gender ideology also affected wives' marital satisfaction, while wives' gender-role ideologies had no effect on either spouse's marital satisfaction.

The key to finding the right balance is learning how to manage work and family so that neither impinges on the other in disruptive ways. We believe that the working couple must proactively establish and maintain a balance between work and family. The couple will be most successful in coming up with a suitable arrangement if they (1) mutually contribute unconditional love, grace, empowerment, and intimacy to their relationship; (2) have an extra dose of cohesion and adaptability; (3) agree on priorities, recognizing what is essential and what is nonessential in their family and work roles; and (4) identify resources within themselves, their marriage, the family, and the wider community to help them meet the demands of their dual roles.

In dealing with work and family conflict, two key dimensions are needed (Frederick and Dunbar 2019). First, role salience is critical. Dual-career couples need to acknowledge that both work and family demands are relatively pressing at a given time. Within a biblical view of marriage, each spouse acknowledges the importance of these demands as well as the individual's need to fulfill these demands. This means that personal identity as both a spouse and a career holder is honored. Discernment, based partly on this personal-identity perspective, enables each spouse to evaluate the actual salience of each sphere's demands.

Role satisfaction is the second dimension needed in balancing work and family conflict. Each partner takes satisfaction in the many or multiple roles they play in life. One's overall satisfaction as a person is not subsumed in either being a spouse or holding a career. One's ultimate satisfaction is being a child of God based on Christ's saving work. Recall the words spoken at Jesus's baptism: "And a voice came from heaven, 'You are my beloved Son; with you I am well pleased'" (Mark 1:11). These words are spoken of each Christian as we are adopted into the family of God via Christ. This is the basis of our ultimate identity, which is expressed as we fulfill our other callings as husbands and wives, mothers and fathers, and earners. As we experience satisfaction in one role, the crossover effect builds endurance for challenges in another role.

A comparison of dual-earner couples from 1970 to 2001 indicates that the proportion of income contributed by wives relative to husbands has steadily increased (Raley, Mattingly, and Bianchi 2006). It is a legitimate question whether a husband's contribution to housework and parenting tasks has correspondingly increased. Some research notes a startling imbalance in dual-earner marriages, as wives continue to do the majority of housework. Those husbands who do contribute describe themselves as "helping out." It appears there is a dire need for dual-earning husbands to not only increase their contribution to home and parenting tasks but also to change their idea of being a helper to taking an active leadership role in parenting.

There are major benefits for both men and women in a dual-earner marriage in which responsibilities are equally shared. The incorporation of relational skills with household tasks further endears men to their families. An important aspect for the man is the knowledge that his intentional choice to be involved as a father leads to validation and appreciation. Also, when the wife relaxes her household standards and parenting expectations, it is much more inviting for the husband to willingly join in. Through the sharing of roles, the wife is not only validated in her work role but more fulfilled in her marriage and her parenting role.

A hard lesson for all dual-earner couples to learn is that they can't do everything! In prioritizing, they must learn to do a "good enough" job. Given the economics of living in the United States, more and more couples are the dual-career type. One reason is that marriage is increasingly delayed due to educational demands and work. Each spouse then maintains their previous commitments, including work, after marrying. Research suggests that work-family conflict is more impactful for single-earner families than dual-career families (Fellows et al. 2016). One important factor for dual-career couples is having social support and a sense of community. They need all the support they can get as they work toward a satisfying and meaningful family life.

A significant part of those family-friendly environments involves the provision of high-quality childcare centers. Many churches are offering such services to their community, meeting a need for many dual-earner parents. An increasing number of young children spend some of their time in day care. We would recommend that parents who send their children to childcare ensure a high degree of values alignment between the parents and the daycare provider. Parents must make every effort to secure high-quality day care as well as be alert to the unique needs of the child in choosing a facility. The relationship established between the parent and the day-care staff is crucial. Children tend to thrive when they have a secure attachment to their parents *and* their parents appreciate the special bond between their child and the day-care worker. Parents and caregivers who are dedicated to staying highly involved in their children's lives will establish mutual trust and work toward the best interest of each child. An important benefit is the perspective that well-trained and experienced teachers have to offer when it comes to developmental issues, routines, discipline, and care.

The Mindset at the Center of Christian Marriage

At the very heart of marriage is the willingness of spouses to let go of their personal agendas so that they can truly listen to what their partners are saying. Philippians 2 describes Christ as emptying himself and taking the form of a servant. *Kenosis*, or emptying, as described in this passage is key to our view of marriage.

It is really a matter of the attitude or mindset of grace and empowerment (Phil. 2:5); this humble posture is characterized by servanthood and keeps relationships and the best interest of others as a precious priority. When both spouses willingly lay down their own interests for the sake of the other, it will organically be a mutual and reciprocal process. The meaning of marriage as mutual edification and ultimately a crucible for sanctification means that each partner is continually challenged to develop the mindset of Christ described in Philippians 2. One's covenant-keeping entails (1) the expression of grace as both partners need forgiveness; (2) mutual empowerment as each partner bears one another's burdens; and (3) deepening intimacy throughout the process.

We should not overlook the Jewish and Eastern traditions that see marriage as a gift for the community as well as for the couple. The family is the foundation of strong societies, and supportive communities beget strong families. It is wise to move beyond our individualistic bias and affirm that the bond of marriage is strengthened when a couple invites a supportive group of people to share in their commitment to their marriage and family life.

In this chapter we have sought to apply biblical principles of relationality to marriage. A three-year longitudinal study of a community sample of 354 married couples by Day and Acock (2013) indicates that marital well-being and religiousness (church attendance, religious practices, belief in God) is mediated by relational virtue and equality. Specifically, not only do religious activities contribute to marital well-being, but religiousness also heightens the relational virtues of forgiveness, commitment, and sacrifice. These relationship virtues in turn contribute to marital well-being.

PART 3

The Expansion
of Family Life

Parenting and Beyond

In this section we move beyond the marriage relationship to parent-child relationships. A strong marital relationship serves as the secure foundation, while children are the building blocks through which the family structure changes during each life stage. It is a universal truth that the couple experiences a dramatic change when children enter—as well as when they exit—the family. In fact, marital adjustment has been found to be at its highest just before the birth of the first child and continues to decline until the last child leaves home (Twenge, Campbell, and Foster 2003). Making the necessary adjustments from the dyad to the triad can be relatively smooth for some couples, whereas the transition to parenthood is a trying time for others.

Summarizing twenty-first-century research, Smock (2010) notes that the "decoupling of marriage and childbearing" draws attention to the fact that there are many pathways to parenthood. Remarking on these demographic changes, Cherlin (2010) found that in 1950 only 4 percent of all children were born outside of marriage, but by 2007, nearly 40 percent of all children were born outside of marriage. Special consideration needs to be given to each unique situation when responding to the particular needs of that family.

Parenting is more difficult than most ever imagine it to be! Building relationships with our children continues to be one of the most rewarding and challenging experiences of a lifetime. It brings both harmony and disharmony to the marriage relationship. Children are also experiencing greater levels of stress and access to information and situations that were unthinkable in previous generations. Parents are facing these pressures external to the family while they try to support the positive development of their offspring.

A major adjustment also occurs during the later stages of family life when adult children leave home (or boomerang back) or when the care of elderly parents brings other kinds of stressors to the couple. Like any sound group, the family must have not only a well-organized structure to function effectively but also one flexible enough to survive the twists and turns of life. The following chapters present some blueprints for successful family living.

Chapter 6 introduces a model of Christian parenting that empowers children to become competent, mature, responsible adults. We look at the pros and cons of some common parenting styles and then offer a biblical model that we believe incorporates the best of these styles. We propose that as children mature, parents must also grow so that there is mutual empowerment and transformation.

In chapter 7, we examine the life of the child from the perspective of several developmental theories. We evaluate how these theories comport with the Christian view of human personhood and indicate important aspects in parenting young children. A primary concern in this discussion is the matter of empowerment.

The topic of chapter 8 is family spirituality. We use this umbrella term to represent the role of the family in inculcating values, morals, beliefs, and religious faith within children.

Chapter 9 deals with the stresses and strains that can develop when adolescence and midlife occur simultaneously. Important to this discussion is the origin and impact of adolescence in modern/postmodern society. Crisis often accompanies these life stages of adolescence and midlife, resulting in a serious clash between the generations.

Finally, in chapter 10 we discuss the dynamics of the family in later life. This begins with the launching of adolescent children, an ambivalent time of life for both parents and children. Parents struggle to let go, while children seek freedom and yet fear leaving the security of their homes. Following this is the postlaunching stage, when parents move into the so-called sandwich generation. At this time, parents feel the squeeze of dealing with both adult children and elderly family members who are physically, emotionally, and/or financially dependent on them. This period of family life involves losses of many kinds, as well as gains reaped from meeting the challenges of changing relationships.

6

Parenting

The Process of Relationship Empowerment

A metaphor of what it means to be a child in contemporary society will help us understand how parents provide empowerment to their offspring. Hyde, Yust, and Ota (2010) offer the metaphor of children as active agents. From birth, children are actively engaging and learning from their parents and their environments. Further, children as agents illuminates how children, in limited yet emerging ways, are developing shared meaning-making systems with their parents. Childhood agency develops as children's bodies and brains grow and they attain more and more competencies.

In most societies, parents simply expect their children to grow up to be normal, healthy adults—no special techniques are deemed necessary. In our modern/postmodern society, however, parents are conditioned to believe just the opposite—we presume we need the help of experts to tell us how to be successful. Reliance on education and experts in diverse fields has subverted the premodern view of parenting. Parents look to websites, pediatricians, and other mental health professionals to identify the optimal path for parenting. This sometimes reduces parents to a state of fear—afraid that they may do something that will have a lasting harmful effect on their children. In this psychologically sophisticated world, we have developed a cult of the expert, keeping our eyes set for authoritative opinion and our ears attuned to the latest wisdom on parenting. Living as we do in a child-oriented society, we are extremely concerned about the parenting role.

One issue here is the transformation of the meaning of parenting. In premodern cultures, the main role of parents was to teach children the family trade. If a child was born to a farmer or blacksmith, the parents would teach the child the skills essential to participate in that business. Further, this would teach children their roles in the community. For modern and postmodern parents, the emphasis is on meeting the needs of children to enhance their flourishing. The modern and postmodern method for ensuring a child's flourishing is to engage them in many activities outside the home. When it was time for Tom's son Nathaniel to attend preschool at the age of three, there was a huge amount of social pressure to decide which was the perfect day care center based on educational outcomes and pedagogy! When the open enrollment day arrived, we went to line up for registration at 5:00 a.m., and we were dismayed to see that there were already fifteen parents ahead of us in line. For preschool day care! The point here is that these types of decisions are assumed to have a profound effect on a child's well-being—that somehow this *single* choice would determine the outcomes of Nathaniel's life.

It is certainly helpful for parents to gain a solid understanding of the biological, psychological, and social development of children so that they have realistic, "age-appropriate" expectations. But in the long run, they need to feel confident in themselves as they nurture, discipline, guide, and relate to their own children. Together, husband and wife must be coleaders in deciding what is best for their children. This develops as they integrate expert knowledge with the personal knowledge that comes from building a secure relationship with their unique children and empowering them to be all they can be.

As contributors to the growing body of expert opinion, we hasten to point out that our quarrel is not with expert opinion but rather with the dogmatism under which some advice is given. We advocate informing parents about child development and parenting methods as well as encouraging them to critically analyze the information and compare it with biblical principles. Parenting is inherently a values-based process. Parents need to listen to and engage with expert advice and opinions and ultimately decide for themselves if and how to apply these opinions in their families. One's identity as a partner and parent will inform how one parents his or her offspring. This identity is crucial because the family is *their family*, and they will inculcate this meaning and identity in their children. Effective parenting must always account for the particular needs of each child and the family as a whole, incorporating or discarding ideas accordingly.

Various New Testament passages describe the Christian life as growth from spiritual infancy to maturity. Theologically, this process is called sanctification, and the goal is becoming more Christlike. The new believer starts as an infant and eventually grows up in Christ. One moves from a state of dependency—in which others model, teach, and disciple—to a mature walk with God. The book of Hebrews describes how new believers need spiritual "milk" like a baby does, and the expectation is that someday they will receive solid food as a mature Christian (Heb. 5:11–14). As this growth occurs, the believer begins to disciple others. Although the believer is always dependent on God and the Holy Spirit in that growth process, there is also a natural progression in maturity, leading the believer to be used by God to serve and minister to others.

The human developmental process encompasses a similar progression from dependency and infancy toward maturity and adulthood. Maturity is often defined as self-sufficiency and independence from one's parents. Most developmental theorists, however, hold that maturity involves more than independence; it entails the capacity to contribute in a positive and constructive way to the good of others. For example, Erik Erikson (E. Erikson 1980; J. Erikson 1997) identifies the virtue of care as the hallmark of adult identity development. In adulthood, the resolution of the struggle between generativity and despair is one of the lengthiest stages. In this stage, individuals identify, develop, and maintain commitments to career, family, and community. These commitments and behavior result in care. However, people may experience regret or lack of concern about career and family, experiencing stagnation. As Donald Capps (2000, 2008) describes it, stagnation results in *acedia*, which is apathy or a profound experience of disinterest in and inability for empathy. This is a spiritual malaise. The spiritual cure for this is renewing one's spirit and understanding one's purpose. This means care is essential to Christian development.

The New Testament describes empowerment as the building up of one another in the Christian faith. It involves loving and serving others and helping them mature spiritually. This description is consistent with the social-science literature regarding the type of parenting that helps children mature. The parenting model we present in this chapter focuses on the parent-child relationship. Each parent and each child is developing and maturing throughout the entire process. We believe that our model, which emphasizes empowering children to maturity, is a needed alternative to models that emphasize control and coercive power. Our model is based on engendering hope and growth in parents and children as they journey together toward maturity.

Speaking for a moment from our personal experience as parents and grandparents rather than as experts, we would challenge parents to concentrate less on the technique of good parenting and more on the process of being a parent. Good parenting is a matter of interacting with our children day in and day out. It is these day-to-day experiences that build our relationships with them. The covenantal bond between spouses forms the basis for the covenantal bond with the children, securing children and parents together. Children experience the truth that their parents are *with* them and *for* them, which provides security even when correction and discipline are needed. Even though the suggestions that follow offer useful guidelines that contribute to an understanding of the child-rearing process, parents can function more freely and openly in their role if they are simply willing to be more genuine with their children.

The Basic Components of Parenting Styles

Now that we have dispelled the notion that there is one correct way to parent children, we will investigate what the social-science literature says about various parenting styles. Parents and other primary caretakers have a significant impact on children's emotional, social, cognitive, and spiritual development. While some parenting styles encourage growth and empowerment, others hinder or block growth either by fostering dependency or by expecting premature self-reliance. Before we analyze these various styles, it will be helpful to examine some of the components that go into them—namely, approaches to discipline and types of leadership.

Approaches to Discipline

Early research into parent-child relationships distinguished between permissive and restrictive parenting. Proponents of permissive parenting, while not denying the need for discipline, stressed that a child's greatest need is for warmth and security. The restrictive school of thought, while not rejecting parental affection, emphasized that a child's greatest need is for discipline, responsibility, and self-control.

Recent literature has taken the same approach but describes the two main dimensions of parenting in terms of responsiveness and demandingness (Carlo et al. 2018). Responsiveness focuses on how parents are engaged emotionally with children's experiences and expressions of feelings. Highly responsive parents tend to be more accepting of the children's actions and feelings and less punitive. Demandingness describes parents who have higher behavioral expectations for their children and consistent enforcement of those standards and expectations. Some of the research on parenting and parenting styles also uses terms like *support* and *control*. Support is defined as making the child feel comfortable in the presence of the parent and giving the child a sense of acceptance and approval as a person. Control is defined as directing the child to behave in a manner desirable to the parents. Examples of control include giving guidelines and setting limits.

Based on the parental support and control dimensions, Diana Baumrind (1996, 2005) identifies three types of parents—authoritative, authoritarian, and permissive—each of which differs in effectiveness in eliciting obedience and responsibility in a child's moral/character development. A number of studies have found that a combination of high levels of support and control—authoritative parenting—is most conducive to developing competency and mental and behavioral health in children and adolescents (Akcinar and Baydar 2014; Larzelere et al. 2013; Pinquart 2017). An interesting finding here is that authoritative parenting is associated with better educational outcomes for children, among other things (Majumder 2016). The authoritarian style (low support and high control) produces children who respect authority but who show little independence and only moderate social competence. Permissive parenting (high support and low control) tends to produce children who lack both social competence and interdependence.

It is important to incorporate both dimensions into the parents' style. Children need both nurturing and emotional support *and* clear expectations and parameters. As parents gain more experience and learn more parenting tools, they begin building their parenting toolbox. We generally encourage more gentle and supportive parenting strategies with children. As behavior escalates, even when parents have been consistent in setting boundaries, they may need to be firmer and more creative in establishing consequences for misbehavior.

Disciplining children takes time, patience, and wisdom. Parents who employ corporal punishment as the primary or even exclusive method of discipline are admitting bankruptcy in disciplinary approaches, demonstrating an inability to be creative and effective. Although coercive punishment does work when parents are attempting to eliminate certain behaviors, it also teaches children that force is what counts. Consistent use of physical punishment eventually leads to dominating or imposing power. This may lead children to retaliate or try to get even. An effective parent wins a child's cooperation by leading rather than coercing.

A comprehensive study of African American, European American, and Hispanic children examined the relationship between physical discipline, emotional support, and behavior problems in children. It was found that parental spanking increased the level of problem behavior in the child over time, but only when maternal emotional support was low. Additionally, corporal punishment was associated with higher degrees of parental frustration regarding children's misbehavior (Irons et al. 2018). Parental support is a key factor in how children respond to spanking. The social-science evidence is becoming more and more conclusive about the overall negative effects of corporal punishment (Larzelere et al. 2010; Gershoff and Grogan-Kaylor 2016). We strongly discourage using physical force with children since there are so many other effective ways of discipline.

Unfortunately, the terms *discipline* and *punishment* are often confused in our society. Some Christians defend physical punishment based on verses such as Proverbs 13:24: "Those who spare the rod hate their children." However, in applying that verse, it is important to consider how the rod was used in the pastoral culture of Old Testament times. It was an instrument to *guide* ignorant sheep, not a means of beating them into submission. Note how the verse concludes: "But those who love them are diligent to discipline them." Discipline is instructive and restorative, used to correct and teach appropriate behaviors. The heart of discipline is to educate children in the proper path.

It is important to recognize that child-rearing patterns considered authoritarian in Western culture might be viewed differently in other cultures. What seems to make for the best disciplinary parenting practice is the certainty or consistency of the practice as opposed to its severity. For example, Asian families frequently exert coercive control because of the demands for high achievement and conformity in the culture. Children in these homes tend to adopt their parents' family and societal values.

The evidence suggests that corporal punishment and physical abuse tend toward more negative child outcomes, and there is only a slight difference in the size of this effect between abuse and physical punishment (Gershoff and Grogan-Kaylor 2016). Continued exposure to corporal punishment is associated with increased adult antisocial behavior, lower educational outcomes, and maladjustment (Gershoff and Grogan-Kaylor 2016; McKinney, Morse, and Pastuszak 2016).

Physical punishment leads to disempowerment, whereas natural and logical consequences lead to empowerment. Punishment is ultimately discouraging to a child. Children who are physically punished are receiving a severe consequence for their action, but there tends to be little instruction or guidance for improvement. Physical punishment emphasizes that the parents are in control of the environment, which reduces a sense of personal agency. The best way to empower children is to have them face the consequences of their behavior and hold them responsible for their actions in a consistent, firm, and loving manner. Recognition of the consequences of one's behavior leads to internal control, whereas punishment focuses on external means.

Logical and natural consequences serve to stimulate children's creative responses. Parents who fail to honor and respect their children will find that their children fail to honor and respect them. The traits of an effective parent include wisdom, vision, a sense of humor, patience, encouragement, and good judgment, not the exercise of superior power. Using everyday situations to teach consequences promotes the child's self-confidence, ability to take others into account, and responsibility for one's own behavior.

In our metaphor of children as agents who are able to influence and engage their social environments, increasing self-regulation is key. Parents have a crucial role in providing emotional support for their children—this is the responsiveness dimension we discussed. Parents must also provide consistent boundaries or standards, which reflect the demanding side of parenting. Erring on the side of permissiveness or responsiveness fosters adults who have difficulty managing their emotions and delaying gratification. Erring on the side of demandingness results in rigid, distant, and domineering adults who have difficulty connecting emotionally with others.

Types of Leadership

Building on research about leadership and small groups, we suggest that *empowered* parenting involves two different types of leadership skills (J. K. Balswick et al. 2003): instrumental and socio-emotional. Instrumental leadership is task oriented, focusing on the things that need to be accomplished in the group. Such leadership organizes activities, sets goals, and generally keeps the group focused on accomplishing those goals. Socio-emotional leadership, by contrast, is person oriented and concentrates on maintaining a healthy relationship among group members. Research indicates that both types of leadership skills are necessary if small groups are to function well. Interestingly enough, it has also been discovered that the two types of skills are rarely found in the same individual.

The studies on instrumental and socio-emotional leadership in small groups apply to the family as well. Instrumental parenting aims at inculcating beliefs, values, and attitudes. It involves teaching children what they must know and how they must behave to be in good standing within the family. Socio-emotional parenting attends to the emotional nature of the relationship between parents and children. Whereas instrumental parenting focuses on tasks and content, socio-emotional parenting focuses on the affective bonding between parent and child (Baumrind 1996).

Alternative Parenting Styles

Having briefly defined parental support and control as well as the instrumental and socio-emotional aspects of parenting, we are ready to combine these two areas to discuss alternative styles of parenting and their effects on children. We will consider various instrumental styles and then several socio-emotional approaches.

Instrumental Parenting

Figure 6 represents the four styles of instrumental parenting. Two dimensions are involved: action and content. Parenting styles can be classified as either high or low in action. That is, some parents engage in and thus demonstrate the type of behavior they want their children to adopt; other parents make no such effort. Parenting styles can also be either high or low in content. Some parents verbally communicate through a rich elaboration of rules, norms, values, beliefs, and ideology; others simply do not bother to teach their children.

FIGURE 6   **Styles of Instrumental Parenting**

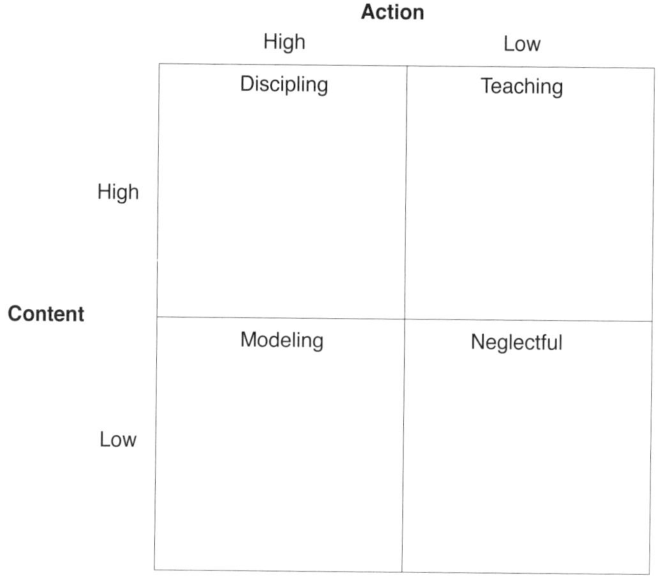

NEGLECTFUL

Parenting that is low in both action and content is the *neglectful* style. Proper behavior is neither displayed nor taught. Because the parents give no direction verbally or otherwise, the children are on their own to latch on to any social norm or form of behavior. The parent who is neglectful in instrumental parenting is also likely to be neglectful in socio-emotional parenting.

This style leaves much to be desired, since the children lack good supportive care and must learn by trial and error to fend for themselves.

TEACHING

Parenting that is low in action and high in content is the *teaching* style. The parent, in effect, says to the child, "Do as I say but don't look to my behavior as a model." Children in such a situation feel that they are being preached at. Though this style may be effective in bringing about the desired behavior in children, it may also breed disrespect for the parents, whose words do not match their lives. As children mature, they become increasingly sensitive to any form of contradictory behavior in their parents. The typical teenager is quick to point out such inconsistency.

Despite its shortcomings, the teaching style is better than the neglectful style. The teaching style becomes a problem for children, however, when the parents' teaching is inconsistent with their behavior. It may be that the parents do not intentionally cause this confusion if they truly believe in and desire to live up to the standards they enunciate but fail to do so.

MODELING

Parenting that is high in action and low in content is the *modeling* style. It also is only partially effective in that a child must rely entirely on observing the behavior of parents to gain a system of values, norms, and beliefs. Modeling does have some advantage over the teaching style, however. While the teaching style lacks behavior to back it up, the modeling style offers the behavior (but with little or no explanation of the values behind it). The old adage that what children learn is "caught rather than taught" applies here, and parents will find that modeling is an effective way to inculcate values and desired behavior in their children. Recent research has verified that modeling does have positive benefits (e.g., Kjøbli et al. 2013).

DISCIPLING

Parenting that is high in both action and content is *discipling*. This style is complete in that parents teach their children by word and by deed. It is curious, however, that while the concept of discipling is popular in the contemporary church, it is rarely used to refer to parental training. The term *discipline*, remember, is related to the word *disciple*, which refers to one who accepts certain ideas or values and leads or guides others to accept them as well. Discipling, then, is a system of giving positive guidance to children.

Socio-emotional Parenting

An important aspect of socio-emotional parenting focuses on the attachment quality of the relationship between parents and children. A resource we highly recommend for parents of young children is the work of Dan Siegel and Tina Payne Bryson. Based on attachment science and an understanding of a child's brain, *The Power of Showing Up: How Parental Presence Shapes Who Our Kids Become and How Their Brains Get Wired* (2020) offers the following building blocks (the four S's) of healthy development: *safe*, providing a place of safe harbor; *seen*, paying attention to positive and negative emotions; *soothed*, being attentive to the hard things they experience and teaching coping skills; and *secure*, providing faithful, ongoing, trustworthy presence. Siegel and Bryson emphasize the significance of parents attuning to children's experiences so that their children experience being felt and known. These experiences emphasize how children respond when one or both of their parents demonstrate affective attunement. That is, children experience a sense of validation when a caregiver responds in a manner that demonstrates attunement. One important way for parents to attune is to remain curious about what their children's behavior is communicating and respond to who they really are, not what parents want them to be.

FIGURE 7 **Styles of Socio-emotional Parenting**

	Support	
	High	Low
High	Authoritative	Authoritarian
Control		
Low	Permissive	Neglectful

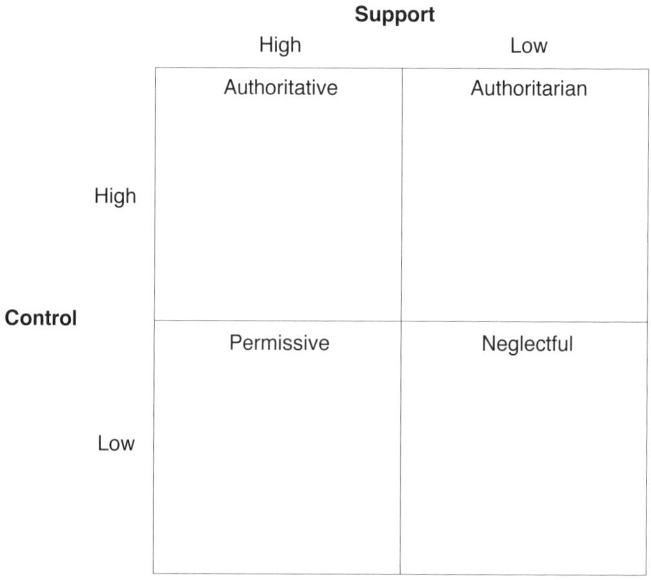

Repeated experiences of positive relational attachment build children's brains to regulate and thrive. Effective and enduring mental health results when parents teach children how to tolerate the inevitable stress and distraction of their young lives through insight, empathy, and emotional and bodily regulation. This model comports well with covenant, grace, empowerment, and intimacy. In a distressing, unsafe, hyper-focused postmodern world, it's not about being perfect parents—it's about showing up, being present, and giving wise guidance. These are important components for connecting and supporting children while also empowering them.

Figure 7 represents the four styles of socio-emotional parenting. Here again there are two dimensions, support and control, each of which can be classified as high or low. The four styles depicted should be thought of as hypothetical rather than precisely representative of the way any one person engages in parenting.

Neglectful

The easiest style to criticize is *neglectful* parenting because of its obvious shortcomings. With low levels of support and control, little bonding develops between parents and children. In many homes, particularly those where economic factors play a devastating role, children are indeed neglected. This parenting style can also be found in homes where our modern, individualistic society leaves little time to meet the demands of caring for and providing sufficient structure for the children. The latchkey child may be a victim of this system. Single parents have little choice and agonize over their lack of time to provide support and exercise control due to the many other demands on them.

There are those who advocate this very free lifestyle for children. They see no need to teach morals; rather, children should experiment and come to their own conclusions about personal values. This philosophy emphasizes the child's right to discover his or her own beliefs and lifestyle and suggests that character is built by allowing children to make their own way in the world.

This low-support, low-control style of parenting is characteristic of disengaged families in which each member's life rarely touches the others in any meaningful way. It also characterizes many urban families in which both parents work outside the home or in which there is only one parent. The tentativeness of many people in making a commitment to another person may be a result of being reared in a neglectful home.

We believe that a home without parental leadership is lacking a great deal. Children who grow up without adequate guidance become fertile ground for authoritarian leaders or cults that prey on neglected young people. Neglected children experience a void regarding their identity and values, making them ripe for manipulation. These individuals hunger for a strong, strict leader to follow and obey without question. Such people are most susceptible to the dictates of an authoritarian figure because they have never experienced bonding with any authority figure. This happens because children are desperate for connection, and they will seek attention, either positive or negative, wherever they can find it.

AUTHORITARIAN

When support is low and control high, we have what is called *authoritarian* parenting. The children are likely to be respectful and obedient to their parents. What is missing, because of a deficiency in the bonding process, is a sense of warmth, openness, and intimacy between parents and children. Authoritarian parenting has been found to be correlated with child behavioral problems (Tan et al. 2012). A study by Gromoske and Maguire-Jack (2012) reported that early spanking (at age one) is predictive of social-emotional development difficulties by age five. In a variation of the authoritarian style, the father is cast in the role of the instrumental leader who expects obedience from his children and teaches them what they need to know, while the mother assumes a socio-emotional role. There is high emotional support in the home, but only on the part of one parent—the one who is not seen as the ultimate authority figure. Compared to those with authoritative parents, children with authoritarian parents tend to have lower educational outcomes and prosocial behaviors like helping others, being sensitive to needs, and offering help before asked (Carlo et al. 2018). This pattern has been found in patriarchal cultures across the world where fathers avoid becoming emotionally close to their children due to prescribed parenting roles.

PERMISSIVE

Where support is high and control is low, we have *permissive* parenting. It assumes that a newborn is like a rosebud, needing only tender love and support to blossom slowly into a beautiful flower. Present-day permissive parenting can be traced back to the ideals of the counterculture movement of the 1960s, which can in turn be traced back to the bohemian morality of a century earlier. The thinking here is that every child has special potentialities at birth that are destroyed by societal rules and standards. Therefore, children need to be allowed to find their own purpose through free expression. During the 1960s, this philosophy was epitomized in the slogan "Do your own thing."

Noticeably absent from the permissive style is any idea that children tend to be self-centered and need parental guidance in learning values and interpersonal skills. Consequently, children raised in permissive homes tend to lack a sense of social responsibility; they also fail to develop interdependence. A permissive parenting style has also been shown to be related to a number of negative child outcomes, including the emergence of children's behavioral problems (Tan et al. 2012).

Authoritative

Authoritative parents combine the best qualities found in the authoritarian and permissive styles. Authoritative parents attempt to direct the child in a rational, issue-oriented manner; encourage verbal give-and-take; explain the reasons behind demands and discipline but also use power when necessary; expect the child to conform to adult requirements but also to be independent and self-directing; recognize the rights of both adults and children; and set standards and enforce them firmly. These parents do not regard themselves as infallible, but they also do not base decisions primarily on the child's desires.

Children thrive in an environment of high support and high control. Carlo et al. (2018) and Pinquart (2017) found that social competence in children increases in matters of self-esteem, academic achievement, cognitive development, lowered externalizing behaviors (acting out), creativity, moral behavior, and instrumental abilities. Children raised in authoritative parenting homes have an increased capacity to make good internal decisions.

Other Impacts of Parenting Styles

Researchers have begun to study the differing impact of parenting styles on children according to the ethnicity and gender of the parents. Rodriguez, Donovick, and Crowley (2009, 195) "showed the majority (61%) of Latino parents as 'protective parents'" and that "while mothers and fathers were similar in their parenting styles, expectations were different for male and female children." Kawabata et al. (2011) observed that children's relational aggression was higher when they were raised by psychologically controlling fathers but not by the same controlling behavior by mothers. Another study of adolescents reported that although "authoritative mothering was found to relate to higher self-esteem and life-satisfaction and to lower depression," for fathering "the advantage was less defined and only evident for depression" (Milevsky et al. 2007, 39).

Parenting styles affect other areas of a child's life as well. As might be expected, children's internet use is highest when the parenting style is permissive and lowest when the style is authoritarian (Valcke et al. 2010). Even when it comes to physical activity, children perceive themselves to have higher fitness competence and value when their parents have a high challenging style in physical activities (Kimiecik and Horn 2012). Parenting styles have also been associated with obesity (Kakinami et al. 2015) and physical activity (Poppert Cordts, Wilson, and Riley 2020).

It should be noted that certain kinds of parental control are more effective and produce better results. For example, a coercive approach that forces a child to act against his or her will usually results in low levels of social competence in that child. Withdrawing one's love to obtain compliance is also ineffective. Inductive control—giving explanations, using reasoning, and encouraging a child's voluntary compliance by avoiding direct conflict of wills—proves to be the most effective approach. Coupling this type of control with strong emotional support produces competent children (Carlo et al. 2018). Coercion has an adverse effect on the development of social competence in children, which supports the type of empowerment we have suggested above.

Biological Factors in Parenting

In chapter 2, we discussed the importance of biological factors in understanding family life, including parent-child relationships. Some parents may wrongly hold to a social deterministic view of parenting—thinking that they have an amazing power to make sure their children grow up to be happy, well adjusted, and free from any developmental difficulties. This sets parents up for harsh judgment of themselves or their children, resulting in sure failure. Instead, child development must be understood as an interplay of biological and social-environmental factors. Parents of a child struggling with hyperactivity, attention deficit, addiction, mental illness, or other developmental challenges should be acutely aware of the biological factors that play a major role in their child's struggle.

Many parents find parenting to be especially difficult during the teenage years, when biological changes enter the relationship dynamics. Significant changes in a teenager's endocrinology system mean that a child's hormones are expressed in mood swings and emotional-sexual struggles. In addition, the brain is still undergoing normal developmental changes during late adolescence and early adulthood. In fact, the brain does not reach adult capacity until the mid to late twenties (Cohen et al. 2016). Adolescents are prone to engage in risky behavior due to their inability to execute higher-order thinking such as planning for the future, controlling impulses, and setting priorities, and that inability impacts their judgment. Of course, this is a cause of concern for parents because these judgments can lead to lifelong consequences.

If that isn't enough, the developing self-structure of teenagers means that they have an increasing desire to make their own decisions. In this struggle for independence, teenagers may strike out in ways that tempt parents to ask themselves, "Where did we go wrong?" Not only do parents need to offer more grace to their children at this stage; they also need to offer grace to themselves. In this spirit we advocate a parenting style that is relational in nature. Open communication and firm guidance are achieved in the context of warm, secure, and caring interaction.

A Biblical Model of Parenting

Having summarized the social-science literature on the effects of various parenting styles, we will now present a biblical model, with the goal of integrating these various materials into a model of biblical parenting.

We believe that a biblical model of parenting can be derived from the scriptural depiction of God as parent. The nature of God is love. God cares for us, is faithful to us, bestows gifts on us, redeems and forgives us, disciplines and grows us, challenges and tests us, comforts and consoles us, and is with us through the difficult times. Taken as a whole, the Bible clearly emphasizes the love and grace that God freely gives (Gen. 6; Ruth; Matt. 9:12; Mark 2:17; Luke 19:1–8; John 3:16; Romans 3:24; 4:16; 5:1–20; Titus 2:11; Hebrews 4). Yet this unconditional love is not free of expectations and demands. God's love includes disciplinary action for our good. God's love as parent bears a striking similarity to the parenting style advocated in the social-science literature: a high degree of support and of inductive (rather than coercive) control.

The actions of God as parent clearly point to a model in which parental love (support) and discipline (control) intertwine to help children develop toward maturity. This model comports well with the theological basis for family relationships that we introduced in chapter 1—covenant, grace, empowerment, and intimacy. Parent-child relationships begin when the parents make an initial covenant (a one-way, unconditional commitment) of love with their child. This covenant makes demands and provides stipulations reflective of God's covenant with Israel and us. Although the infant cannot return this commitment, as the child matures the initial covenant should grow into a mature covenant (a two-way, unconditional commitment). This maturing of the parent-child relationship is possible because the covenant commitment establishes an environment of grace and forgiveness in which parents empower their children and reach new levels of intimacy with them.

Initially, the parents need to maintain both parties' responsibilities in the covenant. The parents provide for the emotional and physical needs of the child as is their duty in the covenant. Children in the covenant initially have no responsibilities. As children grow in competence, their responsibility grows more and more. Further, they increasingly engage intentionally in the covenant relationship. This covenant is characterized by grace—a gift on the part of the parents. Over time, children are exposed to both responsiveness and demandingness, which empowers them by communicating their value and identity in the covenant family. As children take on more and more of the family identity and develop increasing levels of competence, more and more mutual forms of intimacy occur.

This is illustrated by the story of Jesus's baptism (Mark 1), where the covenantal relations of the Trinity are expressed physically. The Holy Spirit is there in the form of a dove, the speech of the Father pronounces love and identity over Jesus, and Jesus is being baptized physically. The covenant relation of the Trinity is Jesus's identity—God the Son. This identity forms the basis of Jesus's actions in ministry—revealing grace and forgiveness, empowering others via healing, preaching, teaching, and discipling, and making intimacy with God possible (Heb. 5).

When each parent's identity is based on Christ, we develop a differentiation of self that is based on our adoption into God's family. Our primary calling as a Christian takes precedence over all other domains in our lives. Differentiation in Christ means that we can parent our offspring in noncoercive and noncontrolling means because of our experience of grace and empowerment in Christ. We can extend grace to our children because of our experience of forgiveness in Christ. We can empower our children as opposed to controlling them as we are discipled in a Christian community under the guidance of the Spirit. Finally, we can experience intimacy as we are fully and authentically known by Christ.

In an ideal situation, the four elements of the parent-child relationship are in a continual process of maturing: intimacy leads to deeper covenant love, which enhances the atmosphere of grace, which strengthens the empowerment process, which leads to deepened intimacy, and so on. This cycle is relational and requires reciprocity, meaning that it is based on the development of competencies in all relational partners. The foundation consists of a faithful commitment and accepting environment where children and parents can be vulnerable and open with each other. This relationship connection promotes the empowerment process in which parents and children learn to serve and to give to each other.

Empowerment is the central element in our biblical model of parenting. Exactly what is involved here? Parents and children are initially at different levels in their relationship. As Ivan Boszormenyi-Nagy and colleagues (Boszormenyi-Nagy 1987, 1996; Boszormenyi-Nagy and Krasner 1986) remind us, this relationship contains ethical obligations. That is, parents are ethically obligated to meet the needs of offspring, and children are in a position to make those ethical demands. Children are not obligated to meet the parents' needs until they are adult peers. Good parenting is the wise exercise of parental position and ability. Empowerment is the process of instilling confidence, of strengthening and building up children to become more powerful and competent. Parents who have been empowered by the unconditional love of God and the Holy Spirit are best able to empower their children.

Jesus redefined power by his teaching and by his action in relating to others as a servant. He rejected the use of power to control others and instead affirmed it to serve others. Using parental power to serve our children involves nurture, guidance, love, discipline, and empowerment.

The capacity to be a servant-leader to others requires a high level of maturity and unconditional love. It demands that a person achieve a maturity going beyond self-sufficiency to interdependence. Abundant life is more than a narcissistic euphoria in which all one's personal needs and desires are met. It involves having a meaning beyond oneself. The admonitions in the New Testament to submit to one another and to love, forgive, serve, and value all of God's people are actually a call to mature living.

The most striking example of mature servanthood is the way Jesus honored children. His example is vital to developing a proper theology of power. Like his approach to children, Jesus related to his disciples in terms of empowerment. He even provided for a continuation of the empowerment process after his departure: "But the Advocate, the Holy Spirit, whom the Father will send in my name, will teach you everything, and remind you of all that I have said to you" (John 14:26). Jesus wanted them to have the capacity and confidence to carry on the message. They had been prepared by his teaching ministry to be independent and by his example to be servants.

Parents who empower their children help them become competent and capable people who will in turn empower others. Empowering parents are actively and intentionally engaged in various pursuits—telling, teaching, modeling, delegating—that equip their children to become confident individuals able to relate to others. Parents who empower help their children recognize their inner strengths and potentials and find ways to enhance these qualities. Parental empowerment is the affirmation of the child's ability to learn, grow, and become all that one is meant to be as part of God's image and creative plan.

Empowerment, from a biblical perspective, does not entail the child's gaining power at the expense of the parent. The view that the supply of power is limited is purely secular. When empowering the children of Israel, God did not give up power but offered it in unlimited supply. The authority (*exousia*) of Jesus flowed from his personhood; it was in no way diminished when he empowered his disciples. Similarly, the authority of parents, which flows from their personhood, is not diminished when they exercise the responsibility to nurture their children to maturity. The process of empowering children does not mean relinquishing parental authority, nor are parents depleted or drained of power when they empower their children. Rather, when empowerment takes place, authority and ascribed power are retained as children develop, grow, and achieve a sense of personal power, self-esteem, and wholeness. Successful parenting results in the children's gaining as much personal power as the parents themselves have. In the Christian context, children are empowered to love God and their neighbors as themselves. They are capable of going beyond themselves to reach out to others.

Find a more detailed account of this biblical model in *Relationship-Empowerment Parenting: Building Formative and Fulfilling Relationships with Your Children* (J. K. Balswick et al. 2003).

The Case for Coparenting

It should be noted here that the *relationship-empowerment model*—our name for the biblical ideal—is most efficiently achieved if both parents bring their respective strengths to the process in a complementary way. There are two types of complementarity. In the case of *longitudinal complementarity*, parents complement each other over time. One parent may be better at dealing with infants or young children, while the skills of the other emerge once the children have developed greater cognitive ability. In the case of *situational complementarity*, parents complement each other on a day-to-day basis throughout their parenting years. Here the situation determines which parental skills are most needed. Thus, at times, the parent who is more capable of helping a child with homework is needed; in other instances, the parent who is more able to provide encouragement when the child lacks self-esteem is needed. Notice that these types of complementarity require a high degree of communication and flexibility. This type of complementarity allows each partner to express his or her needs (intimacy), express grace and forgiveness as challenges arise, and be mutually empowering as talents, skills, and responsibilities are developed and used to parent. All of this is built on the covenant between the relational partners. Complementary parenting offers an advantage in that one parent does not have to meet all the child's needs. The main point is that both parents have an essential role in the empowerment of children.

While children benefit from having both parents involved, it is imperative that parents agree on the basic parenting process. We would warn against parental determinism—the view that parenting is a one-way process—for there is sufficient evidence that "child temperament plays an important role in shaping the coparenting relationships" (Szabo, Dubas, and van Aken 2012, 554). One certainly must take into account the personality dynamics that play a part in the relationship between children and each of their parents.

Parenting that empowers children to maturity is conceptually similar to the New Testament depiction of discipleship. Jesus gathered and trained disciples, empowering them to "go therefore and make disciples of all nations, baptizing them in the name of the Father and of the Son and of the Holy Spirit, and teaching them to obey everything that I have commanded you. And remember, I am with you always, to the end of the age" (Matt. 28:19–20). Parenting follows a similar course. The ultimate reward for parents and children is a relationship that grows into maturity so that when the children have been empowered, they will in turn empower others.

7

Developing a Mature, Reciprocating Self

The outcome of parenting, as was the focus of the previous chapter, is the development of a competent, productive adult. In the United States, the route to this outcome is fraught with concern and challenge. Parents are given many expert opinions—often contradictory—that contribute to this sense of uncertainty about parenting the next generation. This anxiety is further exacerbated by the internet dumping an overload of information on parents, many of whom are ill-equipped to evaluate the quality of the information being provided.

As we mentioned in the preceding chapter, we believe that parents need to resist bowing uncritically before expert opinion and simple formulas that guarantee parenting success. It is more important to develop a parenting philosophy that takes into account cultural beliefs, family of origin (FOO) heritages, personal strengths and limitations (both one's own and those of one's children), knowledge derived from firsthand experience, and common sense. Confidence in one's ability as a parent comes from integrating these elements with the clear findings of child development professionals and solid biblical principles. Parents who wait with bated breath for the next gem of wisdom from the so-called experts are setting themselves up for disillusionment when their offspring do not automatically develop into the ideal children they were promised. Child-rearing is a much more complex process than most people realize.

In chapter 2, we introduced the *family developmental systems perspective*, and in this chapter, we use developmental systems theory (DST) to understand child development (Ford and Lerner 1992; Lerner 2018). Consistent with biblical assumptions about human nature, DST provides an integrative approach to child development.

Many child development theories are limited in that they split explanations of development into oppositional camps—nature versus nurture, individual versus the group or family, mechanistic versus organismic, continuous versus discontinuous (stage) development, and so on. In its emphasis on *relationalism*, DST emphasizes the interaction among all factors that contribute to human development. In other words, DST incorporates the context of the individual's development (family, community, etc.) into understanding how biological, genetic, relational, and psychological factors affect human competence.

Rather than focusing exclusively on the unique contributions of nature or nurture, DST emphasizes the interaction between them as playing a significant role. A proper understanding of child development must consider an *interactive* rather than an additive process. It is not enough simply to add together the influence of the mother, plus the father, plus other family members, plus peers, plus school and church; we must consider the overall impact of all these factors interacting together on the development of a child.

Some key assumptions in DST (Lerner 2018) are that (1) child development includes a multiplicity of biological, cultural, social, and psychological influences; (2) influences are reciprocal in that parents not only affect their child but also are affected by the child at the same time; (3) each child is a unique human; (4) the development of each child is different; (5) children are active choosing agents, participating in their own development; and (6) children are created for community. At the end of this chapter, we revisit these basic assumptions as we critique child-development theories in light of biblical assumptions about being human.

Jack Balswick, Pamela King, and Kevin Reimer (2016) seek to understand human development from a Christian theological viewpoint. In doing so, they note that developmental theories lack a guiding *teleology*, an understanding of the *goal* of development. Implicit in all theories is a *soft teleology*, or the idea of what is optimal human flourishing. There is a lack of consensus regarding this ultimate goal of human development, as each theory and researcher tends to focus on a limited number of variables and theories of human nature. Balswick, King, and Reimer cite this lack of teleology as a *developmental dilemma* resulting from the lack of a theologically informed understanding of development completeness. The naturalistic assumption underlying most developmental theories alludes to *survivalistic* inclinations (humans evolve based on characteristics that best contribute to the survival of the human species) but lacks theological explanation.

A secondary issue tied into the developmental dilemma concerns the difference between description and prescription. Many developmental theorists and researchers attempt to *describe* the natural process of human development over the course of the lifespan. This description is needed to understand and document how humans change over time. When experts try to popularize these theories and research, they are offered as normative or *prescriptive*, meaning that this is how human *should* change over time. A move from description to prescription is a move from science to scientism. It incorporates morality as important questions arise: Does this theory and research contribute a moral good? Does this understanding of development consider cultural and other influences on human development? How does this research reflect naturalistic or mechanistic views of human nature (called psychological anthropology)? Science alone cannot answer the questions of the developmental dilemma—we must propose a theological *telos*.

In response to the developmental dilemma, we begin with the assumption that humans are created to reflect the image of God. The theological dimension of human development is sanctification, or the process of becoming Christlike. While part of that image includes rationality (mind), the *relationality* of God, as exemplified in the relationship among the three persons of the Holy Trinity, is also a core part of that image. Being created in the image of God encompasses a relationality that simultaneously includes differentiation *and* unity. From a theological perspective, the goal or purpose (teleology) is for people to develop a mature, *reciprocating self*—a self that in all its uniqueness engages others in relationships (Balswick, King, and Reimer 2016) that reflect the renewed or sanctified nature of Christ. As Hebrews 1 reminds us, Jesus Christ is the perfect image of God, representing humanity and allowing access to God the Father. Therefore, our understanding of child-development theories centers on how each child develops into a reciprocating, relational self with respect to God and others, as emulated in the incarnation of Christ, the perfected image of God.

Theories of Child Development

Theories of child development consist of systematically organized knowledge accumulated through empirical observation of children. A good theory is like a pair of glasses in that it allows one to focus more sharply on that which is being observed. This is important to remember, as each theory tends to focus on a select aspect or domain of human development. These theories tend to describe distinct aspects of child development, and they shed light on the total developing person when taken together. We draw attention to the major child development theories so that we aren't blinded by one theory while ignoring the others.

To illustrate this point, let us suppose that representatives of the major theories of child development are watching a child playing in the family living room. Although the observers will be exposed to the same behavior, they will not see it through the same set of lenses. Each observer will perceive the child's activity through lenses of predetermined notions about human behavior. The cognitive development theorist will be especially aware of the particular stage of development; the psychoanalytic theorist will look for unconscious motivations in overt behavior; the symbolic interactionist will concentrate on the child's self-concept; the social learning theorist will pay special attention to what the child has learned from observing others. Although it is not a conscious process, all theorists engage in selective perception, viewing the child's actions in accordance with their own general conceptualization of human behavior.

It is also important to discern the goal of each developmental theory. In *The Reciprocating Self* (Balswick et al. 2016), we learn that each stage theory's teleological focus is described in the final stage of development. In other words, the highest accomplishment or the competence that humans should strive for occurs in or is described by the final level of development. We need to understand the Christian-worldview implications of these views of human flourishing in order to discern their relationship to the reciprocal self and becoming more Christlike.

Table 5 compares the major theories of child development that conceptualize development as emerging in specific sequential stages. After presenting brief summaries of each theory introduced in table 5, brief summaries will be given of four important non-stage-specific theories—object relations, social learning, sociocultural, and social ecology. Due to the specific nature of moral development theory and faith development theory, they will be summarized in the following chapter on family spirituality. A good strategy is to consider how these theories are complementary and not just contradictory in yielding insights into the child development process. As a summary, we will compare and contrast the strengths and limitations of each based on biblical assumptions about being human.

Psychoanalytic Theory: Internal Focus

The father of psychoanalytic theory, Sigmund Freud, began by describing the newborn baby as all *id*—a bundle of unrestrained instinctive energy seeking gratification via expression. Although he posited that the id contained

TABLE 5 **Major Stage-Specific Theories of Child Development**

	Psycho-analytic	Erikson (Neopsycho-analytic)	Cognitive Development		
			Piaget	Kohlberg (Moral)	Fowler (Faith)
(0–1½) Infancy	Oral	Trust	Sensorimotor		Undifferentiated
(1½–3) Toddler Stage	Anal	Autonomy	Preoperational	Obedience and punishment	Intuitive-projective
(4–6) Early Childhood	Genital	Initiative			
(7–12) Childhood		Industry	Concrete operations	Individualism and exchange	Mythical-literal
(13–21) Adolescence		Identity	Formal operations	Interpersonal relations	Synthetic-conventional
(21–30) Adulthood		Intimacy		Maintaining social order	Individuative-reflective
(30–45)		Generativity		Social contract and individual rights	Conjunctive
(46–)		Ego integration		Universal ethical principles	Universalizing

both a positive instinct (*Eros*, or life) and a negative instinct (*Thanatos*, or death), Freud described the id as amoral, impulsive, and ruled by unconscious and irrational demands for immediate gratification. In other words, the motivating or animating force for human development is the gratification of one's instinctual drives. Therefore, Freudian psychological approaches are often referred to as drive-reduction models. The id seeks the immediate gratification of these drives regardless of social context. Freud saw parents as attempting to impose their own wishes on the child, which when internalized by the child formed the *superego*. You can imagine the internal struggle between the id wanting immediate gratification and the superego (the internalization of parental wishes) seeking to deny the immediate gratification of impulses of the id. The superego operates as a moral police officer attempting to contain the id, or to find more socially and morally appropriate expressions of id impulses. The third part of the personality, the *ego*, develops out of the struggle between the id and the superego. The ego (self) functions as a type of internal diplomat. The ego attempts to calm the wishes of the id and the superego by finding acceptable ways of rewarding each. The superego rewards the ego by building up self-esteem but punishes the ego with guilt when it does not comply (Freud 1949, 1954).

Parenting from a psychoanalytic perspective can be thought of as a journey through a minefield of potential dangers. If parents are overly rigid and moralistic, they risk suppressing positive aspects of the life force residing in the id. If they are too permissive and fail to provide adequate boundaries for the child, they risk allowing the formation of a child with an inadequate superego, resulting in the unchecked id running wild. Effective parenting is a balance of allowing a child's expression of innate creativity while at the same time taming the child through societal behavioral norms.

According to the psychoanalytic theory of the personality, healthy development is characterized by a strong ego, which can monitor the extreme demands of the id and the superego. During their first six years of life, children move through three developmental stages—*oral*, *anal*, and *genital*—in which they must negotiate their need for gratification with parental and societal approval. In Freud's theory, eros and thanatos are encapsulated in the sexual organs' development. Freud's theory is based in the appropriate expression of id drives that are mainly sexualized in nature (except for the latency stage, where these drives lie in a dormant state). Secure gender identity and self-esteem develop during the *latency* stage (age seven to twelve) if a firm foundation is established during the first six years of life. If earlier conditions were less than ideal, the child may have difficulty relating to others and experience increasing self-doubt and lack of self-esteem. The internal conflicts (id, ego, and superego) are experienced through each stage of the relationship with parents. When relationships with both parents are strong and unwavering, the child will feel a sense of well-being and worth.

Erikson's Neopsychoanalytic or Psychosocial Theory: Infancy through Adulthood

In traditional psychoanalytic theory, the basic personality is thought to be formed by puberty, with minimal change likely thereafter. Two major contributions to our understanding of psychoanalytic human development are provided by Erik Erikson (1968, 1985), who argues that development continues into adulthood. First, Erikson suggests eight developmental stages (as opposed to the five stages proposed by Freud), the last emerging at approximately age forty-five. Erikson focuses on how parents and wider psycho-historical and social factors affect a person's learning each stage-specific developmental task. Mastery of the developmental tasks at each stage is vital to successful achievement of the tasks at the next stage.

The degree of mastery determines the strengths and deficits with which an individual develops. The mastery of these strengths resulted in what Erikson referred to as *virtues* or *vitalities* for the individual. To arrive at maturity (the last stage of development) with a sufficient sense of ego integrity, one must have achieved trust, autonomy, initiative, industry, identity, intimacy, and generativity during the previous seven sequential stages. At the opposite extreme are those individuals who end up in a state of despair because they have experienced mistrust, shame and doubt, guilt, a sense of inferiority, role confusion, isolation, and stagnation sequentially during the developmental stages.

A major strength of Erikson's theory is its recognition of the importance of both familial and extrafamilial influences on human development. Recognizing the cumulative effects of experience throughout the life span, the theory also suggests interventions to help those who have been socially or psychologically deprived at a specific stage of development.

Cognitive Structural Theories

We now turn to cognitive structural approaches to human development. This transition is facilitated by a change in how psychologists understand and study humans. First, we notice that both Freud and Erikson attempt to describe more general human characteristics. Their theories are more global. For example, Freud's theory attempts to explain why people make verbal mistakes (i.e., a Freudian slip) all the way to why a person marries someone else or chooses a specific vocation. Second, in moving toward the cognitive revolution in psychology, theorizing and research focus on more limited human phenomena like language learning or moral development. Finally, there is an increasing emphasis on understanding the interrelationships among biological, neurological, and psychological processes (like thinking) that are reflected in the research. Cognitive structural approaches like those of Piaget, Kohlberg, and Fowler share an emphasis on combining an understanding of the need for brain development to occur before a child is able to achieve a specific level of cognitive, moral, and faith development. In other words, the brain has to have the neurological mechanisms in order for the cognitive, moral, and faith *psychological* processes to be developed.

Cognitive Development Theory: The Child as a Developing Scientist

While cognitive development (CD) theory singles out the cognitive aspects of human development, it should be noted that Kohlberg's moral development model and Fowler's faith process model, while reflected in table 5, will be discussed in chapter 8 as part of the topic of family spirituality. Swiss psychologist Jean Piaget starts with the assumption that children are not merely passive objects but also active agents in constructing their personal reality; that is, they turn all life experiences into action. In a rational fashion, the child continually attempts to make sense of the world. Piaget bases his theory on qualitative data, mainly from observing his own children; he observed how babies make use of their natural reflexes as they contact an object or a person. The child is a "little scientist," learning by acting upon the world. Children are discovering the scheme into which a thing fits so they can act toward it consistently. A ball is to be bounced, but a dog will bark, growl, move away, or bite. Therefore, the child learns to act accordingly by picking up on these cues. The acquisition of language brings a wide variety of new possibilities. With time, the child learns to discriminate between and distinguish parents as "Mommy" or "Daddy" and strangers as "man" or "woman" (or "boy" or "girl"). In analyzing this process, Piaget uses the terms *assimilation*, *accommodation*, and *equilibration*. Assimilation is taking information in and construing it in terms of one's established way of thinking. Whatever is perceived is made to fit into existing schemes. The more refined a scheme, the less likely it is that new pieces of information will be misplaced (Piaget 1932).

However, if children could assimilate experiences only into existing categories, no new scheme would emerge. And because many things do not fit into existing schemes, new schemes must be formed. This is the process of accommodation: altering the existing cognitive structures to allow for new objects experienced. Children continually engage in assimilation and accommodation. The balance between the two is equilibration. People with mature cognitive structures engage in both assimilation and accommodation. People with immature cognitive structures fail to engage in one or the other and thus do not achieve equilibration (cognitive balance).

According to Piaget, cognitive development in a child takes place in four major stages. The first is the *sensorimotor* stage, which covers the period from birth until about two years of age. During this stage, children are primarily focused on basic motor skills and learning to adapt their behavior to their external environment. The child classifies objects by acting upon them. In the process, the child begins to grasp the idea of *object permanence*—that is, to realize that objects that are out of sight have not ceased to exist.

Children also learn to coordinate the different parts of the body during the sensorimotor stage. For example, when trying to reach for an object, they will stand on their tiptoes and stretch their arms as high as they can. Toward the end of the sensorimotor stage, children intentionally engage in goal-directed behavior; that is, they push a chair up to the table and then climb on the chair to get the cookie on the table, all in an orderly sequence.

Mastery of linguistic skills is primary during the *preoperational* stage, in which children are able to name objects, to place words together into meaningful sentences, and to begin to construct a view of reality.

Because the acquisition of language skills is so complex, the thinking and behavior of a child are characterized by unsettledness, fear, and confusion—precisely why this stage is referred to as *pre*operational. For example, the child may conclude that firefighters, since they always appear at the scene of a fire, set fires, or that police initiate trouble. Parents must be mindful that children need help in logically explaining the events they experience. It is natural at this stage for children to think everyone else experiences the world as they do. If they are happy, they project happiness onto everyone else; when they are sad, then everyone else must be sad.

Eventually children are able to move beyond self-focused thinking. At about seven years of age, they reach the stage of *concrete operations*, when thought processes become more stable and consistent. Children at the concrete operations stage can understand the principle of invariance (certain matters of space and weight are in some sense unchangeable regardless of the shape). For example, children at the concrete operations stage understand that the water's volume does not change, no matter the shape or size of the container it is poured into. Children at this stage are also avid collectors since they love to classify and arrange their priceless objects on the basis of color, size, shape, and every other aspect imaginable. This reflects an expanded reasoning ability.

At the *formal operations* stage, children understand causality and can perform scientific experiments. By using deductive reasoning, they formulate hypotheses, carry out experiments, and reach conclusions based on evidence. At this point in children's lives, there is an increased concern for basic values and truths. Formal operations is the teleological trajectory for Piaget. The highest level of human cognitive flourishing is described as the attainment of formal operational thought.

Object Relations Theory: The Child as an Object Needing Love

Even though object relations theory is rooted in psychoanalytic theory, it is useful in understanding the child's development of self within the context of parent-child relationships. Object relations theory emphasizes the development of the self or personality within the context of an infant-caregiver relationship. This is actually the strength of object relations theory compared with classic Freudian approaches. An important assumption of Freud's under-standing of human nature is that drives are satiated by nonspecific objects. This means that any mother could fulfill the drives of any infant. Object relations theory contends that the early interactions of a child and its most intimate caregiver, usually the mother, shape and form personality. That is, the specific mother-child relationship uniquely influences how the child develops.

In object relations theory, there is a shift from *biological* to *interpersonal determinism* and a corresponding change from an internal to a *relational* structural model. Melanie Klein (1932) is a transition figure (Greenberg and Mitchell 1983) in the development of object relations theory and practice. She replaced biological drives with *psychological and relational drives*. Her work brought about a major paradigmatic shift from biological determinism to a perspective that took into consideration the significance of interpersonal interaction.

The core element in Klein's theory consists of the internalization by the child of its relationship with the primary caregiver(s). Klein's theory has similarities with Freud's drive theory, but she changes the essential nature of the drives. Klein posits the essential relatedness of human beings; children are essentially relational in nature (Ogden 1990). Children are born with drives that inherently have objects that can satisfy the drives (Greenberg and Mitchell 1983; Ogden 1990). Klein sees early relationships between mother and infant as primarily an *internal event* for the child, who cannot differenti-ate between the experience and the meaning of the experience (Ogden 1990). "Klein conceives of early infantile experience as nonsubjective (that is, devoid of a sense of 'I-ness')" (Ogden 1990, 27).

Once internalized, the internal object can bring the child comfort or pain. No matter how well the caregiver interacts with the infant, the infant most likely will internalize an object with some negativity. The internalized object then becomes an organizing principle for future interactions. If the child inter-nalizes a good or safe object, he or she will feel secure and will be able to form positive relationships. If the child internalizes an anxious or hateful object, he or she will anticipate having negative experiences in other relationships.

Donald Winnicott's (1971) version of object relations theory strongly em-phasizes that the mother or the caregiver is almost solely responsible for influ-encing the development of the self. He refers to the "holding environment," since a mother provides a physical and psychological space where the baby experiences a sense of well-being. In this secure holding environment, the infant begins to gain a sense of self and other (Grolnick 1990). The mother as an internal object provides a sense of security and safety. If the holding environment is adequate (good enough), the infant's needs are satisfied. A crucial element of this holding environment is how mothers respond to and reflect the experiences of their infants. Parents attuned to the baby's physical and emotional needs provide the foundation for trust and security. The good-enough mother can also find a balance between empathetic gratification of the infant's needs and satisfying her own needs. Parents attuned to the child's needs *mirror* the child's behavior and feelings. For example, a mother is mirroring her child when she produces the same sounds of delight the infant produces when he is lifted into his mother's arms. Rather than ignoring or overwhelming the child, an appropriate response provides an authentication and validation of a child's sense of self.

Transitional space (psychological space) emerges through the process of internalizing the presence of an emotionally attuned but nondemanding parent. The child who has *internalized* the parent as a *good object* has the capacity to be alone. Sometimes a *transitional object* (a special blanket or stuffed animal) can help the child internalize the mother. By symbolizing the calming presence of the caregiver, transitional objects allow toddlers to feel secure even when they are alone.

Transitional space allows for the expression of the true self. The true self is the authentic, spontaneous self, aware and comfortable with his or her uniqueness. The false self is a result of a lack of transitional space. The major contributors to the false self can be seen in the extremes: *absent* parents or *impinging* parents.

In summary, a good holding environment includes a present, mirroring, non-impinging mother; transitional space; and a fostering of the ability to be alone. Transitional space is created by the nondemanding, good-enough mother in a holding environment where she mirrors the child in a non-impinging way.

Social Learning Theory: The Child as Learner

During the past half century, behaviorism has been shaped by the creative research and writing of B. F. Skinner. Skinner (1953) developed what is known as operant conditioning, which is a modification of classical conditioning. Rather than using a stimulus to bring about a desired response, Skinner's model emphasizes reinforcement—that is, a system of rewards for desired behavior and punishments for unacceptable actions. The basic principle here is that consequences shape and maintain behavior. Operant conditioning has proven useful in bringing about changes in behavior.

Social learning theory emphasizes learning by observation rather than through direct reinforcement (Bandura 1977). Children learn how to behave by observing the consequences of the behavior of other people. For example, children learn not to hit other children on the playground primarily by observing that children who do hit others experience negative consequences, such as getting hurt themselves or being reprimanded by a teacher.

Social learning theory also observes that children learn from the modeling of parents and important others in their lives. As role models, parents influence their children in both positive and negative ways. Comparison of direct learning (reinforcement) and indirect learning (observation and imitation of modeled behavior) reveals that modeling is more effective. The application is obvious: effective parents are those who model the behaviors they want their children to implement.

The idea that learning comes through the child's observation and interpretation of behavior implies a self-consciousness and self-determination within the child. Change, then, can be activated both by environmental stimuli and by the child, a discovery that has enhanced learning theory.

In Albert Bandura's concept of *reciprocal determinism*, three factors reciprocally influence one another: *behavior*, the *person* (i.e., one's cognitive makeup), and the *environment*. Children not only change their environment but are being changed by it. Children do not simply react to their parents but act upon them and influence how they parent. The colicky baby elicits a different parenting response than the easy baby does, just as the way the parent deals with the baby affects the baby's response. Although social learning theory doesn't stress innate or biological factors, it views children as actively involved in the construction of their environment and thus in their own developmental process.

Vygotsky's Sociocultural Theory: Parenting as Scaffolding

In the 1930s, in forming a *sociocultural* theory of child development, the Russian theorist Lev Vygotsky concentrated on the relational influences on children as they live in a sociocultural context. Vygotsky paved the way for understanding how *culture* affects development and how language serves as the primary vehicle for the transmission of cultural information. Vygotsky's concept of the *zone of proximal development* is especially helpful in understanding how a child masters a task. The zone contains the range of tasks that a child cannot yet accomplish without the active assistance of parents and others (Vygotsky 1986). The expansion of the child's skill comes through interpersonal relationships since children's immediate potential cannot be magically realized on their own. The child learns new skills each step of the way in the context of relationship support until he or she masters a specific task.

The child is a collaborator, learning new skills through interactions with more cognitively advanced people. Parents must create what Vygotsky refers to as appropriate *scaffolding*. Those who provide an adequate scaffold (not too much or too little support and control) provide an optimal learning environment. The scaffold extends just slightly beyond the child's abilities but never so far beyond as to create unreasonable expectations that end in failure. The concept of scaffolding is similar to the empowerment principle, according to which guidance, assistance, and support are given so the child reaches his or her full potential and mastery. When parents do too much or "take over," the child is disempowered and feels inadequate and dependent. When the child accomplishes a task on his or her own, the parent wisely removes the scaffolding. The child is now competent and confident and has no need to be dependent on the parents.

Children require a high level of interpersonal commitment as they develop. It follows that abused or neglected children often develop negative representations of the self. They have not had sufficient support or scaffolding to reach full maturity. In fact, they need to develop protective strategies for self-survival. Abuse frequently results in the child internalizing the social influences of shame, violence, or emotional abuse that lead to negativity toward others, such as bullying, delinquency, or violence.

Social Ecology: Child Development in the Village

The African proverb "It takes a village to raise a child" is verified in a social ecological theory of child development. Urie Bronfenbrenner (1979) suggests that child development is best understood within four increasingly encompassing ecological systems. At the smallest, most specific level is the *microsystem*, the parent-child relationship. Beyond the microsystem is the *mesosystem*, consisting of social environments such as a child's kindergarten, Sunday school class, neighborhood playgroup, and so on. Each of these settings in and of itself is a microsystem, but the collection of all these microsystems and the relationships between them constitute the mesosystem for the toddler.

Children are also influenced by what occurs in the social environment beyond the settings in which they directly participate. This constitutes their *exosystem*. When both parents are employed outside the home, the child is affected because of parental involvement in these work environments. The child's exosystem consists of all those environments, even when he or she is not a direct participant, because, even from a distance, they affect the parents or the siblings.

Encompassing all three of these systems is the *macrosystem*, best understood as the wider cultural level. Macrosystemic influences are such things as popular culture, the mass media, the government, and moral and religious beliefs and practices in a culture.

According to Bronfenbrenner, "The ecology of human development involves the scientific study of the progressive, mutual accommodation between an active, growing human being and the changing properties of the immediate settings in which the growing person lives, as this process is affected by relations between these settings, and by the larger contexts in which the settings are embedded" (1979, 21).

A social ecological understanding of child development complements the child development approaches that have a more limited focus. Parenting is best understood as part of a web of social relationships that affect the development of a child. As children mature, they become increasingly involved in a variety of settings as they learn to adapt to new environments, roles, and relationships in the process of developmental growth.

A Critique of Child Development Theories in Light of Biblical Assumptions

Although it is beyond the scope of this chapter to present a complete synthesis of the child development theories discussed, it will be helpful to briefly critique them on the basis of how well they comport with biblical teachings on being human. We shall build our critique around three biblical doctrines: (1) humans are in a state of constant internal tension: though created in God's image, they have fallen into sin; (2) humans are active agents who have the capacity to make choices; and (3) humans are created for community.

Internal Tension

None of the theories adequately takes into account the biblical view that humans are distinct from all other living creatures because they carry the image of God within them. Granted, the human condition is marked by sin, and therefore we are a broken image. "Sinning must be understood in the context of its relation to the general human longing for goodness" (Shults 2003, 190). The biblical view of being made in God's image and being marred by sin acknowledges that the human condition is marked by internal tension. As Paul states in Romans 7:21–24, "So I find it to be a law that when I want to do what is good, evil lies close at hand. For I delight in the law of God in my inmost self, but I see in my members another law at war with the law of my mind, making me captive to the law of sin that dwells in my members. Wretched man that I am! Who will rescue me from this body of death?"

In viewing human behavior as part of the natural order, developmental theories refer to internal tension but stop short of using the concept of sin. If the ultimate meaning and purpose of human development is to be understood, we need to know what it means to fall short or miss the mark in human development. In Ray Anderson's theological anthropology, sin is understood in a relational context. He defines sin as "defiance of God's gracious relation to those who bear his image . . . [resulting] in separating persons from the gracious life of God" (1990, 234).

Shame illuminates the experience of sinfulness (Capps 1993) as it is (1) self-involving, (2) self-constricting, and (3) results in estrangement. Sin is self-involving, as it is centered in one's physical being as well as one's thoughts and motivations. Further, sin prevents the flourishing of the person, and the ultimate outcome of sin is alienation or estrangement from others. Sin as the shame experience impacts the *relational* dimension of the image of God—estrangement. Capps (1993) also argues for the *structural* impact of the shame experience—increased psychic depletion of resources as well as the division of the self. Broadly, sin may be conceptualized as an orientation to life that (1) destroys community; (2) impedes God's intentions for the world—human and natural (cosmos); and (3) inhibits or destroys individual well-being (Capps 2000).

In like manner, Shults states that at the "heart of the doctrine of original sin . . . is that each and every person is bound by relations to self, others, and God that inhibit the goodness of loving fellowship" (2003, 309). Humans desire to be related to good objects—this is a core feature of being made in God's image. Human nature is motivated to secure relations with these good objects. The good but sinful human is unable to truly discern what is of ultimate value. This means humans often substitute idols for the ultimate security provided by God—salvation in his Son.

Sin is the condition of failing to be in proper relationship with self, others, and God. Brokenness in relationship is the heart of human sin. Thus, the goals of child development from a Christian point of view are realized in capturing a sense of the relationality in the divine Trinity, as exemplified in the covenant love, grace, empowerment, and intimacy modeled by God for us in the Old and New Testaments.

Capacity to Make Choices

In developmental theories, the capacity to make choices is generally couched in terms of *human agency*. From a theological perspective, human agency is

144

understood in terms of people struggling to live as broken images of God yet being responsible to God and others for their behavior. Child development theorists differ significantly in the degree to which they conceptualize humans as choice-making creatures.

Classic learning theory assumes that children are born as clean slates on which social conditioning imprints the cultural script. In this mechanistic view, people operate on much the same principles as do machines.

Social learning theory leans toward the conviction that children are active organisms who continually act upon and construct their own environments.

The contemporary theories maintain that children are unable to take any action apart from the options presented by their environment. While we can use the wisdom of child development theories to understand human freedom, we must not allow this knowledge to deter us from accepting the scriptural view of free will.

Humans, from a Christian perspective, (1) act intentionally and judge between objects, (2) are motivated by desire for certain goods, and (3) act to attain perceived goods (Shults 2003). "The emerging agent is embedded in a dynamic trajectory in which one finds oneself loving and longing to be loved" (Shults 2003, 191). However, this agent is ambiguously related to the good. Humans have the capability to choose and are inherently motivated to choose. Sin has not removed the ability to choose; it has warped humanity's ability to accomplish good in that choice.

Created for Community

Whereas child development theories have only recently leaned toward the view that children are active organisms or are agents working on the environment, they have been in continuous agreement that human input is necessary if children are to take on human characteristics. Deprived of a human social environment, very little in the biological structure of children would induce them to embrace norms, values, or attitudes. When children are part of a human social environment, however, they take on the attitudes and behaviors of that community.

God created humans to live in community. Imaging God means being in relationships. This is the message from Genesis 1:26, "Let us make humankind in our image," and from Genesis 2:18, "Then the LORD God said, 'It is not good that the man should be alone; I will make him a helper as his partner.'" Relationships are reflected in the Trinity and are modeled in Adam and Eve's relationship. The "be fruitful and multiply" aspect of the creation of humanity is known as the cultural mandate (Gen. 1:28; Wolters 2005), indicating God's desire for humanity to flourish and build community and culture. This core theme of living in community is woven throughout the Old and New Testaments and is central to our theological model of relations. Humans require an empowering community of grace, based on covenant commitment, to provide the security and emotional intimacy all humans need.

In summary, children need not only *a* family; they also need a family of families. This is essentially the New Testament model of what the church is to be to the family—a place where family members are nurtured, empowered, and developed in a community of faith. The covenant community is to care for members as well as to help them mature spiritually.

Parenting Young Children

The major theories of child development provide a basis for discussing important dimensions of parenting young children. In this section we address the matter of how parents can best facilitate the social, psychological, and spiritual growth of their children. In keeping with our theological basis for family relationships, we believe that parents need to provide unilateral unconditional love. This is the indispensable component in the empowerment process. The fundamental qualities—loving, accepting, knowing, and communicating— kindle in children the capacity for mature bilateral commitments. The question of how to empower children comes down to a twofold concern: (1) how to build self-validation and (2) how to discipline.

Unconditional Love and Self-Validation

Children need to be valued for who they are and their unique contributions to their families. When parents have high self-esteem and model mutual regard and cooperation in their marital relationship, they establish a climate in which self-esteem is nourished in their children.

The covenant commitment from parents to children establishes children's identities. As children experience responsiveness and accessibility from their parents, this identity as belonging to the parents is solidified. Covenantal love cements belonging in children. Children learn that they are valued for who they are, not only for how they behave or contribute.

This identity is reflected in our adoption into God's family. In a poignant passage, Paul describes how gentiles and Jews are joined into one family: "So then you are no longer strangers and aliens, but you are citizens with the saints and also members of the household of God, built upon the foundation of the apostles and prophets, with Christ Jesus himself as the cornerstone"

(Eph. 2:19–20). Identity is based on acceptance into God's family; analogically, identity is based on the covenant commitment parents make to their children.

Unconditional love should be shown not only in the parents' commitment to be responsible and faithful in child-rearing tasks but also in verbal and behavioral demonstrations of affection for their children. The children will then begin to recognize that they are loved not only for what they do but also for who they are. This gives them a sense of security and increases the incentive to be cooperative and helpful family members.

Acceptance of Differences Inherent in the Family Constellation

The order in which siblings enter into a family is referred to as the family constellation. Although research is inconclusive about the empirical effects of family constellation on adult personality (Miller, Anderson, and Keala 2004), many therapists emphasize how an individual's birth order affects adulthood. Each position in the family is important, and every child needs to feel secure in his or her place. Particular characteristics accompany each position. For example, the oldest child is usually an achiever since parents tend to give first children special attention and expect them to take responsibility early. Middle children often try to compete with the older sibling(s), but since they cannot catch up, they often achieve in areas untried by the older sibling(s). Sometimes middle children feel squeezed or lost. The family usually caters to the youngest children, who, therefore, tend to be more easygoing and relaxed. The terms *babied* and *spoiled* are usually affectionate labels, but there can also be resentment toward the youngest children. An only child is similar to the oldest child but tends to be more adult in attitudes and actions. Children who come from large families tend to separate themselves into smaller sibling groups.

Every position in the family has certain advantages and disadvantages. The only girl in a family of boys or the only boy in a family of girls may have special privileges and problems. Siblings who are more than five years apart tend to feel separated into different subsystems. And, of course, there is great variability in how each unique family reacts to each individual child.

It is important that every position be respected and that age-appropriate behavior be expected of every child. Parents who exert too much pressure or expect too much burden a child unnecessarily; however, parents with low expectations or who show little faith in a child's abilities provide insufficient stimulation. Neither of these extreme approaches empowers the child.

Older siblings need assurance that their positions in the family are special and secure. Knowing that younger children are not more loved or more valued encourages them to be helpful with their younger siblings rather than jealous or competitive. If middle children are noticed and perceive that they are cherished as special and capable, they will not feel the need to outdo the older children. If the youngest children are given adequate attention and encouraged to accomplish appropriate tasks, they will be able to contribute to the family system without feeling overindulged or coddled. Parents send their children a strong message by believing in them and in their ability to contribute to the well-being of others.

Communication

Parents use verbal and nonverbal communication to show that they respect and value their children. Critical to effective communication is the ability to be genuine. Most children can sense an inauthentic remark because the verbal claim is incongruent with the body language. It behooves parents to be congruent; that is, words, body language, and tone of voice should convey a consistent message. Expressing one's feelings honestly gives children clear and direct messages to which they can accurately respond.

When there is a discrepancy between verbal and nonverbal messages, a child will be confused and frustrated. This is sometimes called the double bind: the child cannot respond to both messages at the same time without being contradictory. The major problem is that neither the parent nor the child talks openly about the confusion, which further obscures the truth. Such distorted communication disrupts family functioning.

Communication will be enhanced if parents use encouraging statements such as, "Mike, you did a fine job of cleaning out the sink," or "Barb, I know it's difficult for you to do those math problems, but you're getting better at it." These messages are very different from negative appraisals, which tend to become self-fulfilling prophecies—for example, "What's wrong with you; don't you know any better?" Such remarks lead to discouragement and uncooperative attitudes.

The most important element of communication is listening. When we are listened to, we feel validated and cared for. Our children also need to be heard and understood. Considering their ideas and caring about their feelings are ways in which parents show they accept their children's perspectives. Taking the time to know how they think and feel leads to deeper understanding. This is the very essence of how children gain the confidence that culminates in self-esteem and good decision-making.

The following illustration demonstrates the supreme importance of listening. When eight-year-old Mario comes home because he has been hurt by his friend Reed, it is important for him to process his feelings with a parent who will listen and try to understand what he feels. This is not a time for the parent to question, scold, make suggestions to fix or repair the relationship, or insinuate that Mario was wrong; nor should the parent march to Reed's house to solve the dispute. Listening is especially helpful because it gives Mario a chance to express and deal with his feelings safely with someone who truly cares about him. Doing so provides a perspective that most likely will enable him to decide for himself how to handle the situation. In other words, listening in this situation allows Mario to become responsible for the relationship. Knowing that parents accept, understand, and support them gives children confidence in themselves. Given such assurance, they will be empowered to act appropriately.

Forgiveness

There are three main types of definitions of forgiveness (Shults and Sandage 2003). First, we can think of the legal aspects of forgiveness, as in eliminating a debt. Second, therapeutic forgiveness focuses on the psychological and relational benefits of going through a forgiveness process. The final definition of forgiveness is redemptive forgiveness, which emphasizes restoration and reconciliation as an outcome of forgiveness. In family relationships especially, there are many opportunities to practice the virtue of forgiveness. Forgiveness in families is redemptive in nature, not therapeutic, as covenant-keeping families empower and exude the grace of forgiveness. Forgiveness is a two-way process: neither parents nor children are perfect, and they all need forgiving when they make mistakes. Every day, we need to admit when we've offended or disappointed someone. Saying we forgive each other is living out grace and acceptance, which is rooted in unconditional loving.

Love You Forever, a wonderful children's book by Robert Munsch (1986), illustrates this kind of love. The boy in this story makes many mistakes throughout his growing years, infancy through adolescence. However, he is assured each night by his mother that he is loved unconditionally: "I'll love you forever; I'll like you for always!" This guarantee of always being accepted, no matter what he has done, gives him the confidence and incentive to love others in the same unconditional way. Such is the love we experience as God's children and ought to extend to our children.

Serving

Empowerment gives children the sense that their contribution to the family is valuable. The perspective that each family member serves and supports the others imparts a feeling of worth and esteem to children and adults alike. When children are expected and encouraged to participate in the functioning of the family, both emotionally and physically, they sense that the family is more than a group of separate individuals. They begin to see themselves as part of a larger system that is greater than all the individual members put together.

When children sense that they are an integral part of the family and that their input is esteemed, they are glad to cooperate and serve. Their contribution will be not only instrumental (doing chores) but also emotional (uplifting the family mood). They will help create family morale, identity, and unity.

Discipline

The Bible uses words such as *love* and *honor* to describe the ideal parent-child relationship. Various Old and New Testament passages also discuss the importance of guidance and correction, and these passages promise that good training will pay off because children will not depart from it. They learn from sound discipline and eventually become self-disciplined, responsible adults.

One helpful method of discipline is the concept of natural and logical consequences (discussed in chapter 6). This method is familiar to us because God dealt with the children of Israel in a similar way. God's people had to face the consequences of their choices and behaviors. There are consequences to be reckoned with when we disobey. The blessing of the covenant was conditional in that they reaped what they sowed (although God's gift of love and grace was unconditional). God has laid down laws such as the Ten Commandments to guide us in rightful living, which will bring meaning to our lives. God has our best interests in mind and knows what will bring fullness and peace and purpose.

In the same way, children learn best when they experience consequences for their behavior, especially if they realize that the rules are a product of their parents' love and concern for them. This is in contrast to training children primarily by punishing their negative behavior, an approach that puts all the responsibility on the parents—they alone make the decision to wield punitive power when they are displeased. It is more helpful for children to come to understand that their misbehavior has specific consequences and that the ultimate responsibility rests with them.

Take the example of five-year-old Alexis in a rocking chair. Rocking back and forth brings pleasure and joy, but if she rocks too hard or becomes too rambunctious, the chair falls over and she suffers the consequences of her action. This experience helps her monitor herself the next time she rocks in the chair. Children find their own limits through these consequences. As they self-correct and set appropriate boundaries for themselves, they are taking responsibility for their actions.

How should parents go about the business of setting up fair and reasonable rules (with logical consequences) to help their children learn limits and eventually become responsible for their own behavior? Children should be given a reasonable limit and told that a specific consequence will be applied if they go beyond that limit. For example, if Ming is given the task of taking the garbage out before dinner, he has a clear task and timeframe. When dinner comes and he has not remembered to take out the garbage, his place at the dinner table is not set (meaning no plates, utensils, cups, etc.). Of course, he will get dinner once he completes his task of throwing away the trash.

Notice how the consequence is logically related to the misbehavior and carried out in a clear and pleasant manner. There is no need for a verbal reprimand, which might well lead parent and child into a useless power struggle and sidetrack attention from the child's responsibility for the consequence. The main point is that the parent does not need to scold or punish but must see to it that the child becomes fully aware of the consequences of the behavior. Additionally, with a clear expectation and consequence, silence allows the child to own the problem and its solution. One important caveat is that the consequence needs to be something the parents can live with. For example, if it is challenging or uncomfortable for parents to withhold dinner until the task is completed, then this approach should be used with some other logical consequence. This allows the child to accept limits and eventually to achieve self-discipline.

Obviously, a crucial point is how the consequences are set up and carried out. The consequences should, of course, be appropriate to the child's age and maturity. Also, parents should not be unduly restrictive and punitive by making rules and regulations that seem unfair or unreasonable to the children. Remember that the certainty of the consequence is more important than the severity.

Here the idea of the family council comes into play. When children are old enough, they should be included in setting up the rules and the consequences of failing to keep them. The family decides together what are reasonable rules and expectations for everyone. It must be an equitable arrangement. For example, if the family rule is "no dishes are to be left in the sink after supper," then every family member must submit to the consequence. Therefore, if the father forgets, he, like any other family member, must wash the dishes the next morning.

When assigning chores, wise parents are flexible and listen to every family member. Perhaps someone is too fussy about how the beds are made, and another too careless in mowing the lawn. If folding laundry is assigned to a teenager, then clear expectations about how to fold the laundry should be provided. However, if a particular family member is too picky about how the laundry is folded, they should either take the chore on themselves or not complain or redo the folding after the teen completes it. Individuals need to complete their tasks to their ability and their preference. These matters need to be discussed together openly in the family council. This is the time and place to set up assignments that are age appropriate and fair. The family council provides an opportunity for children to learn the democratic principles of equality, freedom of speech, and fairness. All members should have input as to whether the emotional needs of the family are being met. Even the youngest child can point out that the family is not spending enough time together having fun and give suggestions for remedying the problem. Or the teenagers may need to point out that since they are older and can handle more independence, it is time to make some changes in policies.

The mode of discipline we have suggested entails personal empowerment. The ultimate goal is mutual empowerment among all family members. Of course, the onus of responsibility will initially be on the parents. They will need to take time with the family, listen to each member, and consider the uniqueness of each child. The parents must be willing to forgive and be forgiven, set an example by submitting to the same requirements asked of the others, and model love and caring behavior, fairness, and consistency. As modeled in the story of the prodigal son (Luke 15), wise parents allow a child the right to choose a behavior despite the consequence to be faced. They know when to step back and allow the consequence to do the correcting, as well as when to intervene to prevent a destructive consequence from exacting its toll.

These principles of the empowerment process involve serving and being served. They are built on a foundation of unconditional love and commitment, operate most successfully in an atmosphere of acceptance and forgiving grace, and result in intimacy through deep knowledge of and communication with one another. People who have been empowered have a competence and self-esteem they can share both in the family and with their community, society, and the world at large.

Once again, God's covenant serves as an analogy. Unconditional faithfulness and love form the foundation. Even though we deserve the consequence of our failure and sin, God offers grace and forgiveness when we fail to meet expectations. Moreover, God provides the Holy Spirit to encourage, empower, and enable us to live according to the law so that the blessing may be ours.

Finally, our hope of intimacy and relationship with the Almighty One renews and revitalizes us. As we grow in this circle of covenant, grace, empowerment, and intimacy, we experience a deeper and more intense level of God's love and of our love for one another. And so does the love within a family deepen as its members implement the empowerment process.

8

Family Spirituality

Nurturing Christian Beliefs, Morals, and Values

In traditional family systems, grandparents played a central role in the spiritual development of the young. The decline of an extended (three-generation) family system changed that, leaving the isolated nuclear family solely responsible for spiritual formation. For the most part, busy modern families have relinquished to other institutions (church and school) the responsibility of teaching moral beliefs and values to their children. Without question, social institutions play a vital role in inculcating values, yet parents are the ones who are directed to "train children in the right way" (Prov. 22:6). We believe spiritual formation begins in the home through everyday interaction practices and patterns of modeling that occur in day-to-day living.

The sometimes-conflicted understanding of education regarding values is described as *secondary socialization* by Peter Berger and Thomas Luckmann (1966). Berger and Luckmann describe how the family is the primary socialization context for children, meaning that children learn values and morals in the family. These values and morals are oriented toward filling important roles in the community. Secondary socialization occurs when children are sent to institutions like schools for education. In modern and postmodern cultures, education is highly valued and inculcates the morals of the dominant culture. Often these dominant values are at odds with the worldviews of families and communities.

The family is indispensable when it comes to building character. How parents live out their faith in the context of the family relationship has an

154

enormous impact. Ideas about how to facilitate this can be found in *Sacred Matters: Religion and Spirituality in Families* by Burr, Marks, and Day (2012).

In this chapter, we use the term *family spirituality* as an umbrella concept to refer to all the ways family members cultivate an understanding of biblical truth, moral beliefs, and values in children. Family spirituality forms the value, moral and ethical, and characterological core of one's identity. Moral values are based on underlying beliefs concerning right and wrong. Ideally, the internal formation of becoming Christlike is manifested in attitudes and behavior that are truly transformative. Although the word *faith* can refer to one's religion, we use it to refer to a personal relationship to God the Father, the Son, and the Holy Spirit. We begin this chapter with a discussion of moral and faith development, using trinitarian concepts as a model for family interaction, and we conclude with an examination of family spirituality as an essential aspect of faith communities.

Moral Development

Building on Piaget's assumption that children reason differently at different stages of development, Lawrence Kohlberg (1963) suggests that moral development is best understood in an analogous way (see table 5 in chap. 7 above). During early childhood, moral decisions are made in terms of *obedience and punishment*. The child obeys rules because to disobey results in punishment. The second stage of moral decision-making—*individualism and exchange*—is slightly refined as the child becomes aware of his or her own individual needs as well as the self-interests of every other family member. A sense of fairness accompanies this realization, and the child is motivated to make moral decisions that show impartiality to each person involved. The capacity to think more abstractly in early adolescence moves one toward the *interpersonal relationships* stage. During this third stage, personal intentions and character traits are taken into consideration in terms of how they affect the relationship when one makes decisions. The fourth stage of moral development involves *maintaining social order*. Now a person comprehends the more complex way that moral judgments maintain social order through laws and societal responsibility. This more abstract understanding emphasizes the fact that laws exist to serve a greater social order.

However, in the next stage—*social contract and individual rights*—the person recognizes that social order does not always equal societal goodness. Therefore, one searches for a criterion higher than the existing social order when making moral decisions. At this point, a person moves on to the highest level of moral reasoning—the *universal principles* stage. Here all people are valued equally, and therefore one bases moral judgment on the principle of the greatest good for the most people. This is known as utilitarianism.

It is clear that Kohlberg's major focus is the *form* of a person's moral reasoning, not the content. His model is epigenetic in that the sequence of moral development moves forward through these stages, never skipping a stage or reverting to an earlier stage. Although stages of moral development might approximate chronological age, Kohlberg acknowledges that it is possible to "get stuck" in a specific stage of moral development and never move forward. Therefore, he reasons, only a small minority reaches the more advanced stages of moral reasoning. This model has been criticized for neglecting the research findings that females tend to make moral decisions more from a personal context rather than simply in consideration of rights and justice. In light of this, some social scientists are interested in getting beyond a cognitive approach by looking at the importance of *moral identity*—one's self-identity as a morally responsible person.

The Handbook of Spiritual Development in Childhood and Adolescence (Roehlkepartain et al. 2005) proposes that moral identity is formed by social influence and most importantly through relationships with others. The authors insist that moral development is not merely a reflection of cognitive ability but primarily the result of a *personal relationship*. These personal relationships or identifications with moral exemplars—individuals who devote their lives to bettering society—form the basis of moral identity. Moral exemplars can be famous people, such as Mother Teresa or Martin Luther King Jr., or simply people who have forsaken personal ambitions to devote their lives to the good of others. The inspirational stories of moral exemplars tell of life-changing experiences, such as serving the poor, that have transformed them (Reimer 2003). While cognitive development is certainly an important dimension of moral decision-making, the role of moral identity has a profound personal impact on a person. Having a relationship with a person of strong moral character is a transformative experience in and of itself.

Therefore, we conclude that a holistic understanding of moral development includes content, cognitive reasoning, and relationships with moral exemplars. What is important for family spirituality is that values, norms, and rules be based on biblical truths and lived out in family relationships.

We would argue that family spirituality fosters what we earlier described as *differentiation in Christ* (DifC) (see "Differentiated Unity: Becoming One and Retaining Uniqueness" in chap. 4). DifC emphasizes that Christians' authentic identity comes from one's relationship to Christ. This identity base is the bedrock from which all behaviors and relationships are built. In other words, DifC forms the basis of identity- or values-based action. Core values and meaning-making are the center of one's identity. DifC provides the value-and-meaning system upon which one engages in value-based action. There will be more on this below.

Faith Development

In his classic work, James Fowler (1981) brings cognitive development theory to his "faith process" mode. He argues that faith is always relational. There is always someone to trust in or be loyal to. Faith, according to Fowler, is an *epistemological process*—a way of knowing. It is a covenantal relationship between an individual, or meaning-making community, and the transcendent Other. It is important to note that Fowler squarely relates the capacity to have faith to the bonding process between parent and child:

> In the interaction of parent and child not only does a bond of mutual trust and loyalty begin to develop, but already the child, albeit on a very basic level, senses the strange new environment as one that is either dependable and provident, or arbitrary and neglectful. Long before the child can sort out clearly the values and beliefs of the parents, he or she senses a structure of meaning and begins to form nascent images . . . of the centers of value and power that animate the parents' faith. As love, attachment, and dependence bind the new one into the family, he or she begins to form a disposition of shared trust and loyalty to (or through) the family's faith ethos. (1981, 16–17)

When parents model covenant love to their children, they expose them to a way of seeing and being in the world. Their provision of a safe, trustworthy environment allows the child to experience loyal and faithful connection, which opens up a meaningful structure for the child. Fowler understands faith as developing through six sequential stages. Infancy begins with *undifferentiated faith*, derived from the infant's initial experience of being sufficiently cared for by parents. The formation of secure or insecure attachments establishes the foundation on which faith is built (and is not counted as one of the six stages). The first stage, *intuitive-projective faith*, emerges during early childhood as language acquisition and emotional development allow a child to imagine through stories. Since logical thinking does not control imagination, reality and fantasy are indistinguishable during this stage. Children begin to form a conscious image of God. The *mythical-literal faith* stage emerges during middle and late childhood. As children begin to reason in a more logical and concrete manner, they can distinguish between fantasy and reality. Children's understanding of God is largely a projection from human characteristics they find present in "godly" characters in stories. Adolescence is characterized by a *synthetic-conventional faith* that allows children to integrate their abstract religious ideas and concepts into a coherent belief system. Developing a personal identity spurs teenagers to incorporate God into that identity, while an increasing capacity for intimacy in personal relationships leads to a desire for a personal relationship with God. Stage 4, *individuative-reflective faith*, emerges as the adolescent transitions into young adulthood. The process of anchoring faith within the self is often accompanied by examining and questioning the unexamined conventional, community-referenced faith of the previous stage. Individuative-reflective faith tends to be both consciously chosen and intellectually based.

Advanced chronological age is no guarantee that one has automatically moved to a new stage of faith. In fact, a majority of young adults do not advance to the *conjunctive faith* stage. During this fifth stage, the need for a rational, intellectually consistent faith is replaced by the acceptance of a faith that includes paradox, ambiguity, and mystery. The black-and-white certainty of the previous stage is replaced by the reality of gray areas.

At this time, one moves toward a deepening of one's relationship with God through spiritual disciplines and practices. It is a time when young people take up a clear devotion to God as their own personal quest rather than riding on their parents' coattails.

The highest developmental stage is *universalizing faith*, reached by few and then rarely before middle to late adulthood. Universalizing faith is characterized by a commitment to overcome division, violence, and oppression, and an ability to transcend specific belief systems. Fowler suggests that a quest for universal justice that moves beyond self-interest can be observed in the lives of people such as Mother Teresa, Martin Luther King Jr., and Mahatma Gandhi.

To summarize Fowler (1996), faith (1) is an integral, human process; (2) underlies the development of beliefs, values, and meanings; (3) provides coherence—a sense of sharing trust and loyalty with others; (4) grounds one's relationship to the ultimate; and (5) provides a coping mechanism for human finitude. This is incapsulated in Fowler's term *centers of value and power* (CVP), which form the basis of faith relationships. These CVPs are crucial in relating individuals with the transcendent other based on family and community relationships.

Although these specific stages of faith development are helpful markers, Fowler maintains that children enter the faith process through the relationships with their parents and primary caregivers, which are so persuasive. Children deprived of trusting and caring relationships are therefore hindered in the development of a mature and trusting relationship with God. The ability to experience God as a loving and trustworthy Parent is related to personal experiences of loving and trusting in and through family relationships. The Christian family plays a crucial role in the development of faith.

A Trinitarian Model of Family Spirituality

Using a trinitarian focus on relationality, we suggest that the core aspect of family spirituality centers on each family member achieving a *differentiated faith*. Differentiated faith in the context of family life is multilayered: first, each family member is differentiated (identity) in Christ; second, each member establishes spiritual differentiation in the context of the family; and third, a differentiated family spirituality develops, which serves as a unifying and transforming process in the life of each family member. This approach also connects and unifies the believer with the Christian community, which is ultimately the context for both the individual and family to flourish spiritually.

Differentiation in Christ

Differentiation in Christ refers to the New Testament emphasis on each believer finding his or her identity and reference in relationship with Christ rather than with other humans. Trusting in Christ's death on the cross for salvation and looking to the Holy Spirit for indwelling and transformation starts the process. DifC is based on being adopted into God's family: the words from Jesus's baptism—"You are my Son, the Beloved" (Mark 1:11)—are said over us when we are adopted into God's family through Christ's saving work. Surrendering one's will to the will of God places Christ at the center of each family member's identity. As the Spirit enters, this individual family member takes on a Christ-centered focus. The apostle John expresses it this way: "He must increase, but I must decrease" (John 3:30). Each family member's personal relationship to Christ and growth in the Spirit enhances family spirituality. Mutual commitment to spiritual transformation keeps family members consciously aware of how God is working in and through each of them and how it affects the family as a whole.

Spiritual Differentiation in the Family

The theological concept of *perichoresis* is based on the reciprocal *interiority* of the divine persons through mutually indwelling and permeating one another. Miroslav Volf (1998) writes that the "internal abiding and interpenetration of the Trinitarian persons . . . determines the character both of the divine persons and of their unity" (208). In a similar way, we suggest, the internal interdependence and mutual indwelling (interpenetration) of the spiritual lives of its members defines a family's spiritual character. Just as the members of the Godhead do not cease to be distinct persons in their unity, neither do family members cease to be distinct spiritual persons in the family. Volf further explains, "The distinctions between them are precisely the presupposition of that interiority, since persons who have dissolved into one another cannot exist in one another" (209). In other words, differentiation makes interiority and interdependency possible.

If family members absorb into one another spiritually, they cease to be distinct spiritual presences to one another. We call this *spiritual fusion*. When members dissolve into one another, they cannot offer unique spiritual perspectives. They relinquish their *uniqueness*, which is based on their personal relationship with Christ. At the other extreme, when the spirituality of family members has little or no mutual impact, spiritual interiority and interdependence are nonexistent. We might call this *spiritual cutoff*. When family members distance or cut off from one another spiritually, they cannot draw on the spiritual resources that could enrich their spiritual lives as a family. The relationship is sacrificed for a pseudo-individuality.

Spiritual differentiation means that each member is ultimately formed through a personal relationship with Christ and God's Spirit. The family supports and nurtures this spirituality, and the family encourages each member to cultivate spiritual meaning individually while maintaining relationships with one another and the local church. DifC means that one is personally called beloved of God and finds his or her identity in Christ and his family, the church. Second, this identity forms the foundation for relating to the family as well as the local church.

In spiritual fusion, the spiritual trials or doubts experienced by one member precipitate a crisis that threatens the faith of the whole family. Hardships necessarily bring questions about the faith to the forefront. These questions produce anxiety as they are perceived to threaten the family's Christian identity. Further, individuals are unable to express honest differences because members are overly invested in being of one mind on spiritual matters. Any expressed difference sends members into a reactive panic mode, and honest doubt and questions are interpreted as a personal affront to the family faith—an existential threat to the family's identity. Such a state of spiritual fusion puts all family members under duress, leading to shaming and judgmental tactics to bring the straying member back into the fold. It might be helpful to make a distinction between spiritual *overdependence* and spiritual *interdependence* among family members.

The opposite end of spiritual fusion is spiritual disconnection and indifference. In this case, a low level of differentiation in Christ leaves family members cut off from one another's spiritual lives. In spiritually cut off families, individual spiritual lives are kept private, as are most personal experiences. Spiritual joys and struggles are not shared, resulting in disconnection. The family misses out on the spiritual meaning that emerges when members openly express their beliefs and spiritual visions. What is needed is neither spiritual *independence* nor spiritual *dependence* but rather spiritual *interdependence*.

The spiritually differentiated family, in contrast to the spiritually fused or cutoff family, allows members to share their spiritual lives in a way that *expands* and *connects*. In other words, this type of differentiated spirituality is *transformative* (Shults and Sandage 2006). Family *relationships* become the means for growth because spiritual differences become a catalyst for spiritual differentiation. In a spiritually differentiated family, the personal faith of each family member can remain firm regardless of what is happening in the life of another member. At the same time, the doubts, struggles, and questioning experienced by one family member can serve as a catalyst for dialogue and personal self-examination before God for the others. Interest, concern, and support are given for the others' spiritual lives. Bringing resources to bear creates a beneficial balanced perspective.

This type of transformative spirituality (Shuts and Sandage 2006) reflects two of the main types of spiritual development. Shuts and Sandage focus on the two-step process of dwelling (togetherness) and seeking (individuality). Times of spiritual dwelling emphasize relationship-oriented activities like fellowship, worship, and connection. In the family, these practices are supportive and reinforce how the family identifies with the Christian story. Times of spiritual seeking are characterized by individuals increasing their knowledge of and relationship with Christ. This intensification aids the individual in making spirituality more personally meaningful. Often times, seeking facilitates isolation and "desert" experiences. Research suggests that individuals with higher levels of DifC tend to have more relational forms of spirituality (Frederick et al. 2016).

Family Spirituality and Sanctification

We believe that healthy spiritual differentiation within the family and among family members offers the greatest potential for a transforming experience. Because of the sheer magnitude of shared life experiences, no other human arena is as potentially powerful to form the inner spiritual life. In a parallel sense, there is no other human arena in which living a Christlike life is more difficult. In the family, we are more exposed than anywhere else, and it is nearly impossible to wear a mask in front of other family members or to fake a spiritual life. Individual spiritual growth is an ongoing and sometimes painful journey that takes place in the demands of actually living together as family. The family becomes a resilient vessel in which a spiritual metamorphosis occurs. Family relationships can become the catalyst for members to grow and to change in response to one another.

It should be noted that family tensions and conflicts can also be the catalysts for healthier forms of spiritual differentiation. Although not pleasant, family tensions and trials allow one to understand oneself more clearly and take responsibility for one's own growth. The family is a safe place where we can encounter others honestly and deal openly with spiritual differences and disappointments. However, if the family is an unsafe arena, spiritual stagnation will result.

Family members become acutely aware of their human frailties in the context of relating to one another. However, living out the biblical components of *unconditional love*, *grace*, *empowerment*, and *intimacy* offer the deepest possibility of being transformed into the image of Christ.

Dealing with Differences in Faith

In this section, we address the issue of diversity of faith commitments within a family. Although one should not assume that the lack of a common faith automatically negates the possibility of family spirituality, it certainly makes it more challenging. Differences in faith commitments can seriously limit family spirituality or place a family at a distinct disadvantage in this area. Under the conditions of diverse faith commitments, spiritual differentiation within a family becomes even more important. Since the adolescent is typically at a development stage in which she or he is trying to develop a personal faith, we use the family with an adolescent child to illustrate this point.

In a spiritually fused family, the teenage child must either conform to the family ideal or risk the dire consequence of fracturing the family's spiritual unity. Since spirituality is foundational to both the individual's identity and the family's, there is intense pressure to maintain this family identity, sometimes at the expense of individual identity. Spiritually fused families have lower thresholds for allowing members to think differently about issues of faith and spirituality, as thinking differently reflects divergent values and consequently a divergent identity. The unfortunate cost for such "spiritual unity" is that the adolescent does not form a personal faith and may be especially vulnerable when he or she leaves home.

We (Jack and Judy) remember when our fourteen-year-old daughter, Jacque, announced at the dinner table that she no longer believed in God. We gulped, tried to remain calm, and listened with interest to what she was saying. We asked questions to help her sort out her ideas. Instead of giving pat answers, we responded to her questions by sharing our beliefs. A few weeks later from our living room, we overheard a conversation Jacque was having with two of her high school–age friends on the front-porch swing. To our amazement, Jacque was reiterating some of our beliefs as well as expressing more clearly her personal belief in God. We realized others were challenging her faith, and she was searching for answers. Much of her questioning about religion during her teenage years was an attempt to make personal a faith she had learned from her parents and church. We were not always cool parents when our teens expressed doubts. Because it is difficult for us to tolerate our own anxiety, we can't help but bombard our children with what we think is correct theology. However, with Jacque we learned to trust in God to be at work in her and to be at work through others as well. We will always be thankful to the youth pastor and a sixty-year-old mentor from our church who allowed our son, Joel, to grapple with faith and ask honest questions without fear. This is how he finally came to a personal faith in Christ.

As we are working on this latest revision, there is intense angst as the COVID-19 pandemic continues to challenge our faith in God. Questions abound regarding the meaning and purpose of God allowing the pandemic to continue. My (Tom's) son Nathaniel is entering his senior year of high school and has felt this angst acutely. Our family has encouraged Nathaniel to develop his faith personally, and we have had many conversations about God's nature and purpose. For Nathaniel, like so many seniors in 2020 and 2021, missing one's friends and many important senior-year activities (especially graduation) looms large. We have adopted a listening approach; it is important for Nathaniel to have space to ask and process the questions, frustration, anger, and grief (anticipated and actual) caused by the pandemic. We are hoping that our relationship with Nathaniel, as well as his connection with God, will sustain him—and all of us—during this uncertain time.

Spiritual insecurity is likely to be at the heart of family spiritual fusion. Insecurity about spiritual differences tends to set up defiant and hostile attitudes toward other family members. Parents may be tempted to ridicule or put down their child's tender beliefs in their attempts to cajole or coerce their child to believe a certain way. Parents may even have a need to punish their wayward child for not conforming to what *they* need him or her to believe. Having a child who holds to a religious belief different from their own may cause them to feel defeated as Christian parents or to be apprehensive about their status in the church community when their children are not following the faith. These self-focused concerns diminish a genuine concern about their child's spiritual well-being.

At the opposite extreme, spiritually disengaged families take a "hands-off" approach in the name of respecting faith differences. Although such evasive tactics succeed in eliminating religious conflict (each family member can go his or her own independent way), they do little to enhance family spirituality. Consciously ignoring the spiritual differences, doubts, questioning, and struggles of other family members renders them "ships passing in the night." Compartmentalizing spiritual dimensions may prevent spiritual conflicts, but it also stifles sharing spiritual joy and meaning as a family unit.

When there is a high level of family spiritual differentiation, children can share spiritual and faith questions with their parents, free of the fear of being rejected. Of course, it is always disheartening when your child seems to reject God. Yet knowing that your children can honestly come to you with doubts and questions means that they are secure in your love. This gives you the best of all possibilities to be with them in their journey of faith.

Family Spirituality Embedded in Supportive Community

Although a family may be able to survive on its own spiritually, we believe it will never thrive without a supportive community. Stanley Hauerwas (1981, 283) describes the church as the *first family* of every Christian by pointing out that we learn "fidelity and love in a community that is sustained by a faithful God." When the family stands alone, it is difficult for it to withstand the onslaught of spiritual distortions from a secular society.

The relationality exemplified in the Holy Trinity is a model for congregational life as well as the family. Identity in Christ, or differentiation in Christ, at the congregational level means there is a healthy degree of *connectedness* as well as a healthy degree of *separation*. Permeable boundaries show respect for individual, couple, and family needs as all people participate in the life of the church. All voices are respected and decisions are made in the best interest of the whole body. This community lives out themes of reconciliation, transformation, restoration, and spreading peace and justice. In other words, the church that is differentiated in Christ embodies the kingdom or reign of God.

A faith community must be invested in the spiritual maturity of all believers (1 Cor. 12:7–12). Baptized by one Spirit into one body, members acknowledge their interdependency and mutual submissiveness (Eph. 5:21). When one stumbles, everyone is affected, just as the healing of one brings blessing to the entire congregation. The community calls members to accountability for destructive patterns of relating and empowers them through care and challenge. The church is a place where a family's differentiated faith is nourished and preserved. It supports the making and keeping of the family members' covenant commitments to one another. Through its multiple resources, the church supports the family's growth through instruction and enrichment opportunities. Colossians 3:12–15 provides a model: "As God's chosen ones, holy and beloved, clothe yourselves with compassion, kindness, humility, meekness, and patience. Bear with one another and, if anyone has a complaint against another, forgive each other; just as the Lord has forgiven you, so you also must forgive. Above all, clothe yourselves with love, which binds everything together in perfect harmony. And let the peace of Christ rule in your hearts, to which indeed you were called in the one body. And be thankful."

The deep undertone of hyperindividualism in modern society is an enormous barrier to faith. It is nearly impossible to hold on to community values in a society that promotes the "I" and the "me" over the "we" and the "us." In fact, community words such as *cohumanity*, *reciprocity*, *interdependence*, and *mutuality* are undervalued and rarely used. This self-focused mentality goes against the Christian ideal of forsaking self for the sake of other. This in itself is a compelling reason for families to join a community of faith that upholds biblical principles. We need all the help we can get to be God-centered and relationship-centered. Being part of a Christian community of care is not just a wise thing to do; it is a necessary spiritual discipline.

Family Spirituality as a Process

The foundational element of family spirituality is covenantal love, which responds to shortcomings with grace and uses personal gifts and strengths for mutual empowerment, resulting in intimate relationships. Family spirituality is not a static state to be achieved but a relational process to be lived out.

In introducing the model of family relationality, we stressed that such a form should be found not only inwardly but also outwardly. As family members are called to love unconditionally, forgive, and empower one another in moving toward greater intimacy, so they are called to do the same with those outside the family. The greatest evidence of strong family spirituality can be seen in the way families reach out to minister to the needs of others.

Family spirituality is an evolving process that corresponds to the major developmental issues of living together as a family. The early stages of marriage establish the foundational spiritual practices. With the arrival of children, family life re-centers around and immerses in teaching and modeling faith. When children become teenagers, parents and children negotiate the meaning of an independent faith. After grown children leave home, both those children and the parents redefine what it means to relate as adult to adult and honor one another's spiritual beliefs. Later in life, a couple's faith extends to grandparenting and elder-care roles, while in the last stage of family life, the finality of death is faced in light of one's faith. At each stage of family life, the potential for individual spiritual growth or stagnation reflects the health of family spirituality and the nature of its corresponding relationality.

The relationship between Jesus and his Father serves as a model. Jesus proclaims in John 17:22–23, "The glory that you have given me I have given them, so that they may be one, as we are one, I in them and you in me, that they may become completely one, so that the world may know that you have sent me and have loved them even as you have loved me." God's desire for family life is for Christ to indwell each family member so that his or her unique spiritual gifts mutually serve and empower the other members. Christ, the cornerstone of faith, is the grounding force that permeates family relationships and the life of the family with sacred meaning.

In anticipation of his death on the cross, Jesus offers us a glimpse of the spiritual differentiation between the Father and the Son. In his time of greatest spiritual anguish, Jesus tells his disciples, "I am deeply grieved, even to death; remain here, and stay awake with me" (Matt. 26:38). He reprimands them for falling asleep rather than joining him in prayer. In his humanity, Jesus seeks comfort and support from his disciples. After they fail him, Jesus prays, "My Father, if it is possible, let this cup pass from me" (v. 39). Jesus faces the anguish of being torn to the breaking point. He desperately wants to be relieved of the upcoming suffering but also agonizes about being separated from his Father in death. But in the intimate connection of prayer and assurance of his Father's love, he willingly submits: "Yet not what I want but what you want" (v. 39).

The text reveals that the Son and the Father have individual wills. Yet the Son's desire is that his will be one with the Father's will. Does the Father feel the anguish and the "sorrow unto death" of the Son? We have no doubt that he does. In a fatherly sense, he is very present through his love and certainly dies with Jesus in that love. However, it is the Son, not the Father, who physically dies on the cross. In a spiritual sense, the Father is there for the Son without depriving the Son of his spiritual purpose. And in the end, after the resurrection, Christ is fully transformed as he becomes one with God. Here we have a glimpse of the differentiated spiritual unity between God the Father and God the Son that can be a model for spiritual differentiation in human family relationships.

9

Adolescence and Midlife

Challenging Changes

The greatest conflicts within the family are likely to occur when children are in their adolescence. One reason is that at the very time children are in the difficult period of adolescence, their parents are likely to be reaching midlife. Research on adult development has shown that reaching midlife is often a time of crisis for adults (Sneed et al. 2012). Thus, the conflict that frequently occurs during the strain of adolescence must be viewed in light of the parental strain as well. Both parents and adolescents are experiencing significant developmental transitions individually, which adds potential stress for the family.

A systemic approach helps us understand the interactive effect of these transitions: adolescent stress does not just add to parental midlife stress—it multiplies it. Further, midlife challenges affect and are constantly affected by adolescent changes. These transitions influence one another, either magnifying conflicts or dampening them. Whenever two or more family members are going through a period of personal crisis simultaneously, the potential for conflict increases exponentially. It is also true that some conflicts with a particular teen may elicit more difficulty than others.

This chapter presents the stressful challenges of adolescence and midlife separately and then considers the special problems that arise when they happen concurrently. We begin with an examination of the factors contributing to the rise of adolescent and midlife strain in our society. "What's the big deal?" the reader may be asking. "People pass through adolescence and midlife in every society. Why make such an issue about them?" But this is not, in fact, the case. True, people in every society pass through the chronological ages corresponding to adolescence and midlife, but these are not distinct stages of life in most societies. We will attempt to explain why our society seems to produce more adolescent and midlife strain than most others.

Adolescence

The Origin of the Adolescent Stage

Western societies initially possessed the cultural equivalent of puberty rites, which marked the transition from childhood to adulthood. Prior to the Industrial Revolution, youth learned to farm or acquired a trade by developing skills through the apprenticeship system. As they both lived with and worked under the watchful eye of the master craftsman, apprentices occupied clear-cut positions. Once the skills were mastered, one was ready for adulthood and marriage. Mastering the skills of one's future trade was the rite of passage into adulthood.

Urbanization and industrialization brought about a slower and more ambiguous passage into adulthood. With the development of factories, the apprenticeship system declined. Factory work did not require a high degree of skill, so youth could begin working independently at an early age. Children began to leave their homes to work in urban factories. Because of the extremely low pay, most of them lived in slum apartments. Alienated from the rest of society, they increasingly became a problem to society. Because these adolescents were disenfranchised from adult life, an adolescent culture emerged.

What in the beginning included just a few urban youth for a brief period of their lives has grown to include virtually all young people in our society. The period in view—the gap between childhood and adulthood, which we call *adolescence*—has also expanded. There are several reasons for this phenomenon. First, as our society has become increasingly technologically oriented, more jobs have been created at the highly skilled level and fewer at the lower level. Thus, young people must continue their education and delay their entrance into the full-time workforce, which would normally award them adult status.

Second, one of the effects of the Industrial Revolution has been the development of the separate spheres of home and work life. The upshot is that home is a place of refuge, relaxation, and enjoyment, where work is a place of toil, difficulty, and challenge. As children are prevented from entering the work sphere until they have sufficient skills and education, adolescence has expanded. This is changing to a certain extent, as technology has been eroding the clear boundaries between work and family life. In some respects, technology (social media, for example) has allowed individuals to be more connected with the world and peers; but it has also increased loneliness, depression, and isolation (Woods and Scott 2016).

Third, the extended family has been replaced by the nuclear family because of high mobility. The nuclear family is a small, fragile unit, isolated from relatives who could provide resources and give young people a sense of stability and belonging. In many families, divorce, separation, or the need for parents to work long hours in the marketplace further complicate the situation. In the present day, nuclear families outsource to churches, agencies, and the local community many needs that extended families once met.

A fourth factor contributing to the expansion of adolescence is the affluence of youth in Western societies today. Either because they earn their own money or because their parents give them money, many young people possess a degree of independence not experienced by any previous generation. The greater independence of youth today goes hand-in-hand with a loss of parental and societal control.

Although these factors did not produce adolescence, they have been instrumental in furthering it. Adolescence came about because social structures developed that slow the movement of youth toward adult status. Concomitant with this arrested development is a lack of meaning in the lives of young people today. Locked out of adulthood, they find their lives void of the meaning that is a part of adult roles. From this vantage, the creation of adolescent subcultures can best be understood.

Adulthood is generally marked by marriage (or having a stable, committed relationship), the end of occupational training, childbearing and rearing, gainful employment, and home ownership (see Townsend 2002 for an excellent discussion of the effect of these markers on gender identity), and adolescence is supposed to equip individuals to attain those markers. Because these markers are increasingly difficult to attain, adolescence has been stretching beyond the traditional end point of eighteen years old and into the mid to late twenties (Kail and Cavanaugh 2017).

There is evidence that, because of a combination of biological and social factors, adolescence is beginning earlier and lasting longer, resulting in the identification of an emerging adulthood stage between adolescence and young adulthood (Kail and Kavanaugh 2017). Formal attempts to define the beginning of adulthood in contemporary society do very little to dispel this confusion. For example, the legal age at which one may marry varies from state to state. In terms of voting privileges and military service, an eighteen-year-old is judged to be an adult. In most states, a young adult is permitted to drive at sixteen and legally allowed to drink alcohol at age twenty-one. It is enlightening to note the age at which a person is regarded as an adult when financial profit is involved. Movie theaters, airlines, and most public establishments that require an admission fee consider a twelve-year-old to be an adult. Teenagers are asked to pay adult prices but are told to wait until they are older to receive adult privileges.

To grow up in the United States can be a free-form experience. Adolescence can be compared to a jam session in which experienced jazz musicians play without a score. They simply improvise as they go along, relying on their skills and experience as musicians to feel the ebb and flow of the music. Unfortunately, being a teen or parenting a teen usually means having little experience or expertise in navigating the crescendo and diminuendo of the sometimes-turbulent improvisation. Unlike the master jazz musician, adolescents follow no clear cultural norms. This explains the rapid change in adolescent fashion and style, whether it be clothes, hairdos, or language.

Adolescence as an Identity Crisis

Although adolescence can be explained as resulting from the social and economic conditions of Western cultures, its effect is most profound at the individual level, where it is often experienced as an identity crisis. This identity crisis is the most important feature of the psycho-social development of adolescents (Erikson 1980, 1997). Our discussion of adolescent stress needs to be tempered by the fact that the media are quick to report on all that is wrong with adolescents but rarely give positive examples illustrating the good things adolescents do (Damon 2004). The popular depiction of adolescence focuses primarily on teenage risk-taking and other negative stereotypes of this life stage.

The creation of an adolescent subculture is an attempt to establish identity. One learns from peer groups what to wear, what music to listen to, what movies to see, what language is "in," and so on. The greater the adolescent's insecurity, the greater the slavish obedience to doing all the right things sanctioned by the peer group.

During the process of differentiation and identity formation, the adolescent is often caught between the family and the peer group. We might think of the family and the peer group as being alternative gravitational forces around which teenagers are orbiting satellites. Young children orbit quite closely around their family, but the orbit becomes wider and wider as the children grow older. As they approach their teenage years, they are increasingly drawn by the alternative gravitational pull of their peer group. As the pull from the peer group intensifies, they sometimes retreat from the family and reorient themselves around the peer group. Parents know quite well when this has happened because their teens usually give more weight to the opinions of their peers than to those of their parents.

The generation gap can be understood as the result of the identity crisis faced by most adolescents. An important aspect of identity development for teens and young adults is technology. As teens communicate more and more online via social media such as Instagram, Facebook, and TikTok, social pressure, almost instantaneous feedback, and pictures and video form the context for identity. We can see distinct changes in the ways in which personal pictures reflect increasing confidence, scope (through sharing), intimacy, and intentionality (Yang and Brown 2016). Social media's role in teen and emerging-adult identity formation is both a positive in that geographical distance is overcome and also a negative, as feedback can be very harsh and overwhelming. Research has identified a strong connection between social media use and depressive symptoms (Nesi and Prinstein 2015). The increasing role of social media has added a dimension to adolescence that many parents are unable to understand. When a teen can receive a million likes and severely negative feedback in the span of a few minutes in his or her own bedroom, caregivers can be at a loss to understand the sometimes-positive and sometimes-negative effects of social media on the teen.

Midlife

Adults continue to pass through individual stages of development throughout their lifetimes. One of the most widely recognized stages is the onset of midlife, used to describe the feeling of not being able to keep up with the vast changes of the postmodern world. The rapidity of social and technological changes tends to shock each new generation. Personal adaptations can reach crisis proportions when we are not prepared for the future.

Technology has had a profound effect on adults in the workforce. Younger workers tend to adopt technology based on their perceptions of how the technology will assist them in accomplishing their tasks. Older workers rely on workplace social norms and the subjective experience of exerting control over the use of the technology (Morris and Venkatesh 2000). Adults in the labor force are especially vulnerable when they realize that the jobs they are trained to do and have been doing for most of their adult lives are becoming obsolete due to the introduction of new technology that boosts productivity. Automobile workers quite understandably experience a crisis when they realize that robots can do much of their work. A similar anxiety plagues managers and other people in the business world. They fear being overtaken by younger, better-trained college graduates, especially in the computer age.

Midlife transition may also be a crisis for people who begin to realize that they will not reach the lofty goals they set years before, goals that represent self-esteem. Erik Erikson (1980, 1997) describes the longest period of one's development as the *generativity versus stagnation stage*. As individuals begin to reflect on their contributions, they invest in caring for their current relationships and work-related developments. Individuals in this stage develop and cultivate the life they have been creating thus far—at work and at home. That is, individuals experience *generativity* by enhancing their relationships with family and further cultivating or growing the tasks and projects they have built. *Care*, as the resulting virtue of this stage, emphasizes the commitment and concern one has in establishing and developing what has been generated. Capps (2008, 126) explains: "Generativity involves an expansion of one's personal interests and emotional attachments to include that which has been generated (conceived, originated, produced, etc.) while stagnation suggests either that nothing has been generated or that, once generated, nothing is being done to insure its survival, growth, or development." This means that individuals make or renew commitments to the investments they have made, whether it be to work, family, friends, or the community. This is known as stewardship from the Christian perspective. Individuals experiencing generativity express care for their contributions to the world. Generativity is achieved when individuals exercise stewardship over their creations.

On the negative side of generativity versus stagnation, individuals experience depletion or emptiness over the lack of meaningful contributions at work and home. In an extreme case, this could result in burnout, but usually individuals begin to lose the sense that work is meaningful and they become increasingly lethargic (Frederick, Dunbar, and Thai 2018). Still others who have worked long, hard hours at their jobs reach midlife only to realize that they have spent little time with their children, who are now nearly grown, and have had little actual influence over them. Some of these hardworking people find that when they do want to relax with their families, they are unable to do so. The crisis in this case is that one has become a slave to work and career.

In his study of career-oriented men, Daniel Levinson (1978) has identified four polarities of midlife transition:

1. *Youth/Age*. Many men in midlife occupy a marginal status: they feel past their youth but are not ready to join the rocking-chair set. They attempt

to appear young by the way they dress or to improve their physique by running or lifting weights.

2. *Destruction/Creation*. Having experienced conflict on the job and being battle scarred and hurt by others, men in midlife may resort to the same tactics. They are aware of the death of friends their age, but at the same time they have a strong desire to be creative as they enter what often proves to be the most productive years of life.

3. *Masculinity/Femininity*. Concern over a physically sagging body is coupled with a desire to become more nurturing.

4. *Attachment/Separateness*. A continued need for bonding with others is balanced by a need to prove that one can get by alone.

Levinson believes that although these polarities exist throughout the entire life cycle, they are accentuated during transition periods. Men who have dealt with these polarities throughout their lives, having met minor crises on a regular basis, do not experience the midlife transition as a crisis period. By contrast, men who have not dealt with them are candidates for a major midlife crisis.

Although much of this is also true of women, Levinson (1996) suggests an important gender difference. For women, midlife transition is less pronounced than for men. This is especially true for women not employed outside the home. Women employed outside the home engage in *gender splitting*, simultaneously holding dichotomous identities. Four common types of gender splitting are *domestic/public*, *homemaker/provider*, *women's work/men's work*, and *femininity/masculinity in individual psyche*. Most of these splits in identity involve women wanting to uphold a traditional view of marriage while also holding an nontraditional view that allows for more independence and equality with men when participating in the public world.

For the woman whose only role has been mother and wife, midlife may be traumatic for other reasons. She may feel her role is being phased out—her maturing children have less need of her, and her husband may no longer appreciate what she is doing in the home. For the woman whose whole identity and self-esteem are based on being a supermother and a superwife, this can be a devastating blow.

Parent-Adolescent Relationships

Having considered the stressful aspects of adolescence and midlife, we are now in a position to consider the interaction between them. To begin with,

173

it should be noted that a family with adolescents is likely to have a double inferiority complex when parent and teen have an insecure identity. This will have an enormous impact on the parent-adolescent relationship.

While the major task during this stage of development concerns identity formation, the following relationship tasks are needed (McGoldrick, Garcia Petro, and Carter 2016):

1. Shifting parent-child relationships to permit adolescents to move into and out of the family system. In other words, adolescents spend more and more time outside the parents' sphere of influence. As a result, adolescents begin to create new relationship and authority networks that may contradict the parents. Parents and adolescents need to negotiate and communicate about these relationship networks that extend outside the family of origin.
2. Refocusing on midlife marital and career issues
3. Beginning the shift toward caring for the older generation

As adolescents gain competence, they expect more and more freedom and responsibility. The family system needs to accommodate the teen entering and exiting the family and engaging with the community as a peer. Further, the teen's growing competence and autonomy allow for parents to reengage as spouses rather than just as coparents. Finally, there is an increasing shift on the part of the parents to care for their own parents. Parents who are confident in themselves do well in making these transitions.

Parents are a source of stability when they encourage these changes as a natural part of their adolescent developing a mature self. Parents in the midst of their own identity crises, however, may not be as understanding or psychologically prepared for the changes. They may personalize the problems and feel angry, rejected, or overwhelmed. In reaction, they may place unnecessary restrictions on their teenagers and dampen the teens' ability to find their own way. It only complicates matters when personal needs in both cases put inordinate strain on the relationship.

One of the factors in parent-adolescent conflicts may be that the parent in midlife and the adolescent are experiencing contrasting physical changes. At a time when the adolescent is developing the physical characteristics of adulthood, the parents are beginning to lose theirs.

There are a variety of other reasons for parent-adolescent conflict. Lack of connection and intimacy between parent and teen is a cause of conflict, especially when interpersonal boundaries are tested. The disagreement peaks in mid-adolescence, around the age of 18, then becomes less intense when realignment occurs in the relationship. This transition occurs when parents and adolescents are able to develop more peer-to-peer type relationships. The teen's sense of identity is supported, and the relationship with the parent is maintained, especially in times of disagreement. The parents emotionally support the teen, and the teen is increasingly responsible for his or her emotional and physical needs. Interestingly, parents tend to view the relationship as more positive and the conflicts as less severe than do the adolescents. The relationships parents maintain with their teens have important consequences for their future relationship. Interestingly, research suggests that teens with more cohesive relationships with their mothers tend to live in closer proximity to the parents, especially in early adulthood (Gillespie and Treas 2017).

Parental Stimuli of Adolescent Rebellion

Sociocultural factors often escalate adolescent strain and rebellion. But while these factors help explain the emergence of adolescence as a general phenomenon in societies around the world, they do not entirely explain why some adolescents go through a period of rebellion and others do not. Evidence suggests that parenting style and structural components within the family contribute to adolescent rebellion (Sogar 2017).

Unwise Child-Rearing Practices

In chapter 6, we compared the effects of four socio-emotional parenting styles. Parenting styles are not directly associated with academic achievement (Pinquart 2016). Parenting styles subtly and indirectly influence academic outcomes. Authoritarian parenting styles are associated with more emotional and behavioral problems and less prosocial behaviors (Kuppens and Ceulemans 2019). Authoritative parenting styles, on the other hand, are associated with fewer behavioral and emotional problems and more prosocial behaviors.

The relationship between parental restrictiveness and adolescent rebellion is far from simple. Adolescent rebellion is highest in very permissive and very restrictive homes, and lowest in homes with a balanced approach to discipline. This may be related to the important task of differentiation. Adolescents are challenged to develop a self in relation—that is, establish a separate self (attitudes, beliefs, and values) while remaining connected with their family. Finding and asserting a clearly defined self is critically important because it is the only way one learns to establish a genuine relationship with parents and others. When an adolescent feels confident as a separate self, he or she has a new capacity to interact in meaningful ways with others.

An example may be helpful here. One of my (Tom's) client families came to me with a "teen defiance" problem. This African American family consisted of a mom, dad, and their only son—a teenager who was sixteen years old at the time they came in for family therapy. The defiance problem concerned identity and membership in the family. The family's identity or core-self consisted in valuing membership in the military as the primary way to serve the public. It was important to their identities as African Americans, as well as being a military family, that their son also follow in their footsteps. For this family, there were generations of elders that sacrificed for the country via military service. As sixteen-year-olds tend to do, the teen began to question whether he wanted to go into the military. The parents, who were highly educated and had spent significant time in the military, were taken aback. They experienced their son's identity question as a challenge to their own identity. Could their son not go into the military and still be part of the family? They immediately became defensive and angry. In my time alone with the teen in therapy, we discussed the meaning of his questioning and how it related to him being a member of the family. In other words, he was questioning his desire to be in the military and if that meant he could no longer be a member of his family. The teen only wanted to investigate and decide whether going into the military was important for him personally. He did not mean to question his parents' ideals or identity. The parents, son, and I were eventually able to have these important identity conversations in a nonreactive, emotionally neutral manner. The teen eventually decided to prioritize going into the military, but he had to do so of his own volition.

In terms of differentiation, the core self of the family needs to be internalized intentionally on the part of the children. This means that they are choosing to adopt the family's values and identity. In families with lower levels of differentiation, identity is either forced onto the children through compliance (restrictive parenting practices) and emotional fusion, or identity is diffused through cutoff and emotional distance (permissive parenting styles).

Ideally, the child moves from complete dependence on the parents to semi-dependence to relative independence and eventually interdependence. The change from dependence to independence tends to proceed smoothly if the parents are moderate in their disciplinary practices. Although younger children seem to thrive on structure, when they become teenagers, they need far more breathing space. If parents continue to be very restrictive, adolescents are likely to rebel out of frustration. Overly restrictive parents hold the reins too tightly and do not allow for a gradual development of self. This creates a situation where independence can be achieved only by a drastic break from the parents. Restrictive parenting fails to provide enough structure/support in the child's process of developing a self. Children in such families may become frustrated or aggressive toward their parents and society in general, acting out in rebellious behavior. Maintaining a good balance of staying connected while supporting differentiation is the goal.

UNSATISFACTORY DIVISION OF PARENTAL AUTHORITY

It is no secret that there is currently much controversy about the best authority pattern in the home. Studies show that the incidence of rebellion tends to be high in homes where either the father or the mother is dominant, moderate where the parents share equal authority, and low where one parent has slightly more authority. We believe that extreme inequality in parental authority results in a state of confusion for the teen. When authority is perceived as being primarily in the hands of one parent, the child may have problems interacting with both parents as authority figures.

Identity development in adolescence can create anxiety among family members as they feel that the family's identity is threatened by the questions the teen is expressing. Confusion may result if the child is not sure where the ultimate authority resides or tries to pit one parent against the other. Power imbalances tend to foster increasing use of triangulation in relationships between the parents and offspring, which indicates a lower level of differentiation (Titelman 2007).

This is why parents need to agree about discipline and stand together as a united front. It is best when teens are crystal clear about their parents being the coleaders in the home. The balance of parental power means that parents consult each other about final outcomes. When both mother and father are actively involved in coparenting, trust is established as they love, discipline, guide, teach, nurture, and empower their children. The key is that parents work in tandem.

Empowering Adolescent Children

Although they may not realize it at the time, parents play an extremely important role in the lives of their teenagers. Parent-adolescent conflict is associated with negative outcomes like emotional and behavioral problems for adolescents (Ehrich, Dykas, and Cassidy 2012). Pamela King and James Furrow (2004) found that young people having a strong sense of shared beliefs, values, and goals with their parents is related to their being altruistic and empathetic toward others. Supportive and encouraging relationships between parents and teens promote empathy and altruism. Positive effects were found for such parental monitoring as setting clear boundaries, establishing clear expectations, and being aware of when their teens left and returned home. Pamela King and Ross Mueller (2004) found that parents significantly influenced their teenager's religiosity.

Delegating responsibility is a challenging task for parents. Fostering teen responsibility is an important aspect of the teen and parents' relationship. To trust one's teenager to make the right choices and to act responsibly is perhaps one of the hardest things a parent is asked to do. It's important to let go as well as to stand firm with teenagers until they reach their full adult status.

Adolescent empowerment depends on parents giving responsibility and adolescents acting responsibly. Adults are an often-overlooked source of empowerment for adolescents. In fact, there may be times of emotional turmoil in the parent-teen relationship when another adult can be more influential than the parents. King and Furrow (2004) found that formal mentoring relationships and informal school, neighborhood, or church relationships are most effective when the relationship between adult and teen is positive and trustful, with open communication and a shared sense of values. Again, adults most positively influence teens when they provide a balance between accountability and guidance on the one hand, and encouragement and affirmation on the other.

Undoubtedly, mistakes will be part of the learning process. But the empowerment process will be most successful, we believe, in parent-child relationships based on covenant commitments. The true test of unconditional parental love occurs when the child reaches adolescence. Where unconditional love prevails, the family lives in an atmosphere of grace. Where there is grace, there is room for failure and the assurance that one will be forgiven and afforded the opportunity to try again. Our teens need to feel our deep affirmation of who they are and acknowledgement of their unique gifts and purpose. This deepens the intimacy between young people and their parents and makes mutual empowerment possible.

10

The Joys and Challenges
of Family in Later Life

Families in *later life* are those that have passed beyond the child-rearing years. The typical parent whose children are in their twenties or thirties can expect to live one-third of his or her life in this particular family life stage. Because of the increase in life expectancy, this stage can last several decades. Many find this time of life an awesome, complex, and arduous journey, especially when there are three or even four generations of family members with which to deal.

The "sandwich generation" describes those "mid-life adults who simultaneously raise dependent children and care for frail elder parents" (Grundy and Henretta 2006). Around the age of fifty, people who are at the peak of their earning capabilities may find it necessary to provide emotional and economic support to both young adult and elderly family members. The responsibility of caring for parents and/or adult children can come as quite a shock, especially after looking forward to a time of freedom to enjoy the fruit of one's active years of labor and raising children. Hoping for a breather after adult children have finally left home, fifty-year-olds may find it burdensome to meet the increasing needs of their adult children and elderly parents. A study of job burnout and couple burnout in dual-earner couples in the sandwich generation revealed "significant differences in burnout type (job burnout higher than couple burnout); gender (wives more burned out than husbands); and country (Americans more burned out than Israelis)" (Pines et al. 2011, 361).

On the positive side, although the phenomenon of living longer results in greater complexity in family relationships, it also opens up the possibility of increased cross-generational family interaction, support, and connection. In this chapter, we describe three separate stages of later life: launching, post-launching, and retirement. We will clarify the unique aspects and typical dynamics of each of these stages.

The Launching Stage

The launching stage is the period when adult children leave home to establish an independent life outside the family. Tasks to be accomplished by the young adult include (1) achieving autonomy in caring for oneself, managing finances, and being a responsible citizen; (2) developing meaningful relationships and support systems; and (3) finding a personal purpose and spiritual meaning in life. If all goes well, young adults prove able to manage their own lives effectively, think and act on their own behalf, take responsibility for their choices, and accept the consequences of their decisions. Other indicators of maturity are the establishment of relationships within and outside the family that lead to mutual interdependence and respect and settling into a career and lifestyle that give personal meaning and satisfaction.

In chapter 7 we noted Erik Erikson's thesis that identity and intimacy are key developmental goals to be achieved by young adults on their way to maturity. Subsequent research has shown that while this sequence (identity then intimacy) holds true for males, the reverse (intimacy then identity) holds true for females. During adolescence, males are more likely to be members of an identifiable peer group, while females are more likely to have made a few close friends. For males, one's rank in the peer group helps to form personal identity; while for females, the emotional bonding and communication between close friends develop intimacy. As a result of these differences during adolescence, the average male enters young adulthood with a firmer sense of identity, while the female has more fully developed intimacy skills. This difference explains why, among those who marry young, husbands struggle more with achieving intimacy and wives with identity. Working on those areas in which one is deficient is essential for young adults at the launching stage.

Adulthood is defined in most cultures as the time when people are held accountable for their behavior in society. It must be remembered that each culture, with its particular beliefs, traditions, and values, determines the pace of the launching period. We must not judge all families by the Western ideal but respect how each unique culture helps its young adults reach the point of accountability. Many circumstances influence the launching of each individual young adult, so we must pay attention to cultural diversity as well as individual differences and oscillations throughout the process from dependence to independence and eventually to mature interdependence.

In chapter 9 we identified some of the normal tensions that arise when parents are grappling with midlife issues just as their children enter adolescence. How well the launching goes is in large measure determined by how well parents and adolescents have addressed and resolved these tensions. We might speak of a *smooth launch* when the adult child who has left home orbits around the family at a safe distance; good connections are maintained, and there are mutually gratifying touchdowns. In a *recalled launch*, everyone seems prepared and ready for the big day, yet complex family circumstances prevent the adolescent from actually getting off the ground. More time is needed to make necessary repairs or to right wrongs before a successful launch can be accomplished. Sometimes there is clearly a blastoff, fueled by anger and dissension, which propels the young adult to a distance beyond the gravitational pull of the family. In such cases, the premature cutoff leaves young adults floundering without support, and it is not surprising that they come crashing back, often having an impact on everyone in their path. Thus, there are sad and incomplete leavings, just as there are happy and satisfying leavings. Perhaps one of the most reliable predictors of the chances for a successful launch is the level of differentiation a youth has achieved while in the home.

There may also be times of renesting, when adult children return home to cohabit with parents due to educational circumstances, financial hardship, or partner breakup (such as death or divorce). Renesting requires that adult children and parents renegotiate their relationship and the accompanying rules of cohabitation. This renegotiation should be based on adult, reciprocal relationships, and not based on parent-child relationships. Some specific aspects of this negotiation should be (1) rent or other renumeration for living in the parents' home, (2) dealing with grandchildren regarding rules and expectations for behavior, (3) the adult child having intimate partners visit, and (4) a plan for relaunching. None of these suggestions should be considered final, but the negotiations should be ongoing, as the reasons for renesting are often complex and multifaceted.

Differentiation is the process whereby an individual assumes his or her unique identity as separate from while remaining connected to the family. Those who approach the launching stage without a clear self-definition can be overly dependent or too cut off and disengaged from their parents. Without a solid, sufficient sense of self, they either pretend that they don't need anybody or they lack the confidence that they can succeed on their own. In contrast, differentiated young adults can assume interdependence in their relationships because they are both separate from yet stay meaningfully connected to their parents.

Transition Tasks

Successful transition through the launching stage is accomplished through four tasks. First, married parents must refocus on their marriage relationship. When the marriage is doing well, an adult child's leaving home unites rather than divides the parents. However, if unresolved issues have caused ongoing tension and disagreements, the marriage may be on shaky ground. If the couple has focused solely on the parenting role, whether through trials or delights, the loss of that role puts them at jeopardy. They may need to face each other and their relationship in new ways. This can lead to growth and a stronger marriage if the couple is able to refocus on their partnership. If not, there is little to keep the marriage vital, and it may disintegrate. Adult children feel the freedom to go forward with their own lives when they are assured their parents have a substantial marriage.

The second task is related to the first: parents and children need to learn to relate to each other as adults. Part of the letting go involves allowing the child to take on a new adult role. Respecting young adults and acknowledging their adult status can be a challenging task for parents. It is especially problematic for parent-child relationships based on authoritarian practices; affirmation of the child's adulthood is more difficult for controlling parents. Easing into an adult-adult relationship is more natural for those working from an empowerment model, since there has been continual affirmation as the child developed toward maturity.

A third task for successful launching is for parents to develop good relationships with their adult child's mate. Often the daughter-in-law/mother-in-law relationship is the most conflicted. One reason may be that mothers tend to be more heavily involved in the lives of their married children. This may be exacerbated when the husband compares his wife to his mother on such matters as cooking, cleaning, and parenting. These comparisons put the daughter-in-law in a no-win situation, since the husband defines "good" in terms of his family of origin. The new wife naturally operates according to *her* family's traditions and tastes.

Also prone to conflict is the relationship between the son-in-law and the mother-in-law. The popular stereotype of a mother-in-law interfering may serve as a self-fulfilling prophecy. The expectation that she will interfere serves to increase the son-in-law's reaction to her involvement with her daughter. The conflict in the son-in-law/father-in-law relationship seems to be centered in the father-in-law's view that the son-in-law is inadequate to provide for his daughter. Indeed, when the son-in-law is perceived by the father-in-law as a good provider, the chances are good that this will be a positive relationship. The least conflictive relationship seems to be between the daughter-in-law and the father-in-law. This relationship is often characterized by mutual acceptance and well-intended humor. Perhaps the relational skills of the daughter-in-law give her an ability to get along with her father-in-law.

The fourth task for successful launching is to resolve issues pertaining to the older generation. When the emotional and economic needs of their adult children have consumed and drained parents, the problems presented by their own aging parents may come as a disturbing reality. Having fewer resources to give may fuel resentment about the needs of aging parents. Taking time to anticipate and prepare for the needs of the elder generation can alleviate some of the frustration.

Contemporary Obstacles to Successful Launching

Clearly, the process of leaving home is not as easy as it once was. In a highly technological society, the majority of well-paying jobs demand a high degree of education, training, and skill. Even adequate entry-level jobs may require a college degree at a minimum. Given the high cost of education and training, the adult child today often needs additional economic help. The pattern of adult children leaving home only to return a few months or years later has given rise to the term *boomerang children*.

The cost of housing also makes it difficult for newly married couples to move into their own homes. This means that adult children frequently ask for financial help from their parents even after they have established themselves in careers and significant relationships. Given this trend of continued financial need on the part of children who have already launched, the contemporary family may be returning to the more traditional extended-family structure.

The Postlaunching Stage

Whenever we (Jack and Judy) visited Jack's parents, a predictable ritual would take place. Dad Balswick would gleefully announce, "I think it's time we washed your car!" Clean cars were a priority for Dad, and our car was sure to need a good washing after traveling three hundred miles. The car-washing ritual dated back to when Jack was a little boy. Dad would hold the hose and give the instructions as Jack did the grunt work of soaping down and scrubbing the car. Now, as an adult, Jack moved back into his little-boy position, while Dad assumed his "father knows best" position. Although this was an innocent ritual, one that Judy thoroughly enjoyed because her father-in-law winked at her as he bragged about how he got Jack to wash the car, it points to an area of struggle during the postlaunching phase. Old patterns of relating can sometimes be hard to take and even more difficult to break during family reunions, especially if the parents fail to relate to their children as adults to adults.

Tom's journey in the postlaunching phase has been similar to Jack's. One challenge when I (Tom) return home is the need to return as a more helpful, caring son as opposed to an adult. Due to my mom's history of strokes, I had to do more caregiving as a child than most of my peers. I learned to wash and fold clothes at an early age. When I return home as an adult, Mom's chronic health issues often become a source of conflict. Having conversations with a parent about what they can and cannot do for themselves is challenging under the best of circumstances, let alone when significant health issues are a part of the picture.

Leaving home is definitely a challenge for both parents and adult children. The fact that launching has taken place doesn't mean that all issues have been clearly worked out between family members. In fact, working out these family relationships is a lifelong process. Making adjustments is difficult because the family is a network of patterns and roles so predictable that they seem cut from a template. And even greater adjustments are required when adult children bring their partners and children into the mix. Old routines will be tested, and new coalitions will bring a mosaic of different interactions and interconnections. Expectations and unspoken messages can leave the new spouse feeling excluded. If parents and their adult children are to have a successful relationship during the launching and postlaunching stages, new roles and patterns must be established. The family should endeavor to create new ways of relating that are also inviting to and include the new members.

An aspect of differentiation is the ability of launched children to be objective about their families and resist the pull that hooks them into the old patterns. Instead of responding in predictable ways of the past, parents and adult children alike need to find appropriate new ways that work best in the current circumstances. A flexible environment allows changes that enhance all relationships so that there is a feeling of well-being and harmony among family members. Rodney Clapp (1993, 86) comments insightfully: "When family is not the whole world, parents can let children go and in turn find themselves reclaimed as parents. Truly letting a child go is hard, not only because of the pain of separation, but because a child fully released will reclaim and reshape the relationship in a way that may not be entirely to the parents' liking." This opportunity for change and growth can increase interconnected-ness and renew the relationship.

Grandparenting

Grandparents have long been depicted as gray-haired, slightly frail, sitting in their rocking chairs, and passing out sugar cookies to their adoring grand-children. Such stereotypes do not fit our modern picture of grandparents be-tween the ages of fifty and sixty-five who dress in blue jeans and tennis shoes as they actively engage with their grandchildren. In view of the amount of financial and emotional support given by grandparents, it is now accurate to describe the North American family as a modified extended family.

Research has provided insights into the changing nature of how grand-parents contribute to their grandchildren as they develop and mature from childhood to adulthood. Infants and toddlers benefit most from secure bond-ing with grandmothers who provide physical and emotional care. During the early school years, grandchildren value what grandparents do for and with them, such as showing love, giving presents, taking them places, and having fun together. In preadolescence, grandchildren continue to value indulgent grandparents but focus on the feelings of connectedness and the family pride they derive from the relationships (Ponzetti and Folkrod 1989).

When the relations between parents and teenagers become strained, grand-parents can be sensitive, nonjudgmental listeners to their grandchildren. It is especially important that grandparents of teenagers listen to the problems relating to self-esteem, affirm their grandchildren's strengths, and demonstrate their care by attending special school events and other performance-oriented activities. An intimate, meaningful relationship between grandparents and teenage grandchildren can be mutually beneficial, contributing to both the grandparents' mental health and the grandchildren's efforts to resolve identity issues. Adult grandchildren and great-grandchildren can benefit from the emotional support given by grandparents and great-grandparents.

What goes around comes around, for those grandparents who actively bond with their grandchildren when they are young can expect their grand-children to be emotionally supportive and concerned about them when they are old. Although granddaughters and grandsons bond equally well with their grandparents, there is a tendency for both to be closer to maternal than to paternal grandparents and to be closer to grandmothers than to grandfa-thers (Hodgson 1995). Since women traditionally take on the role of keeping up relationships with extended-family members and kin, this finding is not surprising.

In traditional nonindustrial societies, most grandparents were highly involved in the lives of their grandchildren. Since parents devoted much of their time to work, the care of children as well as the inculcation of morals, beliefs, and values were frequently the province of grandparents. Indeed, Scripture emphasizes the grandparents' spiritual role of passing on the faith: "I am reminded of your sincere faith, a faith that lived first in your grandmother Lois and your mother Eunice and now, I am sure, lives in you" (2 Tim. 1:5). But because of both the decline of the extended family and the high geographical mobility of industrial society, few grandparents have daily involvement with their grandchildren, let alone the opportunity to pass on their faith. Moreover, in our society, not only the parents but also often the grandparents work outside the home.

The extent to which contemporary grandparents are involved in the lives of their grandchildren varies greatly. Differing circumstances create different styles of grandparenting that can include grandparents as fun seekers, parental surrogates, reservoirs of family wisdom, or even distant figures. Margaret Mueller, Brenda Wilhelm, and Glen Elder (2002) found that grandparents who were most influential and supportive were usually part of a highly cohesive family, had more education, fewer grandchildren, and lived closer to them. Grandparents with a more traditional view tend to be formal figures who take on the role of defining moral behaviors and rules. Grandparents who live a great distance from grandchildren pack a lot into brief visits once or twice a year. They are prone to engage in fun-seeking interaction during those visits but remain background figures for the rest of the year.

Grandparents who live with or close by their grandchildren usually have frequent contact with them. It may be that they serve as surrogate parents for a variety of reasons. And this surrogate parenting is an unfortunate necessity for many in the later-life developmental stage. According to a US census report in 2012, about 10 percent of all children cohabited with grandparents. The number of grandparents who were "grandparent caregivers" or primarily responsible for their grandchildren was roughly 2.7 million (Ellis and Simons 2014). In terms of households, roughly 3 percent of all households include grandparents co-residing with grandchildren. Most of these households are maintained by the grandparent. When Tom was in full-time private practice, grandparents were increasingly seeking parenting education and individual and family therapy to improve parenting. Fortunately, evidence suggests that parenting interventions by grandparents are effective (Sherr et al. 2018). In these cases of surrogate parenting, it goes without saying that grandparents have a great impact on their grandchildren.

Many adults tell heartwarming stories that credit grandparents with providing the love, prayer, values, faith, and beliefs that made all the difference in their lives. The sad news is that when grandparents are divorced, they, and particularly grandfathers, are less involved in the lives of their grandchildren (King 2003). Most grandparents make quite an effort to connect with their grandchildren, even if they are geographically distant. Interest, support, and concern can be communicated through phone and video calls, cards, email, packages, visits, summer trips, and vacations. Regardless of the grandparenting style, most grandparents can be counted on for support in one way or another.

Most adult children turn to their parents for help during times of stress and crisis. Grandparents are called on to fill in the gaps and provide a significant amount of support to their children and grandchildren when divorce occurs. The role of grandparents in the lives of grandchildren can be especially meaningful at transition points, such as leaving home, when the tensions between parents and child are at their highest. Think of the advantage for a child of any age who can draw on unconditional support and love from both maternal and paternal grandparents. Grandparents who have intense relationships with grandchildren during their childhood promote continuation of the relationship into adulthood (Geurts, Van Tilburg, and Poortman 2012a). Parenthetically, it is good to note that intense relationships between grandparents and grandchildren are predictive of adult children supporting their elderly parents (Geurts, Van Tilburg, and Poortman 2012b). Yorgason, Padilla-Walker, and Jackson (2011) found that the emotional and financial support from nonresidential grandparents had a positive effect on their grandchildren.

There are increasing numbers of grandparent-headed households in the United States. Grandparents who assume the responsibility of raising grandchildren face special challenges, including "financial burden, worry, health issues, and freedom restrictions" (Williams 2011, 948). Drawing from a number of research studies on resident grandparents, Strom and Strom (2011, 910) suggest that successful grandparents are able to "establish suitable priorities, recognize the necessary adjustments in their thinking and behavior, and discover how to assess progress by being willing to amend their dreams, get to know grandchildren by spending time together, and adopt a perspective that enables management of stress."

Multigenerational Households

Multigenerational households, consisting of three or more generations living together, are most common during the postlaunching stage. In extended-family systems, such as those in Asian societies, the family by its very nature is multigenerational. In the nuclear-family system of Western societies, multigenerational households are of two types. First is the postlaunching multi-generational household of married children and their offspring who live with their parents or return home after they have been on their own for some time. A second type of multigenerational household forms during the retirement stage, when elderly parents move in with their married children. The dynamics of these two types of multigenerational households may be extremely rich and rewarding or extremely stressful and disruptive. In most cases, there is a mixture of rewards and stress.

In general, families that have not coped well with major transitions in the past are likely to find that multigenerational living amplifies the strain. The stress will be less intense in those multigenerational families characterized by good health, emotional maturity, and self-differentiation. Other factors that can help alleviate stress include adequate material assets, financial security, a house of ample size, access to transportation, and availability of community resources. Among the more beneficial community resources are elder-care programs, day care centers for young children, and a network of extended family, friends, and church members who can step in to provide assistance when needed.

Establishing appropriate boundaries helps combat one of the most potentially troublesome areas within multigenerational households. The homeowners will quite naturally feel that it is their right to establish household rules and boundaries with their adult children, grandchildren, and elderly parents. These rules and boundaries are likely to concern questions of space, household responsibilities, child-rearing or elder-care practices, and time schedules. Although most of the space in the house may be understood as a common living area, it is wise to establish clear guidelines before living together. Taking time for mutual consideration of each individual's needs will help with the negotiation.

During the Balswicks' postlaunching period, our married daughter, son-in-law, and two young grandsons came to live with us for three years. Although we developed clear spatial boundaries from the start, we experienced some humorous moments. Much of the rather large house was open to everyone, but Curtis and Jacob had to be reminded that Grammie and Grampie's bedroom and upstairs living-room areas were private space that was off limits when the doors were closed. We soon learned that our grandsons lived by the letter of the law, so when the door was open just a crack, they would rush in with all the exuberance of young children. One morning, as our grandsons were trying out Judy's hairbrush, comb, perfume, and other items of interest while she was getting ready for work, it was necessary for her to explain that these things belonged to Grammie and were not to be "messed with." After listening to Judy expounding on the boundary rules, Curtis piped up with a serious expression on his face, "And Grammie, when you're in our room, you don't mess with any of our things either!" It was a lighthearted moment, but Judy was quick to reply, "Yes, Curtis, that is right! Grammie and Grampie will knock before we come into your room and ask if we can play with your things!" The boys had learned that boundary issues are a matter of mutual respect.

Other rules concern the responsibility for household tasks such as cleaning, yard work, and meal preparation. In the three years we lived as a three-generation household, our son-in-law took responsibility for house repairs, Jack did the yard work, our daughter cleaned the common living area, and Judy planned the meals, to which we all contributed by cooking and cleaning up. Similarly, when elderly family members move in, it is vital that they contribute to the household in any way they can. For some it may simply be doing a little dusting or clearing the table or gardening or making their beds; the very act of participating gives them meaning. Those unable to help physically can say a prayer or contribute through their presence at family gatherings. They should be affirmed for what they contribute to the family and be told how much they are appreciated.

An area of potential conflict and misunderstanding is caretaking. When it comes to discipline of children, for example, grandparents may tend to take charge. Having strong ideas about parenting since they have already been through the experience, they may find it tempting to criticize the parents' methods. The task facing grandparents is learning how to share knowledge without undermining or disrespecting the parents. Grandparents must also acknowledge that adult children have both the right and the responsibility to raise their children their own way. A sacred rule for the Balswicks was to never interfere with our daughter and son-in-law as they were actively parenting but to share any concerns or suggestions with them in private. Of course, when they were not in the home, we clearly took the leadership role.

Different ideas about caring for elderly parents can also become a serious area of conflict between couples. Making good judgments about what is needed, without being over- or underprotective, is the key. When there are differences that can't be resolved, it is wise to protect the marriage by bringing in substitute caretakers who can ease the load.

When an elderly family member moves into the home, it is essential to discuss some important issues. First, talk openly and honestly about feelings, expectations, strengths, and limitations as you anticipate caring for an aging parent. Get together with one or two close friends to talk through the hopes, fears, and doubts that having this particular parent in the home raises. Discuss the parent's physical and emotional needs and your ability to meet those needs. Consider the role that your sense of obligation plays in the decision to care for your parent and be willing to examine any resentment you may have. It is also vital to spend time reflecting on how the decision will affect your life and your significant relationships. Are there hidden expectations about the extent to which others (spouse, siblings) will be involved? What fears are there about becoming emotionally distant in your relationships as you focus on the needs of the elderly parent? Clearly voicing these concerns helps you be as realistic as possible about the decision. Periodic discussion about how things are going ensures that necessary and appropriate changes are made.

A second set of questions concerns the family as a whole. These questions center on the family's relationship with the aging parent and the impact of the decision on each member. Do they all get along with the elderly individual? Are there particular concerns with any family members that put them at special risk? How will they deal with illness? What feelings of intrusion or resentment are present? These and other questions should be processed in a family meeting. Letting family members voice their fears and concerns as well as their positive attitudes about the decision allows everyone a chance to make it a successful venture.

A third set of questions deals with the adequacy of living space, privacy, and financial resources. Finally, investigating the community resources that can contribute to the well-being of the elderly members of the household will benefit everyone. Such community resources might include transportation programs, senior-activity centers, home-delivered meals, housekeeping services, and home health care.

The Retirement Stage

Couple Satisfaction and Challenge

Most couples report retirement to be a satisfying phase of their lives. Those who are most satisfied engage in rewarding activities and reserve time for themselves. They have fulfilling marriages, a sexual relationship founded on mutual expressions of affection, open communication, and the ability to resolve conflicts. Good communication and compatibility in marriage are most important in preventing stress during retirement. Highly satisfied couples are also fairly healthy, financially secure, and involved with church and friends. Couples in long-term marriages report more affection and intimacy and fewer marital problems, conflicts, and negativity than do couples who have been married fewer years (Cooney and Dunne 2004).

At a time when approximately one out of every two marriages ends in divorce, it is particularly important to discover reasons for long-term marital success. A study of couples who had been married from forty-five to sixty-four years (Lauer, Lauer, and Kerr 1995, 39) reports that essential to success in marriage is an intimate relationship with a mate whose company one thoroughly enjoys. Almost as important are commitment, humor, and the ability to agree on a wide variety of issues. In their review of literature on long-term marriages, T. Cooney and K. Dunne (2004, 138) report that "the same things that make a given couple happy or unhappy early in marriage tend to make them happy or unhappy later in marriage."

Of course, retirement brings with it some notable changes in the marital relationship. As the relationship becomes more equal in power, wives become more assertive, and husbands more concerned with interpersonal relationships (Long and Mancini 1990). Given the additional time that retired couples have to focus on each other and their relationship, it is not surprising that most of the research reports an increase in marital happiness after retirement.

But retirement also tends to highlight the negative qualities of a couple's marriage. Role loss is an inevitable challenge. A workaholic (whether in the home or outside it) who has defined self-worth purely in terms of work will find retirement a difficult time of life. Also, involvement in work may have kept spouses from developing a more satisfying marriage. With time on their hands, a retired couple must confront unresolved marital issues head-on. An annoying habit that was previously tolerated may become unbearable when one must deal with it on a constant basis. Another difficulty for some retired people is insufficient financial resources to maintain their accustomed lifestyle. The most challenging part of retirement involves health and aging bodies. Illness and physical and mental deterioration can sap vitality and much of the joy of living.

One of Tom's favorite couples was facing a challenge during the transition to the husband's retirement. The husband was a Caucasian American, and the wife was Taiwanese. In Taiwanese culture, retirement is viewed very positively. Retirement signals the accomplishment of a lifetime of work and support for one's family. Additionally, aging is viewed more positively in Taiwanese culture than here in the United States. These cultural perspectives influence how the husband more negatively experienced retirement and how the wife had difficulty understanding this life transition. They were both gainfully employed throughout their marriage, even working at the same company. They had been married for over thirty years and had successfully raised and launched three children, two sons and a daughter. Since his retirement, both spouses reported increasing anger and arguments. In discussing the meaning of the retirement, the issues came to light. The wife viewed retirement in solely positive terms—as a much-deserved reward for a lifetime of hard work and providing for the family. The husband would have time to do everything he always wanted—golf, play with grandchildren, vacation. However, the husband experienced retirement as a loss—a loss of an important aspect of his identity. As part of his grieving process, he was experiencing profound sadness, guilt, and purposelessness. When he tried to communicate these feelings to his wife, she had difficulty understanding them, as she viewed retirement very differently. Therapy mostly involved exploring the meaning of retirement and how identity for both partners could expand outside of work.

Minor tensions can arise because retired husbands spend so much time at home. One elderly woman compared the development in her marriage to having an ever-present twin: "He's always right there under my feet! I'm not used to it, and I don't know what to do with him being home all day long." His constant presence interfered with her freedom to socialize with female friends and to run the household on her own. A retired husband with few friends and interests outside the home may find himself at a loss as to how to fill the day and become overly dependent on his wife in retirement.

Retired couples face two major crises: illness and death. The first crisis occurs when one of the spouses becomes seriously ill, making it necessary for the other spouse to become the caregiver. Since husbands are usually older than their wives and women have a longer life expectancy, the wife is more likely to find herself in the caregiver role. Even minor illness can provoke tension when one spouse assumes the burden of caring for the other. The healthy spouse also lives with the fear that the other will get worse and die.

Both physical and emotional illness can greatly affect the quality of a marriage relationship. The increase in life expectancy means that a larger number of people will suffer a debilitating condition such as Alzheimer's or Parkinson's disease. It is estimated that 50 percent of all marriages will reach a point where one of the spouses develops some form of dementia.

As a couple's time and energy focus more on a debilitating illness, their involvement with other couples and friends decreases. At this time, they need assistance from adult relatives. Without help from other family members, the caregiving spouse can become overburdened and stressed beyond the ability to cope. When both spouses are too ill to care for themselves, the extended family must enter the picture to arrange for care.

The death of a spouse is the final phase. Although death can be a relief in the case of a severe illness, it usually comes as a numbing shock to the surviving partner and other family members. Free from the responsibilities of children and work, the lives of elderly partners usually revolve around each other, resulting in mutual emotional and physical dependency. Thus, the death of a beloved partner often leaves the surviving spouse seriously depressed. Frequent crying, withdrawal from others, loss of appetite, sleep disturbances, fatigue, declining health, and lack of interest in life are common symptoms. It is not unusual for a surviving spouse whose health is also failing to give up on life and die shortly after the death of the partner. (For a scholarly discussion of widowhood and its negative effects, see Ennis and Majid 2020.)

It seems that the wider supportive network of friends that characterizes widows, compared to widowers, helps women adjust better to living after the death of their spouse. In addition, older women gain independence through social networks due to their greater potential to "have bridging potential in their networks—between both kin and non-kin contacts" (Cornwell 2011, 782).

Although we might expect that people who are most dependent on their spouses will be more devastated by their deaths, this is not necessarily the case. A study by Carr (2004, 220) found that "women who were most emotionally dependent on their spouses had the poorest self-esteem while still married, yet evidenced highest levels of self-esteem following the loss. Men who were most dependent on their wives for home maintenance and financial management tasks experienced the greatest personal growth following loss." From this we conclude that highly dependent spouses have or can learn the capacity to gain self-confidence when they are forced to manage on their own.

Caring for Aging Family Members

Adult children are called on to care for their dependent elderly members when chronic illness or death strikes. Although such responsibility causes a certain amount of strain, a study of patients with advanced cancer shows that hope is an important ingredient that not only eases one's ability to cope with stressful situations but also reduces caregiving strain (Lohne, Miaskowski, and Rustoen 2012). Extended-family systems take for granted the care of elderly parents by adult children. In nuclear-family systems, care for elderly parents may be more problematic. After their children leave home, parents pride themselves on their desire and ability to live their remaining years by themselves. Single adult children and those in dual-career families may not be able to stay home to care for elderly parents. Some are also caring for boomerang adult children, a situation that leaves little time and energy to take in elderly parents. Health and financial problems may also deter adult children from caring for their elderly parents.

A new perspective on adult children caring for aging family members has been described as *intergenerational ambivalence* (Willson, Kim, and Elder

2003; Pillemer and Luscher 2004). Intergenerational ambivalence is a theory in family gerontology that addresses positive *and* negative features of intergenerational relationships. Ingrid Connidis and Julie Ann McMullin (2002, 565) define *ambivalence* as "socially structured contradictions made manifest in interaction." Family members with fewer options are more likely to resolve ambivalence through acceptance rather than confrontation. Family members exercise agency as they negotiate relationships within the constraints of social structure. One study of middle-aged persons caring for elderly parents found that the caregivers reported more quality of life problems than noncaregivers (Roth et al. 2009).

By comparing and contrasting alternative models of intergenerational family relationships, Vern Bengtson and his colleagues (2002) identify the likely path to intergenerational ambivalence. They conclude that intergenerational relations begin with *solidarity*, the bonds of cohesion that hold a family together, followed by *conflict*, as the ideal relationship evolves into reality, with the intersection of solidarity and conflict resulting in *intergenerational ambivalence* (575).

Modern industrial societies seem to consist largely of modified extended families in contrast to truly nuclear families. Even though parents may live apart from their adult children and grandchildren, they are interdependent and receive emotional, social, and economic support. Thus, the care of aging parents is more a question of how it is to be done than whether it is to be done. The children will inevitably be involved in one way or another.

The sandwich generation is a term that has been coined to refer to couples who are in mid- to late midlife, who may be looking forward to retirement but find themselves caring for both aging parents and children. While their elderly parents may increasingly need financial, emotional, and social assistance, their young adult children may need continued support as they struggle to find financial independence. This dual responsibility can result in couple burnout, especially among dual-earner couples who need to not only balance work and home life but also find time for other family members and their own marriages (Pines et al. 2011). Results from national surveys of women aged fifty-five through sixty-nine in Great Britain and the United States showed "around one-third of the women reported providing help to members of both generations. . . . Having three or more children is associated with a reduced likelihood of providing help to a parent" (Grundy and Henretta 2006, 707).

Although the inclusion of dependent elderly parents can greatly enrich family life, it can also be a psychological, social, and financial burden. As more people live longer, an increasing percentage of health care costs occur in the later years of life. The statistics are staggering. According to the 1990 census, thirteen million Americans were age seventy-five or older. It is estimated that by the year 2040, one in every five Americans will be sixty-five or older. This is approximately seventy million people. There is concern whether Social Security will have sufficient funds to take care of the needs of the elderly in the future.

The cost of placing an elderly person in a convalescent home averages between $30,000 and $50,000 a year. A couple who have worked and saved money over a lifetime may see their nest egg vanish in a matter of years. The inability of such couples and their families to meet the costs is merely the tip of the economic iceberg and a serious concern for our nation.

It is worth noting a gender gap when it comes to taking care of elderly parents. Studies consistently show that adult daughters spend more time giving assistance to their elderly parents than do sons (Sarkisian and Gerstel 2004). A study by Sechrist et al. (2011) found that the quality of the adult daughter–elderly mother relationship was greater when there was greater similarity in religiousness. Women tend to bear more caregiving costs than men and receive more rewards than their spouses in the caregiving process. Although some of the gender difference involves employment obligations, we believe sons as well as daughters need to share the responsibility so that women are not overly burdened in the caregiving process and so that men can experience the rewards.

In chapter 1, we discussed the ideal of a mature bilateral commitment in which the unconditional love shown by parents to their children is reciprocated when the parents age and become socially, emotionally, and physically dependent on their adult children. When this happens, family life has truly come full circle. The Bible speaks of the family's responsibility to care for its most needy members. That this includes elderly parents is made clear in 1 Timothy 5:4: "If a widow has children or grandchildren, they should first learn their religious duty to their own family and make some repayment to their parents; for this is pleasing in God's sight." Lest the reader fail to get Paul's message, he continues with this warning in verse 8: "And whoever does not provide for relatives, and especially for family members, has denied the faith and is worse than an unbeliever."

In the social economy of the early church, it was primarily the responsibility of the family rather than the church to care for the elderly. First Timothy 5:16 reads: "If any believing woman has relatives who are really widows, let her assist them; let the church not be burdened, so that it can assist those who are real widows." The reason given is that the church will then be better able to care for the dependent elderly who do not have family. The clear social ethic found in Scripture is that we are to care for our own family members as well as for those in need through the community of faith.

Terry Hargrave (2005) develops three principles for biblically caring for one's parents. They are (1) responsibility, (2) openhandedness, and (3) evenness. Responsibility focuses on "the honor, respect, and cooperation between parent and child." This devotion "demonstrates how to humbly work together for future generations, and it reminds us how we are expected to do the same in our relationship to God" (73). As parents have invested in their children, children show honor and respect by caring for their parents. Part of this respect is providing care and facilitating the parent's responsibility for things they can manage. Openhandedness is about giving to others what they need, while he or she is also able to receive God's blessings at the same time. Out of the abundance of God's gift of grace, one does not give grudgingly. Evenness is about finding harmony in the midst of stress. This harmony is balance; caring for elderly parents gradually makes more and more demands on the adult children. Considering these three principles together, caregiving is about (1) reciprocity through respecting both the dependent elderly and the caregiving child; (2) balance with the other obligations in the caregiver's life such as spousal, vocational, and parental ones; and (3) honest understanding of both the caregiver's ability and the dependent's needs.

Within reason, the elderly person should have a say in the matter, and their preferences should be taken into account. The elderly parent must be treated with dignity at all times.

Caring for elderly parents is both a privilege and a priority for Christian families and the church community. Granted, making decisions about how to best care for elderly parents is a complex process, and we must do so with respect, honor, and integrity.

Regardless of the social structural arrangements used to care for the elderly, fostering independent living is an important goal. In addressing theological issues in caring for the elderly, Balswick, King, and Reimer (2016) suggest that the family create *zones of proximal capabilities*. In chapter 7, we referred to Vygotsky's *zone of proximal development* concept to describe the range of skills to accomplish in assisting children. In a similar way, a zone of proximal capability helps establish the range of skills an elderly person can accomplish on his or her own or with the help and support of others. As a mirror image of empowerment, family members will increase the scaffolds or helping structures as needed to allow the elderly to continue to be as independent as possible. Sometimes outside caregivers can empower and model patience because family members have a hard time seeing a loved one struggle in an attempt to be independent.

Given the biblical emphasis on community, one can argue that the entire community, rather than merely a few family members, is responsible for the elderly. Some religious groups and denominations are well known for establishing excellent retirement communities to provide for the aging. The overarching biblical principle here is that family members care for their own families. How this is done, within the household or within an elder-care community, depends on social, psychological, physiological, and economic circumstances. God can honor a number of alternative social arrangements. Both approaches—household and community care—have unique strengths and limitations. The important thing is that the dependent elderly be nurtured and loved unconditionally as family, regardless of who is providing the day-to-day care.

PART 4

Gender and Sexuality

Identity in Family Life

This section focuses on two major sources of personal identity: one's gender and one's sexuality. In chapter 11, we discuss the impact of changing gender roles and relations on the family in our society. We examine current explanations of gender differences and then offer a Christian viewpoint. We also offer practical ideas on how Christian families and the church can provide leadership in this area.

In chapter 12, we expound on the fact that God created us as sexual beings and pronounced this very good. God intended that we be authentic and whole in our sexual relationships. After noting sociocultural influences on the development of our sexuality, we present a theological understanding. Finally, focusing on four important aspects of sexual expression—sex and singlehood, masturbation, sexual preference, and marital sexuality—we offer some practical guidelines for achieving wholeness in a broken world.

11

Changing Gender Roles and Relations

The Impact on Family Life

In most societies throughout history, knowing how to be a man or a woman was taken for granted. This is certainly not the case today! Our society is embroiled in debates over what constitutes masculinity and femininity and what the appropriate roles are for each gender. This redefinition of gender roles has caused significant shifts in family life. The marital dyad, where husbands and wives are struggling with conflicting definitions of marital roles, has had to make the most adjustments. Redefining gender roles also extends to parent-child relationships in determining how to relate to and raise sons and daughters in an age when traditional definitions of manhood and womanhood have changed.

In this chapter, we extend our discussion from gender roles to gender relations. Doing so challenges us to understand family life beyond mere definition of roles to relationships established between the genders both within the family and the wider sociocultural context. The four biblical relationship principles (covenant, grace, empowerment, intimacy) and trinitarian theology bring us to the conclusion that relationship surpasses roles. A great deal of flexibility in roles continues to be structured and renegotiated throughout family life.

When it comes to gender relationships, we agree with Mary Stewart Van Leeuwen that we are created from the beginning as males and females for sociability and mutual dominion, equal dignity and mutual respect. The cultural mandates and other dimensions of image bearing in Genesis 1:26–28 are given

201

to both the man and woman, male and female. Together we are called to be God's earthly agents (not separately or hierarchically or in competition, but cooperatively) for engaging in rightful relationships with each other and our world for God's glory (Van Leeuwen et al. 1993).

First, we note the reasons gender roles and relations have been changing and then consider some of the explanations for gender differences. Then we explore the effect that redefinition of gender roles and relationships has on the family. In the process, we reflect on our hermeneutical understanding of the relevant scriptural texts.

Why Gender Roles and Relations Are Changing

There are several reasons why traditional definitions of sexual roles and relations are currently being called into question. The social sciences have demonstrated that many of the traditional characteristics of masculinity and femininity, formerly assumed to be the result of natural development, are in reality a result of cultural conditioning. Increased observation and dialogue with people from various parts of the world have also informed us that most differences between masculinity and femininity are culture bound.

There has also been an increasing separation between the sex assignment of individuals and the gender roles associated with a particular sex. Van Leeuwen (2002) describes six processes or forks that result in adult gender identity. First, *chromosomal* aspects of sex identify one genetically as XX (female) or XY (male). Second, the *gonadal* process entails the forming and development of sexual organs (testes or ovaries). Next, the *hormonal* dimension describes the relative amounts of specific sex hormones. Fourth, *internal accessory* refers to the development of the biological structures that connect the primary sex organs. This is followed by *external genital*, meaning the external physical sex organs (penis or vagina). And sixth is the *pubertal* aspect, which is related to the development of secondary sex characteristics and adult sexual identity. This demonstrates that there is not a direct connection between genetic and biological sex and one's gender identity from a social-science perspective. Gender is defined as a social construct. This means that gender roles are defined by the society that one is in. We see a high degree of differences in gender role expectations when comparing cultures, thus indicating the social—not genetic or biological—origin of masculinity or femininity. For example, a recent editorial in *Nature* (2018), "US Proposal for Defining Gender Has No Basis in Science," argues for the biological science associated with moving from a binary understanding of sex to a continuum of sexual identity. This means that most individuals will identify with the gender traditionally associated with their sex, and there will also be some who will identify with the opposite gender than the one associated with the sex they were assigned at birth.

Workforce changes have also provided an impetus for a shift in gender roles. Dual-earner households represent most families today, so we must also consider the impact of this demographic. This is a crucial concern for children, since the family is the arena in which a child's personal character and gender identity are formed. Young children are continually impacted and develop gender identity by observing the behavior and expectations of male and female figures in their lives. For this reason, we have chosen the family as the context for our discussion of changing sexual roles.

Explanations of Gender Differences

For years, there has been an argument as to whether gender differences are due to heredity or environment—nature versus nurture. This controversy began with the emergence of modern science. With the development of the biological sciences, it was discovered that genetics plays a key role in determining the nature of both plants and animals. Furthermore, not only physical features but also traits of temperament were traced to the genetic packages that children inherit from their parents. Although each individual genetic package was understood to be unique, males and females were thought to possess decidedly distinctive genetic packages.

Behavioral scientists challenged this notion, explaining that gender differences are acquired after birth through cultural conditioning. Both sides of the debate initially assumed an either/or approach, arguing that gender differences are either a result of hereditary factors or a result of environmental factors. As the dividing lines between scientific disciplines have broken down, explanations for gender differences have become less of an all-or-nothing proposition. Contemporary explanations of gender differences are much more complex, and both theoretical sides point to the interactive effect between heredity and environment.

Critical Theory

Critical theory is a sociological analysis of power in relationships. Power is based on having the resources to dominate and control and is thus always being negotiated and reconstructed to keep the dominant group (race, gender) in charge. As a sociological theory, the focus is on the relationships between men and women and how men use institutional and informal power to dominate and control women.

Central to critical theory is the idea of hegemony, the process whereby men keep power by ensuring that everyone sees the world from their point of view. While men are the dominant group and women are the subordinate group, neither of these categories is homogeneous. Only certain men have what the masculine or patriarchal ideology defines as the most desired characteristics: financial independence, physical strength, good looks, toughness, and social status. These men possess hegemonic masculinity. Men who lack these particular masculine characteristics are considered to be of lower status and may be labeled wimps or nerds.

Although all women are a part of the subordinate group, they too differ greatly in relative status. Women who possess the characteristics defined as desirable by the patriarchal ideology (i.e., a pretty face, a shapely body, emotional warmth, submissiveness) experience privilege because they approach ideal femininity. But regardless of how closely a woman approximates ideal femininity, she can never obtain hegemony, for she is not male. Theological, political, and philosophical ideologies combine to justify barring women from powerful positions. For instance, certain religious ideologies maintain that only men can occupy ecclesiastical positions that carry the greatest power.

Michael Messner (2002) provides a heuristic for evaluating the effects of evangelicals adopting hegemonic and privileged forms of masculinity and femininity, respectively. First, one should consider the *cost* of hegemonic masculinity and privileged femininity for evangelicals. Traditional gender ideology is oppressive to males that do not or cannot conform to hegemonic masculinity and to females that do not or cannot conform to privileged femininity. This oppression occurs at both institutional and individual levels. The second area Messner (2002) proposes for understanding the politics of masculinity concerns the *benefits* associated with hegemonic masculinity and privileged femininity. Those who are already in power benefit because they remain in power. As men continue to control access to resources, they will continue to receive benefits for others' labor. Connell (2000) calls this the patriarchal dividend; it is a way to quantify the benefits for hegemonic masculinity and privileged femininity. The final area Messner (2000) describes as being impacted in the politics of masculinity is *diversity*. As an example, the diversity of gender metaphors suggests that evangelicals have many options to choose from in defining their gendered identity (Bartkowski 2000, 2001, 2004; Gallagher 2003; Smith 2000). Bartkowski (2004) identifies four distinct archetypes of Christian masculinity as espoused within Promise Keeper (PK) advice manuals. These types are (1) the rational patriarch, (2) the expressive egalitarian, (3) the tender warrior, and (4) the multicultural man. Despite these diverse gender metaphors, evangelicals demonstrate a preference for the traditional family model with its concomitant gender ideology.

One concerning challenge is that critical theory will never complete or exhaust its power-dynamic analysis. Messner's three aspects allow us to uncover increasingly hegemonic and privileged gender roles in social interactions. At this point, even the denial and questioning of the validity of critical theory is a sign of hegemonic privilege and denial of the effects of systemic oppression. Consequently, there are increasing pushes for acceptance of broader and broader categories and redefinition of gender and sexuality in the name of science without room for critical reflection or honest, data-driven dialogue.

An area of concern with critical theory is the eventual erasure of *any differences* between males and females and men and women. This would contradict the findings of scientists who have identified the following neurological differences between males and females (Jahanshad and Thompson 2017): (1) men tend to have larger brains than women, resulting in certain areas of the brain being larger in size but not in overall volume; (2) females' brains develop earlier than males', especially as they enter puberty; (3) males' brains tend to deteriorate more quickly than females'; and (4) illnesses like schizophrenia, bipolar disorder, and other behavioral disorders affect men and women at differential rates. Critical feminism views sex and gender as independent, and gender being a social construct means that one's gender identity can be whatever the individual wants it to be. This means that men and women are interchangeable. This extreme form of critical feminism is at the root of the transgender debate (Strachan and Peacock 2020).

Biblical Feminism

Biblical feminists are women and men who advocate legal and social changes that would establish the political, economic, ecclesiastic, and social equality of the sexes based on the views of gender as described in the Bible. They are committed to empowering women to identify, develop, and use their gifts for the advancement of God's reign on earth. This is to be done responsibly and without regard to sexual stereotypes.

The excellent work *After Eden* (Van Leeuwen et al. 1993), a book authored by a five-member study group that weds the ideas of critical feminism to biblical feminism, provides an insightful understanding of the structural barriers hindering gender equality. It also presents a biblically informed basis for gender equality as a matter of fundamental Christian justice.

Biblical feminists are committed to raising the consciousness of people within the Christian tradition. They challenge the inequality of hierarchical structures by promoting the ordination of women and gender-inclusive language in the church as well as Bible translations, by attending to the special needs of the disadvantaged poor, and by fighting against the physical and sexual abuse of women and children.

Christian feminists seek reform in and through the church. They urge Christian communities to acknowledge the human suffering of women and to find solutions. They demand that the church encourage all people, regardless of gender, to recognize and affirm that they are endowed by God with gifts and responsibilities to strive for love and justice through service to one another in all realms of life and in all parts of the world.

Organizations such as Christians for Biblical Equality (CBE) have provided a strong voice for evangelicals who advocate equality for all humans. Their methods include issuing challenges, setting up remedial processes, and promoting reconciliation and change. The central difference between biblical feminism and other types of feminism is that its authority is biblical revelation. As men and women reconciled in Christ work together for worthy goals, they will transform the kingdom of God on earth.

One of the main Scriptures that speak the equalitarian understanding of gender is Galatians 3:28. It is helpful to look at this important passage in context:

> Before the coming of this faith, we were held in custody under the law, locked up until the faith that was to come would be revealed. So the law was our guardian until Christ came that we might be justified by faith. Now that this faith has come, we are no longer under a guardian.
>
> So in Christ Jesus you are all children of God through faith, for all of you who were baptized into Christ have clothed yourselves with Christ. There is neither Jew nor Gentile, neither slave nor free, nor is there male and female, for you are all one in Christ Jesus. If you belong to Christ, then you are Abraham's seed, and heirs according to the promise. (Gal. 3:23–29)

The emphasis for biblical feminists is on how gender should not privilege or benefit anyone in the kingdom of God. God's grace is equally applied to men and women, and both have ultimate value to God. Galatians 3:28 reminds us that any human category or division intended to privilege one group over another is obliterated in God's just reign. All need God's grace equally. Biblical feminists are concerned with establishing justice through living one's faith. The essential message of CBE is stated in the introduction to its sponsored book, *Discovering Biblical Equality: Complementarity without Hierarchy*: "Gender, in and of itself, neither privileges nor curtails one's ability to be used to advance the kingdom or to glorify God in any dimension of ministry, mission, society or family" (Pierce, Groothuis, and Fee 2005, 13).

A Radical Proposal for Reconciliation

The common themes in all feminist thinking are (1) the fervent goal of eliminating sexism and (2) the view that gender differences are the product of the fabric of society and culture. Patriarchy has been an obstacle throughout history, blocking the affirmation of women as persons. Frustrated by this obstacle, feminists see the necessity of altering the social and institutional structures that perpetuate the subordinate status of women. Liberation for both women and men from their respective restrictive roles as oppressed and oppressor is the corrective needed to overturn the damage done by patriarchal structures.

Miroslav Volf's (1996) compassionate but tough model on forgiveness offers a powerful ideal for gender reconciliation. The theological starting point is found in the "offense of the cross." It seems outrageous that Christ would make himself totally vulnerable on the cross to create a space in himself for those who were his enemies. Yet he opened his arms and invited the offenders in. Applying Christ's model to the relations between men and women, Volf believes that a "reconciliation with the other will succeed only if the self, guided by the narrative of the Triune God, is ready to receive the other into itself and undertake a readjustment of its identity in light of the other's alterity" (110). This readjustment leads to equal acceptability and equal power between the genders as they make space for the other and move toward true reconciliation.

In this radical approach to reconciliation between men and women, Volf is careful to clarify that forgiveness is not a substitute for justice. What makes confession and repentance so powerful in this situation is the very idea that injustices are being dealt with in the presence of God. Volf's invitation to women and men to let go of the rage and its destructive consequences that eat away at their very souls is crucial because only God can truly forgive. Of course, the choice to no longer see the other as the enemy puts one in a vulnerable position. However, it also means that one is no longer defined by the offender and that one has a new ability to remember rightly. When women and men get beyond excluding each other and reach the point of embrace, there is great hope for the future.

At the heart of the cross was Christ's decision to heal brokenness by no longer keeping offenders as enemies. Volf offers this as a model for groups who define themselves as enemies. For just as God makes room for us, there is hope that when "guided by the indestructible love which makes space in the self for others in their alterity, which invites the others who have transgressed to return, which creates hospitable conditions for their confession, and rejoices over their presence, [women and men will with God's help keep] re-configuring the order without destroying it so as to maintain it as an order of embrace rather than exclusion" (Volf 1996, 165).

Toward an Integrated View of Gender Differences

On the basis of both physiological and social-science research, we can conclude that both *nature and nurture* and the *interaction* between them become important contributors to the formation of femininity and masculinity. We must challenge a single-factor *deterministic* explanation of gender differences. One's natal, chromosomal, gonadal, hormonal, internal and external accessory, and pubertal sexual development play a profound role in one's sexual identity. However, socialization also significantly affects the meanings and behaviors associated with sexual identity.

The interaction of nature and nurture are important in the Christian perspective. The main bodily or physical aspect of human existence is one's sexually differentiated body. "The fundamental human differentiation which constitutes the true order of humanity is necessarily experienced as sexual differentiation, and this is a *determination* of humanity, not an accidental or incidental manifestation of humanity" (Anderson 1991, 51; italics in original). Humanity is being male or female (Strachan and Peacock 2016). That is, structurally speaking, sexuality is the natural state of affairs that determines one's relationships to others and the nonhuman world. From Anderson's perspective, being male or female is primary to one's social relationships.

Social relationships or roles are secondary to one's gendered humanity. This is not to say that social relationships are unimportant. Sexual humanity is true humanity, and gender informs how people relate to one another. An important implication of Anderson's (1991) perspective is that being male and female takes precedence over marital and familial roles. This means that we embody the social roles we find ourselves in based upon our sexually differentiated bodies. This sexual differentiation is the intended, holy, and willful differentiation of the Creator of the universe (Strachan and Peacock 2016). Anderson (1991, 35; italics in original) says, *"that which we call human being is differentiated creatureliness, experienced as a response to the creative divine Word."*

One's sexual, bodily existence is the context for living out the image of God. That is, being male or female forms the central, structural category for differentiated human relationships. This differentiation occurs through God's creative Word and empowerment of humans. Through relationships, humans are to steward and fill the earth. Sexual differentiation provides the somatic experience of both particularity and relatedness. In a profound sense, one's sexual identity is constituted in one's relationships with both the same and opposite sex. This mutuality reconciles males and females to collaborate and complement one another in stewardship of creation and living out family relationships while mutually submitting to the will of Christ.

The most compelling evidence that biological factors account for some gender differences can be found in correlations between the social behavior and the physiological attributes of each gender; gender differences in infants and young children prior to socialization; the emergence of gender differences with the onset of puberty, when physiology and hormonal secretion changes rapidly; stability of gender differences across cultures; and similar gender differences among the higher primates. For other examples of gender differences see Debra Soh's (2020) excellent work, *The End of Gender*. Whereas these findings may seem to reinforce traditional gender stereotypes, they do not deny that the socialization process accentuates these tendencies. The issue here regards society or socialization as *creating* these differences or stereotypes (social construction of gender) or biology as *significantly influencing* the interests and activities of one gender compared to the other.

Genesis 1:27 records the creation of humans: "So God created humankind in his image, in the image of God he created them; male and female he created them." One important implication of this verse is that God created male and female as distinct human beings. We are left to determine exactly what that means and how such differences are to be expressed in male-female relationships. We must turn to the Scriptures for further elaboration on this distinctiveness and then interpret what we find there in light of social-science findings on gender differences. In certain New Testament passages, Paul argues that there are differences between men and women in dress and certain social roles (1 Cor. 11:1–13). These differences are not viewed as a necessary part of the created order, but they are adopted in society. In some passages on how women and men are to relate in households (Eph. 5:21–33), Paul incorporates Roman and Greek household ethical codes and argues that Christians should follow those principles.

Some theologians would argue for specific gender-differentiated household roles or divisions of labor (Köstenberger and Köstenberger 2014; Strachan and Peacock 2016; Strachan 2019). For example, Strachan (2019) identifies these roles for the male as provider, protector, caretaker, and nurturer of the female. One concern with this approach that identifies more traditionally modern male and female divisions of labor as the biblical ideal is that household tasks themselves are difficult to identify as either male or female. More importantly, these modern divisions of household labor may not reflect household division of labor in New Testament times. It is important to maintain the distinctiveness of men's and women's sexual differentiation and how this differentiation results in gender identity and expression. However, we need to be careful to see that God-honoring gender identity may involve different gender expressions as cultures change over time.

The Bible has more to say about Christian temperament in general than it does about distinctions between female and male temperament. Paul writes in Galatians 5:22–23: "The fruit of the Spirit is love, joy, peace, patience, kindness, generosity, faithfulness, gentleness, and self-control." It is noteworthy that our culture considers these attributes to be feminine. On the basis of these verses, we would argue not only that males and females should be more alike but also that males need to develop the qualities that have traditionally been defined as feminine.

Still another means of viewing gender roles from a Christian perspective is to examine the person of Jesus during his earthly ministry. That is to say, what was Jesus really like as a human? To begin with, we read about a person who experienced a wide range of emotions, but compassion and love were pervasive. The compassion of Jesus is seen in his relationships with the blind man, the woman with the issue of blood, the lepers, the bereaved widow, the woman at the well, and children. Consider also his actions toward people in need—feeding the hungry, healing the sick, and reaching out to the lost as to sheep without a shepherd.

The compassion of Jesus was also expressed in his sorrowful emotions during experiences of despair and loss. Jesus wept over Jerusalem because of the unbelief of its people. When he saw Mary and Martha grieving over the death of Lazarus, he openly cried and expressed his own sadness. At other times, Jesus was elated and expressed great joy. When the seventy he had sent out to witness returned, Jesus "rejoiced in the Holy Spirit" (Luke 10:21). He also told his disciples that if they would abide in his love, his joy would be in them (John 15:10–11).

In addition to meekness, Jesus openly expressed anger and indignation. In a world under the curse of sin, he responded appropriately with anger. When he witnessed unbelief, hypocrisy, and acts of inhumanity, he took action. Jesus openly expressed his emotions, whether it was to nurture the little children or to overturn the tables in the temple. The picture that emerges is that Jesus was not traditionally masculine or feminine by our current cultural standards but, rather, distinctively human. He incorporated the characteristics of both masculinity and femininity and presented to the world a model of an integrated and whole person.

Changing Gender Relations and Family Life

The home is one of the main arenas in which males and females live out their gender. As we express our gendered identities in a manner that glorifies God, we need to understand women's and men's roles in family life. A biblical understanding challenges traditional female and male gender roles and offers a corrective to postmodern and critical theory's attempts to erase any meaningful differences between men and women.

Women in Family Life

Western women have traditionally acquired status in our society through being wives and mothers. The dramatic redefinition of work along with men's and women's roles in the workplace has transformed the ways women and men participate in work and family life. Many women experience contradictory expectations when they begin to pursue professional careers or work full time outside the home. Magazines, films, and television add to the confusion by encouraging romance, marriage, and childbearing while at the same time glorifying the independent, career-oriented woman.

The message given to Christian women is that they must have it all. In an effort to do it all, they become superwomen who suffer stress and frustration, especially if they attempt to balance a career and motherhood. The fallout from this might best be illustrated by the titles of popular books written for Christian women such as *Recovering from Biblical Manhood and Womanhood* (2020) and *Beyond Authority and Submission: Women and Men in Marriage, Church, and Society* (2019).

In *The Mommy Myth: The Idealization of Motherhood and How It Has Undermined All Women* (2004), Susan Douglas and Meredith Michaels suggest that there is a "new momism" consisting of a set of standards of success that any mother will find impossible to meet—devoting herself 24/7 to her children with a professionalism that includes the skills of a therapist, a pediatrician, a consumer products safety inspector, and a teacher. In *The Myth of the Perfect Mother* (2004), Carla Barnhill urges mothers to parent without fear or guilt by reclaiming their personhood in Christ. This means viewing motherhood as a spiritual practice and not as a calling. A mother should be judged less on how her children turn out than on how her spiritual practice of mothering is exemplified by the virtues of love, mercy, humility, peace, justice, and compassion. Rethinking the spirituality of mothering goes a long way in combating the cult of the perfect mother.

Whereas husbands may encourage wives to work outside as well as inside the home, they often do not pick up the slack at home, so the woman is left with a double-duty workload—a second work shift. Wilcox (2004) found that married fathers who express the most traditional gender-role beliefs and whose wives also work outside the home spend about three hours less on household labor each week than do egalitarian fathers. We believe that Christians should pursue a path of dual leadership and coparenting. Husbands and wives should be on the cutting edge in working for interdependence and role flexibility in this cooperative venture.

Men in Family Life

The traditional definition of masculinity has also been evaluated negatively by emerging research on men. Men are described as so emotionally restricted that they are often strangers to their wives; fathers are so emotionally absent that they are often more a "phantom man" than a "family man"; boys grow into manhood with a "wounded father" within, resulting from an emotionally distant father they never knew; and what men learn about power, achievement, competition, and emotional inexpressiveness results in their entering relationships with other men with great caution and distrust.

Fatherhood has received careful attention in the past decades. The effect of fatherlessness has been documented as an aspect of social and civic concern since the 1990s. According to 2017 US census data, more than one in four children lived in a home without a father. David Blankenhorn (1995) argues that the decline of the father's role as caregiver, moral educator, head of the family, and breadwinner has been enormous. Although we are cautious about offering a single explanation, there is a wealth of research evidence suggesting that the diminished presence of the father is responsible for increases in a variety of social ills such as juvenile delinquency, youth violence, domestic violence against women, child sexual abuse, children living in poverty and economic insecurity, adolescent childbearing, and unwed pregnancy. In contrast, living with an involved father has been associated with better educational outcomes (Whitney et al. 2017), and father presence in the household is associated with greater emotional and social well-being (Adamsons and Johnson 2013). This does not mean the mere presence of the father is enough to overcome father-absence per se (Schoppe-Sullivan and Fagan 2020). That requires strong fathering, which can have a profound effect on children and all of society (McLanahan, Tach, and Schneider 2013).

More recent definitions of fatherhood describe both the economic and the direct activities associated with it (Schoppe-Sullivan and Fagan 2020). Fatherhood is increasingly understood as providing both direct engagement—including male warmth and responsiveness to children and control or authority—and indirect provision through economic and process needs such as educational opportunities, daily physical resources, and access to parks and recreational activities (Pleck 2010). The emphasis here is on both the emotional and behavioral engagement of the father with his children as well as the indirect provisions of shelter, education, and medical care. Fathers having intimate relationships with their children is crucial to children's well-being. This aspect of fatherhood represents a significant change for men operating with a traditional view of masculinity.

The Christian men's movement Promise Keepers has strongly emphasized emotionally involved fathering as a major plank in its construction of Christian manhood. Men need to be *committed*—especially in their relationships—to Christ, family, and the church. A number of Christian organizations continue to work to strengthen the father in the home.

Bradford Wilcox (2004) notes that when compared with both fathers who do not attend church and fathers from mainline churches, fathers in evangelical churches tend to be warmer and more expressive in their fathering. Family values have become the key markers of evangelical identity. A legitimate question to ask is how evangelical family values and ideology correspond with men's *behavior* in family life. Wilcox uses the term *soft patriarchy* to describe the "softening effect" on men who are regular attendees of conservative churches, shown by greater emotional engagement with wives and children.

Christians in the early church were known for their love of one another. The same should be said of Christian men today; they should be known by their love. Authentic Christian manhood is found in behaviors that reflect the character of Jesus in ways that "seek to support rather than dominate women, empower rather than control younger men, and mentor and complement rather than compete with other men" (J. O. Balswick 1992, 212).

Coparenting: The Need for Mothering and Fathering

Children who live in coparented families have the best of all worlds since they have the presence and involvement of two parents in their lives. Couples who share parenting and household roles experience a high degree of marital happiness, whereas couples who both work but do not share roles at home experience distress. The commitment coparents make to work through various issues about gender-specific parenting and household roles teaches their children about mutual respect, gender equality, and cooperation. Coparenting not only enhances the marital bond but also sends a clear message to children that the parental bond is strong.

A coparenting model begins with the assumption that parenting responsibility should be shared. That is, parenting obligation resides with both mothers and fathers. While recognizing that the mother may have an initial advantage in emotional connectedness through birthing and nursing, fathers can compensate by making special efforts to bond with children. Part of this ownership of parenting emphasizes that mothers and fathers contribute equally to parenting, and this contribution is based on *being a father or mother*. In other words, mothers and fathers make unique parenting contributions to the children. Coparenting will happen only if parents intentionally move toward collaborative parenting, in which fathers are open to learning tasks traditionally reserved for mothers and mothers allow fathers to learn "on the job," resisting the urge to intervene.

Fathers who become involved in the parenting process find that their socioemotional and relational sides develop. This has a positive effect on sons as well, for when fathers set an example of expressing their feelings, their sons also become more expressive. In contrast to the world of work outside the home, where decisions are expected to be based on the rational rather than the emotional, taking care of children inclines men to consider personal and emotional issues, which will affect their work roles as well.

If we take seriously the evidence suggesting that modern society has become increasingly cold, heartless, and impersonal, then the need for the family to be an intimate, nurturing, and caring environment becomes even more obvious. Parents who do daily battle in this impersonal and heartless society often return battered and bruised to the confines of their self-contained, emotionally isolated nuclear family. At the same time, the cultural move toward modernity—extended families, neighborhood networks, community embeddedness—has largely eroded social supports for family members. That is, these aspects of modern family life are commodities that the family purchases to fulfill the needs of the children. This economic approach undermines the premodern emphasis on communal identity. The result is that the nuclear family is often the sole source for meeting its members' emotional needs.

Coparenting is the ideal arrangement for parents, children, and society. Having both parents actively engaged in the parenting responsibilities provides same- and opposite-gender modeling for children. They are able to see authentic, caring, and discipling male and female examples as they grow and learn. Children are able to internalize these models and the positive emotional experiences they provide and pass them on to others.

Sharing the parenting responsibilities and privileges allows men and women to engage in their God-ordained roles as mothers and fathers. It brings balance to the home after a long day's work and school, providing the family with a safe emotional haven in which to recoup. Coparenting challenges and equips men to father in a more emotionally intimate manner and challenges mothers to take on leadership roles in decision-making and discipline. For both women and men, coparenting models for children the self-sacrificial leadership of Jesus Christ.

A Concluding Comment

True Christian womanhood and manhood are not mere reflections of traditional definitions of femininity and masculinity. To help achieve the ideal of true manhood and womanhood, cultures can continue to recognize the distinctions between men and women and at the same time encourage individuals to meet their potentials and goals in life through equal opportunities and responsibilities. Scripture proclaims, "There is no longer Jew or Greek, there is no longer slave or free, there is no longer male and female; for all of you are one in Christ Jesus" (Gal. 3:28). The essential question that we should be asking is at what point our cultural norms prevent both men and women from becoming the fully human persons God intended them to be (Fee 2005). Women and men are both in need of liberation from the gender stereotypes that have hindered growth in personhood. It is important to define gender roles in family life that encourage males and females to flourish and be empowered.

It is important for us to grasp the intentions God had in mind in creating humanity as distinctly male and female (Gen. 1–2). In her essay "Toward Reconciliation: Healing the Schism," Alice Matthews (2005) credits David Scholer with noting that the biblical text that one chooses for one's starting point in the study of a doctrine or issue in Scripture becomes the lens through which one looks at all other texts. The difference between the two positions reflects a difference in hermeneutics—which is determining, through careful exegesis, the original intent of Scripture and applying it to contemporary life. Both positions recognize that culture can bend or alter gender distinctions in ways that the Creator did not intend.

Currently, the Christian community is far from united in its evaluation of the change in gender roles; some Christians say that women should return to their rightful place in the home, while others argue for increased participation by women in all occupations, including the ordained ministry. John Stackhouse (2005) attempts to reconcile these two evangelical positions by suggesting that both sides are wrong—and right! First, egalitarians need to concede that in some of his writing "Paul is maintaining a patriarchal line" (68). Stackhouse goes on to remind his "complementarian friends that the task is to make sense of *all* that Paul says, including the apparently equalitarian verses, some of which appear *in the same passage*" (68). He suggests that, for a reason similar to why Paul did not directly write against the practice of slavery (see Philemon), he at times did not directly write against the patriarchal structure of New Testament times. Stackhouse presents two principles in his paradigm: first, "men and women are equal in every way" (35), and second, "some things matter more than others" (38).

Once again, our theology of relationships is pertinent. Men, women, and children benefit from interacting with one another in a cycle of covenant, grace, empowerment, and intimacy. There must be a joint commitment to one another in a covenant of love working toward the goal of equality. This entails a willingness to forgive and be forgiven of the oppression and antagonism that have existed between the sexes. It takes grace to acknowledge and accept differences of opinion in this area. Other elements are mutual serving and empowerment. Finally, men and women will achieve intimacy in same-sex and opposite-sex relationships as they become free to know and be known by one another. This requires communication and a desire to understand the other so that we may cherish and value who we are as brothers and sisters in Christ. As we become fully developed men and women, others will know that we are Christians by our love for one another.

12

Becoming an Authentic Sexual Self

Becoming an authentic sexual person begins with an understanding of *who* God created us to be as sexual persons. How we behave sexually certainly influences how we define ourselves as sexual beings and vice versa. However, an understanding of what it means to be created as sexual persons in God's image involves much more than a simple assent to or an ability to live according to specified behavioral standards.

Sexuality includes such factors as biology, gender, emotions, thoughts, behaviors, attitudes, and values. The word *authentic* is defined as "real, genuine, believable, and trustworthy" (Balswick and Balswick 2019). We use the term to indicate that sexuality is meant to be a congruent and integral part of a person's total being. Our sexuality must be a real, genuine, believable, and trustworthy part of ourselves, so that we can embrace what God has created and declared to be "very good."

Our sexuality is a product of God's design, but it bears the taint of our fallen nature. In a multitude of ways, this good gift of sex has become perverted and warped in our world. The interplay of societal attitudes and beliefs, cultural structures, and biological factors shapes the inauthentic sexuality inherent in our fallen human condition. In this chapter, we examine some societal and cultural influences on the development of our sexuality. We also present some ideas on how Christians can become more authentic in their sexual personhood and expression.

Societal Attitudes toward Sexuality

Human sexuality is profoundly affected by prevailing societal attitudes. The predominant attitude in the United States has changed throughout history. Our past is often regarded as a time when sexuality was repressed; our modern society, by contrast, attempts to throw off all sexual inhibitions.

While the Puritans have traditionally been blamed for some of the uptightness of past generations, they actually had a quite healthy view of sexuality. They held to a standard of celibacy for the unmarried and monogamy for married people, but they advocated a wholesome sexual expression in the marriage relationship. An example comes from the Groton church leaders in 1675. When a husband announced that he planned to abstain from having sexual relations with his wife as personal penance for disobeying God, the leaders rebuked him, saying he had no right to deny his wife her rights to sexual fulfillment. Sexual expression between spouses was regarded as good, natural, and desirable and therefore not to be withheld, in accordance with 1 Corinthians 7:1–5 (Doriani 1996).

The Victorians, on the contrary, held many sexual taboos and negative attitudes about sex. They attempted to repress anything that appeared to be sexual. Not only were people required to cover their arms and legs in public as a symbol of modesty, but even the legs of furniture were covered with little skirts. A sharp line was drawn between sexual desire and love. A virtuous man was encouraged to wed a woman for whom he had pure thoughts, which meant no sexual desire. Husbands were told that if they really loved their wives, they would refrain from having sex with them too often since sexual relations even in marriage were considered degrading to women.

The expert medical opinion of the day asserted that any sexual desire in a young woman was pathological. The attitude in the 1880s was that decent women do not feel the slightest pleasure during sexual intercourse. The advice columnists of the day indicated that the more a woman yielded to the animal passion of her husband, the more he would lose respect for her. It is not coincidental that one of the most popular songs at the turn to the twentieth century began, "I want a girl just like the girl that married dear old Dad." The dichotomy between sexual desire and love led to a dual arrangement: a man had his sexual needs met by a "bad" woman, but he would only marry a "good" woman. It's no wonder that both men and women believed distorted messages about their sexuality.

Things began to change during the first half of the twentieth century, especially during the 1920s. Shifting attitudes ushered in an era of greater openness toward sexual expression, with a new standard described as permissiveness with affection. Now it was acceptable to acknowledge and express sexual desire and engage in sex when persons felt mutual affection.

For a period following World War II, there was a revolution in American attitudes and interest in sex. This began with the publication of the Kinsey reports: *Sexual Behavior in the Human Male* (1948) and *Sexual Behavior in the Human Female* (1952). There was great interest and fascination with the topic of sex. During this time Hugh Hefner started *Playboy Magazine*, directed to an eager audience of adult males who were ready to jump on the sexual-freedom bandwagon. The magazine (and others like it) had great appeal for men who were obsessed with sexual freedom. Enticed by the centerfold, they were told how to dress, what music to put on, how to mix a drink, and when to turn the lights down. In short, the message was how to get the woman into bed free of emotional attachments. By denying the multidimensional facets of womanhood, this message of freedom reduced women to sex objects.

C. S. Lewis (1960b, 75) compares a sex-obsessed society with a hypothetical society in which people pay good money to view a covered platter sitting on a table. At an assigned time and to the beat of drums, the cover is slowly lifted, and the object underneath is exposed for all to see. To everyone's great delight, a pork chop is revealed. Lewis concludes that something is radically wrong with a society so obsessed with food. Likewise, there seems to be something wrong when a society is so obsessed with sex.

In the 1980s, a slight backlash resulted from sexual overexposure, and a trend toward a new virginity emerged. Women began to question what they had bought into with their newfound sexual freedom; many felt their deeper desire for emotional intimacy had been completely sabotaged. College students wore large red buttons declaring "NO" to casual sex. Many took a second look at how sexual freedom undermines relationships. Christian young people made a pledge of celibacy before their parents and God with a "promise ring" representing their determination to maintain their chastity until their wedding night. Raw, explicit sex had lost its appeal as a shock and stimulus, and people rebuffed the use of sex for entertainment purposes and recreation. The fear of AIDS reinforced the trend to stop promiscuous sex and begin safe practices. Furthermore, the physical risk of STDs associated with unprotected, promiscuous sex led many to declare, "While I like sex, I'm not willing to die for it."

The backlash in the 1980s proved to be short-lived. Using C. S. Lewis's analogy, we might say in regard to sex in the twenty-first century that the platter is no longer covered. Explicit sex is depicted in most forms of popular culture: movies, television, popular music, and so on. The internet allows people to privately consume erotica and pornography. In this computer age, a culture saturated with sex inundates children as well as adults. As harmful as exposure to nudity and sexual innuendoes may be, an even greater harm comes from dishonest messages that depict sexual promiscuity and nonrelational sex as having few or no negative consequences.

The Origin of Sexuality

Not unlike the human personality, human sexuality does not emerge in full bloom in a person. One becomes a sexual being through a multidimensional developmental process. It is evident from social-science research that human sexuality is partly a reflection of the culture within which a person is socialized. In other words, society identifies sexual mores and sexual objects. We are taught to respond sexually to certain objects and symbols in our environment, and this influences how we define ourselves sexually. Our sexuality is also a product of biological, psychological, and experiential factors. We must resist the temptation to give a simplistic explanation of sexuality, one that relies only on either sociocultural or biological explanations.

Human sexuality emerges as part of a complex *interactive developmental* process between biological and sociocultural factors. Figure 8 presents biological factors on the left side and sociocultural factors on the right, with the arrows between the two sides indicating directions of influence and interactions between them. As part of the maturation process, biological and socioemotional-cultural factors individually influence sexual development, and there is also an *interactive* effect. The one-way influences are represented by one-way (⟶) arrows and the interactive influences by two-way (⟷) arrows.

For example, a baby born to a drug-addicted mother is born physiologically addicted to the drug as the drug is able to pass through the placenta into the baby's system. While "crack babies" are physiologically normal in genetic and chromosomal makeup, the sociocultural factors (poverty, abuse, depression, etc.) of the mother abusing drugs result in a chemical dependency in the newborn infant that affects his or her future. Without intervention, this will undoubtedly lead to physical, emotional, and cognitive problems in the development of the child.

A second example involves the development of sexual desire. In response to erotic stimulation (sociocultural), the brain (biological) organizes the behavior that will lead the body to sexual involvement. Incoming sensual stimuli are encoded in the cortex of the brain. The hypothalamus then determines if the stimuli are painful or pleasurable. This determined, the message is sent to the pituitary gland, which controls the adrenal glands and the female and male gonads. If the incoming sexual stimuli are pleasurable, the pituitary gland

FIGURE 8 **An Interactive Developmental Model of Human Sexuality**

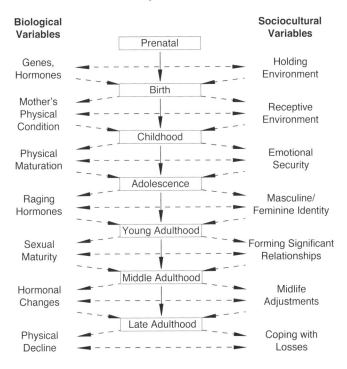

will command the gonads to produce the necessary hormones to begin sexual arousal. However, if the stimuli are painful, the pituitary gland will close the system down. Thus, the social environment greatly influences and affects the brain, which is a biological organ. It is also true, however, that hormone levels can greatly alter the power of external sexual stimuli to bring about erotic arousal within the sexual system. Social and biological factors interact with each other in ways that make it difficult to assess the effect of each separately.

Another example comes from the prepubescent stage, when a variety of changes begin to shape boys' and girls' bodies in different ways, not only between genders but within gender. During this period, boys learn a *boy code* that teaches them to be strong, competitive, and sexually aggressive, while girls learn a *girl code* that teaches them to be nice, cooperative, and sexually modest. There will be differences among boys and among girls, however, to the extent to which these sex-typing codes are learned. Some parents make sharp distinctions between boy and girl behaviors, while others encourage their children to value and emulate both male and female characteristics. At the same time, there are also significant differences in

221

hormone levels among boys and girls. High testosterone levels among some boys and high estrogen levels among some girls set the stage for early development of secondary sexual characteristics (pubic hair, breast and hip development, etc.). The range of gender-typical and gender-atypical behavior during prepubescence can best be understood in terms of both biological and sociocultural influences and the interaction between them. The fact that some boys and some girls prefer male-typical competitive play while others prefer more female-typical relational or nurturing play is most likely the result of both biological *and* sociocultural influences and the interactive effect between them.

Adolescence is a time when hormonal and biological sexual drives begin to take more prominence. Most boys find their masculine identity in male-typical behavior and girls in female-typical behavior. However, there is a wide range of gender-typical and gender-atypical behavior among teenagers. Parental values and spiritual teaching impact this decision as well.

The above example describes the complex interplay between biological drives and processes associated with sexual development and how society channels these drives into gender-segregated activities. Parents tend to take a more protective stance toward their daughters. Girls are warned to show modesty in their apparel; they are instructed to keep their dresses down, their breasts covered, and to guard themselves against sexual advances by boys. In the United States, females bear (no pun intended) more of the costs of pregnancy, childbirth, and rearing than males, so parents and society tend to foster more protective and restrictive practices for females as compared to males.

Although the interaction of the biological and sociocultural contributors to human sexuality is complicated, we offer some generalizations. First, rather than writing about causation, it is more accurate to cite the factors that *contribute* to the development of human sexuality. Second, both biological factors and sociocultural factors contribute to the formation of human sexuality. Third, human sexuality emerges as part of a developmental process, influenced by physiological, psychological, social, and cultural factors. One's beliefs and attitudes based on an effective value system become an important element in developing a healthy sexual self.

The Meaning of Sexuality

Explanations of sexuality are important but incomplete. Moving directly from biological and sociocultural information to value judgments about sexuality is a premature leap. It is one thing to examine sexual behaviors and norms and quite another to make decisions and judgments about moral issues.

222

While biological factors are most crucial in establishing sexuality early in life, sociocultural factors become increasingly significant as the child matures. As children develop the capacity to use language, they correspondingly learn the meaning of sexual attitudes and behavior. An understanding of God's design for human sexuality becomes increasingly important if the individual is to construct a truly meaningful, authentic sexuality. Because the meaning of sexuality is learned within a social context, it is imperative that the family and community powerfully live out and communicate God's design for human sexuality.

Families, churches, communities, and societies vary in the degree to which they reflect God's design and meaning for human sexuality. Since every individual belongs to a variety of groups, many of which offer competing perspectives on human sexuality, internalization of contradictory views is likely. The more the various groups to which the individual belongs consistently reflect God's ideal for sexuality, the more internally consistent will be his or her development of authentic sexuality. Where contradictions exist, our nature as choice-making creatures with emotive, volitional, and moral qualities can help us achieve authentic sexuality.

A Biblical Perspective on Human Sexuality

With this understanding of the development of sexuality, we are now in a place to expand on the biblical meaning of human sexuality. Theologically, human sexuality can be understood as a reflection of God's design for creation. Genesis 1:27–28 declares, "So God created humankind in his image, in the image of God he created them; male and female he created them. God blessed them, and God said to them, 'Be fruitful and multiply, and fill the earth and subdue it; and have dominion over the fish of the sea and over the birds of the air and over every living thing that moves upon the earth.'" This passage shows that the two sexes are distinct in God's design, yet in God's sight they are also equal and to be united as sexual beings. Both men and women are commanded to be fruitful, to subdue the earth, and to rule over the rest of God's creation. The beginning point includes an acceptance of one's unique sexuality, with the ability to acknowledge and be thankful that it is part of God's creation, design, and intention. Our sexuality is good in God's sight.

The biblical account, however, does not end with the *creation* story; it is followed by the *fall*, and then *redemption* and *restoration*. The first chapter of Genesis speaks of the differentiation of male and female and the harmony between them. Human sexuality is a good gift meant to draw us to deeper levels of knowing and being known (ourselves, others, and God). Our bodies are equipped with a nervous system, hormones, physical sensations, and an emotional capacity to help us connect with others. As embodied beings, sexuality incorporates our physiological and spiritual identities, and living *authentically* means expressing our image bearing physically. In this way, our identity is expressed functionally (Strachan 2019). We are born with an innate capacity for sexual pleasure; God's intended design for expressing and experiencing sexuality occurs within an emotionally caring, trustworthy family, and eventually a loving person-centered relationship. Sexuality and spirituality are intricately connected and must not be separated.

After the fall, sexuality was distorted and in need of redemption. In the beginning, Adam and Eve were perfect sexual beings just as God created them to be, yet they fell from that perfect state. Our fallen nature includes our sexuality. It is clear from the Genesis account that the fall has affected both sociocultural and biological life. Forever after, humans must face physical death and various mental and physical consequences of the fall (Gen. 3:17–19).

The comprehensiveness of the fall means that achieving an authentic sexuality involves conflict and struggle for everyone. Brokenness is evidenced in the home through distorted views of sex as well as the reprehensible acts of sexual and physical abuse and neglect. Family structures, along with other social and community structures, all play their part in contributing to the distortion. It becomes difficult to achieve an authentic sexuality in the midst of these distorting influences.

Because these systems are imperfect, we are also imperfect in our sexuality. Some people suffer from deficiencies in the genetic package they have inherited; some lack a sexual wholeness because of inadequate socialization in the home and community; some are victims of societal ills such as rape and pornography.

Despite all the obstacles, the sexual authenticity God intended for us is a goal worth striving for. Authentic sexuality is most attainable for those who are born with a normal genetic and physiological makeup, who are socialized in a home where parents display healthy attitudes regarding sexuality, and who live in a community where societal values are consistent with biblical teaching.

Sexual distortion can take a variety of forms as a result of differing combinations of sociocultural, biological, and spiritual factors. Some people have the disadvantage of living through circumstances that result in a devastating sexual brokenness. This is especially true when sexual encounters have been deeply harmful, creating scars that make healing a long-term process. The good news of the gospel is that we can find hope and wholeness in Jesus Christ, who, having once been wounded for us, shows compassion for and heals our wounds. Christ offers restoration and renews our potential for authentic sexuality.

Sexual Wholeness in a Broken World

The preceding analysis points to the development of sexuality as a complex process of multidimensional factors. Achieving sexual authenticity in a broken world is equally complex. We all have wounds that need to be healed as we struggle to authentically express our sexuality in relationship. In the remainder of this chapter, we will address four aspects of sexual expression that are important concerns to the Christian community: sex and singleness, masturbation, sexual orientation, and marital sexuality.

Sex and Singleness

Not wanting to wrestle with the difficult question of sex and singleness, churches sometimes seek an easy out by declaring that single people should deny their sexuality, or they ignore the question completely. This often leaves Christian singles insufficient guidance as to how they are to live as sexual persons in a singles' subculture that endorses standards in direct contradiction to biblical values.

In 1994, Lewis B. Smedes wrote a book called *Sex for Christians*. He advocates three important principles:

1. The sexuality of every person is meant to be woven into the whole character of that person and integrated into his or her quest for human values.
2. The sexuality of every person is meant to be an urge toward and a means of expressing a deep personal relationship with another person.
3. The sexuality of every person is meant to move him or her toward a heterosexual union of committed love.

Living out these principles keeps sexuality and personhood connected at every level. It also calls to mind our theology of relationships. Sexuality is to be exercised within a context of covenant, an unconditional commitment to a personal relationship. We are challenged to work toward deepening this personal relationship by establishing an atmosphere of grace (acceptance and forgiveness), empowering one another, and increasing the level of intimacy. As Smedes puts it, "Sexual fulfillment is achieved when a personal relationship underpins the genital experience, supports it, and sustains a human sexual relationship after it" (1994, 25–26). This will be our basic premise in discussing premarital sexual relationships.

In the United States today, there are four major standards of premarital sex: (1) sexual abstinence, (2) the double standard, (3) permissiveness with affection, and (4) permissiveness without affection. Although sexual abstinence is the traditional Christian value (and one of the two most strongly held beliefs in the general population), when it comes to behavior, a majority in today's society do not adhere to it. The double standard, which allows premarital intercourse for males but not for females, has declined during the last hundred years. However, in their book *Premarital Sex in America* (2011), Regnerus and Uecker report that the double standard is alive and well today. They explain the persistence of the double standard with two theories: (1) sexual scripts, which define the male role as more permissive than the female role; (2) sexual economics, which presumes that the rational pursuit of reward maximization, rather than love or intimacy, governs the sex lives of young men.

Permissiveness with affection is the viewpoint with the greatest number of proponents in Western societies today. This has to do with sharing more positive feelings and emotional connection leading to sexual intercourse. This also implies a level of exclusiveness and mutuality in expressing affection as well as sex. Permissiveness without affection, which allows casual and recreational sex between two consenting adults, has been a standard in the past few decades, often referred to as "hooking up." A study of 832 college students' experiences with hooking up reveals that women were less likely to consider it a positive emotional experience and that hooking up is a practice associated with "being white rather than a person of color, more alcohol use, more favorable attitudes toward hooking up, higher parental income . . . [and] having hooked up at least once in the past year" (Owen et al. 2010, 653).

We believe that Christians should celebrate their freedom in Christ and be bound by no rules other than those given in Scripture. Starting with the Ten Commandments, it is clear that the Bible holds adultery to be contrary to God's will (DeYoung 2018). While the term *adultery* is usually defined as sexual intercourse between a married person and a person other than the lawful husband or wife, in his Sermon on the Mount Jesus Christ expands the meaning of adultery to include all lust (Matt. 5:27–30; DeYoung 2018).

The New Testament word *porneia*, which is translated "fornication" or "immorality," has traditionally been interpreted as sex outside marriage. Those holding to the position of situational ethics (the guiding principle of which is to maximize love) argue that "fornication" refers to a depersonalized, body-centered sex. Such a definition promotes freedom to engage in sex if it is not depersonalized (love with affection). Although the word may have this meaning in some passages, *porneia* almost always refers to sexual intercourse outside the marriage union.

We interpret the Bible as upholding the restriction of sexual intercourse to the marital relationship. Depending on how engagement and betrothal are defined, specific application of this principle may vary from one society to the next. Historically, girls were often very young at the time of engagement. In contemporary society, however, the trend is to marry at a later age, making it more difficult for older single adults to abstain until marriage.

Another contrast with the past is that societal structures used to help young people meet the biblical standards, but in modern society people of all ages are bombarded with explicit sexual stimuli. The mass media sanction sexual expression before marriage. At the very height of their sexual urges, people who have committed themselves to abstinence before marriage are besieged by such messages.

To add to the confusion, singles must grapple with the gray areas of determining the amount of physical and sexual involvement they will engage in during dating and courtship. This can mean anything from merely holding hands to genital contact just short of sexual intercourse. While the Bible advocates physical affection between Christians in the form of greeting one another with a holy kiss, it does not tell us what makes a kiss holy or how to express affection in a relationship that goes beyond friendship. It is indeed difficult to set up hard-and-fast rules regarding premarital sexual involvement since many factors enter into the situation, such as the couple's age and maturity, the level of their commitment, the length of the engagement, and the closeness to the marriage ceremony.

It is natural and good for a single person to physically express affection for the one he or she loves. Touching is a means of communicating acceptance, love, and care. We learn this from children, who are free to express themselves through touch and open themselves up for expressions of affection. Single adults more often withhold expressions of affection, an important means of affirmation, out of fear of being misunderstood. Unfortunately, this leaves many singles longing for intimate relationships with others that are free of such sexual connotations. Singleness presents a wonderful opportunity for both men and women to develop deep friendships. Reaching an appropriate level of vulnerability in emotional and spiritual and physical relationships with others brings richness to one's life.

Of course, when there is a sexual element to relationships, the couple must negotiate this. It is essential at this point for both individuals to determine to what degree they will be involved, what is appropriate in their relationship, and how to proceed in mutually agreed-upon goals, all the while submitting to the authority of Scripture to guide their discernment process. We present the following guidelines to aid in discerning the expression of sexuality outside marriage.

1. The degree of sexual intimacy should correspond to the degree of love and commitment present in the relationship. Where there is no commitment, a high degree of sexual intimacy is inappropriate. Where there is commitment, being with the person is more important than the pleasure derived from the physical intimacy. In covenant love, commitment to the person and the relationship takes precedence over sexual expression.

2. We tend to desire increased physical involvement in our lovemaking which progresses toward more stimulatation. The ultimate sexual expression is orgasm. The closer a couple gets to that point, the harder it is to retreat to a previous level. The couple needs to be aware of this fact so that they can determine appropriate limits for their physical involvement.

3. Both partners must test their personal motives for the physical involvement and activity. Is the motive for physical involvement to express affection or to sexually excite one's partner and oneself? It does something for the ego of both men and women to know that they can sexually excite another person. As the motive behind physical involvement, such ego gratification has a way of separating sex from personhood, since the goal is not deeper personal connection but satisfaction of one's personal needs.

4. The two people involved must continually communicate about all areas of the relationship. A couple should tread cautiously when the physical dimension develops out of proportion to the social, emotional, psychological, and spiritual dimensions. When the sexual aspect dominates, the other important dimensions are undernourished, and the relationship becomes lopsided, vulnerable, and weak.

5. Both partners should take responsibility for establishing guidelines and setting physical limits. Christian males must reject the societal norm that males should go as far as they can sexually, since it is up to the female to set the limits. Both partners are responsible for their sexual involvement.

6. The two people involved must agree to abide by the limits proposed by the partner with the *more stringent standards*. Such an attitude of respect and caring places the person above the desire for sexual activity.

To sum up our guidelines: the sexual dimension must be put in proper perspective. In 1 Corinthians 6:12–13, Paul says, "'All things are lawful for me,' but not all things are beneficial. 'All things are lawful for me,' but I will not be dominated by anything. 'Food is meant for the stomach and the stomach for food.'. . . The body is meant not for fornication but for the Lord, and the Lord for the body." There are, then, no hard-and-fast laws to govern premarital sexual expression; rather, there is freedom in Christ to make responsible decisions that are in accordance with God's Word up to the limit of sexual intercourse. We must bear in mind that not everything is good or beneficial for us; this is especially true of behavior that comes to have a grip on us. Once again, if sexual involvement becomes the overriding concern, it can lead to the demise of a relationship.

In thinking about premarital sexual involvement, a due amount of attention should be given to the matter of sexual lust and sin. We must neither ignore the subject nor overly concentrate on it. When Paul speaks out against fornication and immorality, he does so in a list of sins that includes greed and overeating. Some people make the mistake of magnifying sexual sin out of proportion. To them it is the great unpardonable sin, but this is not the biblical view. Others yield to the ethics of secular society and minimize sexual sin. It is not easy being single in a sexually oriented society that promotes norms beyond biblical teaching. Single people need to be enfolded into family and community life in ways that accept them as sexual persons with needs for love and intimacy. In turn, they have much to contribute to the community, as they struggle along with everyone else to realize the full potential of their humanity, which includes their God-given nature.

In a mature relationship, there is a mutual responsibility for sexual behavior. This mutuality helps each partner set limits on sexual expression. Leaving the matter up to chance is irresponsible. Although chronological age does not guarantee maturity, it is a general indicator of one's development and differentiation. The younger the person, the more underdeveloped his or her sexuality, and the more confusing sexual involvement can be. Few teenagers are mature enough to sustain a relationship as demanding as marriage. In fact, statistics show a high percentage of teenage marriages in the United States end in divorce. Many who engage in premarital sex do so for the wrong reasons, such as using sex as a substitute for emotional intimacy, to keep a relationship going, or to satisfy a partner. Although sex may offer physical pleasure, fixation on the external act does not satisfy the deepest internal cravings for an intimacy based on covenant love.

In contrast, mutual commitment allows single adults to respond to each other with maturity and respect. A mature sexual relationship incorporates the elements of covenant, grace, empowerment, and intimacy in an ever-deepening cycle that continues throughout life. People who achieve authentic sexuality do not separate sex and personhood but understand that their sexuality is an integral part of who they are. Lauren Winner (2005) argues for the importance of premarital sexual chastity by stressing that sex is communal rather than private—"doing sex in a way that befits the Body of Christ, and that keeps you grounded, and bounded, in the community" (123).

Masturbation

Masturbation (self-pleasuring) seems to be a nearly universal practice for both males and females. In the past, various attempts were made to discourage people from masturbating. Folk wisdom claimed that masturbation had unpleasant consequences: hair loss, warts, pimples, even blindness or impotence. Many young people live with intense guilt over this behavior.

How are Christians to view masturbation? What should parents teach their children about it? Obviously, parents should alleviate the fears and guilt that the myths of the past may have perpetuated. It is natural for children to explore their physical bodies and come to have an awareness of their anatomy. They need to feel positive about their bodies and the sensations they experience when they touch themselves. Healthy attitudes about sexuality begin in the home. Children who get a good start there will grow up with an appreciation of God's gift of sexuality.

It is important to recognize that the Bible is silent on the topic of masturbation and that any case a person builds either for or against it is based on inference. There are three major opinions about the place of masturbation in a Christian's life. The restrictive position is that masturbation under any circumstance is sinful. The permissive position holds that masturbation under any circumstance is healthy and morally permissible, harmful to no one, and a good way to be aware of ourselves as sexual beings. The moderate view holds that masturbation can be both healthy and morally appropriate but also has the potential to be unhealthy and morally inappropriate as well.

We hold this moderate position as most reasonable. Masturbation can be a healthy way for a person without a marital partner to experience sexual gratification or release. God has created humans as sexual beings, so masturbation is one means for them to be in touch with their sexuality. Some common reasons people masturbate are associated with relieving sexual tension, relaxation, or lack of available partners. Sexual pleasuring may be a positive option for married persons who experience separation or the death of a spouse. Accordingly, many Christians need to be freed from the guilty feelings they have about masturbation.

But masturbation is not always psychologically and morally healthy. Compulsive masturbation can lead to addictive, self-defeating patterns. Within marriage, masturbation can be a negative factor if it deprives one's spouse of sexual fulfillment or is used as a way of evading relationship problems. When married partners have different desires regarding the frequency of intercourse, however, masturbation may be a healthy outlet and a loving solution. The relationship must always take priority as the couple faces their sexual differences rather than escapes them.

Another issue to contemplate is the connection between masturbation, fantasizing, and lust. Jesus teaches about this in Matthew 5:27–28: "You have heard that it was said, 'You shall not commit adultery.' But I say to you that everyone who looks at a woman with lust has already committed adultery with her in his heart." Lusting after a particular person may lead to acting out one's desire. This is adultery, and adultery is sin. Lusting should not necessarily be equated with fantasizing, however. Most people fantasize about future possibilities, and masturbation with one's spouse or future spouse in mind can be a helpful way to remain celibate and faithful.

Lusting has more to do with inordinate, inappropriate desire and finding ways to fulfill it. In fantasy, by contrast, one's wish is more general, and there is usually no specific attempt to achieve it. The one who is doing the lusting or fantasizing is usually aware of the difference. The person, for example, who masturbates while fantasizing about having sex with a neighbor's wife turns the lust into action when he makes an advance to her. In this case, fantasy is a precursor to a sinful act. It behooves us to pay attention to our fantasies, so that we can keep them within God's intended purpose.

It may be that a person who craves power fantasizes about sexual conquest. Bringing such a fantasy to awareness makes it possible to consider whether this is God's intended purpose. This particular fantasy disregards God's commandment to love others and not do them harm. In the same way, people who masturbate while viewing erotic pictures ought to consider the moral question of sexual exploitation and consider whether the dehumanizing aspect of the erotic material is in keeping with God's intention for humanity. The rising concern about pornography involves these issues, since the distorted attitudes about women and sex in our culture may lead to an increase in rape and other violent crimes. Again, the Bible admonishes us to cherish and value one another.

These are the kinds of issues for Christians to consider when trying to decide what one is free to do and what is good to do. Each one of us must determine the appropriateness of our fantasies and the effect they have on our whole life. It is possible to monitor our thoughts in the area of sexuality, just as it is possible to make choices about other things we allow to affect us. A person who reads a novel or sees a movie and experiences a romantic fantasy needs to consider if it takes away from the spouse and the marital relationship or increases responsiveness to the spouse in a positive way. The single person needs to decide whether a particular fantasy enhances the hope for a future relationship with a partner whom God has intended or idealizes a phantom person in a role that no ordinary person can fill. The important thing is that we are able to admit when our fantasies are not in keeping with God's intention and to change them to conform to God's plan for us.

In the past, the Christian community has magnified the sins of the flesh out of proportion to other wrongs and given the erroneous impression that sexual sins are far worse than any other sins. It is important to remember that we have been created in the image of God, and we are the children of God who have been made righteous through the blood of Christ. All our sins are forgivable. Regardless of what our past sexual life has been, we can come before God, ask forgiveness, and claim sexual purity in Christ. At the same time, we are responsible for our behavior and must earnestly seek God's help to become whole persons in every aspect of our lives, including sexuality.

Sexual Identity

Sexual attraction is a natural part of a person's sexual development, as well as somewhat of a mystery in terms of who people find attractive. Part of God's design in creating us as sexual beings is that our attractions draw us into deeper personal relationships with others. The vast majority of people identify as heterosexual with opposite-sex attraction. A host of studies have suggested that the percentage of people who identify as gay is much lower (2–3 percent). *Contemporary Perspectives on Lesbian, Gay, and Bisexual Identities* (Hope 2009) estimates that 2 percent of men and 1 percent of women are exclusively same-sex attracted, and 1 percent of men and women are exclusively same-sex in behavior. However, it is estimated that over a lifetime, 6–8 percent of men and 9–10 percent of women have experienced a degree of same-sex attraction, and 5 percent of men and 2 percent of women have engaged in same-sex behavior.

Researchers consistently find no conclusive evidence as to why certain individuals develop same-sex attraction or identity as homosexuals. Eleanor Whiteway and Denis Alexander (2015) state that "no single cause can explain the variety or form of same-sex attraction across genders and cultures" (70). Instead, studies indicate a combination of interrelated bio-social-cultural influences, as well as multiple pathways that lead to same-sex orientation.

A common experience among homosexuals in childhood or adolescence is that of not conforming to traditional gender traits or behavior. The fear of exposure and being labeled "queer" by classmates and family members makes this a confusing and painful time. The attempt to hide same-sex attraction is understandable in a society that exhibits considerable contempt for homosexual and bisexual persons. Ignorance and intolerance unfortunately can lead to homophobic reactions along with acts of hatred and even murder. Hatchel et al. (2019) found that LGBTQ youth were more than three times more likely to have attempted suicide compared with non-LGBTQ peers, and female youth in the psychiatric inpatient facility in the study were twice as likely to have attempted it as male patients. It is reasonable to expect that there is a personal cost to one's mental well-being when living with the fear, hatred, and shame associated with sexual identity.

Believing that God intended heterosexual union as the created norm (Gen. 1–3; Rom. 1:26–27; 1 Cor. 6:9–11), the Christian community has traditionally condemned homosexuality. More recently, alternative responses have emerged in light of the recognition that same-sex attraction is not a choice. Therefore, it is not the orientation that is condemned but the behavior. This has led to the expectation that those who have same-sex attractions choose heterosexual relationship or celibacy. An alternative response is the acceptance of committed, same-sex monogamous relationships. Some advocate for legalization of marriage, ordination, and leadership in the church. Whatever the response, Christians and churches across denominational lines are challenged to be a reconciling force in relating to the gay community.

In doing extensive counseling with the LGBTQ community, Mark Yarhouse (2010), Regent University professor of psychology and director of the Institute for the Study of Sexual Identity, believes it is helpful to distinguish between *attractions*, *orientation*, and *sexual identity*, which he considers to be at the heart of the matter. The first tier, *attraction*, is a descriptive term in which the person has no control over the fact that they are attracted to a person of the same sex. The second tier, *sexual orientation*, is a same-sex attraction that is felt as persistent and durable. Finally, the third tier, *gay identity*, is prescriptive. It involves describing oneself with a label that involves cultural meaning—a formed sexual identity and not just a description. He contends, "*Public* sexual identity is how you identify your sexual preferences to other people or how other people label you, whereas *private* sexual identity is how you identify your sexual preferences to yourself" (39; italics in original). A person with same-sex attractions and orientation may choose an "identity in Christ" as an alternative script that guides life choices. This means following the teachings of Jesus as the model for their lives.

Yarhouse (2010) explains: "I work on what most people can manage and experience change in: I look at how identity develops over time and how it can reflect a person's beliefs and values. I want to help people live their lives and identify themselves in ways that are in keeping with their Christian beliefs and values" (91). He reminds Christians to be humble, to listen carefully and compassionately to the person's developmental story, and to refrain from placing unrealistic expectations on them.

Many deeply spiritual gay Christians wish to be accepted and affirmed in their attraction/orientation/identity. They are looking for churches that offer a safe place of worship, fellowship, and service.

We began this book with our theology of relationships, built on the premise that the original intention of God's creation was heterosexuality. In the Genesis account, the ideal is male and female differentiation and unity: we become one flesh for the purpose of intimacy and procreation. However, since the whole human race is fallen, none of us achieves sexual wholeness in accordance with God's high ideal. Everyone falls short. Homosexuals and heterosexuals alike must strive to find wholeness in their lives in a less than ideal world. Each of us struggles in our own ways for sexual authenticity. In their struggle, some gay Christians believe that God's plan for them is to commit themselves to a lifelong, monogamous homosexual union.

We advocate compassion and support for all people as they move in the direction of God's ideal, and our hope is that God will lead each one of us closer to sexual wholeness. Authentically living out God-glorifying sexuality is a spiritual service to God. This will, of course, be a more painful and difficult process for some than for others. By balancing *truth* and *grace*, we are called to be a place where the world knows we are Christians by our love. Christ is willing to grant to everyone the privilege of walking through that process of finding sexual wholeness.

Marital Sexuality

Sexuality is only one aspect of the marriage relationship. It is authentic and healthy when it is well integrated into a comprehensive pattern of intimacy between the partners. Authentic sexuality is a characteristic of the differentiated unity of marriage. Several principles will prove helpful for couples who want to achieve authentic sexuality in their marriage.

First, the foundation for authentic sexuality in marriage is *mutuality*. This idea is presented in 1 Corinthians 7:4–5: "For the wife does not have authority over her own body, but the husband does; likewise the husband does not have authority over his own body, but the wife does. Do not deprive one another except perhaps by agreement for a set time, to devote yourselves to prayer, and then come together again, so that Satan may not tempt you because of your lack of self-control." Here we see that the Bible urges full mutuality. "By agreement" is a translation of the Greek phrase *ek symphomnou*, which literally means "with one voice" (compare the English word *symphony*). The mutuality mentioned in verse 5 is consonant with Ephesians 5:21, which tells husbands and wives to "be subject to one another out of reverence for Christ."

Authentic marital sexuality can be achieved only if husband and wife are in agreement about their sexual interaction. There is no room for the misguided view that the husband initiates and dominates while the wife submits in obedience. Rather, 1 Corinthians 7:4–5 and Ephesians 5:21 assume mutual desire for and interest in sexual expression. This requires sensitive communication between the couple about their sexual desires. Just as an orchestra plays "with one voice" when each instrument contributes its own unique part and the music is brought together in harmony, so a married couple reaches sexual harmony through communication and sensitive understanding of each other's needs.

Second, the husband and wife need to verbally communicate their sexual feelings and desires. Each spouse needs to know what the other desires sexually; this is not the time for guessing games. Sexuality becomes an expression of emotional intimacy and knowing the other. It is important for couples to communicate about how they can best fulfill each other's sexual needs and desires. Guiding each other through touch and brief words of encouragement during the sexual encounter can be helpful. However, it is also essential that the couple take time to talk about their sexual relationship, so they can evaluate how each is feeling and what may need changing. Open discussion about sexual matters contributes to sexual enjoyment. Obviously, the couple will need to invest time and effort in working together on matters that will enhance the sexual relationship.

Third, there must be no deception or hiding in the sexual encounter. Total openness is essential. There must be no hiding of one's true sexual feelings and desires for the sake of personal advantage. An individual who does not feel attractive may continually bait the partner into affirming him or her in this area. Another kind of game playing is alternately showing signs of sexual interest and disinterest in one's partner. The need to be pursued or the desire to be in control of the relationship often motivates this behavior. Yet another form of game playing is sexual teasing. One partner teases about desiring sex and then resists or is very passive when the other responds with sexual advances. These games end up having a negative impact on the relationship.

Fourth, marital sexuality should include an element of playfulness and spontaneity. A sexual relationship benefits from a sense of uninhibited engagement and non-self-conscious interaction. One of the benefits of playfulness is that it prevents couples from making a production out of sex. Controlling the sexual encounter in such a way that it becomes contrived and serious makes it impossible to respond to each other freely. A spirit of fun, however, keeps the sexual encounter spontaneous and relaxed. A healthy view of oneself and one's body and feelings of comfort with one's partner are vital ingredients of freedom in a sexual encounter. Accordingly, the level of fun in a relationship is often a good measure of the degree of intimacy.

Fifth, it is essential not to become spectators in the sexual encounter. When partners assume a spectator role during coitus, they tend to lose sight of each other. This is a particular problem in a technologically oriented society that emphasizes the importance of using the right methods. This attitude reduces sex to little more than an exercise in techniques. When this happens, sex is like the once-popular paint-by-number kits. The detailed instructions of a sex manual virtually dictate a couple's lovemaking. Just picture a scene in which the wife turns to her husband during lovemaking and says, "Turn back a page, Henry! We must have missed a step because I'm not feeling anything." The whole experience is inauthentic because there is no creative and spontaneous interaction between the spouses. In a very real sense, the personhood of each spouse is lost in the effort to make love by the book. An effort to be technically correct has replaced naturalness between lovers. In authentic sexuality, by contrast, the spouses allow natural feelings, inclinations, and actions to occur without a conscious evaluation of the performance. Both husband and wife are spontaneously engaged in the sexual encounter. Both partners are giving and receiving as they encounter each other in the moment.

Sixth, the greater the sensory pleasure in a relationship exclusive of coitus, the greater the sexual adequacy. This principle refers to the pleasure derived from foreplay. Touch communicates tenderness, affection, desire, warmth, comfort, and excitement. When a couple takes time to touch in ways that invite and increase responsiveness, they find more mutual satisfaction.

Seventh, the more secure the partners feel in their commitment to each other, the more complete their sexual response. Research shows that women and men are most able to invest themselves sexually when they feel secure about the relationship. Inversely, when trust is in question, spouses are less able to achieve an adequate sexual response. Men as well as women desire a sexual involvement that makes them feel warm and secure. Here again we see that trust helps bring about sexual responsiveness and authenticity.

Our discussion of marital sexuality calls to mind our theology of relationships: unconditional love and trust is the foundation of healthy sexuality; acceptance and ability to extend forgiveness in sexual matters is an expression of grace; empowering each other as sexual persons brings mutual regard; and person-centered sexual expression leads to deeper levels of knowing and being known. These four principles will move the couple ever closer to God's ideal of authentic sexuality.

PART 5

Communication

The Heart of Family Life

This section deals with the important dimension of communication. Communication is the heart of family life in that family members interact through verbal and nonverbal exchanges to express their thoughts, wishes, and core emotions. Through their honest expressions of thoughts and emotions, family members come to know one another in very personal ways. When family members communicate and express themselves in their own unique ways, family relationships grow and deepen.

Without the ability to communicate effectively, the family unit quickly becomes a mere collection of individuals whose thoughts, feelings, and desires are nobody's but their own. With an increased ability to communicate, however, the family can become a vibrant system whose members learn to engage in meaningful interaction. In this sense, communication is truly the heart of family life, where members have both the freedom and the skills to deepen their relationships.

Chapter 13 begins with a discussion of why the expression of love is so important to family intimacy. We follow with a section on why expressing love among family members is essential in deepening levels of knowing and being known. We then conclude with the important topic of conflict in family life. Conflict is indeed a normal part of family life, yet there are destructive and constructive ways to work through problems. We describe the five major styles people tend to use when they engage in conflict to help family members recognize the pros and cons of their unique styles. Effective families learn to respect one another's styles but at the same time adjust their ways of dealing with conflict for the good of the relationships. This creative effort is the difference between a satisfactory resolution that connects family members and an unsatisfactory one that distances them.

13

Intimate Communication

Expressing Love and Anger

Intimacy, and specifically intimacy via communication, sets the stage for this chapter. Being able to share thoughts and feelings is crucial to effective family living. By expressing emotions and sharing needs, family members develop an emotional attachment and create opportunities for mutuality and interdependence. The expression of emotions—*anger, hurt, love, joy, sadness, or affection*—is essentially how family members become more intimately acquainted. Expressing and resolving conflict fosters deeper intimacy.

Building intimacy in family relationships is one of the most important, yet one of the most challenging, tasks to do well. A recent approach to understanding the role of emotions in communication is emotional intelligence (EQ). Bar-On (2000) describes how EQ is made up of emotional, social, and personal qualities that allow individuals to identify their emotional experiences and those of others. Further, EQ influences how effectively individuals communicate with one another. Higher levels of EQ allow individuals to manage their emotions while effectively communicating with others. A recent study finds that improvements in EQ levels increased family communication and family satisfaction (Platsidou and Tsirogiannidou 2016).

For a person to share honestly about what is going on internally places one in a vulnerable position. Therefore, the family must be a safe place for members to share. If it is unsafe, members will feel personally threatened and guard others from knowing their true feelings or expressing their real needs. This is especially true of dealing with anger. Anger is a potentially scary emotion, and an unsafe environment will only discourage family members from expressing themselves. And anger expressed in unsafe ways increases feelings of being threatened, and individuals will become more guarded and careful in responding. When the fear of being ridiculed or rejected is more than members can risk, they will undoubtedly protect themselves by keeping their feelings and thoughts to themselves. This creates a distrustful atmosphere in which no one knows what the others are thinking and feeling. Many misunderstandings result from this state of affairs, which stymies family members' interactions. As members keep their distance and remain self-contained, the capacity for significant bonding becomes increasingly remote.

We believe that intimacy is desirable in marriage and family relationships not only as a refuge from the impersonality of society but also as a reflection of the biblical ideal. Genesis 2 describes a pre-fall condition in which intimacy—knowing and being known—brings a deep sense of relationship joy and mutuality. The trinitarian concepts of relationship unity and particularity provide a model for family members to make room in their hearts and lives for each unique family member and their emotions, needs, desires, and thoughts. Dialogue, mutual regard, interest, and engagement lead to increased understanding and interdependent unity. These values are especially important for anger and conflict resolution.

The Effects of Expressing Love

You may ask why it is so important to express to other family members the affection you feel. It assures them that they are lovable and encourages relationship bonding. Humans need to hear and to receive overt expressions of love from the time they are born until the day they die.

Studies of infant development suggest that babies who do not receive expressions of love will be less able to receive or express love to others during their lifetimes. Children who lack sufficient affection (physical touch and nurture), even though they may receive adequate physical care, suffer greatly. Marasmus, a disease in which the body simply wastes away, is prevalent among war victims and orphans. The child fails to develop socially, psychologically, and physically, and death is a frequent outcome. What is important for our purposes is to recognize how essential it is for children to be held, cuddled, caressed, kissed, and hugged as well as to have their physical needs met.

It is well established that children develop self-image based on their perceptions of how others view them. Children are able to love themselves if their parents have expressed love to them both verbally and physically. No one ever outgrows the need for affection and love. As we mature from infancy to adulthood, we have an increased need for verbal affirmation and physical expressions of love.

It is emotionally rewarding for all people to engage with others at a personal and emotional level. Doing so indicates the desire for interaction and interdependency. Psychologically speaking, keeping emotions to yourself actually puts you at risk of losing touch with yourself and others, inhibiting the potential for developing a close, emotional connection with those you love.

Naming and expressing our emotions helps us to communicate directly with those we are in relationship with. This is important because nonverbal communication is ambiguous at best. Using words aids in developing a mutual understanding between relational partners that then interprets nonverbal cues in communication. Additionally, direct communication of emotions helps teach children to name and understand their subjective experience. As they increase in their ability to name their feelings, they are better able to empathize with others. Practicing the expression of emotions increases EQ, which increases intimacy in relationships.

Expressing love is important for all relationships. Just as mutual commitment (covenant) is the basis of secure bonding, communication is the basis for intimacy. Communication is a two-way street. Some family members make valiant efforts to engage but find themselves in a dead end if the other member is unwilling to respond or reciprocate. Some people explain away the problem of expressing themselves with dismissive statements such as "He is just like that" or "She is shy" or "It's in the genes, so I can't expect much." While personality and even shy genes may be part of inexpressiveness, the fact remains that lack of emotional sharing develops into patterns of stifled communication. The possibility of intimacy is crushed, and the relationship stagnates emotionally.

Nonverbal Expressions of Love

Expressions of love can be communicated nonverbally as well as verbally (Chapman 2009; Turner and West 2002). A person can show affection through a hug, a pat on the back, a wink, or some other symbolic gesture. The fact is that we do communicate through our facial expressions, posture, and general body movements. Researchers note that people indicate open- or closed-mindedness through body language. A person who assumes an open and relaxed body posture is likely to be open-minded about the ideas the family is discussing. A family member who sits stiffly upright, tense, with legs crossed and arms folded, is likely to be closed-minded and defensive.

Body language, however, can be misread. The receiver of the message may wonder, "What does that gleam in her eye really mean?" Physical expressions can be misinterpreted as well. A parent may question, "Is my daughter hugging me so tightly because she loves me or because she wants me to delay her bedtime hour?" Symbolic expressions may conjure up suspicion: "Why did he send me these flowers today? Did he just have his secretary order them, or has he really gone out of his way to pick them out?" or "I wonder what's behind all this special attention I'm getting from her tonight." The point here is to take the crucial next step of clarifying the intended meaning so the nonverbal message is crystal clear.

Authentic communication occurs when verbal and nonverbal communication messages are congruent and clear, aiding the development of self-worth and satisfaction for all family members.

Obstacles to Expressing Love

Fear is perhaps the number one reason family members fail to express their love to one another. When we express ourselves freely, we become vulnerable to the other's response. It is not just our feelings that we reveal, but our feelings for the other person. When we communicate love, we place ourselves in an exposed position. It is as if we are emotionally naked, having stripped off our protective armor as we bare our feelings of love. When we let another person know of our love, we may fear he or she won't accept it or reciprocate it. It is a source of dread to be ignored, discounted, or, worst of all, rejected. Past experiences of rejection make it difficult to freely expose ourselves in the present. Acts of love are usually expressed naturally when people spend quality time together. Cultivating intimacy within which love can be expressed comfortably takes much time and intentional effort. Making family time a priority is especially an issue in our increasingly technological society.

Sometimes social and cultural expectations inhibit people from expressing emotions. Norms regarding appropriateness of expression are part of the socialization process. Inborn tendencies (for example, shyness) are reinforced by cultural and gender norms. These expectations become part of the child's self-image and a self-fulfilling prophecy.

Males in many societies learn to value so-called masculine expressions of feelings and to eschew expressions of femininity. They are taught that tenderness and gentleness are feminine. So when a young boy expresses sensitive emotions by crying, his parents may be quick to assert, "You're a big boy, and big boys don't cry!" or "Don't be such a sissy; be a man!" As the boy moves out from the family and into the sphere of male peer groups, the taboo against displaying vulnerable feelings is reinforced. Males should be encouraged to express their vulnerability without facing judgment or ridicule, and females should not bear the burden of drawing out or pursuing males in order for them to express themselves.

On the other hand, females in most cultures are given permission to express languages of love. Female expressions of anger, however, are discouraged because anger is an emotion more acceptable for males. When a woman asserts herself, she is accused of being aggressive; when she gives a strong opinion, she is judged as bossy; when she expresses anger, she is labeled as unfeminine and out of control. These messages that tie certain feelings with gender stereotypes restrict a person's full range of expression.

The important thing is to help both males and females identify their feelings and be able to express them in ways that enhance relationships. Emotional expression is different for females and males, yet it is crucial to building intimacy. It is through expressing our feelings that we learn how others respond to important experiences in their lives. Emotional expressions allow us to gain insight into the character of the other (Roberts 2007).

The Expression of Love in Family Relationships

The emotional bond between child and parent is the most important dimension of child development. Children who are denied a strong emotional bond with their mothers and fathers must go through life compensating for this lack. The most extensive problem for both boys and girls is the lack of a strong emotional bonding with their fathers.

In keeping with their distinct societal roles, mothers and fathers differ in relating to their children (Bi et al. 2018; Schoppe-Sullivan and Fagan 2020). Evidence suggests that these differences begin early and increase through the child-rearing period. Studies show, for example, that mothers tend to engage their babies directly to stimulate responses and to display affection, while fathers tend to read to or watch television with their children. Mothers are also more likely than fathers to hold, smile at, and speak to their infants.

The pattern that seems to emerge from the research on parenting is that mothers are more evenhanded in the affection they show daughters and sons, while fathers treat sons and daughters according to sexual stereotypes. Further, while the disparity in the father's approach toward sons and daughters begins when the children are infants, it increases as they grow older. By the time children reach their teenage years, a father usually views a daughter as someone to be treated in a gentle manner, while a son is treated in a more distant way. It is not surprising that more daughters than sons rate their fathers high in nurturing and giving affection.

These patterns are often maintained into adulthood. Males and females interact differently emotionally, and this often affects marriage. Males who have had more distant fathers may not have the emotional skills to share with their female partners. Females, on the other hand, may experience this as distance in the relationship.

A couple's ability to identify and communicate emotions is related to marital adjustment. Regardless of the total amount, similar levels of self-disclosure point to a healthy marriage. Emotional sharing and intimacy also affect the couple's experience of sexual satisfaction (Yoo et al. 2014). Dissatisfaction and other problems are likely to emerge when there is an imbalance in the amount of self-disclosure.

Although the husband is typically less expressive than his wife, some factors work against a wife's being open and sharing. For instance, the wife's verbal expression of love will diminish over time if her expressions of love are not reciprocated by the husband. When there is an uneven vulnerability in sharing, she will undoubtedly hold back and share less often. In their research, John Gottman and Joan DeClaire (2001) find that one spouse will offer a statement to the other as a bid for greater intimacy—for instance, "I feel like I don't know you." When one spouse reveals himself or herself in an intimate way and the other stands aloof, not responding to the invitation for deeper connection, the spouse who reached out will cease taking steps toward greater intimacy.

Sometimes, expressiveness or non-expressiveness can become a power issue in marriage. If either spouse hides feelings to have more power or if withholding affection becomes an effort to control the other, both spouses lose. Tactics like feigning interest in the relationship in an attempt to gain power will ultimately lead to distance and dissatisfaction in marriage (Gottman and DeClaire 2001). Reduction in marital self-disclosure can occur throughout the relationship's life cycle. Events like the birth of a child bring change. Carrying this additional emotional burden, the wife may express herself less to her husband. As time passes, the child may be able to fill some of the emotional needs of the mother. It is natural for a mother to express herself to a child who returns love, in contrast to a husband who rarely returns affection. It behooves a couple to keep their spousal relationship a priority during transition times in a marriage.

Emotional expression in marriage is key to longevity and satisfaction. Males and females may have learned different ways to express their emotional sides growing up, but marriage affords both partners an opportunity to learn new ways of relating to others. For males, marriage encourages the increasing disclosure of emotional experience. For females, marriage provides a place where they can relate as a peer to another emotional being, sharing but not being responsible for their partner's emotional experience.

Our differentiation in Christ (DifC) model indicates that authentic expression of experience is crucial for facilitating intimate relationships. Our identity as Christians is based on our adoption into God's family. This adoptive relationship grounds our experience and empowers our expression and relationships with others. DifC facilitates two important dimensions of authentically relating to others. First, DifC allows us to actively reflect on and manage our experiences. We are able to gain insight into ourselves, both good and bad, and bring this all to Christ for confession and forgiveness. This aspect of DifC is similar to the emotional regulation aspects of emotional intelligence described above in that it enables us to honestly and authentically develop insight into our sinfulness and confess this to Christ in order to experience his forgiveness more deeply. Second, DifC allows us to live out our core identity as Christ's brother or sister *in relationship with* another. In other words, DifC means authentically living out our identities by relating with others. We share the good and shameful aspects of ourselves with our spouses, and we look to them to do likewise. Authentic sharing and practicing forgiveness draw us deeper into relationship with Christ.

Expressing Anger: Negotiating the Inevitable Conflicts

Expressing anger and resolving conflict provide opportunities for practicing intimate and respectful communication. Strong families are not those that never experience conflict but those that successfully manage conflict when it does arise. Most families, however, approach conflict as a threat to the family system rather than an opportunity for growth. Family conflict resolution can be a significant challenge, and it is to this pressing topic that we now turn.

Simply put, a conflict is a difference in opinion. Family conflict can be individual (i.e., between two family members) or collective (i.e., between two sets of family members). Most family conflict is systemic in nature, centering on changes within and between family systems. Marital conflict, for example, is most likely to occur during the initial years when the spousal system is being formed or during transitional periods involving family restructuring or reforming. As would be expected, parental conflict has the most negative effect on children when focused on parental differences in child-rearing.

Regardless of the marital stage, conflict is greatest when spouses are under stress (Timmons, Arbel, and Margolin 2017). Parent-child conflict is less likely when the parental and sibling subsystems are on solid footing, and more likely when these two subsystems are in flux, such as when children reach their teenage years, when stepfamilies are formed, and so on. Conflict generates more threat and self-blame when there is little family connectedness.

It should also be noted that conflict between subsystems can cause secondary conflict between individuals in the subsystems. For example, parent-teenager conflict can intensify conflict between the husband and the wife around issues of discipline. In stepfamilies, conflicts between child and step-parent bring added tension into the spousal subsystem. Externally, an ex-spouse's dealings with children can cause havoc in the remarriage. However, conflict between subsystems can also unify a subsystem, such as when conflict with parents leads children into coalition or when the remarried couple joins forces to present a united front when dealing with their children or ex-spouses.

A conflict between two family members frequently entangles others (triangling). Strong emotional ties and investment in the outcome make it difficult for the others to stay out of the skirmish. A triangle is formed when noninvolved family members are brought into a conflict to help one member gain power. This side-taking complicates the situation since the matter of the third party's loyalty now intensifies the relationship dispute.

A Destructive Approach to Conflict: Denial

While conflict is neither good nor bad, the way in which it is handled can be destructive or constructive. Denying or failing to deal with conflict is invariably destructive to family relationships. Denial of conflict is like sweeping dirt under a rug. It only appears to eliminate the problem; it does nothing about the behavior that brought about the conflict in the first place. The problem, like the addictive use of drugs, intensifies because the conflict-producing behavior never changes. Denial is destructive on not only the relational level but also the personal level, since those who deny the conflict are also forced to deny their feelings of hurt, disappointment, and anger.

Family members can deny conflict in several ways. One common method is *displacement*: a family member angered or disturbed by another conveniently vents frustrations on a third member. Powerful family members use displacement to take out their frustrations on the less powerful. The younger members on the receiving end often come to the mistaken belief that they are bad and deserve punishment.

Another common form of denial in the family is *disengagement*. In this case, family members avoid conflict by sidestepping sensitive and controversial issues. Disengagement might be initiated by a burst of anger followed by withdrawal, such as when a husband gets mad at his wife, storms out of the house, and drives away in the car, only to return two hours later as if nothing had happened. The husband and the wife never talk about what caused the blowup, and together they collude in the cover-up. Disengagement serves as a barrier to growth in the relationship, and the unresolved conflict may well lead to a severe crisis later.

A more subtle form of denial is *disqualification*, a quick discounting of one's angry reaction. A mother may get mad at her children only to disqualify the legitimacy of her angry feelings by reasoning that she would not have gotten mad if she had slept better the night before. Disqualifiers tend to cover up angry emotions rather than admit them. Like the other forms of denial, disqualification is a barrier to growth and destructive to family relationships.

Constructive Approaches

The first step in dealing constructively with conflict is to admit that the conflict exists. The second step is to decide how to handle the conflict. We will present some basic rules and then discuss conflict resolution and conflict management.

IDENTIFY THE ISSUE

The first rule of dealing constructively with conflict is to identify the real issue. This can be a very difficult task because most family conflicts involve more than a single issue. It is also likely that family members will differ as to what the central issue really is. Little progress can be made until each person involved knows how the others define the conflict. When there are multiple issues, the first tasks are to agree on which one to tackle first and to try to understand how they are all interrelated.

STICK TO THE ISSUE

Once conversation has begun, it is essential to stick to the issue. This may be hard to do, especially when someone brings up a related point that distracts. Tangential issues serve to sidetrack the major issues and only muddy the water, forestalling resolution of the problem.

CHOOSE THE RIGHT TIME AND PLACE

When the family gathers to work out a conflict, it is important that everyone is given the opportunity to participate. The group has come together to listen to each member and to try to understand one another's involvement in the conflict. Each person needs to ask how he or she is contributing to the problem and what can be done individually and collectively to solve it.

If time is available and if emotional intensity is low, some conflicts can be constructively resolved when they arise. In most cases, however, family members need a period for cooling off and must schedule a time for talking that is mutually convenient for everyone involved. If a sixteen-year-old arrives home at midnight, one hour past curfew, the parents would be well advised to wait to deal with the issue until the next day, for they will be tired and angry. This plan accounts for emotional overload and how individuals process emotions, allowing for purposeful and honest communication without the need for defensiveness or disrespect. Then, choose a neutral place, free of interruptions, to resolve the issues. It should be a place where all members feel safe and on an equal footing. Every effort needs to be made to take each family member seriously. Everyone has a valid point and should be given a space to express their point of view, even young children. Parents need to be in charge to see that these rules are followed.

Affirm the Positives

The discussion will proceed much more smoothly if one begins by offering positive affirmation. For example, Manuel has become forgetful about clearing his plate after dinner. However, he has been very good recently about doing his homework without parental prompting. Manuel's parents could directly confront his failure to complete his after-dinner chore: "Manuel, you have not done you dinner chore for the past three days." This is usually where parents give a short lecture on how hard mom works to prepare the meal and how much the parents sacrifice to give Manuel and his sisters a good home. Approaching Manuel in a confrontational manner like this increases anger and blame. But if Manuel's parents begin with a positive affirmation about how they have appreciated his responsibility with his homework, this can help him hear the feedback about his after-dinner chore. There is no need to berate him for the infraction of the rule, and the positive stroke may well elicit a positive feeling and response.

Leave Past Issues in the Past

In the heat of an argument, it is tempting to dredge up past hurts and complaints. Some people have a habit of storing up anger and frustrations, and they are ready to dump them out when conflict occurs. The experience of being dumped on is devastating and will, in fact, negate any progress toward conflict resolution.

Avoid Attacking Behaviors

Name-calling is a sure way to antagonize another person and destroy any chance of reasonable discussion. Examples include calling another person *stupid*, *ignorant*, *silly*, *dumb*, *square*, *childish*, *spoiled*, *compulsive*, *conceited*, or some other derogatory adjective. Using such labels traps people in categories from which they cannot escape. It is disrespectful and prohibits any serious efforts to deal with conflict.

Blaming or accusing others is off-putting. Pointing the finger at others is often a way to avoid personal involvement. Even asking others to vindicate themselves is counterproductive because more often than not, asking "Why did you do it?" is really an attempt to place blame. *Verbal attacks* on areas of personal sensitivity are never warranted. Each of us has emotionally vulnerable areas, and family members generally know one another's sensitive areas. For example, referring to someone's weight or stinginess is a personal attack. Ridiculing or laughing at another family member sends the message that the other's opinion is not worth considering.

Avoid Passive-Aggressive Behaviors

Passive-aggressive behavior, which aims at getting back at another person in indirect, devious ways, is one of the more effective methods of sabotaging a relationship. Picture a Sunday morning, as Mom and Dad are trying to hurry family members so they won't be late for church. Dad has managed to herd everyone to the car except Greg, who happens to be mad at his parents. In response to Dad's call, "Hurry up or you will make all of us late!," Greg very slowly walks to the car, placing one foot in front of the other as if they were made of lead. This is an example of passive aggressiveness—denying one's anger while acting it out in an indirect manner.

Another form of passive-aggressive behavior is feigning weakness, inability, or neediness in order to have an advantage over others. It is a maneuver to play the "poor me" position to get sympathy rather than to take a responsible stance in an argument. If one cannot express anger openly, no resolution is possible, and the anger continues to be acted out in passive ways. The person who behaves in this manner wields a great deal of control in the family.

Avoid Triangles

Suppose thirteen-year-old Kathy and fifteen-year-old Chad are arguing at the supper table. Kathy turns to her mother for support: "Isn't that so, Mom?" She has just attempted to entangle her mother in the argument she is having with her brother. If the mother is wise, she will not allow herself to be drawn into the argument. It is a common practice for two people who are fighting to attempt to bring in a third party to gain an advantage in the argument. In some homes, this has developed into a fine art that thoroughly disrupts the family.

A Biblical Perspective on Anger

It is important to remember that the Bible does *not* say that anger is a sin. Ephesians 4:26 reads, "Be angry but do not sin; do not let the sun go down on your anger." There are two ways, however, in which our anger can become sin. First, if we deny our anger or hold it in, never expressing it, the anger will smolder and build within us. This allows the anger to become sin. Unexpressed anger can lead to resentment, hate, and revenge. Second, anger becomes sin when expressed in abusive ways, either verbally or physically. Physical abuse is, without doubt, sinful behavior. But verbal abuse is also psychologically damaging and sinful. The familiar saying, "Sticks and stones may break my bones, but words will never hurt me," is clearly not true, for abusive words certainly do hurt. The book of James warns that although the tongue is small, its offenses can have disastrous consequences (James 3:1–12).

When anger twists into sin, it is a corruption of the heart. In the Ten Commandments, we read, "You shall not murder" (Exod. 20:13). Jesus transforms this command from a behavioral matter to one of the heart when he teaches about anger: "You have heard that it was said to those of ancient times, 'You shall not murder'; and 'whoever murders shall be liable to judgment.' But I say to you that if you are angry with a brother or sister, you will be liable to judgment; and if you insult a brother or sister, you will be liable to the council; and if you say, 'You fool,' you will be liable to the hell of fire" (Matt. 5:21–22). The emphasis here is on acting out of hatred or spite and disrespecting another who is made in God's image (DeYoung 2018).

In our differentiation in Christ (DifC) model, authentically living out one's identity is a core feature of our relationships. Conflict is going to occur. However, having one's identity based in one's relationship with God through Christ forms the basis of values-based engagement. Assertiveness and awareness of one's needs, one's sins, and one's motivation to act in a Christlike manner inform how relationships function. This reflects the conflict-management literature, which emphasizes assertiveness and concern with individual well-being. Having accepted Christ's forgiveness of our sin, we relate to others in grace and forgiveness. This notion of grace is reflected in the role of empathy and understanding the other in conflict-management literature. DifC facilitates working together based on the desire to live authentic, gracious, Christ-centered relationships. Finally, DifC allows us to know and be known in more and more intimate ways as conflict management reveals our desires (good and bad) and teaches us about the other. Respectful collaboration and learning more about the other are keys to conflict resolution and management.

Conflict Resolution

Research on conflict resolution suggests that it is a process that moves through several stages. In applying this research to the family, Kathleen Galvin, Carma Bylund, and Bernard Brommel (2018) identify six stages:

1. *prior-conditions stage*: the problem arises;
2. *frustration-awareness stage*: a family member comes to realize that another family member is blocking satisfaction of some need or concern;
3. *conflict stage*: the exchange of a series of verbal and nonverbal messages;
4. *solution (or non-solution) stage*: the problem is resolved (or an impasse agreed on);
5. *follow-up stage*: the conflict re-erupts, or hurt feelings and grudges develop; and
6. *resolve stage*: the conflict no longer affects the family system.

Although conflict resolution is a worthy goal, it is part of a difficult process. It is important to remember two caveats. First, conflict resolution focuses as much on the process as on the resolution itself. This means that some conflicts may only resolve themselves after a lengthy process. Second, some conflicts are unable to be resolved in an equitable manner where parties contribute equally to the resolution. A resolution may require one party to sacrifice his or her preferences to maintain the relationship (e.g. whether to have children or the final number of children). These types of conflicts are zero sum; one partner "wins" and the other "loses."

Conflict Management

While some conflict can be resolved, there are perpetual issues in marriage and family that are never really resolved. *Conflict management* is one of the most realistic approaches to handling conflict. Family life is too complex to understand in neat cause-and-effect terms. And conflict is so much a part of this system that it cannot be viewed simply as something that arises within and is then purged from the family. Rather, conflict continually feeds back into the system as a whole. It is, therefore, more realistic to think of conflict as a process to be managed rather than a situation to be resolved.

There are five major styles of conflict management: (1) *Avoidance*, which involves a low degree of both cooperation and assertiveness, is characteristic of individuals we might describe as *withdrawers*. (2) *Accommodation*, which involves a high degree of cooperation and a low degree of assertiveness, is characteristic of *yielders*. (3) *Competition*, which involves a low degree of cooperation and a high degree of assertiveness, is characteristic of *winners*. (4) *Collaboration*, which involves a high degree of cooperation and assertiveness, is characteristic of *resolvers*. (5) *Compromise*, which involves negotiation, cooperation, and assertiveness, is characteristic of *compromisers*. It should be noted that these five styles of conflict management are basic theoretical types. In the real world, styles of conflict management may incorporate many aspects of the different styles.

Each style of conflict management entails specific levels of concern for oneself, for other family members, and for family relationships. The style of conflict management that evidences little cooperation and little assertiveness (avoidance) shows little concern for self, others, and relationships. The style with a high degree of cooperation and a low degree of assertiveness (accommodation) shows high concern for others, less concern for relationships, and little concern for self. The competitive approach shows high concern for self, less concern for relationships, and little concern for others. Collaboration and compromise show high concern for relationships and, accordingly, a balanced concern for self and others.

Most of the research on conflict management has been based on organizations and businesses that are larger and far less personal than a family. Two questions need to be asked at this point: (1) Are the data consistent with the biblical view of how to handle conflict? (2) Are the data applicable to family conflict?

In answer to the first question, we believe the data on conflict management to be consistent with what the Bible says about how Christians are to handle conflict. The Bible most directly addresses this issue in Ephesians 4:25–29: "So then, putting away falsehood, let all of us speak the truth to our neighbors, for we are members of one another. Be angry but do not sin; do not let the sun go down on your anger, and do not make room for the devil. . . . Let no evil talk come out of your mouths, but only what is useful for building up, as there is need, so that your words may give grace to those who hear." Contained in these verses is support for being assertive. We are told that when there is conflict, we should speak truthfully about it. The implication is not to withdraw ("Do not let the sun go down on your anger") or become aggressive ("Be angry but do not sin. . . . Let no evil talk come out of your mouths"). The text lends support to a direct style that shows concern for self, the other, and the relationship.

The verses also point toward unity as the ideal for Christians—we should speak the truth because "we are members of one another." If there is anything that should be characteristic of the body of Christ, it is a spirit of unity or harmony. First Corinthians 12:12 reiterates this idea: "For just as the body is one and has many members, and all the members of the body, though many, are one body, so it is with Christ." We believe that the Bible stresses both assertiveness and cooperation. The best way to deal with conflict, no matter what your natural style, is for both persons to work together with equal concern for self, the other, and the relationship.

Each style of handling conflict has both advantages and disadvantages and, depending on the situation, may be more or less appropriate. As we discuss each style, we will give an example of Jesus using that style. He was, variously, a withdrawer, a yielder, a winner, a resolver, and a compromiser.

Withdrawers

Although avoidance was not the usual style of Jesus, he did withdraw when necessary. When he healed the man with the shriveled hand on the Sabbath, he greatly angered the Pharisees, who "conspired against him, how to destroy him" (Matt. 12:14). Jesus surely could have confronted the Pharisees, as he had on other occasions. But instead, when he became aware of their plotting, he departed (v. 15). There was a similar reaction during the final hours before his arrest, when Jesus anticipated the upcoming conflict. As he and his disciples went to the Mount of Olives, he said to them, "'Pray, that you may not come into the time of trial.' Then he withdrew from them about a stone's throw, knelt down, and prayed" (Luke 22:40–41). We are also told in Luke 5:15–16 that when crowds of people pressed on him with their needs for healing, Jesus would withdraw to deserted places to pray.

There will be times when family members need to withdraw from a conflict to think more clearly about the issue. Sometimes emotions run so high that conflict resolution is impossible. At other times, trivial conflicts need to be set aside for the sake of more pressing family matters. Avoidance can be destructive, however, so the person who withdraws for a time needs to be accountable by promising to come back to deal with the conflict after taking the needed break. In the absence of such a promise, withdrawing sends a signal that the individual does not care enough to work out conflicts.

YIELDERS

In the greatest conflict Jesus had to experience in his life on earth, he yielded himself to be arrested, falsely convicted, and finally crucified. His yielding is evident in the account of his arrest in Matthew 26:50–53. After Jesus had been arrested, one of his companions struck the servant of the high priest and cut off his ear. At that point, Jesus stepped forward saying, "Put your sword back into its place; for all who take the sword will perish by the sword. Do you think that I cannot appeal to my Father, and he will at once send me more than twelve legions of angels?" (vv. 52–53).

Yielding may be appropriate when an issue is far more important to one family member than to the others or when it threatens a relationship. Yielding can also be a self-giving act of putting another person's wishes ahead of one's own. However, when yielding is motivated by a desire to show others how self-sacrificing one is, it can be a form of manipulation. Similarly, yielding out of a fear of rejection or a need to be liked can be detrimental. Yielding to another may also not be in the best interest of that person. The parent who gives in to a child's demands for more candy or to stay up late may be doing the child a disservice.

WINNERS

At times Jesus adopted the approach of a winner. This can most clearly be seen in Matthew 21:12–13: "Then Jesus entered the temple and drove out all who were selling and buying in the temple, and he overturned the tables of the money changers and the seats of those who sold doves. He said to them, 'It is written, "My house shall be called a house of prayer"; but you are making it a den of robbers.'" In this situation, there was no withdrawing, yielding, or compromising. Rather, Jesus acted authoritatively and decisively. The reason for this action, as Matthew makes clear, was that the law of the Lord was being violated.

There will be times when family members disagree on the basis of their principles and assume that the family is strong enough to survive the competition. The danger here is that the real issue may get lost in the battle over principles, and the conflict may degenerate to a personal level at which each party feels the need to win the point to save face. Such competition between family members escalates rather than decreases conflict. It takes a strong family system to survive. Winners often win the battle (the point) but lose the war (the relationship) in the process.

RESOLVERS

During his earthly ministry, Jesus elicited strong reactions. Toward those who reacted against him, such as the scribes, priests, and Pharisees, Jesus assumed a confrontational style. Toward those who reacted positively, he assumed a collaborative style, best seen in his long-term commitment to his disciples.

Since family relationships are long-term commitments, most family conflicts can best be dealt with through collaboration. The advantage of this style is that it offers maximum satisfaction to everyone. The disadvantage is that collaboration takes a lot of time, effort, and emotional energy. It also affords the advantage to a family member who is verbally skilled. In conflicts between siblings, the elder may be able to manipulate the younger one. Five-year-old Carol may be able to resolve a conflict by offering three-year-old Eddie five big nickels for his four small dimes.

In general, family systems benefit from having at least one resolver around who will see to it that conflicts are not swept under the rug. The resolver is often very intense in working through conflicts and will be frustrated when others do not cooperate or have the same amount of determination to settle things. There may be family disruption if the resolver is unable to rest until there is closure on an issue. When the resolver pursues the issue too intently, the others will distance themselves and intimacy will be impaired.

Compromisers

We tend not to see Jesus as a compromiser. Yet when the Pharisees sought to trap him by asking if it was right to pay taxes to Caesar, Jesus replied, "Give therefore to the emperor the things that are the emperor's, and to God the things that are God's" (Matt. 22:21).

Compromise can be the best way to handle conflict when there is inadequate time to work out a collaborative effort. When used too often, however, compromise is too easy an out, leaving all family members less than satisfied. Some family conflicts can be handled best by compromise, such as disagreements about when to serve the evening meal, where to go on vacation, and what television programs to watch. On other issues, compromise is not the best solution. For example, the Kakimotos are planning to move to a different region of the country. Annette wants to live in the heart of the city, where they both will work, while Duane wants to find a twenty-acre plot of land in a rural area some distance from the city. To compromise by living in the suburbs would leave both spouses unhappy. They will need to work together toward a resolution that will afford both of them the essential advantages they are seeking. It will take some creative thought to find such a solution.

Each one of the five styles of handling conflict will prove, at one time or another, to be the most appropriate. It is imperative, then, that family members do not get locked into any one particular style and thus lose their flexibility and capacity for finding creative solutions.

To this point, we have considered individual styles of conflict management. This has been necessary because individual family members differ in the ways they handle conflict. Family conflict must be understood, however, as involving not only the individual members but also the entire family system.

At times, the needs of the family will be met at the expense of the needs of individual family members; at other times, the needs of the individuals will be met at the expense of the needs of the family. Families characterized by compromise and collaboration are the most successful in balancing the needs of individual family members with the needs of the family as a whole. Healthy families also have the combined strengths of flexibility and structure, separateness and connectedness, as well as open and clear channels of communication that permit them to alter their approach to fit the situation.

PART 6

The Social Dynamics of Family Life

The issues of stress, conflict, work, and violence continue to be social dynamics that are part and parcel of family life, and they have been vigorously studied. In this section we turn our attention to the social dynamics of family life. Stress within the family, work and family conflict, and divorce will be the major topics of concern.

In chapter 14 we will examine the relationship between work and family life and how this contributes to burnout.

Family stress is the topic addressed in chapter 15. Every family encounters stress in one form or another. We present a model for understanding stress and demonstrate how family members can work together to solve problems and cope with catastrophes. Christian beliefs and values are crucial resources in times of family stress, providing hope in the midst of despair.

Divorce is a stressful time for families. The high divorce rate in America means that millions will experience the pain and loss that divorce entails. Some of the factors that contribute to this breakdown in family life are discussed in chapter 16. We address the effects of divorce on both couples and children, concluding this chapter with a discussion of the single-parent family. Chapter 17 is devoted to complex families in contemporary society that result from remarriage and blending families. We conclude with a plea for compassion for those family members who attempt to rebuild their lives, noting that Christianity offers the survivors of divorce the hope of restoration and renewal.

14

Work and the Family

Conflict or Collaboration?

Work and family are the two main domains in which individuals spend most of their lives. These two domains provide both stressors and resources that often spill over from one domain to the other. This idea of *spillover* is especially relevant as technology has allowed for the blurring of the boundary between work and family spheres. This chapter will offer a brief discussion of the development of the idea of separate spheres of family and work domains. Next, we will review some of the research that indicates how burnout is a symptom of the conflicts between work and family domains. Third, we will describe a Christian understanding of calling, which provides rich resources for the integration of the boundary between work and family. Finally, several suggestions will be offered incorporating our differentiation in Christ (DifC) model.

The Separate Spheres of Work and Family

In premodern societies, one's life course was primarily determined by gender and class. One of the most poignant examples of this is the choice of a marriage partner. Marriages were arranged for the benefit of the male's family (Clapp 1993; Quale 1988; Yalom 2001). One would not think of choosing one's own marriage partner but would submit and be obedient to the wisdom of the older generation's choice.

The premodern family was seen as an economic center of production. Families in the premodern world functioned to (1) produce goods and services others in the community needed and (2) train children in the skills needed to further that production (Sweet 2014). In premodern families and in more agrarian ones, the family business, whether carpentry or tailoring, was intimately tied to family well-being, as it was housed at the residence. Families taught their children the family trade, and consequently there was no division between the work and family.

The Industrial Revolution profoundly reorganized work and family life. The site of work was divested from the family. Individuals found work at factories and other locations well removed from their place of residence. Consequently, the ideal developed that individuals are capable of earning enough money to reside outside of one's family residence. One implication of this change in work is the idea that remuneration is based on time rather than product (Sweet 2014).

These changes were driven by technological advancements (Frederick and Dunbar 2019). Workers in this historical period began using raw materials in production (coal, oil), and they saw rapid mechanical developments like the steam and internal combustion engine. These technological developments facilitated the creation of a highly trained, specialized workforce. Individual workers were needed who could use and repair the technology beginning to drive the economy outside the family. Thus, workers required more education and skills to fit in to the workforce, meaning that more investment was needed for developing workers with the necessary skills. Not only did technology develop rapidly and demand specialized skills, but capital was increasingly available through familial inheritance and property. An increase in available funds allowed for increased investment in industries and technology. Higher skills meant greater compensation for workers, which ultimately benefited their families.

Rodney Clapp (1993) describes six principles of family life that came into prominence during the Industrial Revolution: (1) the home and family became a place of refuge from the work world; (2) concern for children's well-being increased, especially regarding education and development; (3) the family became the center for identity and value formation; (4) marriage and mate selection were increasingly motivated by love instead of arrangement; (5) the meaning of the marital relationship transformed; and (6) a gendered division of work and family tasks developed, especially the male breadwinner and female domestic roles. These are modern family values because they distinctly separate the spheres of work and family, they place individual choice and preference at the foundation of family formation (e.g., mate selection), and they describe both spouses as rational individuals who are capable of making the best possible choices for their future lives.

With the advent of industrialization, families began to be viewed as a domestic haven against the cruel world of work (Quale 1988). Simultaneously, the view of the family changed from being an economic contributor to a consumer (Sweet 2014). An individual, usually the husband, could be paid enough to support his nuclear family; his children and spouse would no longer need to work outside the household in order to survive. The household would not need to be self-sufficient, because the working man could make enough money to purchase those goods that he and his family needed for survival.

As consumerism and economic resources allowed for the family to be separate from work, gender ideology and work and family gender roles shifted, leading men and subsequently women to increasingly define themselves as economic consumers instead of producers (Cushman 1996). The Industrial Revolution facilitated a profound shift regarding the cultural framework for both the family as well as masculinity and femininity.

What can be called the *domestic framework* for gender roles began taking prominence. This framework holds three overlapping sets of entitlements (Williams 2001). Based in gender essentialism, this framework assumes men are better in the work world due to their competitiveness, while women are better suited for domestic labors due to their ability to care for others. Employers began to demand ideal workers who are willing to work long hours and eschew familial responsibilities like housework and child-rearing.

The second and third entitlements associated with the domestic framework are the male expectation that they can fulfill the ideal worker role and the female expectation that their lives be defined through caregiving (Williams 2001). Only clearly separating work and domestic domains by gender allows males to identify as ideal workers. By entering the workforce as ideal workers, males identify themselves as breadwinners facing a cruel and often hostile world. Breadwinners are expected to take sole responsibility for the economic well-being of their families, and therefore they cannot be expected to also share domestic responsibility. As females remain in the domestic home, they are expected to provide care for husbands/males and children. They are responsible for making the home into a haven for male breadwinners.

Because work and family belong to separate spheres, people experience conflict from both as job demands and family demands increase. In many ways, people are paid for their time away from their families, as exemplified by hourly pay rates. During this paid time, the job or career places many demands on the individual, which often involve the worker applying resources in order to complete tasks. At the same time, the family also makes demands. Parents are expected to attend every recital and basketball game and enroll their children in as many enriching experiences as possible, all the while ensuring their children complete their homework!

Work and Family Conflict Related to Burnout

Work and family conflict (WFC) may culminate in burnout due to the competing demands placed on individuals from both spheres. Burnout was originally defined as the stress response to long-term emotional and interpersonal job stressors (Maslach, Schaufeli, and Leiter 2001). The emphasis in this definition is on the personal or individual's experience of burnout, usually characterized by exhaustion, cynicism, and inefficacy.

As more research pointed to the organizational contributions to burnout, the definition was expanded. Burnout results from a "major mismatch between the nature of the job and the nature of the person who does the job" (Maslach and Leiter 1997, 9). This definition expands on the intrapersonal experience of burnout to include aspects from the organization that contribute to this mismatch, including (1) work overload, (2) lack of control over work, (3) lack of reward, (4) lack of community, (5) lack of fairness, and (6) values conflict (Maslach and Leiter 1997). Higher amounts of things like conflict over organizational values and work overload along with lower levels of personal control, perceived rewards for work, and fairness contribute to higher levels of burnout. One challenge here is that burnout is conceptualized as an experience instead of a discrepancy in social domains. That is, people understand burnout as the experience of exhaustion and often do not focus on the causes in work and family spheres.

The literature on the work-family interface has relied on several overlapping relational concepts. The first one understands the relationship between work and family as characterized by conflict (Allen and Martin 2017; Greenhaus and Beutell 1985). WFC focuses on conflict due to the incompatible demands of role pressure and high expectations from both work and family. A recent study of the relative effects of WFC by Pattusamy and Jacob (2016) found evidence that the negative spillover from work to family is larger than the negative spillover from family to work. However, this effect is mediated by perception of work and family balance. In other words, the effects of WFC on family and job satisfaction are offset by positive perceptions of work and family balance.

The relationship between work and family can be positive, not only negative (Allen and Martin 2017). Both work and family may provide positive and mutually enhancing, enriching resources for individuals. Of course, enrichment can be initiated from either domain: work to family or family to work. Greenhaus and Powel (2006) identify five types of resources that work-family enrichment provides: skills and perspectives, psychological and physical resources, social-capital resources, flexibility, and material resources. These resources are both instrumental (skills and abilities that are directly transferable across domains) and emotional. This means that individuals learn important skills and gain emotional resources in one domain that may spill over to enrich the other domain.

Work-family balance (WFB) has also been used to describe this relationship (Allen and Martin 2017). Following Kalliath and Brough (2008), we understand WFB as one's perception of the *compatibility* and *mutual enrichment* of both work and nonwork activities in accordance with one's values and preferences. This could be thought of as an *authentic* perception of role salience and satisfaction. This means that, to the extent that one is *perceiving the relationships between work and family as predominately compatible and mutually enhancing*, one experiences balance between the two spheres, despite the actual balance between the two spheres. That is, one will perceive and experience greater WFB to the extent that work and family activities are viewed as compatible and to the extent that the individual is able to prioritize his or her role in each domain based on values and preferences. For example, Wolfram and Gratton (2014) conducted a study looking at the effects of WFC on role importance and life satisfaction. They discovered evidence that the most significant negative effects of WFC on life satisfaction occurred when an individual experienced negative WFC and also prioritized one's role in the family.

Greenhaus and Powell (2006) describe two pathways in which skills are transferred between work and home: an *instrumental* and an *affective* path. The instrumental path focuses on the direct transference of enrichment domains such as compromise. The affective path emphasizes the positive effect of resources on happiness or contentment and how positive affect in one role influences the other. For example, individuals learn the skill of flexibility when transitioning from home to school as children. This transition grows an individual's ability to take turns and compromise with others. Flexibility learned at home and reinforced at school becomes an essential skill for working adults. For instance, Sandage and Harden (2011) describe how differentiation of self (DoS) is associated with higher levels of openness to multiculturalism, which plays an important role in compromise and engagement with others. The skills learned at home and at school pay dividends as the individual enters work.

DoS provides the psychological ability to cope with anxiety and stress, and it is established in the family. Family members look to each other to manage and respond to anxiety and stress. These resources focus on functional relationships and togetherness as well as emotion regulation and goal-oriented behavior (Bowen 2004; Jankowski and Sandage 2012; Murdock and Gore 2004; Titelman 2014; Papero 2014). As an example, Murdock and Gore describe how DoS mediates the relationship between resources and coping with stress. In their study, individuals with lower levels of DoS experience more stress, and they have fewer resources for coping with stress. Lower levels of DoS impact the relative amount of anxiety experienced as well as diminish the psychological resources available to cope with that anxiety.

Families characterized by lower levels of DoS engage "instinctual," automatic, and habitual coping patterns, which lead to increased stress and anxiety (Papero 1990, 2014). Families characterized by lower DoS react to stress in rigid, inflexible patterns like (1) triangulation, (2) conflict, (3) distance, and (4) over- or underfunctioning reciprocity. These functional patterns become habitualized and prevent a response to stress based on one's values and goals.

Differentiation of self (DoS), as we have described throughout this book, is arguably the most important family resource for spillover into the work domain. DoS provides the emotional resources that enable an individual to objectively determine the salience of the demands made by a given role. That is, individuals need to objectively and calmly determine which demands are more pressing at a given time as both domains make emotionally charged and pressing demands. Higher levels of DoS allow the individual to respond to demands in a values-based manner (Frederick and Dunbar 2019). Additionally, DoS enhances one's ability to derive personal satisfaction from each domain. This means that emotional strength and confidence are not completely dependent on either domain. The individual has enough of a solid or authentic sense of self that challenges in either domain are not emotionally devastating to the individual (Frederick and Dunbar 2019). In these ways, DoS provides both instrumental and affective paths for resources to spill over between the two domains.

Calling and Differentiation in Christ

Differentiation in Christ (DifC) could be described as the *authentic* expression of one's identity based in Christ. This definition emphasizes the correspondence between one's behaviors and relationships and one's identity in Christ. In terms of identity, being adopted into the family of God via Christ's saving work on the cross is the core self. Living out Christian relationship principles like covenant, grace, empowerment, and intimacy becomes the value base for meaningful action.

Theology provides an important framework for understanding calling, an aspect of Christian identity. There have traditionally been four main definitions of calling (Stevens 1999). The first definition of call is *effectual* and focuses on becoming a Christian. This understanding of calling is synonymous with conversion to Christianity, and the example of the apostle Paul is viewed as paradigmatic (Peace 1999). The effectual call is the primary definition of calling from a Christian perspective.

Second, a *providential* call is embedded in the station, situation, or occupation one is in. In other words, God providentially places individuals in particular locations in order to accomplish particular goals. The stories of Joseph gaining leadership in Egypt (Gen. 37–50), Daniel ascending to a high position in Nebuchadnezzar's court (Dan. 1–5), and Ruth working in the fields of her kinsman-redeemer, Boaz (the book of Ruth), are Old Testament examples of God placing individuals in certain social and political stations for his kingdom purposes (Stevens 2012).

Charismatic calling is the third definition. God gifts or empowers people to accomplish specific tasks (Stevens 1999). These gifts (or *charismata* in Greek) focus on spiritual empowerment for specific situations; examples include being able to speak in a different language (see Acts 2) or healing. These Spirit-provided gifts include talents and abilities as well, meaning that God distributes talents and abilities for humans to work.

The final aspect of calling entails desire or motivation. God's *heart calling* (Stevens 1999, 82) orients one to pursue life paths based on their motivation or desire. Humans have an inner desire to accomplish certain tasks based on the calling of their hearts. In other words, the heart calling fulfills an inner desire or personal motivation to accomplish a task, fulfill a responsibility, or have a certain occupation or station that accomplishes God's purposes.

These definitions have been summarized by Oz Guinness's (2003) description of calling as primary and secondary. Calling is a person's response to the current circumstances of life (relationships, employment, etc.); that response expresses and develops one's abilities and talents with the goal of advancing the kingdom or reign of God. *Primary calling* focuses on identity—effectual call and discipleship. *Secondary calling* describes the physical locations and activities in which one's primary calling is embodied, the social contexts where responsibilities are maintained, and one's opportunities to express gifts and talents.

Frederick and Dunbar (2019) define it this way: "*Calling as we define it is finding one's identity in Christ, and then engaging the world in activities that bring liberation, redemption, and/or stewardship in order to reflect the Kingdom of God here and now*" (74; italics in original). In other words, *calling is an expression of differentiation in Christ.* Basing one's identity on Christ provides the primary calling in one's life. This solid identity based on our adoption into God's family provides resources for managing our emotions and responding to others. Further, we embody this identity in our relationships with others as spouses, parents, children, and coworkers. Our secondary callings are the authentic expressions of our primary calling as a member of God's family.

Christian calling as our primary identity provides the internal resources needed for developing satisfaction in our roles and relationships. To begin with, our sense of self-efficacy and satisfaction is based on our relationship to God in Christ. We are adopted into God's family, and this means that God loves us and is pleased to call us his children (1 John 3:1). This satisfaction allows us to face anxiety, worry, and stress without becoming overwhelmed. That is, our identity in Christ facilitates our emotion regulation so that we can engage in values-based action. Identity is not derived from satisfaction from either work or family roles.

Calling as a secondary expression of identity focuses on role salience. Calling allows individuals to identity the relative importance of demands made from different roles. These demands are able to be objectively evaluated, and the individual is able to respond to them in a values-based manner. The demands are not experienced as overwhelming or pressing, because one's identity is not based on satisfaction from either domain. If one bases identity on satisfaction in a domain, then conflict between domains is experienced as a threat to identity. Responses to this conflict are laden with anxiety, and these responses become habitual patterns. This limits our ability to objectively discern the importance of the demands and determine how God is calling us to respond to the specific circumstances of our lives. The secondary sense of calling provides important resources for discerning which life domain takes precedent, and it facilitates positive spillover from one to the other.

Calling and Image Bearing

Chapter 1 emphasized how the doctrine of the image of God is reflected in vocation. Humanity, as God's image bearers, works to fill the earth, steward its resources, and be fruitful and multiply (Gen. 1:26–28). This image bearing could be viewed in terms of status or ontology (Strachan 2019). Humanity "is the representative of God on earth; to see a man or woman is to see the only living creature made in the image of God" (Strachan 2019, 29). Our actions should reflect our status as image bearers. Or, stated differently, image bearing should be an authentic expression of our identities.

Vocation as an authentic expression of bearing God's image has focused on three different aspects of God's work in the world. James Fowler (1987) describes three main ways in which callings represent authentic expressions of image bearing. First, *governance* is described along stewardship and cultivation lines. Humanity is called to tend the earth and develop the culture. Part of this governance is reflected in the naming of the creatures in Genesis chapter 2. Further, there is a sense that the garden scene is primordial in nature or naive (Wolters 2005). This is evidenced by the overarching trajectory of the Bible, which begins with a garden and ends with a city—the city of God. Humanity engages in governing practices by being responsible with one's resources and fostering practices that seek the benefits of one's creations. Bosses are supportive and encouraging in the development of their employees. Parents encourage the development of their children. Humans reflect God's nature by *caring* for the created world and responsibly cultivating human production, developing culture and technology that are an important aspect of governance—caring for creation. Donald Capps (2000) reminds us that care's foundation is empathy. We understand the effect our actions have on others, and we respond accordingly. Stewardship as cultivation reflects how we care for the fruitfulness of our labors. Care is reflected in our roles as parents, expressing both grace and empowerment. As people identify with Christ and his sufferings, we develop empathy for others.

Image bearing as liberating and redeeming, Fowler's second aspect of calling, focuses on *being for others*. "To be part of the liberative and redemptive work of God means entering into solidarity with Christ and his suffering" (Fowler 1987, 51). Just as Christ entered the human world to defeat the powers of sin and darkness and to reestablish humanity's relationship to God, calling allows us to follow Christ's example to be "for" others. "There is a God, there is a future healed world that he will bring about, and your work is showing it (in part) to others" (Keller 2014, 15). Authentic image bearing reflects redeeming and liberating principles at work and home. We work here to right wrongs and address human problems. Being for others means engaging in practices that foster human flourishing, and this dimension of call focuses specifically on redressing hurt, trauma, and issues that thwart human fecundity.

Partnership or connecting is the third way in which image bearing is expressed. It is fundamental in supporting and upholding the governing and redeeming aspects of work from the Christian perspective. The image of God connects our partnership with God to the world. Connecting is both an internal process and an external focus. Internally, it orients us with our true desires and our sense of God and our relationship to Christ. We live out our inner desires and motivations as a reflection of God's pulling on our heart strings. Partnership uncovers the underlying motivations for our work: Do we labor in response to our God-given commission or do we work out of a desire for personal gain or glory? Externally speaking, we image God in relationships; a key manner in which work expresses this is via collaborative partnerships. Partnering with our spouses and children to develop families characterized by Christian principles reflects this principle of connecting and relationship. These relationships form the covenantal basis of our being, and they express our need for others. Further, collaborating with coworkers and others allows us to reflect authentic relationships at work and utilize these relationships to cultivate culture, create meaningful products, and provide services that will enhance God's kingdom.

The four relationship principles—covenant, grace, empowerment, and intimacy—express these aspects of image bearing as calling: investing in and cultivating the fruits of one's labor. Two of these relationship principles speak directly to expressions of care—grace and empowerment. First, relationships must exude grace. Grace through forgiveness allows relational partners to embody care—I care for you, I want the best for you. Sometimes one's actions have unintended consequences—I hurt you, you hurt me—but we engage in forgiveness. Further, care is mutually empowering. Empowerment as an expression of care allows relational partners to develop important self-knowledge (primary calling). Based on this self-knowledge, one can develop abilities, skills, and talents to thrive in different life areas (secondary callings).

Partnership is based on the type and depth of the relationships that make up marriage and family interactions. Covenant speaks to the depth of one's commitment to the other. This is the "till death do us part" Christian idea. Our commitment to be with and for the other provides the basis of care. Next, intimacy is the ultimate result of care as expressed in covenant, grace, and empowerment. Intimacy deepens as I learn more about my identity and the best ways to express that identity. This type of partnership is the bedrock of Christian marriage and family relationships, and the identity developed in the family spills over into one's identity at work.

The theological understanding of differentiation in Christ provides the foundation for a Christian perspective on calling. Identity based on adoption into God's family provides the primary calling in life, which is expressed secondarily in family and work-related roles. These roles are authentic expressions of our primary calling as they reflect God's commission to us as image bearers to govern, redeem, and partner with others.

Conclusion

Work and family spheres are often fraught with conflict and tension. In a society that is based on productivity, balancing the demands of spouses, children, and bosses presents innumerable challenges. The family provides a unique psychological resource, differentiation of self, that offers both specific skills as well as emotional hardiness, allowing individuals to navigate tensions between work and family life.

Differentiation in Christ is most accurately described in the notion of calling. Calling is illuminated by the doctrine of the image of God, whereby humanity is God's visible representation on earth. This image bearing entails primary calling, which is based on one's identity as a child of God. One's self esteem is based on being a child of God in Christ. Further, being a member of Christ's family provides a meaning-making system that finds its authentic expression in work and family domains. Identity in Christ is expressed as we authentically live out our roles as parents, spouses, and employees.

The primary vehicle for negotiating work and family conflict is role salience and satisfaction. Role salience provides a framework for understanding the relative importance of a demand that comes from either work or family. Role satisfaction, on the other hand, measures the relative personal meaning and well-being derived from either the family or work role. Individuals who are able to derive satisfaction from both roles experience satisfaction spillover, in which the spheres of family and work are mutually enriching.

Calling allows individuals to address both role satisfaction and salience. First, primary calling provides satisfaction and security. This satisfaction is not changeable based on variations in satisfaction from either work or family spheres. Additionally, primary calling provides emotional regulation resources so that one is not reacting to perceived threats to role-derived satisfaction. Second, calling, in a secondary sense, allows one to objectively discern which role is more salient at a given time. This discernment allows one to respond to demands based on one's primary calling. In these ways, calling is an important resource for negotiating work and family conflict.

15

Through the Stress and Pain
of Family Life

Any group whose members have a strong attachment to one another, interact on a regular basis, and go through various changes together can expect to experience stress. The family is such a group. Family stress can be viewed as any upset in the regular routine of the family, which varies from a minor irritation over someone being late for dinner to a major crisis, such as the death of a family member. While family stress itself tends to have an adverse effect on family life, it is also true that stress external to the family can spill over and negatively impact family life. For instance, Buck and Neff (2012) report that couples who must cope with external stress are depleted of time and energy needed to negotiate the day-to-day tensions and adjustments in their own marital or family relationships.

When not dealt with effectively, family strain can have a cumulative, destructive impact. Not surprisingly, family stress correlates with behavioral problems in children (Tan et al. 2012). Many parents who abuse their children were themselves the victims of abuse when they were growing up. Although this finding does not excuse the abusive behavior, it drives home the point that unresolved feelings of powerlessness in parents can take a secondary toll on their children. A related finding, based on the study of caregiver strain in family caregivers of patients with advanced cancer, revealed that hopelessness was related to higher levels of strain (Lohne, Miaskowski, and Rustoen 2012). However, similar events can trigger completely different reactions in different families and their members. What may seem a minor irritation in one family can be a major event in another. It's also the case that families handle stressful situations differently, and neurological research has found that stress can impact each family member in different ways. Even more startling is the finding by Gunnar and Quevedo (2007) that stress in the parent-child relationship can shape a child's neurological system in such a way as to render the child more susceptible to long-term mental and physical health consequences.

A Model for Understanding Family Stress

Attempts to study stress in American families can be traced back to the Depression of the 1930s and to World War II, when millions of fathers were separated from their families. Reuben Hill (1949) proposes that family stress can best be analyzed by considering the interaction of three factors: (1) the stressful event itself; (2) the resources or strengths that a family possesses at the time the event occurs; and (3) the family's perception of the event. In a sense, the event itself (e.g., the war) is the necessary cause but is not sufficient in and of itself to cause family stress. For example, if the alcoholic father is a source of tension in the home, his separation from the family may be perceived as a relief. This is especially true if the mother has sufficient resources to carry out the functions usually performed by the father.

Most models of family stress elaborate Hill's seminal work about how these three factors interact. A good overview of these models can be found in chapters 9 and 10 of *Family Communication* (Segrin and Flora 2005). The major refinement in these models has been an endeavor to understand the coping abilities of the family when confronted by a stressful event. This has placed the focus on the family's recoverability instead of its troubles, and on the family's resources instead of the crisis. A model of family stress that focuses more on the effects of serious individual trauma on the family, such as death, murder, or terrorism, can be found in two books by Don Catherall: *Handbook of Stress, Trauma, and the Family* (2004) and *Family Stress: Interventions for Stress and Trauma* (2005).

Stressful Events

Before we consider how families cope, it is important to gain an understanding of the various types of stressful events that affect most families. A major distinction can be made between predictable events (usually transitions to new stages in family life) and unpredictable events (unexpected and unplanned events). Happy and anticipated events can also be stressful (weddings, births, adoptions, forming new families, leaving home, etc.) because they usher in emotional and physical changes that must be dealt with. Although it is true that the predictability of an event does not eliminate stress, families can make the needed effort to prepare for changes. Transitions in family life not only change each member but the family itself also changes with the entrance and exit of members. These events challenge the family—a system of maturing and changing individuals. The stress generated by the family system causes stress to individuals, and likewise the strains on individuals introduce tension into the family system.

Among the unexpected events that have a devastating impact on families are environmental disasters such as floods, hurricanes, fires, famines, and earthquakes, as well as societal afflictions such as war, terrorism, and economic depression. Individual families have little control over such adversities. These unexpected disasters take a great toll because families and communities are powerless against them. Help is needed from outside sources on a national and international level (Wadsworth 2010).

In a study of experiences that disrupt life in general, not just family life (Holmes and Rahe 1967), forty-three stress-producing events were ranked on a scale from 0 to 100, with a score of 100 representing the greatest amount of stress. It is noteworthy that eight of the twelve most stressful events directly involve family life. The twelve events are death of a spouse, divorce, marital separation, detention in jail or other institution, death of a close family member, major personal injury or illness, marriage, being fired, marital reconciliation, retirement, major changes in the health or behavior of a family member, and pregnancy. Obviously, the major source of personal stress for most people is the family.

A series of stressful events can have a cumulative effect on the family system, especially if the family is unable or unwilling to deal with each event as it occurs. Stress can build up, and eventually a relatively minor incident can burst the floodgates. For example, a teenager who has been irresponsible at home may easily meet his parent's fury when he comes home drunk. A family under financial strain may react out of all proportion to their teen's minor accident because it puts undue stress on the budget.

Resources

A family's ability to cope with stress relates directly to the resources it possesses. Some of these resources are personal in that they reside in the individual family members. An obvious example is the ability to earn an income. Education is a resource that contributes to one's earning power, enhances prestige, and instills self-confidence. Personal maturity coupled with a good education can provide helpful skills in such areas as problem-solving, goal-setting, and strategic planning. Physical and mental health is extremely valuable in times of stress; it provides the needed strength to handle the stressful situation. Characteristics such as self-esteem, a positive disposition, and clearheadedness are resources that can make a difference in a crisis.

The most important resources in coping with family stress, however, are those that reside in the family system. Effective family systems are well connected, have sufficient structure, and yet are flexible enough to adapt to stressors.

Clear and open communication is an important strength that families can draw on during times of crisis. The family that can honestly express ideas and feelings openly can work together to make the needed adjustments.

Some families possess many resources, but the shock of a crisis leaves them stifled and ineffective. They need time and hope offered by others so they can marshal their resources to move forward. The external networks the family has established are the support systems—friends, neighbors, coworkers, church and community groups—they can draw on in times of special need. The necessity of cultivating such outside resources is the reason geographical stability is so important to the family system. A family without such resources is highly vulnerable.

Family Responses to Stress

Families respond to stress in two general ways: *coping* and *problem-solving*. Although the literature on coping is more directly related to the issue of family stress, we believe that the literature on problem-solving is invaluable because it conceptualizes the family's response to stress as taking place in stages.

Coping

Coping refers to what the family and its individual members do with their resources in the face of stress. Sociologist Reuben Hill (1949) developed a model indicating that stress is the result of the interaction among the *event*, the family's *resources*, and their *perception* of the event. Since the degree of success in coping with stress varies significantly from family to family, the following strategy has been proposed.

The first step is to marshal all available resources. Coping strategies may consist of direct action aimed at changing the stressful conditions, a rethinking of the whole situation (including how the stress might be turned into a benefit), or a combination of both of these processes. Take the case of an elderly grandmother who is no longer able to live independently. First, the family considers all the family and community resources available to help with this crisis: retirement homes, elder-care facilities, moving in with a relative, health program options, and so on. While they must consider the initial stress and the adjustment to be made by everyone involved, they also take into account the family strengths and the resources that family members have to offer. It can be a wonderful opportunity for members to extend themselves in new ways. They also see Grandmother as a resource for the family and recognize all the ways each member will benefit from her presence.

If family members are depleted because of other mitigating circumstances, they are not in a position to be a resource in this crisis. For instance, if the husband is frustrated in his job, the teenage daughter is acting out, and the family dynamics are disruptive, they are in no position to take on Grandmother. This would be a poor environment for the grandmother and would likely cause inordinate strain to the family system.

Problem-Solving

Irving Tallman and Louis Gray (1987) present five stages involved in family problem-solving.

1. The family becomes aware of and defines a situation as a problem. The greater the threat to the family's welfare, the more the situation will be perceived as a problem. Families that consider themselves effective problem solvers are quick to perceive threatening situations and deal with them, whereas those that lack confidence in their ability to deal with problems are more likely to deny the seriousness of the situation.

2. The greater the family's confidence that they can solve the problem, the greater will be their motivation to act. In general, families are less likely to recognize and act on problems when stress is either very low or very high. Under very high stress, families tend to engage in defensive avoidance instead of constructive problem-solving. Selective inattention, forgetfulness, missing warning signs, and wishful rationalizations minimize the severity of the problem. Very often, this is the time when the family requires assistance from professional external resources.

3. The family searches for and processes information relevant to effectively solving the problem. On the basis of the information gathered, the family decides which among the many options would be the most effective way to resolve the problem. Unfortunately, they may select the solution that entails the least inconvenience—that is, the least time, money, energy, and resources. Thus, the family may not search for the best possible solution but rather for

a satisfactory one. Taking the time to find the very best option leads to the best outcome.

4. When the selected solution has been tried, the family evaluates its effectiveness. They may decide that the chosen strategy should be continued, revised, or discarded in favor of an alternative strategy. It requires patience and determination to give solutions enough time to work. It is helpful to remember that stress is usually heightened, rather than reduced, during the problem-solving process. However, making needed adjustments to ensure a good solution is also a wise strategy.

5. At this point, the family knows either that the problem has been solved or that the family needs to go back to the drawing board and try another solution. Flexibility ensures that families make needed adjustments or discard what isn't working and try something new. They stay with it until a satisfactory solution is working.

Coping with Catastrophes and Ambiguous Loss

A catastrophe is a stressful event that is sudden, unexpected, and life threatening. The circumstances are beyond the family's control and leave them in an extreme state of helplessness. Because catastrophes occur infrequently, most families are not prepared to cope with them. Wars, terrorist attacks, hurricanes, tsunamis, earthquakes, or pandemics can wipe out whole segments of a population without warning. Survivors are devastated by the sudden losses.

Catastrophes differ from other stressful events in a number of ways (Figley and McCubbin 1983): (1) a family has little or no time to prepare for a catastrophe; (2) the family has no previous experience to help it deal with the situation; (3) there are few resources to draw on to help manage the resulting stress; (4) few other families have experienced a similar disaster and can provide suitable support; (5) the family is likely to spend a long time in a state of crisis; (6) the family experiences a loss of control and posttraumatic stress syndrome resulting from a heightened sense of danger, helplessness, disruption, destruction, and loss; and (7) a number of medical problems (physical and emotional) are likely to occur.

Ambiguous loss is a phrase coined by Pauline Boss (2000, 2010) to refer to unresolved grief that lingers in a family when there is no closure. She describes ambiguous loss as *frozen sadness*, what a family feels when it cannot really know what it has lost. There are two types of ambiguous loss: one involves a family member who is missing, but there is no proof of death or even knowledge of where the person may be, if still alive; the other involves a person who is present in body but whose mind is not, such as is the case with severe dementia, depression, mental illness, or addiction (Boss, Roos, and Harns 2011).

Substantial research has examined the various emotional stages that a family in crisis goes through. Best known is Elisabeth Kübler-Ross's (1970) five-stage process an individual or a family typically goes through when confronted with a loss through death—*denial, anger, bargaining, depression,* and *acceptance.* Although there is agreement that these stages don't always go in order and one must consider the unique grieving process of each family member, it is still helpful to consider these components of grief. *Denial* is often the initial stage, usually characterized as a state of shock in response to the unexpected loss. Family members may appear calm and collected, exhibiting emotions that are even somewhat inappropriate given the severity of what has happened. There can be immediate and acute underlying feelings of numbness. As family members get in touch with the reality of what has happened, they may experience *anger.* To the outside observer, the increased emotional intensity characterizing this time may appear regressive. In truth, it is an honest reaction and a healthy step along the road to emotional healing.

There can be a time of *bargaining* during the crisis. Unable to accept the magnitude of the loss, persons may try to minimize or think a bargaining tactic may change things (e.g., a family that has suffered financial bankruptcy may promise to give more to the church if only God will restore a portion of what has been lost). However, as family members come to realize the full extent of the particular loss, they can become more depressed about what has happened. Often, this is the lowest emotional point. *Depression* is actually an expression of deep sadness and grief about what was lost. Persons can go back and forth through many different emotions (fear, guilt, anxiety, conflict, meaninglessness, feeling out of control, loneliness) in the final move toward *acceptance,* which is known as the angle of recovery. The angle can be depicted as a very steep incline, pointing to a speedy emotional upturn, or as a gradual slope, representing a long, drawn-out recovery period. The angle of recovery depends on the resources the family has at its disposal.

On reaching acceptance, the family may be quite different than it was before the painful event occurred. Reaching acceptance does not mean that family members no longer feel any of the emotions of the other stages of grief, but they are not so immobilized by them. Having been empowered, they can experience increased self-reliance as they make the needed adjustments and plan for the future. The case of ambiguous loss can severely hamper the possibility of a family moving toward recovery.

A crisis can happen to an individual in the family or to the whole family. What is most important is to give help in a way that empowers rather than keeps others dependent. One must treat the person/family with deepest respect rather than taking over, under the assumption that the victim is totally incapable and helpless.

When an entire family suffers a crisis, its members often draw closer together through the common experience. In such a situation, each member mutually gives and receives support. The isolated nuclear family is especially vulnerable during such times, and the Christian community can be invaluable. The challenge is for us to be family to one another so that we can offer Christ's love and support in emotional and physical ways during times of crisis.

Families in Pain

Sometimes, a family feels the disruptive effect of an event so deeply that the term *stress* is an inadequate description. When family members have been hurt to the core of their being, they are in *pain*. Such pain has a far-reaching impact on the life of the family and, if not addressed, may continue from one generation to the next in even greater tragic scenarios.

Like the disciples who asked why the man whom Jesus was about to heal had been born blind, families today often ask similar agonizing questions about their pain. Jesus firmly answered that the man's blindness was not a consequence of anyone's sin. Jesus then took action by responding to the needs of the man in pain (John 9). Like the blind man, we need the One who has the power to heal our deepest hurts. We need God's strength to offset our vulnerability. We need a belief in the God who gives meaning and a perspective to help us survive and eventually get beyond the pain. We need to feel God's compassionate presence suffering with us and lighting the way through our darkest hours.

By banding together, families can constructively work through the deep hurts of life (Balswick and Balswick 1997). In 1 Corinthians 12:26, Paul says that all believers are part of the body of Christ; thus "if one member suffers, all suffer together with it." It works this way in the human family too. When one person suffers, the entire family suffers. The responses of all the family members and the interactions among them during a family crisis need to be acknowledged and reckoned with. A family must not only look for their collective strengths in times of trouble but also deal with those weaknesses that prevent them from helping the hurting one.

Working together and placing Christ at the center, family members can begin a process that will help them regain wholeness:

1. Each family member should gather the courage for self-examination of his or her feelings, thoughts, and behavior under the trying circumstances.

2. The family should ask honest questions about how each member is doing, how each one is affecting the others, and how the family is coping as a whole.

3. Every family member must be allowed to feel the painful experience; the emotions of anger, sadness, and fear about what has happened must be acknowledged rather than denied.

4. Grieving over the losses that have occurred, the family must find the strength to relinquish the concerns they cannot control and to let go of past injuries in order to focus more fully on the present.

Families will be empowered to take responsibility for their behavior once they understand clearly how past events and injuries have contributed to the present pain. Family members often see how their behavior tells a story of unmet needs, fears, and resentments they are trying desperately to resolve. When appropriate, forgiveness will complete the healing and lead to substantial restoration of relationships. Although forgiveness can take many forms and serve different purposes, it should never be superficial or offered lightly. As part of the healing process, forgiveness helps us release the bitterness, anger, and hurt that stifle healing. In some instances, forgiveness of self is the hardest part. Although forgiveness may seem quite an outrageous idea from a human point of view, with God's strength and mercy it is not only possible but it will also prove to be exactly what is needed to bring transforming power to anguished lives.

Christian Belief and Response to Stress and Pain

Our belief systems strongly influence our perceptions of stressful events and our ability to cope with them. The particular influence that Christianity has had in this regard varies over a broad continuum from passive resignation to self-reliant attempts to achieve mastery over catastrophe. At one extreme is a fatalistic view that misuses or misinterprets Paul's teaching that Christians should be content in whatever state they find themselves (Phil. 4:11). Most Western versions of Christianity, in contrast, are very action oriented, emphasizing the responsibility and capability of the believer to take whatever action is needed to alleviate the threatening situation.

An example of the fatalistic view is the theology of positive thinking. It comports well with the societal emphasis on each individual's ability to mentally create his or her own perfect world. Positive thinking comes close to promising a life without any difficulties, but this is incompatible with the reality of a world tainted by sin. To live in a fallen world is to experience stress and pain. In our humanness, we are capable of causing all sorts of burdensome situations for ourselves and for others.

Clichés that admonish us to "turn every stumbling stone into a stepping-stone" and to "turn scars into stars" must not be used to deny the very real disruptions families face. Rightly taken, however, a hopeful and positive view can help reduce stress and keep problems in perspective. To view scars as stars—that is, to change one's perception of a painful event—is healthy when combined with both an awareness of the potential damage the crisis can inflict and a realistic assessment of how the family can manage with the resources available. Such an approach enables the family to take action rather than deny or be paralyzed.

The view that stress or pain is the direct result of a specific sin and/or can be overcome instantaneously through an act of divine healing presents another problem. In reality, most of the events and conditions that distress families, including alcoholism, eating disorders, job loss, parent-child conflicts, and illness, are caused by complex physical, social, and psychological factors. In a general sense, of course, all these stressful conditions stem from our living in a fallen world tainted by sin. But insistence that the cure lies simply in taking action against the sin in individual lives fails to comprehend the pervasiveness of evil and the role that social structures play in producing stress and pain in the world.

True, to deal with stress and pain, we must take action against the sin in our lives, but we must not ignore other realities, such as dysfunction within families, unjust economic systems, the oppressiveness of poverty, and so on. We must adopt a multifaceted approach that recognizes the complexity of the anxieties and pressures of life in the modern world. Awareness of this complexity will make us extremely cautious about claims of instant healing for the deeply painful experiences in life.

In our pill-oriented society, we want instant relief and cure from all that ails us. One aspirin advertisement promises relief "when you don't have time for the pain." Our society promotes the quick fix over the long, hard work required to overcome most of the stress in today's world. To become whole, a healing process must take place in the believer. This healing process, which includes growth in faith and in our relationship to God and others, usually works at a gradual pace.

To think that Christians are immune to stress and pain is not only an unrealistic view but also bad theology. Scripture includes numerous examples of disaster falling on the just and the unjust alike. We need look only at the life of Job to know that evil circumstances come to the righteous and that instant cure is not the norm. What is guaranteed is the compassion of God in every circumstance. God will be present with us through the body of Christ and in the power of the Holy Spirit. This belief can bring deep spiritual hope that helps not only the individual family member but also the entire family. A study done on patients with advanced cancer, for example, found that higher levels of hope were associated with lower levels of strain on the part of family caregivers (Lohne, Miaskowski, and Rustoen 2012).

The two extreme responses to stress that we have examined lead, respectively, to a theology of escapism, in which the Christian tends to withdraw in the face of crisis, and to a theology of activism, in which the Christian tends to be self-reliant to the point of rendering God a mere bystander in the process. What is the biblical response? Scripture suggests that when confronted by a crisis, Christians should not fatalistically resign themselves. For example, when arrested, Paul did not meekly succumb. Instead, he asserted his status as a Roman citizen. Examples from the life of David point to a balance between passivity and activism in the midst of stress. At times David fell on his knees before the Lord, acknowledging that his situation was hopeless without divine intervention. At other times, David took forthright action in the face of extreme difficulties. The balance between passivity and activism can be seen in the story of David and Goliath. Fully aware that without God's help he had no chance against the Philistine, David equipped himself with his sling and five smooth stones.

The same combination of passive reliance and active assertiveness can be seen in the life of Jesus. Faced with imminent arrest, trial, and crucifixion, Jesus retreated to the garden of Gethsemane. Distressed and agitated, he told his disciples that his soul was "deeply grieved, even to death" (Mark 14:34). In his despair, Jesus prayed to his Father, "Remove this cup from me; yet, not what I want, but what you want" (v. 36).

It is important to recall that this very same Jesus had previously gone into the temple and assertively driven out the moneychangers. Enraged at the hypocrisy of the Pharisees, he called them whitewashed tombs, snakes, and a brood of vipers. His language was equally severe when he called Herod a fox, unreceptive audiences swine, and false prophets savage wolves. He did not refrain from taking direct action against the social evils of his day.

Christians need an able response to crisis. An unavoidable part of living in a fallen world, stress should be approached as a time to draw especially near to God and others for support. Although God has not promised an escape from stressful situations, he has promised to be our "refuge in the time of trouble" (Ps. 37:39).

Stressful events often shake up the family system in a way that disrupts the stagnant comfort of routine life. This can be an occasion for growth as

Christians. It can also be a time of increased intimacy among family members and with the body of Christ as a whole. When people are vulnerable, they are often more receptive to the support and love of others. It is essential, then, in periods of adversity to choose a direction that, with God's help, will lead to deeper levels of intimacy, commitment, forgiveness, and empowerment. To help achieve and maintain a balanced perspective, we might also keep in our hearts the simple yet profound prayer of Reinhold Niebuhr (1987, 251):

> O God, give us serenity to accept what cannot be changed,
>   courage to change what should be changed,
>   and wisdom to distinguish the one from the other.

16

Divorce and Single-Parent Families

Families are amazingly resilient. Even in the face of challenging external pressures and intense internal conflicts, they are often able to adapt through a built-in survival mechanism. From an outsider's point of view, a given family may face insurmountable challenges, and yet the members consider the family their primary source of identity and security. The basis of this support and identity is the stability of the parents' relationship. Waite and Gallagher (2000, 323) conclude, "There is substantial evidence that, on the average, being in a satisfying marriage enhances the physical, psychological, social and economic well-being of adults, and that divorcing may involve considerable risk."

There is a concerted effort to emphasize the benefits of marriage even when trouble exists between spouses. In a study released in 2002, Waite and five colleagues analyzed data from the University of Wisconsin's National Survey of Family and Households. They discovered that adults who said they were unhappily married and got divorced were on average still unhappy or even less happy when interviewed five years later, as compared to those who stayed in their marriages. Most of those who stayed in their marriages had on average moved past the bad times and reached a happier stage. After controlling for race, age, gender, and income, the researchers found that divorce usually did not reduce symptoms of depression, raise self-esteem, or increase a sense of mastery over one's life. These findings have been reinforced since 2002 (Kalmjin, 2015). The general conclusion is that divorce does not make unhappily married people happier.

A point does come, however, when spouses divorce because life together is no longer a viable option. This often occurs after a fairly long period of disillusionment or denial, when spouses have ignored or exacerbated their problems. Eugene O'Neill's play *Long Day's Journey into Night* provides a good look at a family engaged in collective denial. They keep talking about each other in totally unrealistic terms. Such defense mechanisms deflect debilitating conflict for the time being but ultimately keep the family from instituting needed change. When built-up anger and bitterness disrupt into violent, abusive interactions, marriage is no longer a safe haven. Without help, the spouses will likely divorce.

Divorce

Demographics

Among developed countries, the United States has one of the higher divorce rates. The annual divorce rate in the United States steadily rose from a low of 1 divorce for every 1,000 married couples in 1860, to a high of 22.5 in 1979. Immediately following World War I, the divorce rate rose noticeably; similarly, following World War II there was a dramatic rise in the divorce rate. These increases reflect both the stress placed on marriages by forced separation and the large number of unstable marriages contracted during the wars. The drop in the rate during the Depression years reflects the costliness of legal divorce. The most dramatic rise in the divorce rate occurred between 1965 and 1979. It was especially pronounced among people under age forty-five. Since that time, the rate of divorce has declined moderately to an estimated rate of approximately 17 divorces for every 1,000 married couples in 2013. This trend has roughly remained steady through 2019 (US Census Bureau 2021).

Since 2000, the rate of divorce has dropped from roughly 4.0 per 1000 to approximately 2.7 per 1000. This reflects a drop from 944,000 divorces from states that report divorce and annulments in 2000 to 746,971 in 2019 (Centers for Disease Control and Prevention, n.d.). The best estimate is that approximately four to five out of every ten current marriages will end in divorce, with the likelihood of divorce being lowest among those who have been married the longest. The average length of marriages that end in divorce is seven years; the rate of divorce is highest for marriages of two to three years' duration.

Although the decline in the divorce rate since 1980 is encouraging, it should also be noted that the number of people choosing to cohabit rather than marry explains this trend in part. Although a high percentage of cohabiting couples separate, such breakups do not affect the divorce rate. The later age of first marriage (twenty-six for women, twenty-eight for men) also contributes to the declining divorce rate. Although it is hard to document, we believe that the positive marriage movement emphasizing the importance of premarital counseling and marital enrichment also accounts for the declining rate of divorce.

Although there is no sure way of predicting whether a marriage will succeed, research has found correlations with a number of demographic factors, such as ethnicity, income, occupation, social class, and level of education that may have a bearing. In 2001, Centers for Disease Control and Prevention reported that 20 percent of first-marriage divorces now occur within five years. Those who marry young, especially in their teens, are much more likely to divorce than those who marry in their twenties. A number of interrelated factors may also be at work here. Couples who marry young are typically from a lower socioeconomic class (which increases the probability of financial difficulties), and they marry after a very short engagement and perhaps because of a pregnancy. Given their stage of individual development, most teenagers are socially and psychologically unprepared for a relationship as demanding as marriage. These trends have continued through 2021.

Next to teenage marriages, the most unstable marriages are those of people who marry after age thirty. Among these divorces, the most common complaints are a lack of agreement and the tendency of the spouse to be domineering and critical. The underlying dynamic here is perhaps that those who marry late in life have become set in their ways and have a hard time adjusting to the expectations of a spouse.

The divorce rate is low among men with little education, increases among those who have had some high school training, and declines among men who have a college degree. In terms of ethnic differences, the divorce rate is highest among Blacks, moderate among Whites, and lowest among other ethnic groups, particularly those of Far Eastern origin. In terms of religion, divorce rates are lowest among Jews, moderate among Catholics, and highest among Protestants. Divorce is more likely when there is a sizable age gap or differences in religion, social class, or ethnic origin.

Causes

There is no single cause of divorce. The reasons are multiple and complex. Some relate to the idiosyncrasies of the individuals; others involve social and cultural factors, such as the demographics we have just noted. Other things being equal, the lower the quality of the marriage, the greater the likelihood the couple will divorce. In other words, low levels of marital satisfaction usually translate into divorce. Therefore, absence of any of the requisites for a strong marriage (e.g., commitment, family support, differentiation, adaptability, forgiveness, mutual empowerment, and intimacy) discussed in prior chapters could contribute to marital failure. Couples who learn conflict-management skills are more likely to work out their differences and stay married.

A seminal work by John Gottman (1994; Gottman and Levinson 2000) projects which couples will likely divorce based on one interview. Gottman tells us divorce is more likely to occur should partners engage in four types of negative communication strategies: criticism, defensiveness, contempt, and stonewalling. Couples that use these negative communication strategies are significantly more likely to divorce. Further, these result in negative affect, which lowers marital satisfaction; lower levels of positive affect also contribute to divorce. This means that couples who divorce tend to experience low levels of positive experience and higher levels of negative communication.

The most frequent motives given for divorce center on relational issues, behavior problems, and problems about work and the division of labor in the home. A recent study in Denmark confirms that similar factors lead to divorce across cultures: lack of love/intimacy, communication problems, lack of sympathy/respect/trust, and growing apart (Strizzi et al. 2020).

A number of factors at the sociocultural level may contribute to a *culture of divorce* and a divorce-prone society. Based on their research on divorce in the Netherlands, deGraff and Kalmijn (2006) observe three important trends in modern societies: the normalization of divorce, the psychologization of relationships, and the emancipation of women. Other factors contributing to a culture of divorce include a decline in viewing marriage as an unconditional commitment, a decline in the social stigma of divorce, the liberalization of divorce laws, increased opportunity for males and females who work together to become romantically involved, and changing gender roles that make wives less dependent economically on their husbands.

When it comes to those who identify as Christian or non-Christian, there seems to be little difference in the prevalence of divorce. However, it does seem to matter when it comes to how devout these people are. A study of over fifteen thousand subjects in Great Britain found that "frequent Christian attendees were 1.5 times less likely to suffer marital breakdown than non-affiliates, but there was no difference between non-attending Christian affiliates and those of no religion" (Village, Williams, and Francis 2010, 327). Bradford Wilcox (2010b, 687) found that "individuals who embraced norms of marital permanency and gender specialization and were embedded in social networks and religious institutions enjoyed high-quality stable marriages." He also found that "couples' in-home family devotional activities and shared religious beliefs are positively linked with reports of relationship quality" (2010a, 963). In her article "Research Disputes 'Facts' on Christian Divorces," Adelle Banks

(2011) pulled together research evidence indicating that the rate of divorce among Christians is significantly lower when persons attend worship regularly. Couples that regularly pray and worship together tend to have more stable and satisfying relationships.

David Popenoe and Barbara Dafoe Whitehead (2003, 2004, 2005) of the Institute for American Values believe that the cumulative effect of divorce has eroded the foundation of American society. They believe the impact of the no-fault divorce policy has made it far too easy to divorce and contributes to a culture that is comfortable with divorce. In addition, the modern/postmodern preoccupation with individualism and self-fulfillment places inevitable tension on marriage today as contrasted to values of covenant commitments and personal sacrifices. Also, unrealistic expectations, lack of egalitarian practices, loss of a community base to support family life, and the emergence of materialism as a dominant value take a toll on marriages. Clearly, there are a multitude of reasons, some direct and some indirect, some conscious and some unconscious, some personal and some societal, that explain why people divorce.

The Process

The divorce process can be a stressful and conflict-ridden time. Any antagonistic or abusive pathology that has previously existed is likely to escalate during and immediately after divorce proceedings, increasing the threat of harm to the children. Divorce and custody proceedings are often accompanied by destructive and adversarial—even abusive—behavioral patterns. The initial phases of divorce and separation are the most dangerous for domestic violence victims. Divorce tends to bring out the worst in partners.

From a legal standpoint, divorce is enacted on a specific date; however, the ending of a marriage typically stretches over several years. As both a public and a private process, divorce is a crisis-producing event. It involves the death of a relationship, and as with most deaths, pain and crisis are common by-products. Although both suffer immensely, generally the man is affected most negatively in the sociopsychological sphere and the woman in the economic.

The divorce process typically follows a four-stage sequence. The first stage is the period before separation, sometimes referred to as the emotional divorce or the erosion of love, which conjures up feelings of anger, disillusionment, and detachment. The second stage is the point of actual separation, which often is accompanied by bargaining tactics, sadness, regret, and depression. The third stage, the period between the separation and the legal divorce, involves legal issues, economic readjustments, continued mourning, coparenting arrangements, reorientation of lifestyle, and a focus on one's own identity and emotional functioning. The fourth and final stage of personal recovery includes a restructuring and restabilizing of lives, opening up to new possibilities and goals. This time may include a "second-adolescence" phase of being single and being involved in the dating scene again.

The emotions people experience in the four stages of a divorce are like the emotions experienced during the stages of coming to grips with the death and dying of a spouse. Although the marriage has ended, the two individuals are still alive, however, and their relationship with their children has not ended, keeping them involved with each other after the divorce.

The Effects on Children

It is no surprise that parents' conflictual relationships negatively impact children. In fact, divorce is a very common adverse childhood experience (ACE) that has long-term effects (Felitti et al. 2019). Divorce is reported to diminish psychosocial well-being in children. This diminished well-being tends to result in negative academic achievement (Potter 2010). Yu et al. (2010) found that marital conflict and divorce can affect the quality of the relationship between the mother and her children. The negative effect on children's development begins early, at the "in-divorce" stage according to Kim (2011). Afifi, Schrodt, and McManus (2009) discovered that children were emotionally affected by the fact that their parents talked negatively to their children about their divorced spouse. Children of divorce also experience more behavioral problems (Weaver and Shofield 2015).

There are factors other than divorce, however, that contribute to greater problems for children of divorce. For example, Vousoura et al. (2012) warn about the overall level of psychopathology in the family prior to divorce as a stronger contributor to childhood depression than divorce. Some research suggests that the economic effects of divorce have a greater effect on childhood mental illness than the disruption of divorce (Auersperg et al. 2019; Strohschein 2012).

We acknowledge that when there is a high level of violence in the home, divorce sometimes saves lives and the well-being of children. All things being equal, however, we believe children need and deserve to grow up in a family with two parents who love them and who love each other. Research on two-parent families documents the positive advantage this arrangement gives to children (Waite and Gallager 2000; Haskins 2013; Wilcox 2014). Since divorce hurts the relationship between parents and kids, it must always be a drastic last resort. Children must be a priority so we can protect them and provide the attention they need when divorce does occur. The covenant commitment extends to our children, a biblical truth that corresponds to the finding that when children experience a positive attachment with their parents, they have fewer adjustment problems and adjust better at each phase of their parents' divorce and eventual remarriage.

The crucial question is, What is in the best interest of children? The long-term impact of divorce on children has been debated for the past forty years. Some researchers are more optimistic than others about the adaptability and resilience of children, while others point to the negative effect that divorce continues to have on them. Up until the late 1970s, there was some attempt to downplay the negative effects of divorce on children. This attitude was based on research suggesting that children may be better off in a happy one-parent home than in an unhappy two-parent home. The home supposedly became a more stable, less disruptive environment once the neglectful or abusive father or mother was removed.

At this time, research indicates that children from divorced homes fare worse than children from intact homes. However, the reason for this can be debated. One view is that the real harm to children comes from a conflicted marriage, in which children have experienced trauma created by the psychopathology of their parents. In support of this view are Robert Gordon's (2005) findings that the direct negative effect of divorce is more short term, with children of divorce appearing less harmed after long-term adjustment. Gordon believes that the impact of divorce on children is fleeting and that the long-lasting psychological problems displayed by children of divorce in adolescence and adulthood reflect more the preexisting marriage and the continued conflict between ex-spouses. Lisa Strohschein (2005) reports that even before divorce, children whose parents later divorce exhibit higher levels of anxiety/depression and antisocial behavior than children whose parents remain married. She did note, however, that there were "divorce specific" increases in anxiety and depression. Another study (VanderValk et al. 2005, 533) reports "a further increase in child anxiety and depression but not antisocial behavior associated with the event of parental divorce itself."

Most researchers agree that the trauma created by the divorce itself and the resulting anxiety and uncertainty is harmful to children. A well-documented longitudinal study by leading divorce researchers Mavis Hetherington and John Kelly (2002) found that the changes in everyday life following divorce do have an initial negative impact on the children. The greatly altered behavior of their parents during and soon after divorce (dating phase) is a particularly difficult time. It takes most parents two or more years to recuperate from divorce, and during this time of adjustment both parents struggle with personal self-esteem needs. In the study, some spouses were prone to sexual acting out, vengeful deeds against the former spouse, emotional outbursts, periods of depression, and fearful concerns about their future and their finances. This period of transition takes a toll on the children because parents are often not available to help them make emotional adjustments.

Children also have adjustment problems in the first year after divorce, and they may exhibit acting-out or acting-in behaviors. Girls frequently recover in the second year, while boys may continue to have adjustment problems throughout adolescence, especially if they live with their mother in a single-parent home. Though dependent on her, boys go through coercive cycles and tend to be more aggressive and noncompliant. Single-parent mothers and daughters tend to become very close emotionally until the onset of adolescence, which brings conflict over sexual behavior and individuation (Hetherington and Kelly 2002). When conflict between parents continues after the divorce, children are often caught in the middle. Paul Amato and Tamara Afifi (2006, 222) conclude that "research on divorce has found that adolescents' feelings of being caught between parents are linked to internalizing problems and weaken parent-child relationships."

The body of divorce research supports both views; namely, children are harmed by what transpires in unhappy and conflictive marriages, but they also suffer because of divorce itself. This means that both highly conflictual marriages and families *and* divorce have the potential to seriously harm children. The term *double-exposure effect* refers to how the *divorce event* and *parental distress* contribute *independently* to child and adolescent distress (Storksen et al. 2006). Regardless of the source of the harm, the evidence indicates that children of divorced homes are burdened more than children of intact homes.

Long- and Short-Term Divorce Adjustment

Hetherington and Kelly's longitudinal project, which spanned three decades, led them to conclude that divorce should not be viewed as a momentary event but rather "as a lifelong process that has a continuing influence throughout the stages of divorce, single parenthood, remarriage, and stepfamily life" (2002, cover). They indicate that going through a divorce takes a toll on all family members because of the many changes, challenges, and losses they experience during that time. The years immediately before and after the divorce especially carry high risks in terms of emotional, personal, and health issues. It seems that the father's absence is more disruptive to boys than to girls, and the father's withdrawal from child-rearing may damage the child's recovery.

Hetherington and Kelly report that by six years after divorce, over half of the women and 70 percent of the men had remarried, with over three-quarters of them believing the divorce had been the right thing to do. They contend that the vast majority of children of divorce (75–80 percent) are resilient and doing well. They criticize studies that take averages—for example, "20–25 percent of kids of divorced families have behavior problems compared to 10 percent of non-divorced"—because these studies capitalize on the "twice as many" but fail to point out that 75–80 percent are not having problems, and therefore the vast majority are doing well (Hetherington and Kelly 2002).

The evidence of both the long- and short-term effects of divorce has been documented well by Judith Wallerstein (2005) and her colleagues. They conclude that "stressful parent-child relationships in the post-divorce family together with the enduring effects of the troubled marriage and breakup lead to the acute anxieties about life and commitment that many children of divorce bring to relationships in their adult years" (401). Later in life, children of divorced parents seem to be at greater risk for divorce (Segrin, Taylor, and Altman 2005). Nair and Murray (2005) report that mothers raised in divorced homes had lower income levels and lower levels of education compared with their counterparts from intact families and were less likely to use authoritative parenting styles.

In light of the long-term effects of divorce, we would do well to heed Connie Ahrons's (2004) suggestion that "good divorces" allow adults and children to continue to live relatively harmoniously as a family. She notes that divorce reorganizes a family but does not destroy it. In fact, many children of divorce believe that their parents' decision to divorce was the right one, and most do not wish their parents had remained married. However, the ideal of a good divorce should be tempered by the study (Amato, Kane, and James 2011) reporting only modest support for the good-divorce hypothesis, with the greatest benefits being a smaller number of behavior problems among children and closer ties to their fathers. In other words, a good divorce means that children's well-being is of paramount importance during the divorce process.

Best-Case Scenarios

From a Christian perspective, we must ask what the best-case scenario can be for spouses and children when divorce becomes a reality. Here we focus on conditions under which divorce is least troubling. It has been established that children adjust better when parents discuss the possibility of divorce beforehand and continue to discuss the situation after the divorce occurs. Obviously, the less hostility between the parents during the divorce process, the better the child's adjustment. Divorced parents who maintain an affable relationship with each other and show continuous love and support of their children lessen the disruptive effects of their divorce. The quality of the parents' postdivorce communication is essential to good adjustment in children.

Another key indicator of how well a child will adjust to divorce is the custodial parent's effectiveness in the role of single parent. When custodial fathers expect obedience and good behavior and operate with mutual respect and affection, children do better. Giving in to children and trying to make up for the pain of the divorce leaves them less secure than when the father takes a clear leadership role. It is vital that the parent who has not been awarded custody spend quality time with the children.

Joint custody and split custody are two creative attempts to promote continued involvement by both divorced parents in the lives of their children. The results have been mixed, but for the most part when both parents take cooperative and mutual responsibility, the children fare better. This arrangement can work well when a couple maintains a good relationship, but it does not succeed when parents continually fight and have disputes over the children and custody arrangements. Although children in joint custody tend to exhibit greater self-esteem than do those in sole custody, primary custody by the parent of the same sex in most cases seems to be a more beneficial arrangement for the child.

In split custody, each parent assumes the care of one child (or more). It is sometimes reasoned that girls need to be with their moms and boys with their dads. However, sibling separation and the formation of parent-child coalitions may in the long run hurt rather than help the adjustment process.

A Christian Approach to Divorce

Divorce, while not condoned in Scripture, has become common in today's world. For this reason, we want to offer a Christian response. Throughout this book, we emphasize that marriage and family relationships should be based on a mutual covenant. God desires permanence in marriage, and married Christians must do all that they can to uphold their marriages. This ideal for Christian marriage is an honorable aspiration that can be achieved by God's grace and through the power of the Holy Spirit.

However, we would be remiss if we didn't acknowledge that there are no perfect people and none completely live up to this ideal. All marriages are composed of two imperfect people who fail each other to one degree or another. All couples struggle with their relationships. While many learn to deal successfully with marital conflict and find the healing needed through therapy and community support, others are unable to overcome the obstacles of violence, disrespect, abuse, bitterness, addictions, cold detachment, and neglect. Brokenness heaps on brokenness and anger; hurt and bitterness begin to take on a life of their own. These marriages tend to spin in reverse—from conditionality to emotional distance to possessive power to conditional love and an atmosphere of law—and eventually the marriage is severed.

Wherever Jesus talks about divorce (Matt. 5:31–32; 19:3–9; Mark 10:2–12; Luke 16:18), the clear thrust is that marriage is of the Lord and not to be broken (Wenham 2020). It is also important to acknowledge a range of Christian views on divorce and remarriage. The highly accessible *Divorce and Remarriage: Four Christian Views*, edited by Wayne House (1990), presents the arguments on divorce and remarriage. Christ calls couples to fidelity in marriage as a lifelong commitment; he does not have in view, however, a marriage of legalism that entails only commitment to the institution and not to the relationship. Marriage is a human structure, and we must never focus more on preserving a structure than on caring about the individual spouses. Jesus did not condemn the woman at the well for her unsuccessful marriages and relationships but offered redemption and a new beginning (John 4).

The New Testament focuses on grace and forgiveness and hope. The message of restoration must be generously offered to those who have gone through the pain of broken relationships. We advocate for the pastoral support of Christians who have gone through divorce. As we have seen, divorce negatively impacts everyone involved. The church should come alongside those experiencing divorce, offering hospitality and encouragement in word and deed. Romans 3:23 indicates that "all have sinned and fall short of the glory of God," meaning that we should not be judgmental of our brothers and sisters who have experienced divorce. At the same time, there is a real, tangible need for aid, especially in the first couple of years after divorce.

Single-Parent Families

Single-parent households can be defined as either mother or father living alone with their children, bringing children into a cohabiting situation, or sharing living arrangements with others (extended family or other single or married people). The parent who lives in the same household with his or her dependent children is referred to as the custodial parent, while the noncustodial parent is the one who does not live with the children. There is evidence that whether they live in the home or not, grandmothers especially are becoming the default caregivers after divorce.

As trends of divorce have increased, so have single-parent homes. Every year approximately one million children become part of a single-parent home. The percentage of children under age eighteen living with a single parent has risen from 9 percent in 1960 to 28 percent in 2004. The changing proportion went from 22 percent in 1960 to 56 percent in 2004 among Blacks and from 7 percent to 22 percent among Whites (Popenoe and Whitehead 2005).

These trends have continued into the later part of the 2010s (Centers for Disease Control 2020). For example, about 15.76 million children lived with single mothers. About 3.23 million children lived with single fathers. These trends have been decreasing from the peak in 2012. It should also be noted that due to remarriage, many children from single-parent homes eventually become part of reconstituted families.

The first two years following a divorce can be an especially fragile period in the single-parent home as both the custodial parent and the noncustodial parent adjust to new roles. The degree of harmony or conflict between the parents is the major factor in how stressful this period will be. The hurt, anger, sadness, and depression that occur with a divorce affect the single parent at an emotional level especially in the first few years, making it more difficult for divorced parents to attend to the needs of their children. With their security undermined, they can feel unsure of themselves in many areas. Two major stressors accompany the adjustment to being a divorced person with children: *not enough time* and *not enough money*.

Not Enough Time

The common complaint of not enough time only intensifies when the solo parent is called on for double duty. At the practical level, this means something has to give. Single parents lack the time needed to juggle work, parenting, household tasks, and a personal life. Being deprived of a mate to share the parenting responsibilities, the single parent often feels both lonely and overwhelmed. Some single mothers give more to their children and take less care of themselves, which explains the common complaint among single mothers that they have little left over for themselves.

As hard as single parents try, their children are often shortchanged. The term *latchkey children* describes youngsters who are on their own and lack adult supervision for a large portion of time, even when living with the custodial parent. Because of the difficult circumstances of single parenthood, living in a single-parent home can be a lonely existence for children and place inordinate responsibility on them. Given less attention and guidance than they require, such children are disadvantaged when it comes to educational, occupational, and economical provisions.

Noncustodial Parents

Potentially, but rarely in reality, the noncustodial parent equally shares parenting responsibilities with the custodial parent. Those parents who truly put the good of their children first find a way to overcome differences with the ex-spouse and remain involved, caring, and supportive parents. Sadly, face-to-face involvement by noncustodial parents in the lives of their children consistently decreases with time. A major cause of the declining involvement is often the development of a new relationship for the father.

Economic and emotional abandonment of children by their fathers may cause many of divorce's most damaging effects. Mothers rarely abandon their children when they abandon marriage, but fathers often move away or fail to pay child support. Since children ordinarily do not live with their father after divorce, his absence can be detrimental to both sons and daughters. One main issue with postdivorce father absence is reflected in nurturance and involvement. Popenoe and Whitehead (2003) reported that only one in six children saw their father as often as once a week in the first year after divorce. Ten years after the breakup, more than two-thirds of the children report not having seen their father for a year. Income for mothers and children declines about 30 percent, in contrast to fathers, who gain 10–15 percent in personal income.

These trends continue as children age. Fewer adolescents than younger children belong to single-father households (King, Boyd, and Pragg 2018). For adolescents in single-mother families, belonging and attachment to mothers is reflected in lower levels of marijuana and tobacco use, lower levels of alcohol use, fewer depressive symptoms, and less delinquency. In other words, secure attachment between single mothers and their children is associated with lower levels of drug use and delinquency as compared with single mothers with less secure attachment styles. For adolescents living with their fathers only, these teens experienced lower depressive symptoms, lower marijuana use, and less delinquency compared with teens living with mothers only. In other words, single father households are associated with lower drug use and delinquency compared with single mother households, even ones with more secure attachment patterns. The divorced father's closeness to the noncustodial mother did not provide the same level of support for adolescent well-being as even single-parent families. That is, the level of closeness between two divorced parents trying to coparent still does not provide the same level of support as single-parent families where one parent is no longer engaged in parenting. Fathers who stay engaged with their children after divorce reap the benefits of a higher quality relationship with them.

Not Enough Money: The Link between Single Parenthood and Poverty

Although the lack of sufficient income adversely affects all types of low-income families, the negative effect is especially pronounced among single-parent families (Conger, Conger, and Martin 2010). Perhaps the greatest difficulty experienced by single parents is a lack of economic resources. Whatever the path to single motherhood (divorce, death of a spouse, unwed pregnancy), it is estimated that approximately two-thirds of single-parent mothers live below the poverty level. The Brookings Institution found that finishing high school, getting married, and then having children has prevented 98 percent of the American population from experiencing poverty (Sawhill and Haskins 2003).

It is sobering that the majority of those who divorce live below the poverty level. Lack of sufficient education or skill often means that the single parent's employment demands physical and emotional energy with little left over for the care of the children. As a way to alleviate economic stress, some single mothers remarry prematurely, only to face a second divorce. Finding employment, especially when one is not educated or trained, is an enormous burden. On top of this, the single mother must deal with the logistics of making ends meet, perhaps face the need to relocate, and take care of the emotional and physical needs of the children, which means she has little time to maintain a social life.

The discouraging evidence is that falling into single-parent family status often begins a downward spiral to deep poverty that persists from one generation to the next (Blalock, Tiller, and Monroe 2004). Such single-parent families are caught in a *culture of poverty*, a concept denoting a way of life that ensues when people are forced to adapt to poverty.

Poverty affects children's physical and mental health. Children in poverty tend to have more dietary concerns, stress, and lowered physical health (Pascoe et al. 2016). These trends follow for lower educational outcomes as well as mental illness. Children from families with lower socioeconomic status had lower academic achievement, even in the earliest years of school.

One study found that married mothers had more education, were older when giving birth to their children, showed better psychological adjustment, were more financially secure, and had more social support than cohabiting or single mothers (Aronson 2004).

This bleak account of single-parent families should be balanced by the fact that, in spite of the extreme difficulty resulting from the lack of economic resources and time, some single-parent families function quite effectively. This is especially true when the noncustodial parent contributes financially and takes an active role in the lives of the children. Single mothers also fare better when grandparents step in to serve as surrogate parents to the children (Harper and Ruicheva 2010).

Although the research presented above paints a grim picture, single-parent families offer strengths as well. One of Tom's most diligent clients was a single mother trying to raise her son. Gabriella brought her son Juan into treatment after increasing anger outbursts at school and home. Juan was especially angry at his day care counselors and was slowly becoming angrier and angrier at his mother and teachers. Prior to becoming so angry, Juan described himself as wanting to be a good boy again, and he wanted to love his mom and dad. One of the main issues was that Juan's dad began making and breaking promises after he divorced Juan's mother. Juan had a hard time understanding and dealing with these broken promises. Further, Gabriella was trying to earn enough money to live on, and she was also trying to support Juan's education. During therapy, we implemented more proactive strategies like setting boundaries with Juan's father. We also processed Juan's anger and grief over the divorce. We practiced identifying patterns and relationship triangles to increase Juan's insight into his anger triggers. We also implemented a school strategy where Gabriella would take the initiative in reaching out to Juan's teachers regularly for progress reports. We also praised Gabriella and Juan's resilience and strengths at coping with a very difficult situation. Juan was able to see how well his mom supported him, and he learned how to regulate his emotions and respond in a more appropriate manner.

Family Values and Valuing Families: A Christian Response

The reality is that more and more children are growing up in single-parent families. This is partly due to the decreasing number of individuals getting married before having children and to the prevalence of divorce and separation. As we have been describing, the effects of single-parent families are challenging for children especially. A biblical ethic of family must include the mandate that each member in society is to be cared for—that truly none must be left behind. The radical redefinition of family by Jesus leaves no room for an ethic that allows Christians to draw the line at caring only for their own families. This is a reversal of Cain's refusal to be his "brother's keeper" in Genesis 4:9. We are in fact called to care for our brothers and sisters. The Christian community should be a resource for those in need, especially for children in single-parent households that may be struggling with tangible needs.

A disturbing finding by Marquardt (2005) is that children found the church to be less than helpful in the divorce process. For those children attending church at the time their parents divorced, two-thirds said that no one, neither clergy nor congregational members, reached out to help.

Kristen Harknett (2006, 171) has identified private safety nets—"the potential to draw upon family and friends for material or emotional support if needed"—as a major advantage that some single mothers have over others. She found that single mothers who do not have such safety nets are more prone to depression and lack of self-esteem and self-confidence. The Christian community can serve as a safety net for single-parent homes and make a significant difference to these families.

Many families are doing well, even after the disruption that occurs as a result of divorce, death, or abandonment. When both custodial and noncustodial parents take seriously their covenant with their children, there will be great reward for all concerned. Extended-family members and church community members can take the role of mentor and empower children from single-parent families. Other resources in the larger community can bring needed support, such as Big Brother/Big Sister programs, after-school activities (sports, music, art), church youth groups, and tutoring services. Welfare agencies at the local, state, and federal level can also offer substantial help that can make a difference in the lives of those family members.

17

Complex Families in Contemporary Society

We can no longer assume that a family consists of two parents and their children. Family types now include single parents living with their children full- or part-time; stepfamilies with his, hers, and their children full- or part-time; foster families; cohabiting couples with children; married or cohabiting couples without children; households of singles and married people with or without children; multigenerational family structures; and same-sex marriages/partnerships. Holding a narrow definition of *family* undermines the importance of these families. In this chapter, we examine the complex dynamics that occur in newly formed families and note the important qualities that keep them resilient. Diverse conditions (individual differences, quality of relationships among members, family environments, unique stressors, cultural and religious beliefs) affect the success or the failure of these families to thrive.

In our postmodern era, newly formed families face unique challenges. The ability to adopt creative living arrangements that meet the needs of each family and its members is the key to successful integration. Postmodern family life resembles a theme park. There are many different attractions available, and they are all competing for the attention of each family member.

Embracing differences, irregularity, and diversity necessitates permeable boundaries. Making room for each family member and his or her significant relationships (coming in and going out) challenges the structure of these families. Adapting to the changing needs of the members is quite a balancing act. Establishing family identity in the midst of making space for noncustodial parents and extended-family members and friends is not an easy task. Increased family forms introduce increased stress among family members.

Our rapidly changing technological society impresses on us the need to be proactive in keeping all families functioning at an effective level. When the multifaceted interests, abilities, gifts, and talents represented by each member become resources for the good of the whole, the family has achieved a greater goal.

A View from Trinitarian Theology

The changing nature of newly formed family structures does not change the interaction principles introduced in our trinitarian theology. Identity is the core feature of the family, and it is the core feature of differentiation in Christ. Our security as a child of God through Christ forms the basis for our being (identity) and doing (relating). In the postmodern world, reciprocal relationships may be more complex; however, they are more essential. Foundational to all interactions, regardless of the family structure, are the biblical relationship principles of covenant (establishing trust, belonging, and security); grace (living in a constant state of acceptance and forgiveness); empowerment (building one another up to reach God-given potential); mutual interdependence (differentiated unity); and intimacy (communicating in ways that establish deep connections and intimate sharing among members).

As our identity in Christ forms the core of our identity, we are able to make covenants with our partners and children. The main vehicle or mode of living out our identity in Christ is our value base. This base leads us to form covenantal relations typified by grace, empowerment, and intimacy. The ultimate goal is to authentically reflect our identity in Christ via our relationships for doxological purposes. In other words, we glorify God by relating authentically—in congruence with our identity. Diversity and distinction are exemplified in the Trinity. Further, the doctrine of the image of God evidences God's desire for diversity. It begins with the created order—manifold expressions of flora and fauna—and it culminates with humanity—"male and female he created them" (Gen. 1:26–28). Both fathers and mothers *must* remain faithful in their covenant commitment to their children even when the spousal covenant has been broken. Every family member prioritizes the best interest of other members. The interdependence of working together for the good of the whole strengthens newly formed families.

Interdependence means that new family members must learn to depend on one another and work together. They will experience the benefits and blessings when they feel part of and responsible for working toward a well-functioning family. Indeed, grace (acceptance and forgiveness) must abound during the process of coming together and then living together. Mutual empowerment will become a primary focus as family members show respect for differentiation as well as engage in cooperative efforts for the good of the whole family. Interdependence will be achieved when each member contributes rather than focusing on individual rights. Because all members have an important place and purpose in the family, each one reaps the benefits of intimate connection.

Newly Formed Couple

Although an estimated 80 percent of people who divorce eventually remarry, the timing of remarriage is often delayed due to postdivorce cohabitation, especially with multipartnered forms of cohabitation (Xu, Bartkowski, and Dalton 2011). Although these marriages have a slightly greater risk of dissolution than do first marriages (Bramlett and Mosher 2001), being remarried seems to bring restoration and renewal to most. Linda Waite's research (Waite et al. 2002) indicates that those who divorce or are widowed regain many of marriage's benefits when they remarry. Although parental remarriage can be difficult and even catastrophic for some children, most divorced men and women hope to be in a committed relationship with a spouse who loves, values, and supports their children.

An increasingly common pattern is for divorced persons to move into a cohabiting relationship either instead of or before a second marriage. Johnson, Anderson, and Aducci (2011) use commitment theory to explain why some choose to remarry rather than cohabit. They found that those who value interpersonal dedication move toward remarriage, while those who adhere to constraint commitment (feeling "stuck in" rather than valuing the relationship) choose cohabitation.

Second-marriage transition is a unique challenge for newly married spouses, and many are ill prepared to meet it. Trust is often a casualty of divorce, and individuals looking to enter into new relationships after a divorce are often wary. Building trust is more difficult in second marriages due to hurt that often lingers from dissolved first marriages. Those in second marriages often identify lack of trust in their first marriage as an issue that prompts them to increase trust while dating and establish trust in their remarriage. The fundamental truth is that the newly formed marriage is the most fragile relationship, yet the most important link, in forming the new family. The newly married couple may feel shaky in light of several external factors that have an immediate impact on them. Yet being prepared for the reality of joining their

---

Dealing with Loss and Grief

- Fear is often a by-product of loss.
- Anger is often a by-product of fear.
- Take time to talk about the losses.
- Take time to grieve the losses.
- Don't shortchange the process—take all the time needed.

---

two families means they must honestly anticipate the common challenges and stand solidly together as they enter this new phase of life.

Janet, a widow of three years, began dating Terence, a widower of two years, who fell head over heels in love with her. Their first marriages had been strong, and each felt the profound loss of a beloved partner. They each had children who would be part of the remarried family. As they began to antici-pate a future together, Janet noted that Terence had not fully grieved the loss of his wife. "I can live with her memory but I cannot live in her shadow," she told her counselor. A new marriage was not possible until the loss was fully grieved. She knew that living with an idealized ghost is a no-win situation. Janet was astutely aware she could never live up to an image, nor could she or would she want to replace the deceased spouse. Her own differentiated sense of self gave her a solid place to stand on her beliefs. She challenged Terence that he and his children had not sufficiently grieved their loss, and until they did, they could never make room for her. Also Janet's younger son, Curt, had formed a special relationship with his mother since his older siblings were in college. After his father's death, he had played an important role in his mother's life and was not ready to relinquish it. Clearly, he was not ready for a relationship with a stepfather. Working these issues out in therapy gave this couple the best chances to take their time until there was clear readiness for these two families to come together. Timing is everything.

In a divorce situation, a major chapter has ended, and each family must make numerous changes to separate from an old life and establish a new one. Similar to the grieving process accompanying death, there is also a grieving process of letting go of the past before one is able to embrace the future. After divorce, spouses are acutely aware of the pain of a broken covenant and the unfinished emotional business accompanying that relationship. The high divorce rates for second marriages are enough to keep people from entering a new covenant before they are ready. If the pain and grieving are denied or dismissed in the throes of a new romance, however, people may plunge into a new relationship before they are emotionally ready. This is a disastrous step because without insight and changed behavior, problems will only repeat.

Fortunately, many enter a second marriage after personal examination and understanding about the past relationship that ended in divorce. They have developed a differentiated self and can thus choose more carefully the second time around. Instead of repeating patterns, they have done the emotional work required to enter the new marriage with valued assets. In cases of both divorce and death, the following reminders are helpful for family members to keep in mind as they grieve their losses.

Second-Marriage Dynamics

Modern cultural ideology and norms about stepfamilies can have a negative impact on relationships. The first five years of forming the new family are the most troublesome, and during this time the couple is at greatest risk for divorce. Therefore, it is important that the couple enter marriage with optimistic strength to face head-on the realities of forming a new family. Alert to second-marriage dynamics, they can avoid making common mistakes.

Knowing the value of and being skilled in communication and conflict resolution will put the couple on the right path of interpersonal relating. What both spouses have learned in the former relationship will pay off in second-marriage dividends. Such spouses are not foolhardy, approaching the marriage with blinders on, but are realistic and have their eyes wide open, aware of what it takes to make marriage work. Prior planning regarding living arrangements (his, hers, or a new home), financial provisions, dealing with one or more ex-spouses, and extended-family visiting rights will help smooth a sometimes rugged path. In many ways, divorce prepares the newly formed relationship to deal with the economic aspects of the relationship in ways that first marriages are often unprepared for.

The marriage is the most fragile unit of the newly formed family and therefore must be protected through a covenant commitment that builds relationship security. It is particularly important that the new relationship develops a sense of "we-ness," which forms the basis of the covenant. In other words, this new differentiated unity needs to form the core selves for the spouses. Each partner needs to be honest about their wounds and experiences in the previous marriage. Further, each partner needs to feel secure in the new relationship. As this new relational identity forms, other relationships will necessarily need to be modified. New partners will be introduced to relatives, and the family of origin will receive a new extended member. Additionally, new partners often immediately become parents, which creates a need to engage with the previous spouse and their extended family regarding child custody and child-rearing practices. The covenant identity of the new relationship functions as a base of operations for each partner in negotiating these new relationships.

Building a marriage grounded in sound biblical principles also renews enthusiasm. The couple is well beyond the romanticizing of younger days and brings both wisdom and knowledge to the family dynamic. Although living alone may have led to independent living, their desire and choice is to bring togetherness and separateness into a balanced interdependency.

Remarriage can be an incredible source of healing. Being accepted, cherished, and nurtured by one's new spouse enhances connection and is reassuring. A new sexual relationship with a consistent partner, shared activities, and a meaningful life are a great contrast to the lonely days. Discovering a new couple identity and protecting it with all one's might is well worth the effort. Reaching out for support from family and friends helps safeguard the sacredness of the new commitment.

Newly Formed Family

The terms *blended*, *binuclear*, *reconstituted*, and *stepfamilies* are used in the literature to refer to homes in which children from a previous marriage reside. Although we often refer to *newly formed families* as a way to acknowledge a variety of families (foster, cohabiting, etc.), here we use *reconstituted* and *stepfamilies* interchangeably as terms that have developed over the years. Connie Ahrons (Ahrons and Rodgers 1987) coined the term *binuclear* to give a positive view of being part of a reconstituted family. Such a family has two nuclei, both of which are essential to the progress of the family as a whole and the well-being of the children.

Regardless of the terms we use, a major challenge facing newly formed families concerns *ambiguity of status*. A history of shared experiences that maintained the first families is missing. The boundaries of reconstituted families must be more permeable to include everyone invested and involved in the lives of family members. Adding to the complexity of ambiguity of status is the fact that parental authority and economic responsibilities shared by two households open up emotional battles of divided loyalties and affection. On the other side, second spouses may use this ambiguity to engage in triangulation by attempting to connect with the child or children against the ex-spouse. It is in the best interest of the children that parents do not use them as pawns in a continuing effort to sabotage the other biological parent. Even though

Ideas for Newly Formed Families

- Discover an identity of your own as a family.
- Create holidays and traditions unique to this family.
- Plan fun times/vacations/activities together.
- Experience faith practices and worship as a family event.

family members yearn for less ambiguity, it is a condition that needs to be accepted and lived with.

The lack of clearly defined norms regarding newly acquired relationships can be daunting. Children can feel torn when living with a stepmother or a stepfather while their biological mother or father lives elsewhere. Moreover, ambiguity is also an issue for the former wife and her current husband (or a former husband and his current wife), children's grandparents, and family friends with whom close ties have been established.

In research designed to identify resilience in remarried families, Greeff and DuToit (2009) found the following eight factors associated with resilience: supportive family relationships, affirming and supportive communication, a sense of control over outcomes in life, activities and routines that help the family to spend time together, a strong marriage relationship, support from family and friends, redefining stressful events and acquiring social support, and spirituality and religion within the family. Further, stepfamily cohesiveness, expressiveness, and harmony are associated with higher levels of relationship satisfaction. Stepfamily functioning plays a stronger role than stepparent-stepchild relationship quality in determining relationship satisfaction (Ganong et al., "Stepfathers' Affinity Seeking," 2019).

The task is to build a newly formed family with a distinct history that includes fresh traditions, rituals, and experiences that become unique to them. In the process of living together, the family creates an identity that becomes a shared blessing.

Unrealistic Expectations

Another source of difficulty in any newly formed family is *unrealistic expectations*. It is important to keep in mind the differences between first marriages and families and repartnered marriages and stepfamilies. There are five main dimensions of difference (Papernow 2018). First, insider/outsider positions are emotionally intense and long lasting. That is, individual roles are maintained, and they are highly emotional. For example, fathers and mothers remain as parents, but they may remarry and bring in other sets of in-laws that remain part of the stepfamily. Second, children in stepfamilies struggle with loss and change, and their loyalty to each parent is frequently strained during the divorce and remarriage. Remarriage may bring up unresolved issues from the divorce, and children will also need to engage with the parent's new partner. These transitions may bring out many unconscious conflicts, which may affect their relationships with new family members. Third is consistent parenting, which will be discussed below. Fourth, stepfamilies must build a new family culture while respectfully navigating previously established cultures. In other words, stepfamilies need to establish a unique identity. Finally, other parents outside the household (ex-spouses) are part of the family, meaning that the parenting system includes the biological parents and stepparents.

A natural source of difficulty is the tendency for stepchildren to be more tolerant of the mistakes of their natural parents than of the mistakes of the stepparents. Most likely, history with their biological parent gives them more familiarity and confidence in that relationship. Of course, the child may also have sustained serious damage by a biological parent, which keeps that child skeptical and distant. But, in general, society conditions children to trust their own parents, and therefore they will quite naturally be more suspicious, overcautious, and even resentful of the stepparent or foster parent.

Themes in children's literature put the wicked stepmother or stepfather in a bad light. Less often do we read stories or see films about the positive role a stepparent or a foster parent plays in the life of a child, so no matter

---

Unrealistic Expectations about Stepfamilies and Foster Families

- Our stepfamily/foster family will function just like our first family.
- There will be instant love among all family members.
- Everything will quickly fall into place; adjustments will be easy.
- The children will be as happy about the remarriage/new family as we are.
- The stepchildren/foster children want a relationship and will be easy to get along with.

how loving and caring, stepparents are often rebuffed. Knowing this will keep the stepparent/foster parent from trying too hard or pushing too soon for a relationship. Patience is the key. Resist the temptation to move quickly into a parental role and take time to be a friendly adult who cares about the children. A stepparent can never win if he or she tries to compete with an idealized parent who, in the eyes of the child, is perfect. The sidebar lists some common unrealistic expectations that will add perspective. Most important is learning how to get along with stepchildren/foster children and taking time to develop a relationship with them.

It can be immensely helpful for couples to anticipate the tough emotional and physical adjustments that are inevitable during the first few years. Rather than crumble under the illusion of unrealistic expectations, the couple establishes a united front to face the reality of the situation. Family cohesion is not the first goal for stepfamily success. The ability to stay flexible is the golden rule. This gives family members the necessary time to get used to one another gradually, so that they can define their roles and relationships accordingly. Family cohesion can be achieved only through the mutual respect and regard that occurs when the newly formed family is living together. Bartolomeo Palisi and his colleagues (1991) found that the couple's being realistic as well as possessing negotiation skills that lead to united decisions regarding stepchildren are predictors of remarriage adjustment.

Parents Taking Leadership

How a family navigates structural change is influenced by cultural, socio-economic, religious, and cross-generational values and attitudes. Regardless of these influences, family leaders must do whatever they can to protect and provide for the children. Inevitable environmental and relationship changes place the parenting roles in a continual state of flux. Maintaining sufficient structure and stability counterbalances the frequent moving between households. Although leadership of the family lies with the biological parent(s) for the most part, stepparents or surrogate parents play an essential part in leadership decisions.

Research indicates that it is extremely important for the biological mother and father as well as the stepparents to be involved in the lives of the children. Parenting values and practices are a key element to be negotiated in newly formed families. The literature shows that quality and quantity time spent with children has a positive effect on their overall health and resilience. Establishing a foundation of trust and a sense of belonging are crucial in the life of a child. Even after disruptions such as death or divorce, a secure attachment established early in life gives children the capacity to build on that initial bonding (Bell 1974; Bell and Ainsworth 1972).

Clear communication is crucial for creating a stepfamily. The biological parent and stepparent need to create a new identity that incorporates the losses associated with the divorce, especially for the children. Further, there needs to be a frank discussion regarding how they will incorporate the other biological parent *as a parent*. On top of this, a plan is needed regarding the role of the child's other family members from the other biological parent. How will Christmas vacations be handled? When will the child visit his or her grandparents from the other biological parent? These discussions need to take place without the child.

The biological parent and the stepparent also need to establish an identity with the child. This way, the child will be able to engage in a meaningful and proactive way with each. The child may begin adopting the new identity as he or she is part of this new, expanded family. This new identity provides a secure platform for clear communication. This is crucial as clear communication supports both relationship satisfaction and positive outcomes, at least for teens (Pace et al. 2015).

Cooperation and collaboration place the emphasis on teamwork in reconstituted families. The leaders set the pace for harmonious interactions. Basic agreement requires constant communication, commitment, and mutual accountability. Learning to work through differences takes persistence and perseverance. Because children are often part of two family systems, they must learn to cooperate and fit in as contributing members in both homes. Teenagers may contribute by assuming a role in childcare, younger

---

Guidelines for Leadership

- Be united in your leadership roles.
- Don't initiate major changes (rules and routines) too soon.
- Establish clearly defined rules in a timely manner.
- Be flexible and adaptable when possible.
- Use a weekly family council time to negotiate family goals.
- Stand together on goals and expectations decided in the family council.
- Create strategies for making decisions, negotiating solutions, and resolving problems.

children through performing household chores. The entire family may choose to prepare meals as a cooperative venture, everyone pitching in to clean up, and so on. Consulting with children and teens about family responsibilities and rewards brings them into the process as contributing members who also express their preferences and privileges. When family rules are determined in a democratic way, each member has input and takes responsibility in the cooperative venture. Schedules, lists, routines, and structure help organize the family, while adaptations are made in response to the needs of its unique members. Communicating individual and family needs becomes the joint responsibility of every member and the family as a whole.

Stepparents/Stepchildren

It will come as no surprise that the quality of the stepparent-stepchild relationship greatly affects the couple relationship. Age is a moderating factor; the younger the children are during the remarriage, the greater the likelihood of success.

Children quite normally experience strain between loyalty to their natural parents and to their stepparents. Stepparents who no longer live with the children from their first marriage may also struggle with loyalty issues. Perhaps moved by guilt to be better parents with the new family, they become more intense, which actually hinders establishing a relationship with their stepchildren.

Balancing the demands of parenting and personal desire for adult companionship and romance can be a tension for divorced parents. In their study of divorced custodial mothers' orientation toward repartnering, Anderson and Greene (2011) found a continuum from more child-focused to adult-focused mothers. They found that "mothers who are more adult focused tend to be older, more educated, more likely to be employed outside the home, and exiting marriages of longer duration" (741). Predictably, adult-focused mothers report spending less time in joint activities with their children and having lower rapport with them.

Many studies indicate that children can and do form close emotional connections with stepparents. To be successful, stepparents must take sufficient time to form relationships with each child (Ganong, Coleman, and Jamison 2011). The transition experience provides a stabilization process in which stepfamily members begin to think of themselves more as a family unit. When studying thirty-two stepdaughters and seventeen stepsons, Ganong, Coleman, and Jamison (2011) found that the degree to which stepchildren engage in relationship-building and relationship-maintaining behaviors with stepparents corresponds with their positive evaluation of the stepparents' contributions.

According to Mavis Hetherington and John Kelly (2002), making a good transition into parenting involves the stepparents' ability to consider themselves initially as secondary parents. It is especially important for the stepparent to be a warm and supportive friend and refrain from taking on a strong disciplinary role in the beginning. The point is to let the biological parent continue in the disciplinary role and to simply back this role rather than be the one who determines it. The couple is the architect of the newly formed family, and when the spousal relationship is well formed, their joint leadership sets the right tone for the rest of the family. Agreement between stepparents about the rules and roles is a solid building block for discipline strategies and interaction with the children.

The positive stepparent-stepchild relationship keeps members connected and united rather than distant and fragmented. Establishing appropriate boundaries and working out a cooperative relationship with former spouses also goes a long way in keeping the marital dyad strong. In contrast, highly charged, conflicted, or negative relationships with former spouses negatively affect the new couple's relationship (Shafer et al. 2013).

Stepfathers/Stepchildren

In most cases, the mother brings children into the reconstituted family. Thus, the most problematic relationship is usually between the stepfather and the stepchildren. Stepfathers tend to be either very much involved with or disengaged from their stepchildren. Stepfathers who build relationships with stepchildren tend to have more cohesive relationships with the biological parent as well as higher levels of relationship satisfaction (Ganong et al., "Stepfathers' Affinity Seeking," 2019).

Initially, both boys and girls tend to be somewhat resistant to a stepfather coming into the home. Over time, he is likely to win them over, especially if he does not take a strict disciplinarian role but works hard to build relationships with his stepchildren. Hetherington and her colleagues (1982) found that boys are generally more open to a stepfather, whereas girls tend to resist his intrusion into their special mother-daughter relationship. Teenage daughters of divorcées seem to have difficulty interacting in appropriate ways with stepfathers, even though they desire and seek male attention.

According to research, girls make a better adjustment after divorce if they are cared for by their mothers, and boys make a better adjustment if they are cared for by their fathers. It seems that girls in the custody of their fathers and boys in the custody of their mothers profit from remarriage. The arrival of stepparents enhances their social development.

William Marsiglio (2004) did a conceptual analysis using in-depth interviews, exploring stepfathers' experiences in claiming stepchildren as their own. Trying too quickly to construct an unrealistic "we-ness" or isolating oneself in the outsider position hinders the process. Because of the complexity of each situation, the stepfather needs to be wise in establishing a quality, stable connection with stepchildren. In this study, the majority of the men expressed a reasonably strong connection with their stepchildren and took responsibility in practical ways in the home regarding money, discipline, protection, guidance, childcare, and affection. "It was shared daily contact and practical involvement in their stepchildren's lives that altered their views in almost imperceptible ways" (37). The feeling of "we-ness" developed through joint activities in everyday situations. It seems stepfathers grew closer to their stepchildren as time went on and as they began to think of themselves in the fatherly role. Making an unconditional commitment to the stepchildren and gradually spending time with them helped the stepfathers see the stepchildren as their own.

Some important interrelated benchmarks that emerged in stepfathers claiming stepchildren as their own concerned timing, degree of deliberativeness, degree of identity conviction as a stepfather, having a range of roles in their lives, being mindful of their needs, and seeking recognition in public as a stepfather (Marsiglio 2004). The biological mother's influence is also important to the stepfathers' success. When she encourages connection and expects him to take responsibility for her children, it opens an opportunity for him to develop feelings for them. In a real sense, she is making it easy for the stepfather to have a relationship with her children when she asks him to pick up the kids after school, help with homework, and take part in the discipline.

Being a stepparent is an extremely demanding job. You must be relentless in your compassion for the children and refuse to view them as "out to get you." Trying to create one big, happy family is an erroneous goal, so stepparents should live with the realistic goal of doing everything possible to live in harmony in the newly formed family. The perseverance, courage, patience, and sacrifice usually offer great rewards.

Marital Tension over Stepchildren

The not-so-surprising news is that one falls in love with the person he or she marries but not necessarily with his or her children. Thus, engaging each other's children may be the most difficult aspect of remarriage. Even when you know you have a lot to offer as a parent, your confidence is easily destroyed by the indifference or rejection of your spouse's children. Often the stepparent is seen as the unwanted intruder. Stepchildren may automatically spurn and even ridicule your attempts at nurture. When children have been emotionally hurt and disillusioned with life, they hold on to unrealistic fantasies that parents will reunite and make everything better. They can be fiercely determined to defeat the stepparent. This is new territory for both parents and children. No one is ever prepared for such disruption, which has the power to devastate the new marriage.

Such explosion over who has priority—the spouse or the children—creates startling tension between the remarried spouses. Similar marital struggles in a first marriage do not take on such emotional dimensions because the children are the couple's own. As good as the marriage may be, guilt, anger, and trouble over children can take a serious toll on any marital relationship.

In a stepfamily situation with adolescents, a further complication is that adolescents are entering the life stage when it is common to question, engage in conflict with parents, and challenge authority figures. Under these circumstances, adolescent stepchildren believe the new parent has no right to discipline them. Every attempt must be made to neutralize the dichotomous good parent/bad stepparent thinking so that stepparents can be effective in their leadership.

Lawrence Ganong and Marilyn Coleman (2004) found that stepfamilies are more complex than previously thought, and they can function successfully in different ways. However, when stepfamilies are able to construct an identity of their own, and the members can establish relationships with one another, they are well on their way. The study shows that the nature and quality of the stepparent-stepchild relationship depends on several factors, such as the stepparent's investment in the relationship, the stepchild's willingness for the relationship, the relationship with the nonresidential parent, and time available.

Summary

Ronald Deal (2002, 70) uses the analogy of a Crock-Pot to describe the stepfamily. He writes: "It takes time and low heat to make an effective combination of ingredients. When ingredients are thrown together in the same pot, each is left intact, giving affirmation to its unique origin and characteristics. Slowly and with much intentionality, the low-level heat brings the ingredients into contact with one another. As the juices begin to flow together, imperfections are purified, and the beneficial, desirable qualities of each ingredient are added to the taste. The result is a dish of delectable flavor made up of different ingredients that give of themselves to produce a wondrous creation."

Stepfamilies are "a work in process"! The concept of differentiation helps us put to rest the idea of a blended, bland family. Only when each member is able to contribute his or her distinctiveness will there be a rich flavor to taste. Relationships with stepchildren develop over time. They set a pace that cannot be hurried.

Take it one small step at a time. It takes time for each family member to adjust to new living conditions and new roles, rules, and responsibilities. It takes time to get to know one another, develop trust, and begin a shared history. It takes time to find a sense of belonging, interdependence, and identity as a newly formed family unit. Learning to trust the time factor gives spouses permission to relax, lower expectations, go with the flow, and enjoy the moments of progress. Be patient. Be ready to listen with compassion. Persevere, and remember to use humor, laughter, and play in developing relationships with stepchildren.

All families struggle to rearrange busy schedules to be together, but it takes an even more intentional effort for stepfamilies to make these connections. It requires tremendous openness and flexibility to address the unique needs and desires of each member in the midst of establishing family routines and rituals that bond them together. A highly effective way to formulate a family identity is to create family traditions, rituals, and celebrations around significant holidays. When family members come together for such events, they each bring a unique presence. Be it a birthday celebration at a special restaurant, a church advent service, or an annual trip to the beach or the mountains, it brings history and harmony to the newly formed family.

Learning to apply the concepts and principles discussed throughout this book—empowerment, acceptance, grace, intimacy, and loyalty—will lead to stepfamily growth. Showing empathy and tolerance for one another, putting

---

Routines, Rituals, Traditions

- Invite the children to help create traditions and rituals.
- Welcome their ideas and follow their suggestions.
- Give adolescents leadership roles.
- Allow time for family ties to evolve.
- Make weekly, monthly, and yearly opportunities for connection.

the best interest of others on a par with one's own, and giving of oneself out of care and concern for others develops not only character but also closeness.

The rewards are great when the members of the newly formed family can establish meaningful relationships and join in cooperative projects. Finding mutual meaning in spiritual life forges a bond that gives the family a significant purpose beyond itself. See chapter 8, which discusses family spiritual life, for more ideas about this process.

PART 7

Family Life
in Postmodern Society

Any meaningful understanding of the family must integrate analysis at both the micro and macro level. We have focused mainly on microfamily issues—looking inside the family for an understanding of its dynamics. We turn now to an analysis of macrofamily issues—looking outside the family to explore the relationship between the family and the wider social context. Through this exploration, we will see that many microfamily issues are, in reality, a reflection of macrofamily issues.

In chapter 1, we developed a theology of family relationships based on the biblical concept of covenant. Now we move beyond the family to examine the broader social context. The contemporary family lives in a world of urbanization, bureaucracy, and technology—developments that make covenant commitment increasingly difficult. Modernity, first, and then postmodernity have profoundly affected contemporary family life. Rather than replacing modernity, postmodernity exists as a layer upon modernity, as both interact in their effect on the family. Chapter 18 introduces major aspects of modernization (an issue first addressed in the 1950s and 1960s) and their profound negative influence on contemporary family life. Not only has covenant commitment eroded within the family, but the very structures intended to support and maintain this ideal have collapsed. In chapter 19, we discuss postmodernity's effects on family life and present a biblical response to modernity and postmodern thought. We suggest ways in which broad social structures can, and must, incorporate covenant commitment. Only by recapturing the covenantal meaning of living in community, whether localized or universal, can the family be strong. We need a family-friendly society.

18

Biblical Family Values in a Modern and Postmodern World

"It was the best of times, it was the worst of times." Charles Dickens's description of revolutionary change in eighteenth-century France aptly characterizes the family in the United States and around the world today. It truly is the best of times and the worst of times. The contemporary family is an institution of contrasts and contradictions. Although the current divorce rate in modern nations is virtually as high as ever, more married couples than in the past report satisfaction in their relationships. At the very time that millions of children are living in broken families, there is also an unprecedented emphasis on love and intimacy in family relationships. And just as some are celebrating the freedom and openness brought about by new family forms, others are horrified at the decline of the family.

Don Browning, M. Christian Green, and John Witte (2006) document how the major world religions are currently wrestling with questions of the purpose and meaning of marriage and family life in modern society. In focusing on the American family, Steven Tipton and John Witte (2005) suggest that the family is indeed in trouble and can be rescued only by reintegration into a just moral order of the larger community and society. They argue that beyond merely upholding traditional family values, we must come to terms with increasing family diversity. However, this poses a challenge as family values do not necessarily integrate into larger community and societal morals.

The successive effects of modernity and postmodernity have also led to contradictions in the family. Our society has traditionally espoused a very

317

optimistic view of the future, based largely on faith in progress. However, what once was heralded as the path to a utopian future is now being blamed for the decline of the family and the quality of life in our postmodern world. Along with this lament for the family, we must also be cautious when valuing the family too highly. We are challenged to be creative in promoting biblical relational ideals in family life.

Modernity Defined

A concept as inclusive and encompassing as *modernity* is difficult to define. One line of thought ties modernity closely to technological development. Renowned sociologist Peter Berger conceives of modernity as closely linked to technology. His view has been summarized by James Hunter (1983, 6): "Modernization is to be understood . . . as a process of institutional change proceeding from and related to a technologically engendered economic growth. . . . Modernity is the inevitable period in the history of a particular society that is characterized by the institutional and cultural concomitant of a technologically induced economic growth." As a consequence of modernity and increasing technological advances, Peter Berger (1990) describes how sacred, religious understandings of the natural world are becoming less and less meaningful. The "sacred canopy" of a religious worldview is disappearing as humanity is able to exert increasing control and certainty over the natural world through science and technology.

Other theorists understand modernization as social change in various spheres. Neil Smelser (1973, 748), for example, sees modernization as occurring "(1) in the *political* sphere, as simple tribal or village authority systems give way to systems of suffrage, political parties, representation, and civil service bureaucracies; (2) in the *educational* sphere, as the society strives to reduce illiteracy, and increase economically productive skills; (3) in the *religious* sphere, as secularized belief systems begin to replace traditionalist religions; (4) in the *familial* sphere, as extended kinship units lose their pervasiveness; (5) in the *stratificational* sphere, as geographical and social mobility tends to loosen fixed, ascriptive hierarchical systems."

The sociological concept of modernization reflects both evolutionary theory and structural functionalism. Evolutionary theory assumes that a society advances from a simple to a complex state. This process is usually described as "development," regarding traditional agrarian communities with minimal technological innovation as undeveloped. Modernization, then, is conceived as occurring in stages. We might imagine, for instance, a five-stage progression beginning with an *agrarian society*, *preconditioning for takeoff*, *takeoff*, *drive to maturity*, and finally *high mass consumption*.

Structural functionalism assumes that as economic development takes place, new social and cultural forms must emerge. It argues that new institutional forms are desirable and necessary in view of the changes in economic life. Some Christians, who see God-given ideals behind traditional social institutions, experience modernity as a threat. While the threat is real, modernity also affords the opportunity to examine existing social structures and re-create them in light of the biblical ideal.

The Crisis and Challenge of Modernity

A primary feature of modernity is the disintegration of traditional forms in regard to values, behavior, and expectations. With this breakdown of traditional forms comes the responsibility to create new institutional structures. And with this opportunity come threats of social, moral, and intellectual chaos, making the creative task of reconstructing institutions overwhelming. This tension leads us to only see the threats of modernization rather than to face up to modernity.

Social scientists continue to debate the origins and moving forces of modernization. While some theorists believe that modernization is fueled primarily by economic and technological forces, others point out that ideological changes have made modernization possible. We believe that modernization unfolds in a dialectical manner, fed by both material and ideological aspects of life. No part of society and culture is autonomous; no social entity develops purely in terms of its own internal organization. This is true of every major structural unit of contemporary society—the church, the family, the economy, education, and politics.

Although there is interaction among all the major dimensions of life, the economic and technological are dominant in present-day Western society. The other dimensions of life have been cast into a responsive, rather than a leading, role. However, the various internal crises of modernization may lead to changes in the current balance of power. For example, the issue of moral legitimation in modern society may lead to a new role for religious and moral institutions. Many question whether a society built on moral pluralism and its attendant moral uncertainty can maintain itself. The crisis of secularization may lead to an awareness of the need for a new moral, if not religious, consensus in modern society.

In developing a framework to analyze the modern situation, we consider four dimensions of sociocultural life: *consciousness, communication, community*, and *commodities*. Modernization is rooted largely in economic reality (commodities); changes at this level are reflected at the other levels of sociocultural life. Each level also sends feedback to the others. The dialectical model we are suggesting is similar to a general model of social structure in which each part is conceived as influencing and being influenced by every other part. We hasten to add that these dimensions should be considered as analytical constructs only. They should not be reified and considered separate components of reality.

In facing up to the challenge of being modern, we must address all areas of life. We have chosen these four dimensions because they are the settings in which major crises are occurring in our world today. We will first explore the general dilemma posed in each of these layers of sociocultural life and then turn our attention to the specific negative effects on the family.

Consciousness

Consciousness refers to the individual's subjective experiences, including thoughts, beliefs, images, and emotions. Crises in this area can occur both within and between individuals—both subjectively and intersubjectively.

Within the individual, consciousness is fragmented among different spheres of life. The individual must negotiate between the impersonal competition of the marketplace and the intimacy of friendship and family, between rationality in the school and faith in the pew, between the fast-paced solutions of multimedia and the routine open-endedness of daily life. Under such circumstances, even the best minds and the most stable personalities can quickly lose a sense of centeredness, a clear grasp of meaning and reality.

This fragmentation of thought has resulted in a disjunction between faith and life. We ask: How do our beliefs and values affect the structure of our lives? Do competing values and beliefs shape different areas of our lives? Do our commitments and beliefs as Christians distinguish us from others? People in this era live in a state of cognitive dissonance. We have adapted to apparently inconsistent beliefs and lack of congruency between values and behavior. For example, interpersonal commitments and intimacy are highly valued, but relationships are unstable. Many Christians speak about having compassion for the poor but avoid people in need. To paraphrase the apostle Paul, we are trapped in a sociological "body of death," doing not the good we want, but the evil we do not want—and we do not understand our actions (Rom. 7:15–25).

A diversity of worldviews is available to us. The more modern we become, the more we are aware of this diversity and the more relative our views appear. Berger (1983) refers to this as the pluralization of consciousness. For some, this opens the door for a challenging dialogue with others to help in the construction of one's personal value system. This can be an awesome and lonely task. Others try to mold a new consensus, either by creating a new synthesis through dialogue or by cutting the dialogue short and imposing their own beliefs on the other participants. Another possible way of proceeding is subjectivization. As Hunter (1982, 40) puts it, "When the institutional routines and ideologies are rendered implausible, modes of conduct and thought, *morality included*, are deliberated. If institutions no longer provide consistent and reliable answers to such questions as 'What do I do with my life?' 'How do I raise my children?' 'Is it acceptable to live with a member of the opposite gender outside of marriage?' etc., the individual must necessarily *turn inward* to the subjective to reflect, ponder and probe for answers. The process of 'turning inward' is the process of subjectivization." As Hunter further suggests, the process of subjectivization is not negative—it is simply a structural feature of modern society. It can, however, foster "an incessant fixation upon the self . . . [an] abiding absorption with the 'complexities' of individuality" (40).

Communication

Communication in modern society both shapes and reflects the fragmentation, pluralization, and subjectivization of modern consciousness. Significant symbols—terms that everyone understands in precisely the same way—are the basis of communication. But in modern society, we cannot assume that everyone understands a term in precisely the same way. Even the words *family* and *church* have a variety of meanings that can arouse emotional debate. The denotative, or referential, meanings of words vary considerably; consider the multitude of meanings of the word *love*. The connotative, or associative, meanings are even more diverse. Lack of consensus on meanings creates a dilemma. On the one hand, our diverse backgrounds and uniqueness as individuals make communication more necessary than ever. On the other hand, our lack of significant symbols makes communication equally problematic.

A variety of questions arise in the context of our attempts to communicate: How can we communicate if we cannot assume that others will understand our words as we understand them? How is dialogue possible if there is no shared basis of interpreting language? Are our vocabularies authentic? How free are we to create new vocabularies and to give new meanings to words? What is the relationship between experience and language? Can we trust the very process of communication? Will language become, like advertising, one more technique to mystify and control others?

The difficulties of communicating are compounded today by the proliferation of technical and professional languages, which mystify the nonspecialist. We also see attempts to transcend the traditional means of symbolic communication through various forms of nonverbal communication. For the most part, everyday language and conversation are impoverished because of the difficulty of capturing complex and confusing realities in simple words.

Community

Although the ideal of community and family life might differ in the various faith traditions, modernity has fragmented the sense of community and family life. Many people have lamented the breakdown of homogeneous and geographically based communities as the major crisis of the modern era. Without such communities, we have no means of social control and are thus vulnerable to our own moral laxity. People are in search of a new home or community so that they can find meaning and purpose. What is often forgotten when we grieve the loss of traditional communities, however, is the provincialism and lack of autonomy that characterize them. Isolated villages and tribal groups are noted for their ethnocentrism.

Concurrent with the disintegration of community life is the centralization of economic and political functions in corporate and governmental bureaucracies. The picture that emerges is of the isolated individual and the nuclear family confronted with the faceless image of mass society. The community that once mediated between the individual and larger institutions is no longer there. Judicial and political institutions are increasingly called on to settle family, church, and community disputes. Government encroachment into areas previously considered private or sacred has become a serious social question to which there are no apparent answers.

Some social scientists have suggested that networks are the modern substitute for traditional communities. Friends, coworkers, and social, educational, cultural, and religious groups—together these networks can satisfy all or almost all of the individual's needs. However, networks tend to be unstable and specialized and thus lack the virtues associated with community: unconditional commitment and a sense of belonging that encompasses the whole of a person's life.

There is a wide range of responses to the disintegration of traditional communities. At one extreme is the trend toward a self-contained individualism that denies dependence on others and makes no commitment to them. At the other extreme, people form communities around a common value, such as economic sharing, family life, or religious devotion. Those in the middle search for a sense of community in institutional contexts such as the church, where the community metaphor is familiar, and in homogeneous neighborhoods such as suburban housing developments, where names like Homewood, Pleasantdale, and Community Heights imply commonality and identity.

Commodities

In advanced capitalism, the economic sphere has been largely secularized. Economic life develops unguided by any particular religious ideology. This differentiation of economic life is characteristic of modern institutions. The fragmentation of consciousness, complexity of communication, and disintegration of community make an integration of life around economics seem viable. Remaining unanswered is the question of whether or not a society based solely on economic and political consensus can maintain itself.

Economic principles do dominate modern social life. As the principles and values associated with economic life enter other areas (political, educational, and interpersonal), we see a pattern of the "commodification" of social life developing, where achieving quality social relationships comes to be seen as merely using the right techniques of relating. When emphasis on commodities results in the alienation of the worker, the intrinsic meaning of work is lost. When work becomes only a means to the end of making money, it becomes a moral criterion for judging people. The twin phenomena of careerism and consumerism, two evidences of these trends, are found at the center of economic, church, and family life.

The Impact of Modernity on the Family

With this basic understanding of modernity, we can now examine the dilemmas it poses for the family, as well as the false hopes it has generated (see table 6).

TABLE 6 **The Impact of Modernity on the Family: Dilemmas and False Hopes**

Impact of Modernity	Dilemmas for the Family	False Hopes
Fragmentation of Consciousness		
Fragmentation of thought Disjunction between faith 　and life Religious and moral 　pluralism Subjectivization	Crisis in morality and authority Dichotomy between private and 　public life	Traditionalism: restoring 　the family of the past Cult of the expert Privatization

Impact of Modernity	Dilemmas for the Family	False Hopes
Complexity of Communication		
Decline of significant symbols Mystifying technical language Impoverished conversation	Diverse backgrounds and linguistic styles Generation gap	Overreliance on techniques of communication Isolation of communication from regular activities
Disintegration of Community		
Disintegration of traditional community life Lack of social control Individuals confronted by bureaucracy and mass society Government encroachment into private matters	Isolated nuclear family Lack of community support and control Increased family dependence on mass institutions Development of a youth culture Little parental stake in children's marriages Lack of ties between extended families Diminished parental authority Equalization of power within the family	The family as a self-contained unit Extrafamilial care of children, the elderly, and handicapped Alternative family forms
Dominance of Commodities		
Integration of society around economic values Separation of economic from church life "Commodification" of social life Dominance of technical means	The family as the unit of consumption instead of production Separation of work and family life Individual and family worth determined by economics	Assessment of the fair market value of housework Community through consumption The family as the center of cottage industry Full employment for both husband and wife (careerism)

Fragmentation of Consciousness

THE PROBLEM

The fragmentation of consciousness has produced a crisis in the areas of morality and authority within the family. Each family must construct its own value system, usually without the support of the extended family. Difficulties are especially likely to arise when children reach their teenage years and begin to compare their family's system of morality with that of their friends. Parents are placed in the position of having to defend their view of morality against the view of their children's peers. The crisis in authority brought about by the fragmentation of consciousness also includes questions of the authority of the extended family over the nuclear family and of the husband over the wife. The current redefinition of sex roles comes into play here.

The fragmentation of consciousness has also led to a dichotomy between public and private life. In traditional societies, there tends to be little separation between the two; the primary social unit in both work and private life is one and the same—the family, the clan, or the tribe. In contrast, the recent separation of work and private life has led to two levels of social functioning. While working, individuals experience others as relatively impersonal beings and themselves as anonymous functionaries (Berger, Berger, and Kellner 1973, 34). This anonymity precludes any involvement on a plane higher than what might be described as pseudointimacy. People attempt to find genuine intimacy, meaning, and fulfillment in their private lives. But we suspect that modernity may have so weakened the private institution of the family that even here intimacy and fulfillment are not possible.

False Hopes

As the Christian community has felt the crisis created by the fragmentation of consciousness, a major response by conservatives has been traditionalism—an attempt to restore the family to what it was in the past. With the confusion created by modernity, many Christians are quick to hold up the nineteenth-century American version of the family as the biblical ideal. We believe that this is a false hope because it is less the biblical perspective on the family in modern society than a defense of what the family has been in the past. Christians commonly fall into the trap of assuming that the particular family form existing in their culture is God's ideal. They read their own cultural standards into Scripture and accept all biblical accounts of family life as if they were normative. But some of the accounts of how the family was organized during biblical times were never intended to dictate how it should be organized in all cultures at all times.

A second response to the fragmentation of family consciousness is to rely on expert opinion, another false hope. Parents often experience a crisis in confidence and are unwilling to trust their common sense out of fear that they may be doing something wrong in rearing their children. Such self-doubt frequently occurs in the Christian community, where many parents hold to a deterministic view of parenting: they wrongly believe that correct parenting is a guarantee of God-fearing children. Unfortunately, this view is reinforced by a variety of self-proclaimed experts, who attract large numbers of parents eager to be relieved of the agonizingly difficult task of parenting in modern society.

Another false hope is the privatization of family life, an offshoot of the dichotomy between private and public life. When couples or families construct self-centered meaning, it can be an artificial reality that does not comport with external reality. The privatization of family life can easily lead to an amoral familism, where the family is so preoccupied with its own concerns that it fails to serve far needier people. The amoral privatized family dishonors the biblical concept of family life.

Complexity of Communication

THE PROBLEM

The complexity of communication in modern society saps vitality from family life. That there is no exact universal understanding of words such as *family, love, parenting, intimacy,* and *sharing* complicates communication and relations. To the extent that a husband and a wife come from diverse backgrounds or experience differing patterns of growth, they will encounter difficulty in communication. It may very well be that the seemingly unending search for intimacy in contemporary society is an attempt to fill a void resulting from a lack of shared experiences.

Parents with teenage children are quick to realize that a good part of what is referred to as the generation gap is in large measure a gap in communication. With the emergence of the adolescent subculture come not only new meanings for old words (*cool, hot, tight, square, rad*) but also new words (*dope, lit, low-key, hi-key, cash money, swag, epic, epic fail*). To appreciate the complexity of communication among adolescents, one must realize that there is no monolithic adolescent subculture; rather, there are adolescent subcultures (stoners, jocks, rockers, new wavers, surfers, goths, and straight edge), each developing its own style of communication (much of it nonverbal).

FALSE HOPES

Overreliance on the techniques of communication is a common response to the complexity of communication in the family. One need only glance at the many how-to books written on marital and family communication to realize the heavy emphasis placed on technique. But a focus on technique can actually reduce communication. Spouses may find themselves talking about talking rather than engaging in genuine dialogue. The overreliance on technique has spread even into the area of sexual communication; manuals promise a couple complete sexual fulfillment if they will only follow the suggested step-by-step procedure.

Another response to the complexity of communication is to isolate communication from our customary activities. Many parents, realizing the need to explain to their children the reasons for family rules and values, set aside time for discussion rather than having such conversations as a natural part of life together. Essentially, then, family communication is removed from the normal course of activity and becomes one more task for the modern family. It is better to explain family rules and values whenever a suitable occasion presents itself. Communication will be greatly improved if it is embedded in the common experiences of developing family relationships.

Disintegration of Community

THE PROBLEM

The nuclear family has replaced the extended family in most modern societies. With the uprooting of the nuclear family from its extended family, clan, or tribal base comes the loss of community support and control of family life. The isolated nuclear family in modern society is a very fragile system. Gone is the day-to-day support provided by the extended family. The young married couple must go it alone. With no one else to share in the task of childcare, the absence of either husband or wife (or both) from the home can be severely disruptive. In their review article on understanding families with children, Crosnoe and Cavanagh (2010, 8) point to the need to "better situate families within neighborhoods . . . [so that] we can know more about the places that families live over time, how they influence what goes on inside the family, and how family life is experienced by youth."

The lack of community moorings has freed family members to become part of social networks over which the family has very little control. As mentioned previously, teenagers have become part of adolescent subcultures.

Modern ideology has set the individual above the traditional community in an emphasis on individual growth and the nuclear family over extended family. Modern ultra-individualism, with its lack of accountability to the community, increases the fragility of the family in terms of relationship support and connection.

FALSE HOPES

At least three responses to the disintegration of community prove to be false hopes. First, some families become self-contained units. They attempt to meet every need internally. They develop their own ideology, strive for economic self-sufficiency, and become deeply enmeshed. The self-contained family is an unrealistic ideal that is doomed to fail in modern society. It is also inconsistent with Jesus's definition of family (Mark 3:31–35).

Out of necessity, other families in modern society are turning to extra-familial institutions for the care of dependent members. Many of these families are fractured units that do not have the resources needed to provide adequate care for children, the elderly, or the disabled. In other instances, the stress on individualism and personal self-fulfillment prevents family members from actively assuming caretaking responsibilities. They ignore the fact that the quality of care that large institutions can give needy people rarely measures up to the New Testament standard of *koinonia* (fellowship, community).

The third response has been the development of alternative family forms. It is true that family forms must change in response to modernity; to think otherwise is to accept the traditional American family as the biblical ideal, instead of merely one among several equally justifiable cultural alternatives. Christians must be aware, however, that, as a result of modernity's secularizing influence, many alternative forms tend to suit the demands of individual self-fulfillment. Alternative forms need to be evaluated in terms of scriptural authority as well as in terms of whether they suit the best interest of individuals, family, and society.

The emergence of genetic technologies such as artificial insemination, in vitro fertilization, surrogate motherhood, external gestation, and cloning makes it possible for one person or any combination of persons to form a family for a newborn child. Any use of genetic technology must be based on a covenant commitment to have children. The continued development and application of genetic technology in reproductive efforts must also be assessed vis-à-vis their effect on the communal aspects of family life.

Dominance of Commodities

THE PROBLEM

A major effect of the dominance of commodities has been to change the family from the basic unit of production to the basic unit of consumption. It is rare to find family members together for the purpose of producing; it is equally rare to find family members together for any purpose other than consuming. The world of work and family life are separated; this is, as we have seen, one of the symptoms of the fragmentation of consciousness.

Another effect of the dominance of commodities is that the ability to acquire them is the chief determinant of the worth of individuals and families. Others gauge us by our success in the marketplace, and we gauge ourselves by how much money we earn relative to others. In many instances, a raise is needed more to build self-esteem than to meet financial obligations.

False Hopes

There have been various responses to the dominance of commodities in modern society. Some have argued that true equality for housewives can be achieved only by the state paying a wage for their work or to assess the market value of their housework in terms of the money earned by their husbands. Although we do not negate marital equality as a biblical ideal, we believe that even this less radical suggestion is a compromise with the view that marriage is based on social exchange, both partners seeking to gain more from the relationship than they give up. We do not deny that this is the basis for many modern marriages; we believe, however, that it flies in the face of the biblical ideal of mutual submissiveness.

Some families wrongly believe that they can create a sense of community solely through consumption—for example, by watching television or going to a movie together. We do not deny that some activities of this nature can play a small role in producing a sense of community; we do deny, however, the naive assumption that the family that consumes together blooms together.

The role of technology for the family of the future is mixed. While the family has benefited from a breakdown of rigid work/family spheres, the almost constant contact with work and other outside influences plays a large, negative role in the family. As we write this, technology has enabled us to continue working on this manuscript during the COVID-19 pandemic of 2020; this ability to work remotely has been a blessing. However, the availability of work almost 24/7 has the potential to erode the boundaries between family time and work time, thus increasing work and family conflict. The positive coping methods families develop, as well as the negative effects of being isolated for more than a year, remain to be seen. Technology has played both a positive and negative role.

Another false hope is the phenomenon of careerism. Careerism, whether only one or both spouses are involved, falsely equates individual worth with career success. Careers, like money, can detract from the establishment and maintenance of intimate relationships within the family and society as a whole.

This modern age has brought about important changes that have made life easier for most people; yet consciousness is fragmented, communication is overly complex, the traditional community has broken down, and there is an obsession with commodities. The family is in a wretched predicament, since most attempts made to ameliorate the situation have proved to be false hopes. In the closing chapter, we consider the impact of postmodernity and the further erosion of biblical family values. We conclude with a call for purposeful change built on biblical principles.

19

Creating a Family-Friendly Society

In the previous chapter, we considered the social environment of the contemporary family. By examining the effect of modernity on the family, we gained an understanding of why it is difficult to live according to biblical ideals. What is needed is a positive environment that strengthens family life.

In this chapter, we propose ideas for creating a healthy environment for family life. Fundamental changes must be made in two general areas: (1) families must make a determined response to modernity; and (2) community and societal structures must incorporate the biblical ideals of *koinonia* and *shalom*.

Inadequate Responses to Modernity

Modernity has greatly challenged and changed the family. We cannot simply succumb to the march of progress by adjusting the family lifestyle in accordance with innovations introduced into society. Rather, the challenges—fragmentation of consciousness, complexity of communication, disintegration of community, and dominance of commodities—make it imperative that we develop fresh insights into creating a positive environment in which the family can give glory to God and through their relationships show evidence of the salvation and freedom offered in Christ Jesus. This redemption, which enables us to meet the challenges of modernity, was purchased at a great cost and requires a thoughtful response.

It is important to keep in mind that redemption is an unfolding creative work of God in the lives of individuals, families, and societies. We need release from our bondage to commodities, which in turn will make reconstruction of community possible, which will provide an arena for revitalization of communication, which will eventually lead to reintegration of consciousness.

In contemplating the restoration of the family, we must have a general acquaintance with previous attempts that have proven to be false hopes. One general category consists of reactionary endeavors to return the family to an idealized past. These efforts are based on twin fallacies: (1) that the nineteenth and early twentieth centuries were a golden age of family life; and (2) that the traditional patriarchal family represents the biblical ideal for society today. This approach ignores the complexity of the issues. Its attempts to reconstitute the past overlook the dominance of commodities, the disintegration of community, the complexity of communication, and the fragmentation of consciousness. Instead of stumbling into the pitfall of idealizing a particular cultural and temporal form of the family, we must recognize the forces of modernity and respond creatively. We must move beyond traditional and modern views of family life.

Postmodern thinking represents a second category of response. Rejecting both a return to the family of an idealized past and the certainty of modernist thinking, this approach embraces the potential good and usefulness of a variety of alternative family forms. Postmodernity represents a radical response to the excessive emphasis on rationalism found in modernity and sees truth as what is in the eye of the beholder—that is, what one experiences. Postmodernity can be a useful corrective to the certainties of modernity, which promote human reason as the basis for a universal human morality. However, in its extreme form, postmodernity also has the potential to undermine family values and structures because it takes an all-inclusive point of view.

Postmodernists do not regard the general laws of nature as grounds for accepting or rejecting ideas. Viewing reality as multilayered, they believe there are many ways of knowing, many flavors of truth. Although the Christian perspective is acknowledged as one possible view, many others are considered equally acceptable. Postmodernism sees danger in accepting one truth or morality over the myriad of other options; to do so is regarded as restrictive and intolerant. Ironically, this is in itself a restrictive and intolerant position (Lee 2004). That is, the perspective of the "truth-teller" takes precedence over the objective truth that is being told. It stands in contrast to a Christian worldview that focuses on continued compliance with God's revelation.

Herman Bavinck (2019) captures the sentiment: Worldviews are fluid and adapting. Worldviews are constantly being confronted with the truth that God created the world with a definite goal and purpose. Humans need to reflect and adapt their worldviews to this purpose, that God has intentionally created the cosmos for his benefit and glory. God's purpose in creation is most clearly revealed in Scripture. This emphasis on worldviews means that we are constantly in an evaluative process: To what does my worldview conform? How do I conform my worldview to Christianity and postmodernity, especially when there are points of tension between the two? Christians acknowledge their limited ability to know the truth perfectly; however, there is an objective truth outside the perspective of the perceiver. Christians are continually trying to conform to this truth. This means that worldviews are fluid and adapting in more fully apprehending God's truth.

A strict postmodernist view leaves little ground on which to evaluate the morality of one family form or process over against another, since all alternatives are equally acceptable. The problem, of course, is that postmodernism cannot adequately respond to the number of abusive and harmful family systems that we know exist. We must stand for a morality that keeps the best interests of all family members in mind and recognizes the potential for evil as well as good in the various systems.

While modernity seeks to assess family life on the basis of scientific and naturalistic assumptions, postmodernity embraces every cultural form of family life. To avoid the modernist pitfall of idealizing a particular cultural and temporal form of the family, postmodernity goes to another extreme and dashes any hopes of finding criteria to assess family morality.

We, as Christians, uphold a reality. We must, then, have a good understanding of both modern and postmodern thinking so that we can rightly evaluate their benefits and hazards. To embrace modernity or postmodernity uncritically leaves one in the position of choosing human perspectives over God's perspective. We believe that Christians must recognize the positive and the negative forces of both modernity and postmodernity and then formulate a biblically based response.

Toward a Radical Response to Modernity and Postmodernity

Release from Bondage to Commodities

The first step toward a healthy environment is to free ourselves from the dominance of commodities (see table 7). One need not be a Marxist to acknowledge that capitalism dominates all of modern life. We are a people for whom the term *productivity* automatically connotes commodities. Clearly, the restoration of family life cannot be accomplished without liberation from the pervasive influence of our economic system.

TABLE 7 **Creating a Positive Family Environment**

Challenges of Modernity	Christian Responses
Dominance of Commodities	Release from Bondage to Commodities 　Employment programs that give priority to relationships 　Family sacrifice of socioeconomic goals 　Church support 　Mutual empowerment (rather than social exchange) as the basis of 　　family relations
Disintegration of Community	Reconstruction of Community 　Effective boundaries around the family 　Emphasis on the inclusiveness of the family
Complexity of Communication	Revitalization of Communication 　Family communication during shared activities 　Development of family rituals
Fragmentation of Consciousness	Reintegration of Consciousness 　Dependence on the beliefs and values provided by the church 　Openness to people who are different 　Service and witness to Christ

Without a revolution to free us from our bondage to commodities, we will inevitably be pulled toward conformity to the system that promotes it. Technology, money, careers, and material growth have become spiritual forces in society. We cannot count on society to adopt our Christian values; rather, we must be willing to sacrifice and risk appearing foolish in resisting the power of worldly values.

Christian employers can take the lead. They can, for example, establish policies that provide ways for their employees to give priority to family relationships. One option is to offer flexible schedules for both mothers and fathers who desire to be with young children. A strategy that reverses the two-hundred-year-old trend of giving economic institutions priority over parenting would make a significant contribution. Such a program could involve concessions for difficult pregnancies, maternity/paternity leave, and childcare on the premises. Excellent health care and disability coverage as well as good retirement programs go a long way to help families at all stages. Such measures would inevitably cost the company in monetary profits, but gains would be realized in the strengthening of family relationships, in the employees' personal well-being, and in their loyalty to the company. Employees would benefit from the commitment, care, and empowerment provided by their employers.

Commitments from employers to the welfare of their employees need corresponding commitments from employees to produce high quality work. The present economic system, which makes the profit motive the major consideration, works directly against the development of any sense of loyalty or pride in the quality of work performed. A philosophy of productivity that pressures employees to put in long hours away from home also hurts family life. Christian employers must provide, in addition to salary, a context in which employees receive incentives and rewards for creative service and quality rather than quantity in this work.

Within the family itself, a focus on relationships and a sharing of resources with others must replace consumerism and careerism. This would require (in addition to an attitude of mutual submissiveness, empowerment, and servanthood) a willingness to forgo the socioeconomic status and security that we have been conditioned to achieve for ourselves and our families. A basic assumption of middle-class American society is that we are obligated to hand down to our children a certain social status and economic security. Family life is oriented toward this goal. A decision to sacrifice socioeconomic status in order to live more simply will be perceived as a threat to the existing order. The children involved, other family members, and friends may criticize someone who takes a lower-paying job in order to spend more time with the family or to serve the community.

It is not easy to buck the system and make personal relationships and serving others higher priorities than making money. Our society respects people with high-paying jobs but seldom prizes those who choose relationships as their supreme goal. A typical case in point is parents who choose to stay home with their children out of dedication to the parenting role. These parents are often judged negatively for not being employed outside the home. A single parent who makes such a decision may have the additional stigma of living at the poverty level.

The church must offer its blessing to any individual willing to make sacrifices. Such support and backing will minimize the impact of these sacrifices and protect the individual from the brute economic forces of modern society. Churches can offer sustenance to families that commit themselves to relational goals. They can also provide quality day care for the children of parents who need to be employed outside the home. Further, the church should be sensitive to the special needs of families that have added emotional or financial burdens. The resources provided by a caring community can be of enormous benefit to families who are mentally or physically challenged, to those suffering from chronic mental or physical health problems, and to the elderly coping with frailty and death.

Reconstruction of Community

The typical nuclear family in the United States is a partial community at best. It is plundered on one side by the demands and intrusions of mass society and on the other by an individualism that has become increasingly self-centered. What is needed most is a recapturing of the biblical perspective of what it means to be a family. In this regard, two points that may at first appear to be paradoxical need to be made.

First, the reconstruction of family life needs to take place in a secure environment with effective boundaries. The family needs protection from the intrusion of a multitude of forces that currently encroach on it and sap its vitality. We have already mentioned the necessity of protecting the family from economic institutions. A similar appeal could be made regarding governmental, educational, and even religious institutions. In trying to meet all the demands with which these institutions bombard it, the family is fractured. Family members need a central place where they can gather and be nurtured in an environment of acceptance, intimacy, and mutual concern.

Second, the reconstruction of community can take place only when the concept of family is regarded as inclusive rather than exclusive. Whereas servanthood and commitment are meant to begin in the family, the Bible presents a moral imperative that expands our circle of caring to an expanded awareness and concern for others. In fact, on occasion Jesus speaks of leaving, dividing, and even hating one's family. Luke 12:52–53 says, "From now on five in one household will be divided, three against two and two against three; they will be divided: father against son and son against father, mother against daughter and daughter against mother, mother-in-law against her daughter-in-law and daughter-in-law against mother-in-law." The point here is that loyalty must transcend one's immediate family and extend to the Christian community as a whole. The family and church community extend to the wider community as well.

Revitalization of Communication

Communication is vital in reconstructing our community life and reintegrating our consciousness. It should reflect both our individual uniqueness and our shared values and activities. In the intimacy of the family or church community, we have a place where we can be naked and not ashamed (Gen. 2:25), a place where we can be who we are, free from all the demanding requirements of the outside world. Here is a place where family members can relax and be comfortable in a supportive and encouraging atmosphere. Here they do not have to hide but can be honest and real before the other members of the family. Families grounded in the principle of mutual servanthood exemplify the spirit of Christian community.

Family communication must be liberated from overreliance on techniques and obsession with words. Communication must be contextualized—that is, become an organic part of daily family life—rather than being a separate activity unto itself. Communication is more than active listening techniques; it develops within a family and provides a context for family identity in fostering meaning-making. Living in community involves individuals and families in person-centered engagement. These activities provide a natural context in which to share stories, experience life, and learn from each other.

Creating or rediscovering family and church rituals for special occasions is an excellent way to break down barriers between people and symbolize family values. At Christmastime, for example, celebrating the spiritual aspects of the season through symbolic acts, art, plays, song, and dance creates solidarity in which all members participate. This intimate time of togetherness is also an opportunity for each family member to express personal uniqueness. Worshiping together as a family in a multigenerational service enhances mutuality and togetherness.

Reintegration of Consciousness

Individuals are able to integrate their experiences only if a plausible system of beliefs and values is available to them. The isolated nuclear family is incapable of developing and maintaining such a system. The church can help by providing a coherent structure of beliefs and values so that the family can achieve a reintegration of consciousness. Spiritual formation takes place in the context of the worshiping community.

Another means of achieving reintegration is for the church and the family to be open rather than closed systems. The nuclear family can develop fictive kin—people who, though they are not blood relatives, are taken in as extended-family members. Church members should seize the opportunity to become world Christians rather than focusing only on the plight of their own groups. The church is challenged to learn about Christians around the world and respond to them as brothers and sisters in Christ. Embracing different cultures and races and employing their gifts and leadership enriches the worshiping community of faith. Wherever there are poor and oppressed people, the Christian community has an opportunity to reach out with acts of compassion as well as with monetary and political support. During the COVID-19 crisis, for example, churches joined together in efforts to provide food for those in need, enhancing the life of the church body even though they were not meeting in the church building.

Through service and witness to Christ, we have a great hope of reintegrating our lives. We must keep in mind, however, that the disintegrating effects of modernity will be overcome only in part in the present world. Perfection will come in the future. "For we know only in part, and we prophesy only in part; but when the complete comes, the partial will come to an end. . . . For now we see in a mirror, dimly, but then we will see face to face. Now I know only in part; then I will know fully, even as I have been fully known" (1 Cor. 13:9–12).

The fact that change will be only partial and imperfect in our human social systems is no excuse for retreat from a radical response to modernity. It is essential that Christians neither deny nor be paralyzed by the serious disruptive effects of postmodernity. They must be both realistic and optimistic. Contemporary society is currently staggering from the blows of modernity and postmodernity. Within this context, the people of God must call for and serve as salt and light, affecting the transformation of American culture.

Support Structures

Our focus in this chapter has been on how a biblical family structure can be created in the face of modern/postmodern society. But the family does not exist in a vacuum; it is vitally connected, for better or for worse, with community and society.

The family, the community, and society are interrelated support structures. We have suggested that a trinitarian theology and the four relationship principles of covenant, grace, empowerment, and intimacy are biblical themes on which to pattern family life. We believe that the corresponding biblical ideals for community and society are *koinonia* and *shalom*.

Extended Families

Families need caring communities in which they can find a sense of identity and social support. In cultures where the extended family is the basic social unit, nuclear families have a built-in support community. The basic social unit is in large measure determined by the level of societal complexity.

There are two lines of thought regarding the future of the family in postmodern societies. The pessimistic view is that the fragile, isolated, nuclear-family system will become even weaker. Those making this prediction suggest alternatives, such as nonmarital cohabitation and temporary marriages, which would provide the flexibility needed in contemporary society. The optimistic, utopian view is that the emerging electronic revolution will serve to reunite work and family life. As parents work at home on computers and teach their children, they will develop closer relationships. Apprentices learning the work will come to live within the home for a while, and nonrelated extended families will emerge. Although some of these developments are occurring today, only a minority of families benefit.

Koinonia in Communities

The New Testament concept of *koinonia* refers to a community in which Christians are united in identity and purpose. In the New Testament prototype, members of the church voluntarily shared all their possessions. They joined in both *politeia* (civic life) and *oikonomia* (family life). *Koinonia* came to represent a new type of community between the all-inclusive, impersonal state and the exclusive, blood-based household.

We believe that families need the support of *koinonia*. Mass societies, characterized by impersonalization, urbanization, industrialization, rationalization, dehumanization, relativism, bureaucratization, and secularization, make *koinonia* difficult. Churches that practice *koinonia* emphasize small groups and the relational themes of covenant, grace, empowerment, and intimacy. The members of these groups take time to know one another and care for one another in a variety of ways. They also reach out to the greater community and general society. A recent study reported that married couples benefit most when there is a *koinonia*-like overlap between the network of friends of the husband and the wife. When one's spouse had more contact with the other's network members, one was more likely to "(a) view the spouse as a reliable source of support, (b) open up to the spouse, and (c) discuss health issues with the spouse" (Cornwell 2012, 229).

The Church

The primary locus of *koinonia* is the church. In form the church should resemble a family; its members, after all, are described as the children of God and brothers and sisters in Christ. Paul writes, "And I will be your father, and you shall be my sons and daughters, says the Lord Almighty" (2 Cor. 6:18); and "So then you are no longer strangers and aliens, but you are citizens with the saints and also members of the household of God" (Eph. 2:19).

The church, then, is to be a family to families and a source of identity and support for isolated nuclear families. In becoming a community of faith, the church must avoid the pitfall of exclusivity and the tendency to accept only certain types of people. It must welcome the widowed, the orphaned, the handicapped, the poor, the single person, and broken people and families. Social-science research is beginning to give clear evidence of the positive effect when this is practiced in the church; as an example, a recent study reported that greater religious participation of single mothers correlated with more positive children's behavior and the less likelihood of problem behaviors (Petts 2012).

The church can become a family to families if it follows several principles: (1) The church must be a place of diversity, including people of various social classes, races, ages, backgrounds, and religious experiences. (2) The church needs to be a place where people can get to know one another intimately. Opportunities need to be provided for people to share their burdens and joys in small groups. (3) The church must create (or re-create) roles for all its members. Working together as multigenerational teams (young and old) to focus on spiritual formation, worship, hospitality, peace, justice, and so on is a good example of using a diversity of gifts (differentiation) to serve the whole body.

What can the church do to ensure that everyone feels at home? Single people need to be integrated into the body as mature equals who give of their talents to serve the church community. Married and adult singles should view one another as rich resources as they form relationships to deepen faith through fellowship and service. Mentoring or spiritual friendships can be established to encourage and empower others in their growing faith. Women must be encouraged to freely exercise their gifts in the church. The gap between clergy and laity must be minimized so that the pastorate is not viewed as a more important career or calling. Thus, clergy need to be willing to share the ministry, and parishioners need to accept responsibility and opportunities for ministry.

In short, the empowerment process must be practiced in the church. Participatory Bible studies and sermons can focus on communal church life and ways in which to love, forgive, serve, and know one another. Further, individuals should have the freedom to express their faith creatively. The decline in traditional symbols and language is an opportunity to explore and experiment with new worship expressions. We must be liberated from our fixation on words or the old ways of doing things, which has impoverished communication, and be more open to diverse ways of expressing God's love. As an inclusive family of families, the church should welcome worship and the arts, including the contributions of artists, poets, dramatists, and dancers.

Shalom in Society

Society is larger than, more abstract than, and more distant from the family than is community. It encompasses political, economic, educational, and religious institutions, each of which entails a complex hierarchy and roles regulated by an integrated set of norms. While it might be easy to picture how communities can be vital sources of support for family life, it is more difficult to imagine ways in which mass society and its institutions can be sources of support.

There is a grave need to build a society in which institutions promote the well-being of the family. Perhaps more than anything else we need a fresh understanding of the role of society in family life as depicted in the Old Testament. In contrast to our modern individualistic emphasis, family members in ancient Israel held a strong sense of corporate solidarity and identity with the wider community. The family household was not separate from but was formed, shaped, and sustained by society.

The Old Testament concept of *shalom* characterized Israelite society. *Shalom* is usually translated "peace." However, this peace is to be understood not merely as absence of conflict but as the promotion of human welfare in both material and spiritual ways. Such a society is poignantly described in Isaiah 11:6–8:

> The wolf shall live with the lamb,
>> the leopard shall lie down with the kid,
> the calf and the lion and the fatling together,
>> and a little child shall lead them.
> The cow and the bear shall graze,
>> their young shall lie down together;
>> and the lion shall eat straw like the ox.
> The nursing child shall play over the hole of the asp,
>> and the weaned child shall put its hand on the adder's den.

Shalom is present in a culture characterized by justice and righteousness as well as peace. For example, chronic unemployment and oppression of the poor needs to be eliminated before *shalom* is present. One way to deal with poverty is to provide the poor with food, shelter, and clothing. Although this is all well and good, if the underlying causes of poverty are not dealt with, *shalom* is still not achieved. *Shalom* entails giving the poor a means of helping themselves. A society characterized by *shalom* does not treat people unjustly, nor does it disempower or patronize them. It takes action in terms of housing and work opportunities.

Shalom is present when social structures empower the family. *Shalom* is not present when economic institutions demand time at the expense of one's family; move employees every two years, making it impossible to establish roots in a community; or provide the unemployed no opportunities to earn a living. *Shalom* is not present where oppression, racism, and discrimination prevent minorities from gaining access to jobs. *Shalom* is not present when the elderly are denied sufficient resources and health benefits or when divorcées and their children live at the poverty level and laws make it difficult to stay connected with their children. We could go on and on about the multitude of other ways societal structures damage family life.

Hope for the Family and Society

Stable and strong family life can be achieved by recapturing and practicing the biblical concept of the family, which entails covenant love and manifestation of that love through grace, empowerment, and intimacy. God intends for covenant love, the basis for intrinsic moral authority, to be supremely experienced and exemplified in the context of the family and society. Our own society has increasingly come to depend on coercive political and economic means of control, demonstrated by the fact that social relationships are characterized more by contract than covenant, more by law than grace, more by compulsion than empowerment, and more by alienation than intimacy.

The cornerstone of the moral order of society is families based on covenant love, which manifests itself in sacrificial acts for others. Self-giving begins with the family, spilling over to enrich and order society. Our Lord Jesus taught and modeled that we must extend covenant love to our neighbors: "When Jesus saw his mother and the disciple whom he loved standing beside her, he said to his mother, 'Woman, here is your son.' Then he said to the disciple, 'Here is your mother.' And from that hour the disciple took her into his own home" (John 19:26–27). Our challenge in relationships is to so forgive, empower, and intimately know one another that Jesus would want to send his mother to be part of our family.

Bibliography

Aarskaug, R., W. Keizer, and T. Lappegard. 2012. Relationship quality in marital and cohabiting unions across Europe. *Journal of Marriage and Family* 74:389–98.

Adams, B. 2004. Families and family study in international perspective. *Journal of Marriage and Family* 66:1076–88.

Adamsons, K., and S. K. Johnson. 2013. An updated and expanded meta-analysis of nonresident fathering and child well-being. *Journal of Family Psychology* 27 (4):589–99. https://doi.org/10.1037/a0033786.

Adele, D. 2009. The interplay of biology and the environment broadly defined. *Developmental Psychology* 45:1–9.

Adler-Baeder, F., and B. Higginbotham. 2004. Implications of remarriage and stepfamily formation for marriage education. *Family Relations: Interdisciplinary Journal of Applied Family Studies* 53:448–58.

Afifi, T., P. Schrodt, and T. McManus. 2009. The divorcee disclosure model (DDM): Why parents disclose negative information about the divorce to their children and its effects. In *Uncertainty, information management, and disclosure decisions: Theories and application*, edited by T. Afifi and W. Afifi, 402–25. New York: Routledge/Taylor and Francis Group.

Ahrons, C. 2004. *We're still family: What grown children have to say about their parents' divorce*. San Francisco: HarperCollins.

Ahrons, C., and R. Rodgers. 1987. *Divorced families: A multidisciplinary developmental view*. New York: Norton.

Akcinar, B., and N. Baydar. 2014. Parental control is not unconditionally detrimental for externalizing behaviors in early childhood. *International Journal of Behavioral Development* 38:118–27. https://doi.org/10.1177/0165025413513701.

Allen, T. D., and A. Martin. 2017. The work-family interface: A retrospective look at 20 years of research in JOHP. *Journal of Occupational and Health Psychology* 22:259–72. https://doi.org/10.1037/ocp0000065.

Amato, P., and T. Afifi. 2006. Feeling caught between parents: Adult children's relations with parents and subjective well-being. *Journal of Marriage and Family* 68:222–35.

Amato, P., and J. Cheadle. 2005. The long reach of divorce: Divorce and child well-being across three generations. *Journal of Marriage and Family* 67:191–206.

Amato, P., J. Kane, and S. James. 2011. Reconsidering the "good divorce." *Family Relations* 60:511–24.

Anderson, E., and S. Greene. 2011. "My child and I are a package deal": Balancing adult and child concerns in repartnering after divorce. *Journal of Family Psychology* 25:741–50.

Anderson, K. 2010. Conflict, power, and violence in families. *Journal of Marriage and Family* 72:726–42.

Anderson, R. 1982. *On being human: Essays in theological anthropology.* Grand Rapids: Eerdmans.

———. 1985. The gospel of the family. Fuller Theological Seminary. Unpublished manuscript.

———. 1990. *Christians who counsel: The vocation of holistic therapy.* Grand Rapids: Zondervan.

———. 1991. *On being human.* Pasadena, CA: Fuller Seminary Press.

Anderson, R., and D. Guernsey. 1985. *On being family: Essays on a social theology of the family.* Grand Rapids: Eerdmans.

Armor, D. 2003. *Maximizing intelligence.* New Brunswick, NJ: Transaction Publishers.

Aronson, S. 2004. The mother-infant relationship in single, cohabiting, and married families: A case for marriage? *Journal of Family Psychology* 18:5–18.

Auersperg, F., T. Vlasak, I. Ponocny, and A. Barth. 2019. Long-term effects of parental divorce on mental health–A meta-analysis. *Journal of Psychiatric Research* 119:107–15. https://doi.org/10.1016/j.jpsychires.2019.09.011.

Aunola, K., and N. Jari-Erik. 2005. The role of parenting styles in children's problem behavior. *Child Development* 76:1144–59.

Bach, G., and P. Wyden. 1968. *The intimate enemy: How to fight fair in love and marriage.* New York: Morrow.

Balswick, J. K., and J. O. Balswick. 1997. *Families in pain: Working through the hurts.* Grand Rapids: Revell.

———. 2019. *Authentic sexuality.* 3rd ed. Downers Grove, IL: InterVarsity.

Balswick, J. K., J. O. Balswick, B. Piper, and D. Piper. 2003. *Relationship-empowerment parenting: Building formative and fulfilling relationships with your children.* Grand Rapids: Baker Books.

Balswick, J. O. 1992. *Men at the crossroads: Beyond traditional roles and modern options.* Downers Grove, IL: InterVarsity.

Balswick, J. O., and J. K. Balswick. 1987. A theological basis for family relationships. *Journal of Psychology and Christianity* 6 (3):37–49.

———. 1995. *The dual-earner marriage: The elaborate balancing act*. Grand Rapids: Revell.

———. 2006. *A model for marriage: Covenant, grace, empowering, and intimacy*. Downers Grove, IL: InterVarsity.

Balswick, J. O., P. King, and K. Reimer. 2016. *The reciprocating self: Human development in theological perspective*. 2nd ed. Downers Grove, IL: InterVarsity.

Bandura, A. 1977. *Social learning theory*. Englewood Cliffs, NJ: Prentice Hall.

Banks, A. 2011. Research disputes "facts" on Christian divorces. *Christian Century* 128:17.

Barber, B., H. Stolz, and J. Olsen. 2005. Parental support, psychological control, and behavioral control: Assessing relevance across time, culture, and method. *Monographs of the Society for Research in Child Development* 70:1–137.

Barnhill, C. 2004. *The myth of the perfect mother: Rethinking the spirituality of women*. Grand Rapids: Baker Books.

Bar-On, R. 2000. Emotional and social intelligence: Insights from the emotional quotient inventory. In *The handbook of emotional intelligence*, edited by R. Bar-On and J. D. A. Parker, 363–88. New York: Wiley.

Bartkowski, J. P. 2000. Breaking walls, raising fences: Masculinity, femininity, and accountability among the Promise Keepers. *Sociology of Religion* 61:33–53.

———. 2001. *Remaking the godly marriage: Gender negotiation in evangelical families*. Piscataway, NJ: Rutgers University Press.

———. 2004. *The Promise Keepers: Servants, soldiers, and godly men*. Piscataway, NJ: Rutgers University Press.

Bartle, S. E. 1993. The degree of similarity of differentiation of self between partners in married and dating couples: Preliminary evidence. *Contemporary Family Therapy* 15 (6):467–84. https://doi.org/10.1007/BF00892293.

Barton, S. 1996. Biblical hermeneutics and the family. In *The family in theological perspective*, edited by S. Barton, 3–23. Edinburgh: T&T Clark.

Baumrind, D. 1996. The discipline controversy revisited. *Family Relations* 45:405–14.

———. 2005. Taking a stand in a morally pluralistic society: Constructive obedience and responsible dissent in moral/character education. In *Conflict, contradiction, and contrarian elements in moral development and education*, edited by L. Nucci, 21–50. Mahwah, NJ: Erlbaum.

Baumrind, D., R. Larzelere, and P. Cowan. 2005. Ordinary physical punishment: Is it harmful? Comment on Gershoff (2002). *Psychological Bulletin* 128:580–89.

Bavinck, H. 2019. *Christian worldview*. Translated by N. G. Sutanto, J. Eglinton, and C. C. Brock. Wheaton: Crossway. Originally published in 1904.

Beck, A. T. 1989. *Love is never enough*. Reprint. New York: Harper Perennial.

Beck-Gersheim, E. 2002. *Reinventing the family: In search of new lifestyles*. Malden, MA: Blackwell.

Bell, R. 1974. Contribution of human infants to caregiving and social interaction. In *The effect of the infant on its caregiver*, edited by M. Lewish and L. Rosenblum, 1–19. New York: Wiley.

Bell, S., and M. Ainsworth. 1972. Infant crying and maternal responsiveness. *Child Development* 43:1171–90.

Bellah, R., R. Madsen, W. Sullivan, A. Swidler, and S. Tipton. 1985. *Habits of the heart: Individualism and commitment in American life*. Berkeley: University of California Press.

Bem, D. 1996. Exotic becomes erotic: A developmental theory of sexual orientation. *Psychological Review* 10:320–35.

Bengtson, V., R. Giarrusso, J. Mabry, and M. Silverstein. 2002. Solidarity, conflict, and ambivalence: Complimentary or competing perspectives on intergenerational relationships? *Journal of Marriage and Family* 64:568–76.

Berger, B., and P. Berger. 1983. *The war over the family*. Garden City, NY: Doubleday.

Berger, P. 1983. From the crisis of religion to the crisis of secularity. In *Religion and America: Spiritual life in a secular age*, edited by M. Douglas and S. Tipton, 14–24. Boston: Beacon.

———. 1990. *The sacred canopy*. Reprint. Norwell, MA: Anchor.

Berger, P., B. Berger, and H. Kellner. 1973. *The homeless mind: Modernization and consciousness*. New York: Random.

Berger, P. L., and T. Luckmann. 1966. *The social construction of reality: A treatise in the sociology of knowledge*. Norwell, MA: Anchor.

Bernhardt, P., J. Dabbs, J. Fielden, and C. Lutter. 1998. Testosterone changes during vicarious experiences of winning and losing among fans at sporting events. *Physiology and Behavior* 65:59–62.

Bi, S., E. Haak, L. Gilbert, M. El-Sheikh, and P. Keller. 2018. Father attachment, father emotion expression, and children's attachment to fathers: The role of marital conflict. *Journal of Family Psychology* 32 (4):456–65. https://doi.org/10.1037/fam0000395.

Bianchi, S., and M. Milkie. 2010. Work and family research in the first decade of the 21st century. *Journal of Marriage and Family* 72:705–25.

Bimbaum, R., L. Lach, D. Saposnek, and R. MacCulloch. 2012. Co-parenting children with neurodevelopmental disorders. In *Parenting plan evaluations: Applied research for the family court*, edited by K. Kuehnie and L. Drozd, 270–329. New York: Oxford University Press.

Binstock, G., and T. Arland. 2003. Separation, reconciliation, and living apart in cohabiting and marital unions. *Journal of Marriage and Family* 65:432–43.

Blalock, L., V. Tiller, and P. Monroe. 2004. "They get you out of courage": Persistent deep poverty among former welfare-reliant women. *Family Relations* 53:127–37.

Blankenhorn, D. 1995. *Fatherless America: Confronting our most urgent social problem*. New York: Basic Books.

Blanton, P. 2001. Marital therapy and marital power: Constructing narratives of sharing relational and positional power. *Contemporary Family Therapy: An International Journal* 23:295–308.

Blissett, J. 2011. Relationships between parenting style, feeding style and feeding practices and fruit and vegetable consumption in early childhood. *Appetite* 57:826–31.

Bonhoeffer, D. 1995. *The cost of discipleship*. Translated by H. Fuller. New York: Simon & Schuster. Originally published in 1937.

———. 1997a. *Creation and fall; Temptation: Two biblical studies*. Translated by J. C. Fletcher. New York: Simon & Schuster. Originally published in 1937.

———. 1997b. *Letters and papers from prison*. Translated by E. Bethge. New York: Touchstone Books. Originally published in 1970.

Booth, A., and D. Johnson. 1988. Premarital cohabitation and marital success. *Journal of Family Issues* 9:255–72.

Borchet, J., A. Lewandowska-Walter, P. Połomski, A. Peplińska, and L. Hooper. 2020. We are in this together: Retrospective parentification, sibling relationships, and self-esteem. *Journal of Child and Family Studies* 29:2982–91. https://doi.org/10.1007/s10826-020-01723-3.

Borrowdale, A. 1996. Right relations: Forgiveness and family life. In *The family in theological perspective*, edited by S. Barton, 203–17. Edinburgh: T&T Clark.

Boss, P. 2000. *Ambiguous loss: Learning to live with unresolved grief*. Cambridge, MA: Harvard University Press.

———. 2010. The trauma and complicated grief of ambiguous loss. *Pastoral Psychology* 59:137–45.

Boss, P., S. Roos, and D. Harns. 2011. Grief in the midst of ambiguity and uncertainty: An exploration of ambiguous loss and chronic sorrow. In *Grief and bereavement in contemporary society: Bridging research and practice*, edited by R. Neimeyer, D. Harris, H. Winokuer, and G. Thornton, 163–75. New York: Routledge.

Boszormenyi-Nagy, I. 1987. *Foundations of contextual therapy*. New York: Brunner/Mazel.

———. 1996. Relational ethics in contextual therapy: Commitment to our common future. In *Martin Buber and the human sciences*, edited by M. Friedman, 371–82. Albany: State University of New York Press.

Boszormenyi-Nagy, I., and B. R. Krasner. 1986. *Between give and take: A clinical guide to contextual therapy*. New York: Brunner/Mazel.

Boszormenyi-Nagy, I., and G. M. Spark. 1984. *Invisible loyalties*. New York: Brunner/Mazel.

Bowen, M. 2004. *Family therapy and clinical practice*. New York: Jason Aronson.

Bramlett, M., and W. D. Mosher. 2001. *First marriage dissolution, divorce, and remarriage. United States: Advanced data from vital and health statistics* (No. 323). Hyattsville, MD: National Center for Health Services.

Bronfenbrenner, U. 1979. *The ecology of human development: Experiments by nature and by design*. Cambridge, MA: Harvard University Press.

Brown, S. 2004. Family structure and child well-being: The significance of parental cohabitation. *Journal of Marriage and Family* 66:351–67.

Brown, S., L. Sanchez, S. Nock, and J. Wright. 2006. Links between premarital cohabitation and subsequent marital quality, stability, and divorce: A comparison of covenant versus standard marriages. *Social Science Research* 35:454–70.

Browning, D., M. Green, and J. Witte Jr. 2006. *Sex, marriage, and family in world religions*. New York: Columbia University Press.

Browning, D., B. Miller-McLemore, P. Couture, B. Lyon, and R. Franklin. 1997. *From culture wars to common ground: Religion and the American family debate*. Louisville: Westminster John Knox.

Browning, S. 1994. Treating stepfamilies: Alternatives to traditional family therapy. In *Stepparenting: Issues in theory, research, and practice*, edited by K. Pasley and M. Ihinger-Tallman, 175–98. Westport, CT: Praeger.

Buck, A., and L. Neff. 2012. Stress spillover in early marriage: The role of self-regulatory depletion. *Journal of Family Psychology* 26:698–708.

Buechner, F. 1992. *Listening to your life: Daily meditation with Frederick Buechner*. San Francisco: Harper.

Buehler, C. 2006. Parents and peers in relation to early adolescent problem behavior. *Journal of Marriage and Family* 68:109–24.

Bumpass, L., R. Raley, and J. Sweet. 1995. The changing character of stepfamilies: Implications of cohabitation and nonmarital childbearing. *Demography* 32:425–36.

Burr, W., L. Marks, and R. Day. 2012. *Sacred matters: Religion and spirituality in families*. New York: Routledge/Taylor and Francis Group.

Buss, D., ed. 2005. *The handbook of evolutionary psychology*. New York: Wiley.

Cade, R. 2010. Covenant marriage. *Family Journal* 18:230–33.

A Call to a New Conversation on Marriage. 2013. www.americanvalues.org/marriage-a-new-conversation/a-call-to-a-new-conversation-on-marriage.php.

Canfield, K. 2006. *The heart of a father: How dads can shape the destiny of America*. Chicago: Northfield.

Capps, D. 1993. *The depleted self: Sin in a narcissistic age*. Minneapolis: Fortress.

———. 2000. *Deadly sins and saving virtues*. Eugene, OR: Wipf & Stock.

———. 2008. *The decades of life: A guide to human development*. Louisville: Westminster John Knox.

Carlo, G., R. M. B. White, C. Streit, G. P. Knight, and K. H. Zeiders. 2018. Longitudinal relations among parenting styles, prosocial behaviors, and academic outcomes in U.S. Mexican adolescents. *Child Development* 89 (2):577–92. https://doi.org/10.1111/cdev.12761.

Carlson, M. 2006. Family structure, father involvement, and adolescent behavioral outcome. *Journal of Marriage and Family* 68:137–54.

Carr, D. 2004. Gender, preloss marital dependence, and older adults' adjustment to widowhood. *Journal of Marriage and Family* 66:220–35.

———. 2005. The psychological consequences of midlife men's social comparisons with their young adult sons. *Journal of Marriage and Family* 67:240–50.

Carr, D., and K. Springer. 2010. Advances in families and health research in the 21st century. *Journal of Marriage and Family* 72:743–61.

Casey, B., N. Tottenham, C. Liston, and S. Durston. 2005. Imaging the developing brain: What have we learned about cognitive development? *Trends in Cognitive Science* 9:104–10.

Catherall, D. 2004. *Handbook of stress, trauma and the family*. Hove, East Sussex, UK: Brunner-Routledge.

———. 2005. *Family stress: Interventions for stress and trauma*. Hove, East Sussex, UK: Brunner-Routledge.

Centers for Disease Control and Prevention. 2020. *Marriage and divorce*. https://www.cdc.gov/nchs/fastats/marriage-divorce.htm. Accessed August 19, 2020.

———. n.d. Provisional number of marriages and marriage rate: United States, 2000–2019. National Center for Health Statistics (website). Accessed March 5, 2021. https://www.cdc.gov/nchs/data/dvs/national-marriage-divorce-rates-00-19.pdf.

Chao, R. 1994. Beyond parental control and authoritarian parenting style: Understanding Chinese parenting through the cultural notion of training. *Child Development* 65:1111–19.

Chapman, G. 2009. *The five love languages: The secret to love that lasts*. Chicago: Northfield.

Cherlin, A. 2004. The deinstitutionalization of American marriage. *Journal of Marriage and the Family* 66:848–61.

———. 2010. Demographic trends in the United States: A review of research in the 2000s. *Journal of Marriage and Family* 72:403–19.

Clapp, R. 1993. *Families at the crossroads: Beyond traditional and modern options*. Downers Grove, IL: InterVarsity.

Clingempeel, W., and E. Brand-Clingempeel. 2004. Pathogenic-conflict families and children: What we know, what we need to know. In *Handbook of contemporary families: Considering the past, contemplating the future*, edited by M. Coleman and L. Ganong, 244–61. Thousand Oaks, CA: Sage.

Cobb, N., J. Larson, and W. Watson. 2003. Development of the attitudes about romance and mate selection scale. *Family Relations* 52:222–31.

Cohen, A. O., K. Breiner, L. Steinberg, R. J. Bonnie, E. S. Scott, K. Taylor-Thompson, M. Rudolph, et al. 2016. When is an adolescent an adult? Assessing cognitive control in emotional and nonemotional contexts. *Psychological Science* 27 (4):549–62. https://doi.org/10.1177/0956797615627625.

Colby, A., and W. Damon. 1995. The development of extraordinary moral commitment. In *Morality in everyday life: Developmental perspectives*, edited by M. Killen and D. Hart, 342–70. New York: Cambridge University Press.

Coltrane, S. 2004. Fathering: Paradoxes, contradictions, and dilemmas. In *Handbook of contemporary families: Considering the past, contemplating the future*, edited by M. Coleman and L. Ganong, 224–43. Thousand Oaks, CA: Sage.

Comiskey, A. 2003. *Strength in weakness: Overcoming sexual and relational brokenness*. Downers Grove, IL: InterVarsity.

Conger, R., K. Conger, and M. Martin. 2010. Socioeconomic status, family processes, and individual development. *Journal of Marriage and Family* 72:685–704.

Connell, R. W. 2000. *The men and the boys*. Berkeley: University of California Press.

Connidis, I. 2001. *Family ties and aging*. Thousand Oaks, CA: Sage.

Connidis, I., and J. McMullin. 2002. Sociological ambivalence and family ties: A critical perspective. *Journal of Marriage and Family* 64:558–67.

Cooney, T., and K. Dunne. 2004. Intimate relationships in later life: Current realities, future prospects. In *Handbook of contemporary families: Considering the past, contemplating the future*, edited by M. Coleman and L. Ganong, 136–52. Thousand Oaks, CA: Sage.

Coontz, S. 2004. The world historical formation of marriage. *Journal of Marriage and Family* 66:974–79.

Cooper, S. 1999. Historical analysis of the family. In *Handbook of marriage and family*, edited by M. Sussman, S. Steinmetz, and G. Peterson, 13–38. New York: Plenum.

Copen, C., K. Daniels, J. Vespa, and W. Mosher. 2012. First marriages in the United States: Data from the 2006–2010 national survey of family growth. *National Health Statistics Reports* 49 (March 22). United States Department of Health and Human Services.

Cordova, J., C. Gee, and L. Warren. 2005. Emotional skillfulness in marriage: Intimacy as a mediator of the relationship between emotional skillfulness and marital satisfaction. *Journal of Social and Clinical Psychology* 24:218–35.

Cornwell, B. 2011. Independence through social networks: Bridging potential among older women and men. *Journals of Gerontology Series B: Psychological Sciences and Social Sciences* 66B:782–94.

———. 2012. Spousal network overlap as a basis for spousal support. *Journal of Marriage and Family* 74:229–38.

Cowdery, R., and C. Knudson-Martin. 2005. The construction of motherhood: Tasks, relational connection, and gender equality. *Family Relations* 54:335–45.

Cox, H. 1984. *Religion in the secular city: Toward a postmodern theology*. New York: Simon & Schuster.

Cozolino, L. 2014. *The neuroscience of human relationships: Attachment and the developing social brain*. 2nd ed. New York: Guilford.

Crano, W., and J. Aronoff. 1978. A cross-cultural study of expressive and instrumental role complementarity in the family. *American Sociological Review* 43:463–71.

Crosnoe, R., and S. Cavanagh. 2010. Families with children and adolescents: A review, critique, and future agenda. *Journal of Marriage and Family* 72:594–611.

Crowder, C. 1996. The family reunion: Reflections on the eschatological imagination. In *The family in theological perspective*, edited by S. Barton, 329–44. Edinburgh: T&T Clark.

Cushman, P. 1996. *Constructing the self, constructing America: A cultural history of psychotherapy*. Boston: Addison Wesley.

Damon, W. 2004. What is positive youth development? *The Annals of the American Academy of Political and Social Science* 59:13–24.

Danzinger, C. 1976. *Unmarried heterosexual cohabitation*. New Brunswick, NJ: Rutgers University.

Davies, J. 1996. A preferential option for the family. In *The family in theological perspective*, edited by S. Barton, 219–36. Edinburgh: T&T Clark.

Day, H. D., S. A. St. Clair, and D. D. Marshall. 1997. Do people who marry really have the same level of differentiation of self? *Journal of Family Psychology* 11 (1):131–35. https://doi.org/10.1037/0893-3200.11.1.131.

Day, R., and A. Acock. 2013. Marital well-being and religiousness as mediated by relational virtue and equality. *Journal of Marriage and Family* 75:164–77.

Deal, R. 2002. *The smart step-family: Seven steps to a healthy family*. Bloomington, MN: Bethany House.

Deater-Deckard, K. 2011. Families and genomes: The next generation. *Journal of Marriage and Family* 73:822–26.

Debrot, A., W. Cook, M. Perre, and A. Horn. 2012. Deeds matter: Daily enacted responsiveness and intimacy in couples' daily lives. *Journal of Family Psychology* 26:617–27.

Deddo, G. 1999. *Karl Barth's theology of relationships: Trinitarian, christological, and human; Towards an ethic of the family*. New York: P. Lang.

DeGraff, P., and M. Kalmijn. 2006. Divorce motives in a period of rising divorce: Evidence from a Dutch life-history survey. *Journal of Family Issues* 27:483–505.

DeLeire, T., and K. Kalil. 2005. How do cohabiting couples with children spend their money? *Journal of Marriage and Family* 67:286–95.

DeMaris, A., and W. MacDonald. 1993. Premarital cohabitation and marital instability: A test of the unconventionality hypothesis. *Journal of Marriage and Family* 55:399–407.

DeMaris, A., L. Sanchez, and K. Krivickas. 2012. Developmental patterns in marital satisfaction: Another look at covenant marriage. *Journal of Marriage and Family* 74:989–1004.

Dennison, R., S. Koerner, and C. Segrin. 2014. A dyadic examination of family-of-origin influence on newlyweds' marital satisfaction. *Journal of Family Psychology* 28 (3):429–35. https://doi.org/10.1037/a0036807.

Denton, M. 2004. Gender and marital decision making: Negotiating religious ideology and practice. *Social Forces* 82:1151–80.

DeYoung, K. 2018. *The Ten Commandments: What they mean, why they matter, and why we should obey them*. Wheaton: Crossway.

Dick, D., A. Agrawal, M. Schuckit, L. Eierut, A. Hinrichs, L. Fox, J. Mullaney, et al. 2006. Marital status, alcohol dependence, and GABRA2: Evidence for gene-environment correlation and interaction. *Journal of Studies on Alcohol* 67:185–94.

Dodson, L., and J. Dickert. 2004. Girls' family labor in low-income households: A decade of qualitative research. *Journal of Marriage and Family* 66:318–32.

Doherty, W. J. 1996. *Soul searching: Why psychotherapy must promote moral responsibility*. New York: Basic Books.

Dollahite, D., L. Marks, and M. Goodman. 2004. Families and religious beliefs, practices, and communities: Linkages in a diverse and dynamic cultural context. In *Handbook of contemporary families: Considering the past, contemplating the future*, edited by M. Coleman and L. Ganong, 411–31. Thousand Oaks, CA: Sage.

D'Onofrio, B., and B. Lahey. 2010. Biosocial influences on the family: A decade in review. *Journal of Marriage and Family* 72:762–82.

Doriani, D. 1996. The Puritans, sex, and pleasure. In *Christian perspectives on sexuality and gender*, edited by A. Thatcher and E. Stuart, 33–51. Grand Rapids: Eerdmans.

Douglas, S., and M. Michaels. 2004. *The mommy myth: The idealization of motherhood and how it has undermined all women*. New York: Free Press.

Dunn, J. 1996. The household rules in the New Testament. In *The family in theological perspective*, edited by S. Barton, 43–63. Edinburgh: T&T Clark.

Eccles, J., and J. Gootman. 2002. *Community programs to promote youth development*. Washington, DC: National Academy Press.

Echlin, E. 1996. Ecology and the family. In *The family in theological perspective*, edited by S. Barton, 291–305. Edinburgh: T&T Clark.

Ehrich, K., M. Dykas, and J. Cassidy. 2012. Tipping points in adolescent adjustment: Predicting social functioning from adolescents' conflict with parents and friends. *Journal of Family Psychology* 26:776–83.

Ellis, R. R., and T. Simmons. 2014. Coresident grandparents and their grandchildren: 2012. Population Characteristics. October 2014. https://www.census.gov/content/dam/Census/library/publications/2014/demo/p20-576.pdf.

Ellison, C., A. Henderson, N. Glenn, and K. Harkrider. 2011. Sanctification, stress, and marital quality. *Family Relations* 60:404–20.

Ennis, J., and U. Majid. 2020. The widowhood effect: Explaining the adverse outcomes after spousal loss using physiological stress theories, marital quality, and attachment. *The Family Journal* 28 (3): 241–46. https://doi.org/10.1177/1066480720929360.

Erikson, E. 1963. *Childhood and society*. New York: Norton.

———. 1968. *Identity: Youth and crisis*. New York: Norton.

——— . 1980. *Identity and the life cycle*. New York: Norton.

———. 1985. *The life cycle completed*. New York: Norton.

Erikson, J. M. 1997. *The life cycle completed*. Extended version. New York: Norton.

Fee, G. 2005. Male and female in the new creation: Galatians 3:26–29. In *Discovering biblical equality: Complementarity without hierarchy*, edited by R. Pierce, R. Groothus, and G. Fee, 172–85. Downers Grove, IL: InterVarsity.

Felitti, V. J., R. F. Anda, D. Nordenberg, D. F. Williamson, A. M. Spitz, V. Edwards, M. P. Koss, and J. S. Marks. 2019. Relationship of childhood abuse and household dysfunction to many of the leading causes of death in adults: The adverse childhood experiences (ACE) study. *American Journal of Preventive Medicine* 56 (6):774–86.

Fellows, K. J., H. Chiu, E. J. Hill, and A. J. Hawkins. 2016. Work-family conflict and couple relationship quality: A meta-analytic study. *Journal of Family and Economic Issues* 37 (4):509–18. https://doi.org/10.1007/s10834-015-9450-7.

Ferree, M. 2010. Filling the glass: Gender perspectives on families. *Journal of Marriage and Family* 72:420–40.

Figley, C., and H. McCubbin. 1983. *Coping with catastrophe*. Vol. 2 of *Stress and the family*. New York: Brunner/Mazel.

Fincham, F., and S. Beach. 2010. Marriage in the new millennium: A decade in review. *Journal of Marriage and Family* 72:630–50.

Fisher, H. 1996. The origin of romantic love and human family life. *National Forum* 76:31–34.

———. 2002. Lust, attraction, and attachment in mammalian reproduction. *Human Nature* 9:23–52.

Fisher, H., A. Aron, D. Mashek, H. Li, and L. Brown. 2002. Defining the brain systems of lust, romantic attraction, and attachment. *Archives of Sexual Behavior* 31:413–19.

Flavell, J. 1963. *The developmental psychology of Jean Piaget*. Princeton: Van Nostrand.

———. 1985. *Cognitive development*. 2nd ed. Englewood Cliffs, NJ: Prentice Hall.

Fletcher, A. 1996. The family, marriage and the upbringing of children in Protestant England. In *The family in theological perspective*, edited by S. Barton, 107–28. Edinburgh: T&T Clark.

Fletcher, G. J. O., J. M. Tither, C. O'Loughlin, M. Friesen, and N. Overall. 2004. Warm and homely or cold and beautiful? Sex differences in trading off traits in mate selection. *Personality and Social Psychology Bulletin* 30:659–72. https://doi.org/10.1177/0146167203262847.

Flora, J., and C. Segrin. 2003. Relational well-being and perceptions of relational history in married and dating couples. *Journal of Social and Personal Relationships* 20:515–36.

Flurry, L., and A. Burns. 2005. Children's influence in purchase decisions: A social power theory approach. *Journal of Business Research* 58:593–601.

Ford, D., and R. Lerner. 1992. *Developmental systems theory: An integrative approach*. Newbury Park, CA: Sage.

Forward, S., and J. Torres. 1986. *Men who hate women and the women who love them*. New York: Bantam.

Fowers, B. J., K. H. Montel, and D. H. Olson. 1996. Predicting marital success for premarital couple types based on Prepare. *Journal of Marital and Family Therapy* 22:103–19.

Fowers, B. J., and D. Olson. 1992. Four types of premarital couples based on Prepare. *Journal of Family Psychology* 6:10–21.

Fowler, J. 1981. *Stages of faith*. New York: Harper & Row.

———. 1987. *Faith development and pastoral care*. Minneapolis: Fortress.

———. 1992. Perspectives on the family from the standpoint of faith development theory. In *Christian perspectives on faith development*, edited by J. Astley and L. Francis, 320–26. Grand Rapids: Eerdmans.

———. 1996. *Faithful change: The personal and public challenges of postmodern life*. Nashville: Abingdon.

Franchini, B., R. Poinhos, K. Klepp, and M. de Almeida. 2011. Association between parenting styles and own fruit and vegetable consumption among Portuguese mothers of school children. *The British Journal of Nutrition* 106 (6):931–35.

Francis, J. 1996. Children and childhood in the New Testament. In *The family in theological perspective*, edited by S. Barton, 65–85. Edinburgh: T&T Clark.

Frederick, T. V. 2015. Forgiveness and mental health practice. *Mental Health, Religion & Culture* 18 (5):418–24. https://doi.org/10.1080/13674676.2015.1077210.

Frederick, T. V., and J. O. Balswick. 2011. The sexual division of household labor. *Psychology* 2 (5):509–16. https://doi.org/10.4236/psych.2011.25079.

Frederick, T. V., and S. Dunbar. 2019. *A Christian approach to burnout caused by work and family conflict: Calling, caring, and connecting*. Lexington: Lexington Books.

Frederick, T. V., S. Dunbar, and Y. Thai. 2018. Burnout in Christian perspective. *Pastoral Psychology* 67:267–76. https://doi.org/10.1007/s11089-017-0799-4.

Frederick, T. V., S. Purrington, and S. Dunbar. 2016. Differentiation of self, religious coping, and subjective well-being. *Mental Health, Religion & Culture* 19 (6):553–64. https://doi.org/10.1080/13674676.2016.1216530.

Freud, S. 1949. *An outline of psychoanalysis*. New York: Norton.

———. 1954. *The origins of psychoanalysis: Sigmund Freud's letters*. New York: Basic Books.

Friedman, R., and J. Downey, eds. 2002. *Sexual orientation and psychoanalysis: Sexual science and clinical practice*. New York: Columbia University Press.

Furnham, A. 2009. Sex differences in mate selection preferences. *Personality and Individual Differences* 47:262–67.

Furstenberg, F., and A. Cherlin. 1991. *Divided families: What happens to children when parents part.* Cambridge, MA: Harvard University Press.

Gallagher, S. 2003. *Evangelical identity and gendered family life.* New Brunswick, NJ: Rutgers University Press.

Galvin, K., C. Bylund, and B. Brommel. 2018. *Family communication: Cohesion and change.* 10th ed. New York: Routledge.

Gangel, K. 1977. Toward a biblical theology of marriage and family. *Journal of Psychology and Theology* 5:55–69, 150–62, 247–59, 318–31.

Ganong, L., and M. Coleman. 2004. *Stepfamily relationships.* New York: Kluwer Academic/Plenum.

Ganong, L., M. Coleman, and T. Jamison. 2011. Patterns of stepchild-stepparent relationship development. *Journal of Marriage and Family* 73:396–413.

Ganong, L., T. Jensen, C. Sanner, L. Russell, and M. Coleman. 2019. Stepfathers' affinity seeking with stepchildren, stepfather-stepchild relationship quality, marital quality, and stepfamily cohesion among stepfathers and mothers. *Journal of Family Psychology* 33 (5):521–31. https://doi.org/10.1037/fam0000518.

Ganong, L., T. Jensen, C. Sanner, L. Russell, M. Coleman, and A. Chapman. 2019. Linking stepfamily functioning, marital quality, and steprelationship quality. *Family Relations* 68 (4):469–83. https://doi.org/10.1111/fare.12380.

Gershoff, E. 2002. Corporal punishment by parents and associated child behaviors and experiences: A meta-analytic and theoretical review. *Psychological Bulletin* 128:539–79.

Gershoff, E., and A. Grogan-Kaylor. 2016. Spanking and child outcomes: Old controversies and new meta-analyses. *Journal of Family Psychology* 30 (4):453–69. https://doi.org/10.1037/fam0000191.

Geurts, T., T. Van Tilberg, and A. Poortman. 2012a. The grandparent-grandchild relationship in childhood and adulthood. A matter of continuation? *Personal Relationships* 19:267–78.

———. 2012b. Older parents providing child care for adult children: Does it pay off? *Journal of Marriage and Family* 74:239–50.

Ghate, D., and N. Hazel. 2002. *Parenting in poor environments: Stress, support and coping.* London: Jessica Kingsley Publishers.

Gillespie, B. J., and J. Treas. 2017. Adolescent intergenerational cohesiveness and young adult proximity to mothers. *Journal of Family Issues* 38 (6):798–819. https://doi.org/10.1177/0192513X15598548.

Gilley, S. 1996. Chesterton, Catholicism and the family. In *The family in theological perspective*, edited by S. Barton, 129–47. Edinburgh: T&T Clark.

Gilligan, C. 1982. *In a different voice: Psychological theory and women's development.* Cambridge, MA: Harvard University Press.

Gillis, J. 2004. Marriages of the mind. *Journal of Marriage and Family* 66:988–91.

Gordon, R. 2005. The doom and gloom of divorce research: Comment on Wallerstein and Lewis (2004). *Psychoanalytic Psychology* 22:450–51.

Gottman, J. 1994. *What predicts divorce? The relationship between marital processes and marital outcomes.* Hillsdale, NJ: Erlbaum.

———. 1995. *Why marriages succeed or fail.* New York: Simon & Schuster.

———. 1999. *The marriages clinic: A scientifically based marital therapy.* New York: Norton.

———. 2011. *The science of trust: Emotional attunement for couples.* New York: Norton.

Gottman, J., and J. DeClaire. 2001. *The relationship cure.* New York: Crown.

Gottman, J., and R. W. Levenson. 2000. The timing of divorce: Predicting when a couple will divorce over a 14-year period. *Journal of Marriage and Family* 62 (3):737–45. https://doi.org/10.1111/j.1741-3737.2000.00737.x.

Grabovac, A. D., M. A. Lau, and B. R. Willett. 2011. Mechanisms of mindfulness: A Buddhist psychological model. *Mindfulness* 2:154–66. https://doi.org/10.1007/s12671-011-0054-5.

Greeff, A., and C. Du Toit. 2009. Resilience in remarried families. *American Journal of Family Therapy* 37:114–26.

Greeff, A., and H. Malherbe. 2001. Intimacy and marital satisfaction in spouses. *Journal of Sex and Marital Therapy* 27:247–57.

Greenberg, J. R., and S. A. Mitchell. 1983. *Object relations in psychoanalytic theory.* Cambridge, MA: Harvard University Press.

Greenhaus, J. H., and N. J. Beutell. 1985. Sources of conflict between work and family roles. *Academy of Management Review* 10:76–88.

Greenhaus, J. H., and G. H. Powell. 2006. When work and family are allies: A theory of work family enrichment. *Academy of Management Review* 31:72–92.

Grenz, S. 2001. *The social God and the relational self: A trinitarian theology of the imago Dei.* Louisville: Westminster John Knox.

Grolnick, S. 1990. *Work and play of Winnicott.* San Francisco: Jossey-Bass.

Gromoske, A., and K. Maguire-Jack. 2012. Transactional and cascading relations between early spanking and children's social-emotional development. *Journal of Marriage and Family* 74:1054–68.

Group for the Advancement of Psychiatry, Committee on Preventive Psychiatry. 1989. *Psychiatric prevention and the family life cycle.* New York: Brunner/Mazel.

Grundy, E., and J. Henretta. 2006. Between elderly parents and adult children: A new look at the intergenerational care provided by the "sandwich generation." *Ageing and Society* 26:707–22.

Guinness, O. 2003. *The call: Finding and fulfilling the central purpose of your life.* Nashville: Thomas Nelson.

Gunnar, M., and K. Quevedo. 2007. The neurobiology of stress and development. *Annual Review of Psychology* 58:145–73.

Hadden, B. W., C. R. Agnew, and K. Tan. 2018. Commitment readiness and relationship formation. *Personality & Social Psychology Bulletin* 44 (8): 1242–57. https://doi.org/10.1177/0146167218764668.

Hamner, T., and P. Turner. 1990. *Parenting in contemporary society.* Needham Heights, MA: Allyn and Bacon.

Hardy, N. R., K. L. Soloski, G. C. Ratcliffe, J. R. Anderson, and B. J. Willoughby. 2015. Associations between family of origin climate, relationship self-regulation, and marital outcomes. *Journal of Marital and Family Therapy* 41 (4):508–21. https://doi.org/10.1111/jmft.12090.

Hargrave, T. 2005. *Loving your parents when they can no longer love you.* Grand Rapids: Zondervan.

Hargrave, T., and S. Hanna. 1997. *The aging family: New visions in theory, practice and reality.* New York: Brunner/Mazel.

Harknett, K. 2006. The relationship between private safety nets and economic outcomes among single mothers. *Journal of Marriage and Family* 68:172–91.

Harper, S., and I. Ruicheva. 2010. Grandmothers as replacement parents and partners: The role of grandmotherhood in single parent families. *Journal of Intergenerational Relationships* 8:219–33.

Harrison, C. 1996. The silent majority: The family in patristic thought. In *The family in theological perspective*, edited by S. Barton, 87–105. Edinburgh: T&T Clark.

Hart, C., L. Newell, and S. Olsen. 2003. Parenting skills and social-communicative competence in childhood. In *Handbook of communication and social interaction skills*, edited by J. Greene and B. Burleson, 753–800. Mahwah, NJ: Erlbaum.

Haskins, R. 2013. Three simple rules poor teens should follow to join the middle class. Brookings Institution. March 13, 2013. https://www.brookings.edu/opinions/three-simple-rules-poor-teens-should-follow-to-join-the-middle-class/.

Hatchel, T., K. M. Ingram, S. Mintz, C. Hartley, A. Valido, D. L. Espelage, and P. Wyman. 2019. Predictors of suicidal ideation and attempts among LGBTQ adolescents: The roles of help-seeking beliefs, peer victimization, depressive symptoms, and drug use. *Journal of Child and Family Studies* 28 (9):2443–55. https://doi.org/10.1007/s10826-019-01339-2.

Hauerwas, S. 1981. *A community of character: Toward a constructive Christian social ethic.* Notre Dame, IN: University of Notre Dame Press.

Hawkins, A. J., V. L. Blanchard, S. A. Baldwin, and E. B. Fawcett. 2008. Does marriage and relationship education work? A meta-analytic study. *Journal of Consulting and Clinical Psychology* 76 (5):723–34. https://doi.org/10.1037/a0012584.

Hersey, P., and K. Blanchard. 1988. *Management of organizational behavior*. 4th ed. Englewood Cliffs, NJ: Prentice Hall.

Hetherington, E., M. Cox, and R. Cox. 1982. Effects of divorce on parents and children. In *Nontraditional families: Parenting and child development*, edited by M. Lamb, 233–88. Hillsdale, NJ: Erlbaum.

Hetherington, E., and J. Kelly. 2002. *For better or for worse: Divorce reconsidered*. New York: Norton.

Heuveline, P., and J. Timberlake. 2004. The role of cohabitation in family formation: The United States in comparative perspective. *Journal of Marriage and Family* 66:1214–30.

Hiebert, P. 1978. Conversion, culture and cognitive categories. *Gospel in Context* 1:4.

Hill, R. 1949. *Families under stress*. New York: Harper & Row.

Ho, M., J. Rasheed, and M. Rasheed. 2004. *Family therapy with ethnic minorities*. 2nd ed. Thousand Oaks, CA: Sage.

Hochschild, A. 1989. *The second shift*. New York: Viking.

Hocker, J., and W. Wilmot. 1985. *Interpersonal conflict*. Dubuque, IA: William C. Brown.

Hodgson, L. 1995. Adult grandchildren and their grandparents: The enduring bond. In *The ties of later life*, edited by J. Hendricks, 155–70. Amityville, NY: Baywood.

Holman, T., J. Larson, and S. Harmer. 1994. The development and predictive validity of a new premarital assessment instrument: The preparation for marriage questionnaire. *Family Relations* 43:46–52.

Holmes, T., and R. Rahe. 1967. The social readjustment rating scale. *Journal of Psychosomatic Research* 2:213–18.

Hope, D. A., ed. 2009. *Contemporary perspectives on lesbian, gay, and bisexual identities*. Nebraska symposium on motivation 54. New York: Springer.

Horton, M. 2006. *Introducing covenant theology*. Grand Rapids: Baker Books.

———. 2012. *Pilgrim theology: Core doctrines for Christian disciples*. Grand Rapids: Zondervan.

Hosley, R., K. Canfield, S. O'Donnell, and G. Roid. 2008. Father closeness: Its effect on married men's sexual behavior, marital, and family satisfaction. *Sexual Addiction and Compulsivity* 15:59–76.

House, H. W., ed. 1990. *Divorce and remarriage: Four Christian views*. Downers Grove, IL: IVP Academic.

Hsu, A. 1997. *Singles at the crossroads*. Downers Grove, IL: InterVarsity.

Huang, P., P. Smock, W. Manning, and C. Bergstrom-Lynch. 2011. He says, she says: Gender and cohabitation. *Journal of Family Issues* 32:876–905.

Hunter, J. 1982. Subjectivization and the new evangelical theodicy. *Journal for the Scientific Study of Religion* 21:39–47.

———. 1983. *American evangelicalism: Conservative religion and the quandary of modernity*. New Brunswick, NJ: Rutgers University Press.

Hyde, B., K. Yust, and C. Ota. 2010. Defining childhood at the beginning of the twenty-first century: Children as agents. *International Journal of Children's Spirituality* 15 (1):1–3. https://doi.org/10.1080/13644360903565342.

Institute for American Values. 2013. A call for a new conversation on marriage: An appeal from seventy-five American leaders. http://www.americanvalues.org/marriage-a-new-conversation/index.php. Accessed May 5, 2013.

Irons, L. B., H. Flatin, M. T. Harrington, T. Vazifedan, and J. W. Harrington. 2018. Parental self-assessment of behavioral effectiveness in young children and views on corporal punishment in an academic pediatric practice. *Clinical Pediatrics* 57 (10):1183–90. https://doi.org/10.1177/0009922818764926.

Jahanshad, N., and P. M. Thompson. 2017. Multimodal neuroimaging of male and female brain structure in health and disease across the life span. *Journal of Neuroscience Research* 95 (1–2):371–79. https://doi.org/10.1002/jnr.23919.

Jankowski, P. J., and S. J. Sandage. 2012. Spiritual dwelling and well-being: The mediating role of differentiation of self in a sample of distressed adults. *Mental Health, Religion, and Culture* 15:417–34.

Jarrett, R., and S. Jefferson. 2004. Women's danger management strategies in an inner-city housing project. *Family Relations* 53:138–47.

Jayson, S. 2010. Report: Cohabiting has little effect on marriage success. *USA Today*, March 2, updated October 14, https://usatoday30.usatoday.com/news/health/2010-03-02-cohabiting02_N.htm.

Johnson, M. D., J. R. Anderson, and C. J. Aducci. 2011. Understanding the decision to marry versus cohabit: The role of interpersonal dedication and constraints and the impact on life satisfaction. *Marriage and Family Review* 47:73–89. https://doi.org/10.1080/01494929.2011.564525.

Johnson, S. 2008. *Hold me tight: Seven conversations for a lifetime of love*. New York: Little, Brown.

Jones, S., and M. Yarhouse. 2007. *Ex-gays? A longitudinal study of religiously mediated change in sexual orientation*. Downers Grove, IL: IVP Academic.

Kail, R. V., and J. C. Cavanaugh. 2017. *Essentials of human development: A life-span view*. 2nd ed. Boston: Cengage Learning.

Kakinami, L., T. A. Barnett, L. Séguin, and G. Paradis. 2015. Parenting style and obesity risk in children. *Preventive Medicine* 75:18–22. https://doi.org/10.1016/j.ypmed.

Kalliath, T., and P. Brough. 2008. Work-life balance: A review of the meaning of the balance construct. *Journal of Management and Organization* 14:323–27.

Kalmijn, M. 2015. Relationships between fathers and adult children: The cumulative effects of divorce and repartnering. *Journal of Family Issues*, 36(6), 737–59. https://doi.org/10.1177/0192513X13495398.

Kaplan, L., C. Hennon, and L. Ade-Ridder. 1993. Splitting custody of children between parents: Impact on the sibling system. *Families in Society* 74:131–43.

Kawabata, Y., L. Alink, W. Tseng, M. Van IJzendoom, and N. Crick. 2011. Maternal and paternal parenting styles associated with aggression in children and adolescents: A conceptual analysis and meta-analytic review. *Developmental Review* 31:240–78.

Kear, J. S. 1978. Marital attraction and satisfaction as a function of differentiation of self. Doctoral dissertation, California School of Professional Psychology, Fresno.

Keller, T. 2014. *Every good endeavor: Connecting your work to God's work.* New York: Penguin.

Keller, T., and K. Keller. 2013. *The meaning of marriage: Facing the complexities of commitment with the wisdom of God.* New York: Penguin.

Kerckhoff, A., and K. Davis. 1962. Value consensus and need complementarity in mate selection. *American Sociological Review* 27:295–303.

Kerr, J. 2005. Poverty rate continues to rise. *Pasadena Star-News*, August 31, sec. B.

Kerr, M. E., and M. Bowen. 1988. *Family evaluation.* New York: Norton.

Kettler, C., and T. Speidell, eds. 1990. *Incarnational ministry: The presence of Christ in church, society, and family.* Colorado Springs: Helmers and Howard.

Killen, M., and D. Hart, eds. 1999. *Morality in everyday life: Developmental perspectives.* New York: Cambridge University Press.

Kim, H. 2011. Consequences of parental divorce for child development. *American Sociological Review* 76:487–511.

Kimball, G. 1997. Empowering parents: How to create family-friendly workplaces, schools, and governments. Unpublished manuscript.

Kimiecik, J., and T. Horn. 2012. Examining the relationship between family context and children's physical activity beliefs: The role of parenting style. *Psychology of Sport and Exercise* 13:10–18.

King, P., and J. Furrow. 2004. Religion as a resource for positive youth development: Religion, social capital, and moral outcomes. *Developmental Psychology* 40:703–13.

King, P. E., and R. A. Mueller. 2004. Parents' influence on adolescent religiousness: Spiritual modeling and spiritual capital. *Marriage and Family: A Christian Journal* 6:413–25.

King, V. 2003. The legacy of a grandparent's divorce: Consequences for ties between grandparents and grandchildren. *Journal of Marriage and Family* 65:170–83.

King, V., L. M. Boyd, and B. Pragg. 2018. Parent-adolescent closeness, family belonging, and adolescent well-being across family structures. *Journal of Family Issues* 39 (7):2007–36. https://doi.org/10.1177/0192513X17739048.

King, V., and M. Scott. 2005. A comparison of cohabiting relationships among younger and older adults. *Journal of Marriage and Family* 67:271–85.

Kinsey, A. 1948. *Sexual behavior in the human male.* Philadelphia: Saunders.

———. 1952. *Sexual behavior in the human female.* Philadelphia: Saunders.

Kjøbli, J., S. Hukkelberg, and T. Ogden. 2013. A randomized trial of group parent training: Reducing child conduct problems in real-world settings. *Behaviour Research and Therapy* 51 (3):113–21. https://doi.org/10.1016/j.brat.2012.11.006.

Klein, M. 1932. *The psychoanalysis of childhood.* London: Hogarth.

Kohlberg, L. 1963. Moral development and identification. In *Child psychology: Sixty-second yearbook of the National Society for the Study of Education*, 277–332. Chicago: University of Chicago Press.

Kornhaber, A. 1996. *Contemporary grandparenting.* Thousand Oaks, CA: Sage.

Köstenberger, A. J., and M. E. Köstenberger. 2014. *God's design for man and woman: A biblical-theological survey.* Wheaton: Crossway.

Kotva, J. J., Jr. 1996. *The Christian case for virtue ethics.* Washington, DC: Georgetown University Press.

Kübler-Ross, E. 1970. *On death and dying.* New York: Macmillan.

Kulik, L. 2011. Does cohabitation matter? Differences in initial marital adjustment among women who cohabited and those who did not. *Families in Society* 92:120–27.

Kulu, H., and P. Boyle. 2010. Premarital cohabitation and divorce: Support for the Trial Marriage Theory? *Demographic Research* 23:881.

Kuperberg, A. 2014. Age at coresidence, premarital cohabitation, and marriage dissolution: 1985–2009. *Journal of Marriage and Family* 76 (2):352–69. https://doi.org/10.1111/jomf.12092.

Kuppens, S., and E. Ceulemans. 2019. Parenting styles: A closer look at a well-known concept. *Journal of Child and Family Studies* 28 (1):168–81. https://doi.org/10.1007/s10826-018-1242-x.

Lal, A., and S. Bartle-Haring. 2011. Relationship among differentiation of self, relationship satisfaction, partner support, and depression in patients with chronic lung disease and their partners. *Journal of Marital and Family Therapy* 37 (2):169–81. https://doi.org/10.1111/j.1752-0606.2009.00167.x.

Lam, C., A. Solmeyer, and S. McHale. 2012. Sibling differences in parent-child conflict and risky behavior: A three-wave longitudinal study. *Journal of Family Psychology* 26:523–31.

Lamb, G. E. 2017. Fatherlessness: Implications for God's word, church, and world. *Christian Education Journal* 14 (1):99–108. https://doi.org/10.1177/073989131701400109.

Larson, J., and R. Hickman. 2004. Are college marriage textbooks teaching students the premarital predictors of marital quality? *Family Relations* 53:385–92.

Larson, J., and T. Holman. 1994. Premarital predictors of marital quality and stability. *Family Relations* 43:228–37.

Larzelere, R. E., J. Cox, B. Ronald, and G. L. Smith. 2010. Do nonphysical punishments reduce antisocial behavior more than spanking? A comparison using the strongest previous causal evidence against spanking. *BMC Pediatrics* 10:10. https://doi.org/10.1186/1471-2431-10-10.

Larzelere, R. E., and J. Merenda. 1994. The effectiveness of parental discipline for toddler misbehavior at different levels of child distress. *Family Relations* 43:480–88.

Larzelere, R. E., A. S. Morris, and A. W. Harrist, eds. 2013. *Authoritative parenting: Synthesizing nurturance and discipline for optimal child development.* Washington, DC: American Psychological Association.

Lareau, A. 2003. *Unequal childhoods: Class, race, and family life.* Berkeley: University of California Press.

Lauer, R., J. Lauer, and S. Kerr. 1995. The long-term marriage: Perceptions of stability and satisfaction. In *The ties of later life*, edited by J. Hendricks, 35–41. Amityville, NY: Baywood.

Laumann, E., J. Gagnon, R. Michael, and S. Michaels. 1994. *The social organization of sexuality: Sexual practices in the United States.* Chicago: University of Chicago Press.

Lee, C. 1998. *Beyond family values: A call to Christian virtue.* Downers Grove, IL: InterVarsity.

———. 2004. Agency and purpose in narrative therapy: Questioning the postmodern rejection of metanarrative. *Journal of Psychology and Theology* 32:221–31.

Leidy, M., N. Guerra, and R. Toro. 2010. Positive parenting, family cohesion, and child social competence among immigrant Latino families. *Journal of Family Psychology* 23:252–60.

Leman, P. 2005. Authority and moral reason: Parenting style and children's perceptions of adult rule justifications. *International Journal of Behavioral Development* 29:265–70.

Lerner, R. 2018. *Concepts and theories of human development.* 4th ed. New York: Routledge.

Levine, J. 1997. *Working fathers: New strategies for balancing work and family.* Reading, MA: Addison-Wesley.

Levinson, D. 1978. *The seasons of a man's life.* New York: Knopf.

———. 1996. *The seasons of a woman's life.* New York: Knopf.

Lewin, E. 2004. Does marriage have a future? *Journal of Marriage and Family* 66:1000–1006.

Lewis, C. S. 1958. *The allegory of love: A study of medieval tradition.* New York: Oxford University Press.

———. 1960a. *The four loves.* New York: Harcourt Brace.

———. 1960b. *Mere Christianity.* New York: Macmillan.

Lewis, R., and G. Spanier. 1979. Theorizing about the quality and stability of marriage. In *Contemporary theories about the family*, edited by W. Burr et al., 269–94. New York: Free Press.

Lindahl, K., and N. Malik. 2011. Marital conflict typology and children's appraisals: The moderating role of family cohesion. *Journal of Family Psychology* 25:194–202.

Lindsey, E., Y. Caldera, and M. Colwell. 2005. Correlates of coparenting during infancy. *Family Relations* 54:346–59.

Loades, A. 1996. Dympna revisited: Thinking about the sexual abuse of children. In *The family in theological perspective*, edited by S. Barton, 253–72. Edinburgh: T&T Clark.

Lohne, V., C. Miaskowski, and T. Rustoen. 2012. The relationship between hope and caregiver strain in family caregivers of patients with advanced cancer. *Cancer Nursing* 35:99–115.

Long, J., and J. Mancini. 1990. Aging couples and the family system. In *Family relationships in later life*, edited by T. Brubaker, 2nd ed., 29–47. Newbury Park, CA: Sage.

Loughlin, G. 1996. The want of family in postmodernity. In *The family in theological perspective*, edited by S. Barton, 307–27. Edinburgh: T&T Clark.

Loving, T., K. Heffner, J. Keicolt-Glaser, R. Glaser, and W. Malarkey. 2004. Stress hormone changes and marital conflict: Spouses' relative power makes a difference. *Journal of Marriage and Family* 66:595–612.

Luke, C., R. Miller, and G. McAuliffe. 2019. Neuro-informed mental health counseling: A person-first perspective. *Journal of Mental Health Counseling* 41 (1):65–79. https://doi.org/10.1774/mech.41.1.06.

Maccoby, E. 1999. *The two sexes: Growing up apart, coming together*. Cambridge, MA: Belknap.

MacKay, D. 1974. *The clockwork image*. Downers Grove, IL: InterVarsity.

Macklin, E. 1987. Nontraditional family forms. In *Handbook of marriage and the family*, edited by M. Sussman and S. Steinmetz, 317–53. New York: Plenum.

Majumder, M. A. 2016. The impact of parenting style on children's educational outcomes in the United States. *Journal of Family and Economic Issues* 37:89–98.

Manning, W. 2004. Children and the stability of cohabiting couples. *Journal of Marriage and Family* 62:674–87.

Manning, W., and J. Cohen. 2012. Premarital cohabitation and marital dissolution: An examination of recent marriages. *Journal of Marriage and Family* 74:377–87.

Manning, W., and P. Smock. 2000. Swapping families? Serial parenting and economic support for children. *Journal of Marriage and Family* 62:112–22.

Marcia, J. 1980. Identity in adolescence. In *Handbook of adolescent psychology*, edited by J. Adelson, 159–87. New York: Wiley.

Markman, H., S. Stanley, and S. Blumberg. 1994. *Fighting for your marriage*. San Francisco: Jossey-Bass.

Marquardt, E. 2005. *Between two worlds: The inner lives of children of divorce*. New York: Crown.

Marsiglio, W. 2004. When stepfathers claim stepchildren: A conceptual analysis. *Journal of Marriage and Family* 66:22–39.

Maslach, C., and M. Leiter. 1997. *The truth about burnout: How organizations cause personal stress and what to do about it.* San Francisco: Jossey-Bass.

Maslach, C., W. Schaufeli, and M. Leiter. 2001. Job burnout. *Annual Review of Psychology* 52:397–422.

Matson, F. 1966. *The broken image.* New York: Braziller.

Matthews, A. 2005. Toward reconciliation: Healing the schism. In *Discovering biblical equality: Complementarity without hierarchy*, edited by R. Pierce, R. Groothuis, and G. Fee, 494–507. Downers Grove, IL: InterVarsity.

Mauldon, J. 1992. Children's risks of experiencing divorce and remarriage: Do disabled children destabilize marriages? *Population Studies* 46:349–62.

McAdams, D. P. 1997. *The stories we live by.* New York: Guilford.

McBride, B., G. Brown, K. Bost, N. Shin, B. Vaughn, and B. Korth. 2005. Paternal identity, maternal gatekeeping, and father involvement. *Family Relations* 54:360–72.

McGee, E., and M. Shevin. 2009. Effect of humor on interpersonal attraction and mate selection. *Journal of Psychology: Interdisciplinary and Applied* 143:67–77.

McGoldrick, M., N. Y. Garcia Preto, and B. Carter, eds. 2016. *The expanded family life cycle: Individual, family, and social perspectives.* 5th ed. Upper Saddle River, NJ: Pearson.

McKinney, C., M. Morse, and J. Pastuszak. 2016. Effective and ineffective parenting: Associations with psychological adjustment in emerging adults. *Journal of Family Issues* 37 (9):1203–25. https://doi.org/10.1177/0192513X14537480.

McLanahan, S., L. Tach, and D. Schneider. 2013. The causal effects of father absence. *Annual Review of Sociology* 39 (1):399–427. https://doi.org/10.1146/annurev-soc-071312-145704.

McLean, S. 1984. The language of covenant and a theology of the family. Paper presented at the Consultation on a Theology of the Family, Fuller Theological Seminary.

McRae, S. 1997. Cohabitation: A trial run for marriage. *Sexual and Marital Therapy* 12:239–73.

Mead, M. 1966. Marriage in two steps. *Redbook* 127:48–49.

Messner, M. A. 2002. *Taking the field: Women, men, and sports.* Minneapolis: University of Minnesota Press.

Middleton, J. R. 2005. *The liberating image: The imago Dei in Genesis 1.* Grand Rapids: Brazos.

Milevsky, A., M. Schlechter, S. Netter, and D. Keehn. 2007. Maternal and paternal parenting styles in adolescents: Association with self-esteem, depression and life-satisfaction. *Journal of Child and Family Studies* 15:39–47.

Miller, R. B., S. Anderson, and D. K. Keala. 2004. Is Bowen theory valid? A review of basic research. *Journal of Marital and Family Therapy* 30 (4):453 66. https://doi.org/10.1111/j.1752 0606.2004.tb01255.x.

Minnotte, K. L., M. C. Minnotte, and D. E. Pedersen. 2013. Marital satisfaction among dual earner couples: Gender ideologies and family-to-work conflict. *Family Relations* 62 (4):686–98. https://doi.org/10.1111/fare.12021.

Mintz, S. 2004. *Huck's raft: A history of American childhood.* Cambridge, MA: Harvard University Press.

Montoya, R. 2008. I'm hot, so I'd say you're not: The influence of objective physical attractiveness on mate selection. *Personality and Social Psychology Bulletin* 34:1315–31.

Moreira, J. F. G., and E. H. Telzer. 2015. Changes in family cohesion and links to depression during the college transition. *Journal of Adolescence* 43:72–82.

Morris, M. G., and V. Venkatesh. 2000. Age differences in technology adoption decisions: Implications for a changing work force. *Personnel Psychology* 53 (2):375–403. https://doi.org/10.1111/j.1744-6570.2000.tb00206.x.

Mueller, M., B. Wilhelm, and G. Elder. 2002. Variations in grandparenting. *Research on Aging* 23:380–88.

Munsch, R. 1986. *Love you forever.* Scarborough, ON: Firefly.

Murdock, N. L., and P. A. Gore. 2004. Stress, coping, and differentiation of self: A test of Bowen Theory. *Contemporary Family Therapy* 26:319–35.

Musick, K., and L. Bumpass. 2012. Reexamining the case for marriage: Union formation and changes in well-being. *Journal of Marriage and Family* 74:1–18.

Nair, H., and A. Murray. 2005. Predictors of attachment security in preschool children from intact and divorced families. *Journal of Genetic Psychology* 16:245–63.

Nature. 2018. US proposal for defining gender has no basis in science. 563:5. https://doi.org/10.1038/d41586-018-07238-8.

Nesi, J., and M. J. Prinstein. 2015. Using social media for social comparison and feedback-seeking: Gender and popularity moderate associations with depressive symptoms. *Journal of Abnormal Child Psychology* 43 (8):1427–38. https://doi.org/10.1007/s10802-015-0020-0.

Ngee Sim, T., and L. Ping Ong. 2005. Parent physical punishment and child aggression in a Singapore Chinese preschool sample. *Journal of Marriage and Family* 67:85–99.

The NICHD Early Child Care Research Network, ed. 2005. *Child care and child development: Results from the NICHD study of early child care and youth development.* New York: Guilford.

Niebuhr, R. 1987. *The essential Reinhold Niebuhr: Selected essays and addresses.* Edited by McAfee Brown. New Haven: Yale University Press.

Nock, S. 1998. *Marriage in men's lives.* New York: Oxford University Press.

Noller, P., and J. Feeney. 2002. Communication, relationship concerns, and satisfaction in early marriage. In *Stability and change in relationships*, edited by A. Vangelisti, H. Reis, and M. Fitzpatrick, 129–55. New York: Cambridge University Press.

Nomaguchi, K., and M. Milkie. 2003. Costs and rewards of children: The effects of becoming a parent on adults' lives. *Journal of Marriage and Family* 65:356–74.

Norwood, R. 1985. *Women who love too much: When you keep wishing and hoping he'll change*. Los Angeles: J. P. Tarcher.

Nuttall, A., K. Valentino, and J. Borkowski. 2012. Maternal history of parentification, maternal warm responsiveness, and children's externalizing behavior. *Journal of Family Psychology* 26:767–75.

Oetzel, J., and S. Ting-Toomey. 2006. *The Sage handbook of conflict communication: Integrating theory, research, and practice*. Thousand Oaks, CA: Sage.

Ogden, T. H. 1990. *The matrix of the mind: Object relations and the psychoanalytic dialogue*. Lanham, MD: Rowman and Littlefield.

Olson, D. 1988. Family types, family stress and family satisfaction: A family development perspective. In *Family transitions*, edited by C. Falicov, 55–80. New York: Guilford.

———. 1998. *Prepare/Enrich counselor's manual, version 2000*. Minneapolis: Life Innovations.

———. 2011. FACES IV and the circumplex model: Validation study. *Journal of Marital and Family Therapy* 37:64–80.

Olson, D., D. Sprenkle, and C. Russell. 1979. Circumplex model of marital and family systems: Cohesion and adaptability dimensions, family types, and clinical applications. *Family Process* 18:3–28.

Omoto, A., and H. Kurtzman, eds. 2005. *Sexual orientation and mental health: Examining identity and development in lesbian, gay, and bisexual people*. Washington, DC: American Psychological Association.

Orford, J., A. Copello, R. Velleman, and L. Templeton. 2010. Family members affected by a relative's addiction: The stress-strain-coping-support model. *Drugs, Education, Prevention and Policy* 17:35–43.

Orthner, D., H. Jones-Sampei, and S. Williamson. 2004. The resilience and strengths of low-income families. *Family Relations* 53:159–67.

Owen, J., and F. Fincham. 2011. Young adults' emotional reactions after hooking up encounters. *Archives of Sexual Behavior* 40:321–330.

Owen, J., G. Rhoades, S. Stanley, and F. Fincham. 2010. "Hooking up" among college students: Demographic and psychosocial correlations. *Archives of Sexual Behavior* 39:653–63.

Pace, G. T., K. Shafer, T. M. Jensen, and J. H. Larson. 2015. Stepparenting issues and relationship quality: The role of clear communication. *Journal of Social Work* 15 (1):24–44. https://doi.org/10.1177/1468017313504508.

Palisi, B. J., M. Orleans, D. Caddell, and B. Korn. 1991. Adjustment to stepfatherhood: The effects of marital history and relations with children. *Journal of Divorce and Remarriage* 14:89–106.

Papernow, P. 1993. *Becoming a stepfamily: Patterns of development in remarried families*. San Francisco: Jossey-Bass.

———. 2018. Clinical guidelines for working with stepfamilies: What family, couple, individual, and child therapists need to know. *Family Process* 57 (1):25–51. https://doi.org/10.1111/famp.12321.

Papero, D. 1990. *Bowen family systems theory*. Needham Heights, MA: Allyn and Bacon.

———. 2014. Emotion and intellect in Bowen theory. In *Differentiation of self: Bowen family systems perspectives*, edited by P. Titelman, 65–81. New York: Routledge.

Parker, B. E. 2018. Typology and allegory: Is there a distinction? A brief examination of figural reading. *The Southern Baptist Journal of Theology* 21:57–83.

Parott, T., R. Giarrusso, and V. Bengtsen. 1994. What predicts conflict in parent-adult child relationships? Paper presented to the American Sociological Association, Los Angeles.

Parrott, L., and L. Parrott. 2015. *Saving your marriage before it starts: Seven questions to ask before and after your marriage starts*. Anniversary ed. Grand Rapids: Zondervan.

Parsons, S. 1996. Feminism and the family. In *The family in theological perspective*, edited by S. Barton, 273–90. Edinburgh: T&T Clark.

Pascoe, J. M., D. L. Wood, J. H. Duffee, A. Kuo, and Committee on Psychosocial Aspects of Child and Family Health, Council on Community Pediatrics. 2016. Mediators and adverse effects of child poverty in the United States. *Pediatrics* 137 (4).

Patton, J., and B. Childs. 1988. *Christian marriage and family: Caring for our generations*. Nashville: Abingdon.

Pattusamy, M., and J. Jacob. 2016. Testing the mediation of work-family balance in relationship between work-family conflict and job and family satisfaction. *South African Journal of Psychology* 46:218–31. https://doi.org/10.117/0081246315608527.

Peace, R. V. 1999. *Conversion in the New Testament: Paul and the Twelve*. Grand Rapids: Eerdmans.

Peleg, O., and M. Yitzhak. 2011. Differentiation of self and separation anxiety: Is there a similarity between spouses? *Contemporary Family Therapy* 33 (1):25–36. https://doi.org/10.1007/s10591-010-9137-z.

Pellerin, L. 2005. Applying Baumrind's parenting typology to high schools: Toward a middle-range theory of authoritative socialization. *Social Science Research* 34:283–303.

Perelli-Harris, B., and N. Gassen. 2012. How similar are cohabitation and marriage? Legal approaches to cohabitation across Western Europe. *Population and Development Review* 38:435–67.

Peterman, D. 1975. Does living together before marriage make for a better marriage? *Medical Aspects of Human Sexuality* 9:39–41.

Peterson, E. 2005. *Christ plays in ten thousand places: A conversation in spiritual theology*. Grand Rapids: Eerdmans.

Peterson, G., and B. Rollins. 1987. Parent-child socialization. In *Handbook of marriage and the family*, edited by M. Sussman and S. Steinmetz, 471–507. New York: Plenum.

Petts, R. 2012. Single mothers' religious participation and early childhood behavior. *Journal of Marriage and Family* 74:251–68.

Phillips, J., and M. Sweeney. 2005. Premarital cohabitation and marital disruption among White, Black, and Mexican American women. *Journal of Marriage and Family* 67:296–314.

Piaget, J. 1932. *The moral judgment of the child*. London: Kegan Paul, Trench, Trubner.

Pierce, R., R. Groothius, and G. Fee. 2005. *Discovering biblical equality: Complementarity without hierarchy*. Downers Grove, IL: InterVarsity.

Pillemer, K., and K. Luscher, eds. 2004. *Intergenerational ambivalences: New perspectives on parent-child relations in later life*. Amsterdam: Elsevier.

Pines, A., M. Neal, L. Hammer, and T. Icekson. 2011. Job burnout and couple burnout in dual-earner couples in the sandwiched generation. *Social Psychology Quarterly* 74:361–86.

Pinquart, M. 2016. Associations of parenting styles and dimensions with academic achievement in children and adolescents: A meta-analysis. *Educational Psychology Review* 28 (3):475–93. https://doi.org/10.1007/s10648-015-9338-y.

———. 2017. Associations of parenting dimensions and styles with internalizing symptoms in children and adolescents: A meta-analysis. *Marriage and Family Review* 53 (7):613–40. https://doi.org/10.1080/01494929.2016.1247761.

Piper, B., and J. K. Balswick. 1997. *Then they leave home: Parenting after the kids grow up*. Downers Grove, IL: InterVarsity.

Pipher, M. 1994. *Reviving Ophelia*. New York: Ballantine.

Pittman, F. 1997. Just in love. *Journal of Marital and Family Therapy* 23:309–12.

Plaskow, J. 1980. *Sex, sin and grace: Women's experience and the theologies of Reinhold Niebuhr and Paul Tillich*. Lanham, MD: University Press of America.

Platsidou, M., and E. Tsirogiannidou. 2016. Enhancement of emotional intelligence, family communication, and family satisfaction via a parent educational program. *Journal of Adult Development* 23 (4):245–53. https://doi.org/10.1007/s10804-016-9240-y.

Pleck, J. H. 2010. Paternal involvement: Revised conceptualization and theoretical linkages with child outcomes. In *The role of the father in child development*, edited by M. E. Lamb, 58–93. New York: Wiley.

Ponzetti, J., and A. Folkrod. 1989. Grandchildren's perceptions of their relationships with their grandparents. *Child Study Journal* 19:41–50.

Pootman, A., and M. Mills. 2012. Investments in marriage and cohabitation: The role of legal and interpersonal commitment. *Journal of Marriage and Family* 74:357–76.

Popenoe, D., and B. Whitehead. 1998. Life without father. In *Lost fathers: The politics of fatherlessness in America*, edited by C. Daniels, 33–49. New York: St. Martin's Press.

———. 1999. Challenging the culture of fatherlessness. In *The fatherhood movement: A call to action*, edited by W. F. Horn, D. Blankenhorn, and M. B. Pearlstein, 17–26. Lanham, MD: Lexington Books.

———. 2002. *Should we live together? What young adults need to know about cohabitation before marriage: A comprehensive review of recent research*. 2nd ed. Piscataway, NJ: National Marriage Project. Executive summary, http://national marriageproject.org/resources/should-we-live-together/.

———. 2003. *The state of our unions: The social health of marriage in America, 2003*. New Brunswick, NJ: National Marriage Project at Rutgers University.

———. 2004. *The state of our unions: The social health of marriage in America, 2004*. New Brunswick, NJ: National Marriage Project at Rutgers University.

———. 2005. *The state of our unions: The social health of marriage in America, 2005*. New Brunswick, NJ: National Marriage Project at Rutgers University.

Poppert Cordts, K., A. Wilson, and A. Riley. 2020. More than mental health. *Journal of Developmental and Behavioral Pediatrics* 41 (4):265–71. https://doi.org/10.1097/DBP.0000000000000755.

Post, S. 1994. *Spheres of love: Toward a new ethics of the family*. Dallas: Southern Methodist University Press.

Potter, D. 2010. Psychosocial well-being and the relationship between divorce and children's academic achievement. *Journal of Marriage and Family* 72:933–46.

Quale, G. R. 1988. *A history of marriage systems*. Westport, CT: Greenwood.

Rabin, C. 1996. *Equal partners, good friends*. New York: Routledge.

Raley, S., M. Mattingly, and S. Bianchi. 2006. How dual are dual-income couples? Documenting change from 1970 to 2001. *Journal of Marriage and Family* 68:11–28.

Ramey, S. 2005. Human developmental science serving children and families. Edited by Sharon Landsman Ramey. *Child Care and Child Development: Results from the NICHD Study of Early Child Care and Youth Development*. New York: Guilford.

Regnerus, M., and J. Uecker. 2011. *Premarital sex in America: How young Americans meet, mate, and think about marriage*. New York: Oxford University Press.

Reimer, K. 2003. Committed to caring: Transformation in adolescent moral identity. *Applied Developmental Science* 7:129–37.

Reinhold, S. 2010. Reassessing the link between premarital cohabitation and marital instability. *Demography* 47:719–33.

Rhoades, G., S. Stanley, and H. Markman. 2006. Pre-engagement cohabitation and gender asymmetry in marital commitment. *Journal of Family Psychology* 20:553–60.

———. 2012. The impact of the transition to cohabitation on relationship functioning: Cross-sectional and longitudinal finding. *Journal of Family Psychology* 26:348–58.

Riesman, D. 1950. *The lonely crowd*. New Haven: Yale University Press.

Riina, E., and M. Feinberg. 2012. Involvement in childrearing and mothers' and fathers' adjustment. *Family Relations* 61:836–50.

Roberts, M., and S. Powers. 1990. Adjusting chair timeout enforcement procedures for oppositional children. *Behavior Therapy* 21:257–71.

Roberts, R. C. 2007. *Spiritual emotions: A psychology of Christian virtues*. Grand Rapids: Eerdmans.

Rodriguez, M., M. Donovick, and S. Crowley. 2009. Parenting styles in a cultural context: Observations of "protective parenting" in first-generation Latinos. *Family Process* 48:195–210.

Rodríguez-González, M., E. A. Skowron, E. A. Cagigal de Gregorioc, and I. Munoz San Roquec. 2016. Differentiation of self, mate selection, and marital adjustment: Validity of postulates of Bowen Theory in a Spanish sample. *American Journal of Family Therapy* 44:11–23. https://doi.org/10.1080/01926187.2015.1099415.

Roehilkepartain, E., P. King, L. Wagener, and P. Benson. 2005. *The handbook of spiritual development in childhood and adolescence*. Newbury Park, CA: Sage.

Rogerson, J. 1996. The family and structures of grace in the Old Testament. In *The family in theological perspective*, edited by S. Barton, 25–42. Edinburgh: T&T Clark.

Rogge, R., and T. Bradbury. 2002. Developing a multifaceted view of change in relationships. In *Stability and change in relationships*, edited by A. Vangelisti, H. Reis, and M. Fitzpatrick, 229–53. New York: Cambridge University Press.

Rollins, B., and D. Thomas. 1979. Parental support, power, and control techniques in the socialization of children. In *Contemporary theories about the family*, edited by W. Burr et al., 1:317–64. New York: Free Press.

Rosenfeld, M. J., and K. Roesler. 2019. Cohabitation experience and cohabitation's association with marital dissolution. *Journal of Marriage and Family* 81:42–58. https://doi.org/10.1111/jomf.12530.

Rosenfeld, M. J., and R. Thomas. 2012. Searching for a mate: The rise of the internet as a social intermediary. *American Sociological Review* 77 (4):523–47. https://doi.org/10.2307/41723048.

Rosenfield, S. 1992. The costs of sharing: Wives' employment and husbands' mental health. *Journal of Health and Social Behavior* 33:213–25.

Rossi, A. 1984. Gender and parenthood. *American Sociological Review* 49:1–19.

Roth, D., M. Perkins, V. Wadley, E. Temple, and W. Haley. 2009. Family caregiving and emotional strain, associations with quality of life in a large national sample of middle-aged and older adults. *Quality of Life Research* 18:679–88.

Rovers, M., L. Kocum, S. Briscoe-Dimock, P. C. Myers, S. Cotnam, T. Henry, E. Kwasniewski, and D. Sheppard. 2007. Choosing a partner of equal differentiation: A new paradigm utilizing similarity and complementarity measures. *Journal of Couple & Relationship Therapy* 6 (3):1–23. https://doi.org/10.1300/J398v06n03_01.

Sandage, S. J., and M. G. Harden. 2011. Relational spirituality, differentiation of self, and virtue as predictors of intercultural development. *Mental Health, Religion, and Culture* 14:819–38. https://doi.org/10.1080/13674676.2010.527932.

Sanik, M., and T. Mauldin. 1986. Single versus two parent families: A comparison of mothers' time. *Family Relations* 35:53–56.

Sarkisian, N., and N. Gerstel. 2004. Explaining the gender gap in help to parents: The importance of employment. *Journal of Marriage and Family* 66:431–51.

Sassler, S. 2010. Partnering across the life course: Sex, relationships, and mate selection. *Journal of Marriage and Family* 72:557–75.

Satir, V. 1983. *Conjoint family therapy*. 3rd ed. Palo Alto, CA: Science and Behavior Books.

Sawhill, I. V., and R. Haskins. 2003. Work and marriage: The way to end poverty and welfare. The Brookings Institution. September 1, 2003. https://www.brookings.edu/research/work-and-marriage the-way-to-end-poverty-and-welfare/.

Scheirer, M. 1983. Household structure among welfare families: Correlates and consequences. *Journal of Marriage and Family* 45:761–71.

Schindler, H., and R. Coley. 2012. Predicting marital separation: Do parent-child relationships matter? *Journal of Family Psychology* 26:499–508.

Schmeer, K. 2011. The child health disadvantage of parental cohabitation. *Journal of Marriage and Family* 73:181–93.

Schoppe-Sullivan, S. J., and J. Fagan. 2020. The evolution of fathering research in the 21st century: Persistent challenges, new directions. *Journal of Marriage and Family* 82 (1):175–97. https://doi.org/10.1111/jomf.12645.

Schrodt, P. 2009. Family strength and satisfaction as functions of family communication environments. *Communication Quarterly* 57:171–86.

Schwarz, P. 1994. *Peer marriage: How love between equals really works*. New York: Free Press.

Scriven, M. 1968. Putting the sex back into sex education. *Phi Delta Kappa* 48:485–89.

Sechrist, J., J. Suitor, N. Vargas, and K. Pillemer. 2011. The role of perceived religious similarity in the quality of mother-child relations in later life: Differences within families and between races. *Research on Aging* 33:3–27.

Segrin, C., and J. Flora. 2005. *Family communication*. Mahwah, NJ: Erlbaum.

Segrin, C., M. Taylor, and J. Altman. 2005. Social cognitive mediators and relational outcomes associated with parental divorce. *Journal of Social and Personal Relationships* 22:361–77.

Shafer, K., T. M. Jensen, G. T. Pace, and J. H. Larson. 2013. Former spouse ties and postdivorce relationship quality: Relationship effort as a mediator. *Journal of Social Service Research* 39 (5):629–45. https://doi.org/10.1080/01488376.2013.834284.

Sherr, L., K. J. Roberts, S. Hothi, and N. Balchin. 2018. Never too old to learn: Parenting interventions for grandparents; A systematic review. *Cogent Social Sciences* 4 (1). https://doi.org/10.1080/23311886.2018.150862.

Shults, F. L. 2003. *Reforming theological anthropology: After the philosophical turn to relationality*. Grand Rapids: Eerdmans.

Shults, F. L., and S. J. Sandage. 2003. *The faces of forgiveness: Searching for wholeness and salvation*. Grand Rapids: Baker Academic.

———. 2006. *Transforming spirituality: Integrating theology and psychology*. Grand Rapids: Baker Academic.

Sider, R. J. 2005. *Scandal of the evangelical conscience: Why are Christians living just like the rest of the world?* Grand Rapids: Baker Books.

Siegel, D. J. 2020. *The developing mind: How relationships and the brain interact to shape who we are*. 3rd ed. New York: Guilford.

Siegel, D. J., and T. Payne Bryson. 2020. *The power of showing up: How parental presence shapes who our kids become and how their brains get wired*. New York: Ballantine.

Sillars, A., D. Canary, and M. Tafoya. 2004. Communication, conflict, and the quality of family relationships. In *Handbook of family communication*, edited by A. Vangelisti, 413–46. Mahwah, NJ: Erlbaum.

Sim, T., and L. Ong. 2005. Parent physical punishment and child aggression in a Singapore Chinese preschool sample. *Journal of Marriage and Family* 67:85–99.

Skinner, B. F. 1953. *Science and human behavior*. New York: Macmillan.

Skowron, E. A. 2000. The role of differentiation of self in marital adjustment. *Journal of Counseling Psychology* 47 (2):229–37. https://doi.org/10.1037/0022-0167.47.2.229.

Smedes, L. 1994. *Sex for Christians*. Revised ed. Grand Rapids: Eerdmans.

Smelser, N. 1973. Processes of social change. In *Sociology: An introduction*, edited by N. Smelser, 2nd ed., 671–728. New York: Wiley.

Smith, C. 2000. *Christian America? What evangelicals really want*. Berkeley: University of California Press.

Smock, P. 2000. Cohabitation in the United States. *Annual Review of Sociology* 26:1–26.

———. 2004. The wax and wane of marriage: Prospects for marriage in the 21st century. *Journal of Marriage and Family* 66:966–73.

———. 2010. Diversity in pathways to parenthood: Patterns, implications, and emerging research directions. *Journal of Marriage and Family* 72:576–93.

Sneed, J., S. Whitbourne, S. Schwartz, and S. Huang. 2012. The relationship between identity, intimacy, and midlife well-being: Findings from the Rochester adult longitudinal study. *Psychology and Aging* 27:318–23.

Sogar, C. 2017. The influence of family process and structure on delinquency in adolescence: An examination of theory and research. *Journal of Human Behavior in the Social Environment* 27 (3):206–14. https://doi.org/10.1080/10911359.2016.1270870.

Soh, D. 2020. *The end of gender: Debunking the myths about sex and identity in our society*. New York: Simon & Schuster.

Stackhouse, J. 2005. *Finally feminist: A pragmatic Christian understanding of gender.* Grand Rapids: Baker Academic.

Stanley, S., G. Roades, and H. Markman. 2006. Sliding versus deciding: Inertia and the premarital cohabitation effect. *Family Relations* 55:499–509.

Stanley, S., S. Whitton, S. Sadberry, M. Clements, and H. Markman. 2006. Sacrifice as a predictor of marital outcomes. *Family Process* 45:289–303.

Stassen, G., and D. Gushee. 2003. *Kingdom ethics: Following Jesus in contemporary context.* Downers Grove, IL: InterVarsity.

Stephen, T. 1994. Communication in the shifting context of intimacy: Marriage, meaning, and modernity. *Communication Theory* 4:191–218.

Stephens, L. 1996. Will Johnny see daddy this week? An empirical test of three theoretical perspectives of postdivorce contact. *Journal of Family Issues* 17:466–94.

Stevens, R. P. 1999. *The other six days: Vocation, work and ministry in biblical perspective.* Grand Rapids: Eerdmans.

———. 2012. *Work matters: Lessons from Scripture.* Grand Rapids: Eerdmans.

Storksen, I., E. Roysamb, T. Holmen, and K. Tambs. 2006. Adolescent adjustment and well-being: Effects of parental divorce and distress. *Scandinavian Journal of Psychology* 47:75–84.

Strachan, O. 2019. *Reenchanting humanity: A theology of mankind.* Fearn, Ross-shire, Great Britain: Mentor.

Strachan, O., and G. Peacock. 2016. *The grand design: Male and female he made them.* Fearn, Ross-shire, Great Britain: Christian Focus Publications.

———. 2020. *What does the Bible teach about transgenderism?* Fearn, Ross-shire, Great Britain: Christian Focus Publications.

Strait, J. G., J. G. Sandberg, J. H. Larson, and J. M. Harper. 2015. The relationship between family-of-origin experiences and sexual satisfaction in married couples. *Journal of Family Therapy* 37 (3):361–85. https://doi.org/10.1111/1467-6427.12007.

Strizzi, J. M., S. Sander, A. Ciprić, and G. M. Hald. 2020. "I had not seen Star Wars" and other motives for divorce in Denmark. *Journal of Sex and Marital Therapy* 46 (1):57–66. https://doi.org/10.1080/0092623X.2019.1641871.

Strohschein, L. 2005. Parental divorce and child mental health trajectories. *Journal of Marriage and Family* 67:1286–1300.

———. 2012. Parental divorce and child mental health: Accounting for predisruption differences. *Journal of Divorce and Remarriage* 53:489–502.

Strom, P., and R. Strom. 2011. Grandparent education: Raising grandchildren. *Educational Gerontology* 37:910–23.

Struening, K. 2002. *New family values: Liberty, equality, diversity.* Lanham, MD: Rowman and Littlefield.

Su, A. J. 2019. Finding balance as a dual-career couple. *Harvard Business Review.* July 29, 2019. https://hbr.org/2019/07/finding-balance-as-a-dual-career-couple.

Suggate, A. 1996. Ideology, power and the family. In *The family in theological perspective*, edited by S. Barton, 237–52. Edinburgh: T&T Clark.

Sweet, S. 2014. *The work-family interface: An introduction.* Thousand Oaks, CA: Sage.

Swensen, C. 1994. Older individuals in the family. In *Handbook of developmental family psychology and psychopathology*, edited by L. L'Abate, 202–17. New York: Wiley.

Szabo, N., J. Dubas, and M. van Aken. 2012. And baby makes four: The stability of coparenting and the effects of child temperament after the arrival of a second child. *Journal of Family Psychology* 26:554–64.

Tallman, I., and L. Gray. 1987. A theory of problem solving applied to families. Paper presented at the Theory-Methodological Workshop. National Council on Family Relations, Atlanta.

Tan, T., L. Camras, H. Deng, and M. Zhang. 2012. Family stress, parenting styles, and behavioral adjustment in preschool-age Chinese girls. *Early Childhood Research Quarterly* 27:128–36.

Tanner, S., and T. Bradbury. 2012. Marital interaction prior to parenthood predicts parent-child interaction 9 years later. *Journal of Family Psychology* 26:479–87.

Tarpley, M. 2011. The Christian family crisis in the United States and its implications for medical decision making. *Christian Bioethics: Nonecumenical Studies in Medical Morality* 17:299–314.

Teachman, J. 2003. Premarital sex, premarital cohabitation, and the risk of subsequent marital disruption among women. *Journal of Marriage and Family* 65:444–55.

Thatcher, A. 1999. *Marriage after modernity: Christian marriage in postmodern times.* New York: New York University Press.

Thomson, E., and U. Colella. 1992. Cohabitation and marital stability: Quality or commitment? *Journal of Marriage and Family* 54:259–67.

Timmons, A., R. Arbel, and G. Margolin. 2017. Daily patterns of stress and conflict in couples: Associations with marital aggression and family-of-origin aggression. *Journal of Family Psychology* 31 (1):93–104. https://doi.org/10.1037/fam0000227.

Tipton, S., and J. Witte Jr. 2005. *Family transformed: Religion, values, and society in American life.* Washington, DC: Georgetown University Press.

Titelman, P., ed. 2007. *Triangles: Bowen Family Systems Theory perspectives.* Philadelphia: Haworth.

———. 2014. The concept of differentiation of self in Bowen theory. In *Differentiation of self: Bowen family systems perspectives*, edited by P. Titelman, 3–64. New York: Routledge.

Townsend, L. L. 2000. *Pastoral care with stepfamilies: Mapping the wilderness.* St. Louis: Chalice.

Townsend, N. 2002. *Package deal: Marriage, work and fatherhood in men's lives.* Philadelphia: Temple University Press.

Treas, J. 2000. Sexual infidelity among married and cohabiting Americans. *Journal of Marriage and Family* 62:48–60.

Trost, J. 1975. Married and unmarried cohabitation: The case of Sweden, with some comparison. *Journal of Marriage and Family* 37:677–82.

Tuason, M. T., and M. L. Friedlander. 2000. Do parents' differentiation levels predict those of their adult children? and other tests of Bowen theory in a Philippine sample. *Journal of Counseling Psychology* 47 (1):27–35. https://doi.org/10.1037/0022-0167.47.1.27.

Turner, L., and R. West. 2002. *Perspectives on family communication.* 2nd ed. Boston: McGraw-Hill.

Twenge, J., W. Campbell, and C. Foster. 2003. Parenthood and marital satisfaction: A meta-analytic review. *Journal of Marriage and Family* 65:574–83.

Udry, J. R. 1988. Biological predispositions and social control in adolescent sexual behavior. *American Sociological Review* 53:709–22.

US Census Bureau. 2020. Historical living arrangements of children. https://www.census.gov/data/tables/time-series/demo/families/children.html. Accessed August 8, 2020.

———. 2021. Historical marital status tables. https://www.census.gov/data/tables/time-series/demo/families/marital.html. Accessed January 14, 2021.

Valcke, M., S. Bonte, B. DeWever, and I. Rots. 2010. Internet parenting styles and the impact on internet use of primary school children. *Computers and Education* 55:454–64.

Valentine, K. A., N. P. Li, A. L. Meltzer, and M.-H. Tsai. 2020. Mate preferences for warmth-trustworthiness predict romantic attraction in the early stages of mate selection and satisfaction in ongoing relationships. *Personality and Social Psychology Bulletin* 46:298–311. https://doi.org/10.1177/01461672198550.

van Houdt, K., and A. Poortman. 2018. Joint lifestyles and the risk of union dissolution: Differences between marriage and cohabitation. *Demographic Research* 39:431–57. https://doi.org/10.4054/DemRes.2018.39.15.

VanderValk, I., M. DeGoode, C. Maas, and W. Meeus. 2005. Family structure and problem behavior of adolescents and young adults: A growth-curve study. *Journal of Youth and Adolescence* 34:533–46.

Van Laningham, J., D. Johnson, and P. Amato. 2001. Marital happiness, marital duration, and the U-shaped curve: Evidence from a five-wave panel study. *Social Forces* 79:1313–41.

Van Leeuwen, M. 1990. *Gender and grace: Love, work and parenting in a changing world*. Downers Grove, IL: InterVarsity.

———. 2002. *My brother's keeper: What the social sciences do (and don't) tell us about masculinity*. Downers Grove, IL: InterVarsity.

Van Leeuwen, M., A. Knoppers, M. Koch, D. Schuurman, and H. Sterk. 1993. *After Eden: Facing the challenge of gender reconciliation*. Grand Rapids: Eerdmans.

Village, A., E. Williams, and L. Francis. 2010. Does religion make a difference? Assessing the effects of Christian affiliation and practice on marital solidarity and divorce in Britain, 1985–2005. *Journal of Divorce and Remarriage* 51:327–38.

Visher, E., and J. Visher. 1996. *How to win as a stepfamily*. New York: Brunner/Mazel.

———. 1997. *Stepping together: Creating strong stepfamilies*. New York: Brunner/Mazel.

Volf, M. 1996. *Exclusion and embrace : A theological exploration of identity, otherness, and reconciliation*. Nashville: Abingdon.

———. 1998. *After our likeness: The church as the image of the Trinity*. Grand Rapids: Eerdmans.

Vousoura, E., V. Verdell, P. Warner, and C. Baily. 2012. Parental divorce, familial risk for depression, and psychopathology in offspring. *Journal of Child and Family Studies* 21:718–25.

Vygotsky, L. 1986. *Thought and language*. Edited and translated by E. Hafmann and G. Vakar. Cambridge, MA: MIT Press. Originally published in 1937.

Wadsworth, S. 2010. Family risk and resilience in the context of war and terrorism. *Journal of Marriage and Family* 72:537–56.

Waite, L., D. Browning, W. Doherty, M. Gallagher, Y. Law, and S. Stanley. 2002. *Does divorce make one happy? Findings from a study of unhappy marriages*. New York: Institute for American Values.

Waite, L., and M. Gallagher. 2000. *The case for marriage: Why married people are happier, healthier and better off financially*. New York: Doubleday.

Walker, K., C. Pratt, and L. Eddy. 1995. Informal caregiving to aging family members. *Family Relations* 44:402–11.

Wallerstein, J. S. 2005. Growing up in the divorced family. *Clinical Social Work Journal* 33:401–18.

Wallerstein, J. S., and S. Blakeslee. 1989. *Second chances: Men, women, and children a decade after divorce*. New York: Ticknor and Fields.

———. 1995. *The good marriage: How and why love lasts*. New York: Houghton Mifflin.

Wallerstein, J. S., and J. Kelly. 1980. *Surviving the breakup: How children and parents cope with divorce*. New York: Basic Books.

Wallerstein, J. S., J. M. Lewis, and S. Blakeslee. 2001. *The unexpected legacy of divorce: The 25 year landmark study*. New York: Hachette.

Watson, J. 1930. *Behaviorism*. Revised ed. Chicago: University of Chicago Press.

Watters, E. 2003. *Urban tribes: A generation redefines friendship, family, and commitment*. New York: Bloomsbury.

Weaver, J. M., and T. J. Schofield. 2015. Mediation and moderation of divorce effects on children's behavior problems. *Journal of Family Psychology* 29 (1):39–48. https://doi.org/10.1037/fam0000043.

Wenham, G. 2020. *Jesus, divorce, and remarriage: In their historical setting*. Bellingham, WA: Lexham.

Wenzel, A., and T. Emerson. 2009. Mate selection in socially anxious and nonanxious individuals. *Journal of Social and Clinical Psychology* 28:341–63.

Whiteway, E., and D. Alexander. 2015. Understanding the causes of same-sex attraction. *Science & Christian Belief* 27:17–40. https://www.scienceandchristianbelief .org/serve_pdf_free.php?filename=SCB+27-1+Whiteway+Alexander.pdf.

Whitney, S. D., S. Prewett, Z. Wang, and H. Chen. 2017. Fathers' importance in adolescents' academic achievement. *International Journal of Child, Youth, and Family Studies* 8 (3):101–26. https://doi.org/10.18357/ijcyfs83/4201718073.

Wilcox, B. 2004. *Soft patriarchs, new men: How Christianity shapes fathers and husbands*. Chicago: University of Chicago Press.

———. 2010a. The couple that prays together: Race and ethnicity, religion and relationship quality among working-age adults. *Journal of Marriage and Family* 72:963–75.

———. 2010b. Is love a flimsy foundation? Soulmate versus institutional models of marriage. *Social Science Research* 39:687–99.

———. 2011. *The state of our unions: The social health of marriage in America*. The National Marriage Project at the University of Virginia. Charlottesville, VA.

———. 2014. The new progressive argument: For kids, marriage per se doesn't matter. Institute for Family Studies. September 15, 2014. https://ifstudies.org/blog/for -kids-marriage-per-se-doesnt-matter-right/.

Wilcox, B., and S. Nock. 2006. What wives want. *Inside UVA Online*, http://virginia .edu/insideuva/2006/04/happiness.html.

Williams, J. 2001. *Unbending gender: Why family and work conflict and what to do about it*. New York: Oxford University Press.

Williams, M. 2011. The changing roles of grandparents raising grandchildren. *Journal of Human Behavior in the Social Environment* 21:948–62.

Willson, A., M. Kim, and G. Elder. 2003. Ambivalence in the relationship of adult children to aging parents and in-laws. *Journal of Marriage and Family* 65:1055–72.

Winner, L. 2005. *Real sex: The naked truth about chastity*. Grand Rapids: Brazos.

Winnicott, D. 1971. *Playing and reality*. London: Tavistock.

Witte, J., Jr. 1997. *From sacrament to contract: Marriage, religion, and law in the Western tradition*. Louisville: Westminster John Knox.

Wolfram, H. J., and L. Gratton. 2014. Spillover between work and home, role importance and life satisfaction. *British Journal of Management* 25:77–90. https://doi.org/10.1111/j.1467-8551.2012.00833.x.

Wolters, A. M. 2005. *Creation regained: Biblical basics for a Reformational worldview.* 2nd ed. Grand Rapids: Eerdmans.

Wolterstorff, N. 1980. *Education for responsible action.* Grand Rapids: Eerdmans.

Woo, H., and R. Raley. 2005. A small extension to "Costs and rewards of children: The effects of becoming a parent on adults' lives." *Journal of Marriage and Family* 67:216–21.

Woods, H. C., and H. Scott. 2016. Sleepyteens: Social media use in adolescence is associated with poor sleep quality, anxiety, depression and low self-esteem. *Journal of Adolescence* 51:41–49. https://doi.org/10.1016/j.adolescence.2016.05.008.

Xu, X., J. Bartkowski, and K. Dalton. 2011. The role of cohabitation in remarriage: A replication. *International Review of Sociology* 21:549–64.

Yalom, M. 2001. *A history of the wife.* New York: HarperCollins.

Yang, C., and B. B. Brown. 2016. Online self-presentation on Facebook and self-development during the college transition. *Journal of Youth and Adolescence* 45 (2):402–16. https://doi.org/10.1007/s10964-015-0385-y.

Yarhouse, M. A. 2010. *Homosexuality and the Christian: A guide for parents, pastors, and friends.* Minneapolis: Bethany House.

Yoo, H., S. Bartle-Haring, R. D. Day, and R. Gangamma. 2014. Couple communication, emotional and sexual intimacy, and relationship satisfaction. *Journal of Sex and Marital Therapy* 40 (4):275–93. https://doi.org/10.1080/0092623X.2012.751072.

Yorgason, J., L. Padilla-Walker, and J. Jackson. 2011. Nonresidential grandparents' emotional and financial involvement in relation to early adolescent grandchild outcomes. *Journal of Research on Adolescence* 21:552–58.

Youngmin, S. 2003. The well-being of adolescents in households with no biological parents. *Journal of Marriage and Family* 65:894–909.

Yu, T., G. Pettit, J. Lansford, K. Dodge, and J. Bates. 2010. The interactive effects of marital conflict and divorce on parent-adult children's relationships. *Journal of Marriage and Family* 72:282–92.

Index